# Shaping the City, 2nd Edition

Taking on the key issues in urban design, Shaping the City examines the critical ideas that have driven these themes and debates through a study of particular cities at important periods in their development.

As well as retaining crucial discussions about cities such as Los Angeles, Atlanta, Chicago, Detroit, Philadelphia, and Brasilia at particular moments in their history that exemplified the problems and themes at hand like the mega-city, the post-colonial city and New Urbanism, in this new edition the editors have introduced new case studies critical to any study of contemporary urbanism – China, Dubai, Tijuana, and the wider issues of informal cities in the Global South.

The book serves as both a textbook for classes in urban design, planning and theory and is also attractive to the increasing interest in urbanism by scholars in other fields. Shaping the City provides an essential overview of the range and variety of urbanisms and urban issues that are critical to an understanding of contemporary urbanism.

**Rodolphe El-Khoury** is an urban designer and historian. He is Associate Professor and Canada Research Chair in Architecture and Urban Design at The University of Toronto. El-Khoury is also a partner in Khoury Levit Fong, an award winning practice that has gained international recognition for innovative design.

**Edward Robbins**, trained as an anthropologist, is Professor of Urbanism in the Institute of Urbanism, The Oslo School of Architecture and Design who has written and taught extensively about the relation of design to social theory and practice. Presently he is engaged in working on the challenges posed by cities in the south, especially the issue of poverty.

# Shaping The City, 2nd Edition

## Studies in History, Theory and Urban Design

**Edited by**
**Rodolphe El-Khoury and Edward Robbins**

Routledge
Taylor & Francis Group

LONDON AND NEW YORK

Second edition published 2013
by Routledge
2 Park Square, Milton Park, Abingdon, Oxon OX14 4RN

Simultaneously published in the USA and Canada
by Routledge
711 Third Avenue, New York, NY 10017

Routledge is an imprint of the Taylor & Francis Group, an informa business

British Library Cataloguing in Publication Data
A catalogue record for this book is available from the British Library

Library of Congress Cataloging-in-Publication Data
A catalog record has been requested for this book

ISBN: 978-0-415-58458-6 (hbk)
ISBN: 978-0-415-58462-3 (pbk)

Typeset in Univers Light
by Wearset Ltd, Boldon, Tyne and Wear

MIX
Paper from
responsible sources
FSC
www.fsc.org    FSC® C013056

Printed and bound in Great Britain by
TJ International Ltd, Padstow, Cornwall

# Contents

# Contents

# Contributors

**Jonny Aspen** is an Associate Professor at the Oslo School of Architecture and Design

**Joan Busquets** is Architect Barcelona, Martin Bucksbaum Professor in Practice in Urban Planning and Design at the Harvard Design School

**Teddy Cruz** is Professor in Public Culture and Urbanism at the University of California, San Diego, Visual Arts Department

**Farès el-Dahdah** is Associate Professor at Rice University, School of Architecture

**Keller Easterling** is Professor at Yale University, School of Architecture

**Victor J. Jones** is an Assistant Professor at University of Southern California

**Rodolphe El-Khoury** is Associate Professor at University of Toronto, John H. Daniels Faculty of Architecture, Landscape and Design

**Adrian Blackwell** is Assistant Professor at University of Waterloo, School of Architecture

**Rem Koolhaas** is founder of the Office for Metropolitan Architecture

**Edward Robbins** is a Professor at the Oslo School of Architecture and Design

**Mitchell Schwarzer** is a Professor at California College of the Arts

**Paulette Singley** is an Associate Professor at Woodbury University,

**Jonathan D. Solomon** is Associate Professor at Syracuse University

**Contributors**


**Richard M. Sommer** is Dean of the John H. Daniels Faculty of Architecture, Landscape and Design, University of Toronto

**Charles Waldheim** is Chair of Landscape Architecture at the Harvard Graduate School of Design

**Sarah Whiting** is Dean of the School of Architecture at Rice University

# Acknowledgments

The editors would first and foremost like to thank all the authors who contributed to this volume.

The editors and publishers also gratefully acknowledge the following for their permission to reproduce material in the book.

Rem Koolhaas, "Atlanta" © 1995, Rem Koolhaas and The Monacelli Press, Inc, was first published in S,M,L,XL, by Rem Koolhaas and Bruce Mau, The Monacelli Press, Inc, New York.

"Abu Dhabi and Dubai: World City Doubles" is adapted and updated from a text published as "Extrastatecraft" from Perspecta 39, "Re_Urbanism" (2007).

Among several peers, colleagues and friends who have contributed critical insights and expert knowledge to the book the editors especially recognize and thank George Baird, Robert Levit, Jennifer Schirmer, and Nader Tehrani.

We thank the book's production team for flawlessly orchestrating the publication of the work: Caroline Mallinder, Michelle Green, and Sarah Wray for the first edition; Louise Fox, Nicole Solano, and Fredrick Brantley for this second edition.

# Introduction

*Rodolphe El-Khoury and Edward Robbins*

In the face of dramatic urban transformations, there has been a growing concern about how to develop a lively and engaging urban life. The rub, however, for designers is how to represent and make sense of this urban reality, how to comprehend it as an artifact that can be constructed and transformed, and how to make real the physical stage upon which urban socio-spatial practices are played out.

The challenge emerges out of the incalculable complexity of what we call the "urban," composed as it is of so many different actors, groups, and institutions, and so many layers making up the sites and places of our cities. Adding to this complexity is the way different agents, forms, and practices create different sites that although not reducible to each other often inhabit the same location. Imagine the old 42nd Street in New York with its multiplicity of people; locals, tourists, day workers, prostitutes, johns, pimps, drug addicts and pushers, street vendors and more, sharing little in the way of practices and pre-dilections but all found on 42nd Street amid its porno theaters, legitimate businesses, restaurants, and central transportation hub. At the other extreme, there are urban places that often are completely segregated and homogeneous in their form and social reality; gated neighborhoods, suburban enclaves, and public housing projects for the very poor. At critical points, this multitude of different realties makes up an entity that we might conceive of as a whole. While this whole sets out a structural framework to which we all respond, it neither penetrates nor circumscribes all aspects of our local cultural and social practices. It is because we are all part of the same urban universe yet live often in parallel worlds that are connected in different ways to the whole and to each other that it is problematic at best to think of the urban as a singular reality. More to the point, the whole is ephemeral; it is as if, to paraphrase Karl Marx, all that is solid is continually melting into air.

This helps to explain why we find so many different and conflicting viewpoints among urban designers, architects, planners, and urban theorists about the city. It may be that "Everyone knows what is meant when we speak of … the 'corner' of a street, a 'marketplace', a shopping or cultural 'centre', a 'public place', and so on."[1] What everyone knows, however, may not be the same. The same place is often the site of antinomian discourses and contradictory and conflicting practices. The urban can neither be defined and understood through its reality as a whole nor adequately described by reference to its many fragments and parts. It is neither total nor partial, its elements neither wholly intertwined nor totally unrelated. The city is the multiple of its many parts and the whole of its many multiple sites and practices.

Equally as critical, there is an almost Manichean sensibility regarding the urban. As Thomas Gieryn points out:

> Urban places have been described as the locus of diversity, tolerance, sophistication, sociation, public participation, cosmopolitanism, integration, specialization, personal network-formation, coping, frequent spontaneous interactions, freedom, creativity…. But urban places have also been described as the locus of anonymity, detachment, loneliness, calculating egoism, privatization, formalized social controls, segregations, individualism, withdrawal, detachment, parochialism, disconnections, isolation, fear, seclusion, mental illness…[2]

This inclination to emphasize the urban as the site of one or another condition results in a tendency to ignore or underplay the complexity and even contradictions that underlie urban life. The street life of the city center and the coming together of strangers so popular with so many intellectuals living in older and gentrified city centers with their many and different forms of cultural consumption and social engagement, for example, is one reality. Another reality is that of the ghetto where so much of the street life we see is an escape from the desolation and despair embodied in the broken down and decrepit interiors of the buildings people inhabit. It may be useful to recall, even romanticize, the great centers of traditional cities: they provide many of us with what is a most engaging and exciting life. Equally as important to recall is that these centers of great wealth are but the flip side of miles of urban misery: for every new and exciting gentrified neighborhood, every revived urban center, there are new slums on the city's margins often as the consequence of urban renewal elsewhere. But even this is a simplification for poverty reaches out and affects the center in the figures of street people and beggars, and street life becomes less a coming together of strangers and more a contested terrain between us and those who are other. And, the slum streets with their despair also support a wealth of social engagement and cultural interchange, creativity, and joy.

The same, it could be said, holds for those for whom the traditional neighborhood and the image of the small-town street are exemplars of meaningful and successful urbanity. Forgotten, though, are the xenophobia, the racism, the malicious gossip, and the oppressive restrictions of the small and the local. Yet again it is reductive to so condemn the small and the local. Main streets and local neighborhoods even as they create bounded worlds offer what is best of the urban, full of the strong social engagement and supports that make the city such a rich and engaging social and cultural environment.

That may be why there are so many differing and even conflicting views about urban form and what and how we should plan for it among architects, planners, and urban designers. Some emphasize the mega-scale of the city while others place great emphasis on the city as a townscape (or as contained neighborhood). While some argue for the necessity of keeping things compact and well ordered and excoriate what they see as sprawl, others see the extension of the city as a natural and unproblematic reality. For some the city is best seen as a machine for others as an ecology and for still others as a splintered whole.

Yet, even though there exists a broad range of conflicting views about the urban, the complex and multiple realities go unrecognized by architects, planners, and urban designers. What we should continually engage when dealing with the urban is its many and different publics, its heterogeneous and often conflicting mix of peoples all demanding a public voice. It is, we should always keep in mind, an amalgam of different realities. Each of the many different actors who make up the urban often inhabits the same location, each has its own sense of urbanity and each has its own ideas about what constitutes good urban form. The notion that we can develop some clear and universal ideal or plan for the good city in a society like our own is a chimera. Designers and planners today, in ways that are new and unique, face not the design of a city singular, but the realities of similarity and difference.

Thus our collection of essays! None of the authors claims to represent the city in its entirety but looks at different cities with different optics. It is a collection that is devoted to both analyses and descriptions of one or another city in one or another aspect and to generating a plural sense of that which we might call "THE CITY" in an attempt to address, if not completely answer, the question posed by Michel de Certeau, that is, how "To think the very plurality of the real and to make that way of thinking the plural effective?"[3] This book is the result of a series of conversations that we, the editors (one an anthropologist and the other a designer), have had over the years about the shaping of cities and the making of particular cities and their parts. We felt that most books about urban design dealt primarily either with urban form as a kind of autonomous phenomenon or with urban design as a technical and professional field. There was strong agreement that there was little in the literature that addressed the contradictions and dilemmas of urban design as a polymorphous and transdisciplinary practice. We were certainly aware that there could be no one book about urban design that could claim to encompass the whole and all its parts. What we hoped we could do was present a series of essays that, in different ways and by addressing different themes from different perspectives, would provide an introduction to the rich variety and contradictions that are a part of the shaping of the city – i.e. urban design.

We wanted to address the rich variety of critical issues and approaches within urban design, which can be epitomized by different cities. We therefore asked the contributors to present visions and ideas of urban design associated with the different cities or historical moments that they have come to exemplify. The goal was to derive from the context vivid demonstrations of theoretical constructs in their physical and/or cultural manifestation, not exhaustive historical accounts or analytical descriptions of the cities themselves. Thus what follows are not complete descriptions of the urban design of particular cities, but a series of chapters that find in each city a lesson that demonstrates a particular way of reading the city and the consequent strategies that may be deployed in reshaping it. Although it is critical to emphasize the variety and complexity of urban design, we need to be constantly reminded that there are a number of core issues that have reappeared in negotiating the persistent challenges and opportunities of rapidly growing cities in the modern world. The essays in this book engage a number of those critical themes.

Central to much urban design is the belief that an understanding of the planning process is central to any discourse about the city, as demonstrated in the work of Whiting and Sommer. Others would argue that there is a danger in an uncritical adherence to planning regulations, and this is addressed by Schwarzer. A number of the chapters struggle with the tension between the plan and its reality. El-Dahdah reveals that what appears as a rigid plan provides a context for its mutation. Waldheim argues that what we see as an unstructured process for shaping the city is rather a highly determined result of the laws of capital. For Singley, the lack of structure is a problem of representation. What appears as an absence of plan is the result of methods of mapping that simply do not address this new form of urban design. Robbins deplores the reactionary infatuation with "neighborhood" and "community" while Koolhaas relishes the erosion of traditional urban cores by suburban typologies.

In this second edition of the book we took the opportunity to include themes and perspectives that have gained in relevance since the initial publication to become an important part of the evolving debate on the city. Easterling and Blackwell consider in radically different views the staple urban phenomenon of the new century: mushrooming cities in Special Economic Zones. Cruz looks at the tensions and contradictions of transborder urbanism – another staple of the new economy. Aspen frames the decline of public space while Solomon questions its relevance in groundless and increasingly mediated urban environments.

It is critical for the design of this book that different themes and ideas are associated with different styles of writing and presentation. Just as different theories of urban design are associated with different contexts, different ideas about urban design are perforce related to a variety of intellectual approaches and styles of writing consistent with those approaches. For some contributors a more formal and social-scientific approach was appropriate; others preferred a more journalistic, plannerly, or literary style. The variety is not accidental. It seemed to us, as editors, important to present a volume that not only encompasses the variety of forms of urban design, different urban contexts and different ways of understanding the shaping of the city, but also allows the reader to engage the range of stylistic and textual approaches that attempt in various ways to make sense of urban design. All the variety, though, leads to one theme: urban design and its role in shaping the city.

## Notes

1   Lefebvre, 1991, p. 16.
2   Gieryn, 2000, p. 476.
3   De Certeau, 1984, p. 94.

Chapter 1

# Abu Dhabi and Dubai – World City Doubles

*Keller Easterling*

The nation-state often portrays itself and its network of cities as an ultimate form. Yet as power continues to amass and disperse in recurring patterns as it has throughout the ages, world capitals preside over empires and regions, as well as nations. Some are city-states unto themselves.

In the fabled pairings of, for instance, Beijing and Shanghai, Washington, DC and New York, Ankara and Istanbul, the national capital is the more sober inland location that stands in contrast to its market partner, often a maritime city with a long record of promiscuous trading and cosmopolitan intelligence. The mercantile city is sometimes cast as the sister city or the shadow entity, seemingly ceding power and official jurisdiction so that it can grow extra-national power outside the cumbersome regulations of government. Yet contemporary versions of this sister city are not merely alter egos of the national capital, but often something more like independent city-states – the descendants of Venice or Genoa when they were trading centers of the planet. Recombining urban power genetics into yet another species of urbanism, they exceed the interests of global financial centers such as London, New York, Frankfurt, or Sao Paulo.[1] They also exceed the requirements of the fabled "region state" – the financial and trans-shipment nexus of late-twentieth-century globalization theory.[2] Some contemporary world cities like Hong Kong and Singapore are not only the crossroads and destinations of national expedition and franchise but also the centers of global franchises that have property nested in holding companies and national territories all around the world. Their agents of franchise may be global trade conglomerates (e.g. Singapore's PSA or Hong Kong's Hutchison Port Holdings) that are the modern descendants of organizations like the Dutch or British East India Companies. Merging the techniques of freeport traders, pirates, and mercenaries, the free zones of the new world city create legal habitats for contemporary trade that naturalize the insertion of extra-national territory within national boundaries.

While Western superpowers have perhaps grown accustomed to the idea that world cities like Singapore or Hong Kong are much more than the product of their own colonial ventriloquism, an emergent world city like Dubai presents an unusual political foundation and an abrupt conflation of ancient and contemporary worlds. The usual pairing of Abu Dhabi and Dubai as capital city and mercantile city would appear at first to follow familiar models. The two play their roles well until it becomes clear they are both capital city and world city in another time and dimension. The United Arab Emirates (UAE) is a feder-ation of some of the world's last functioning kingdoms, having skipped the most bombastic chapters in the grand history of national sovereignty. During the very centuries that nations have emerged as a dominant framework, so too have substantial networks of transnational business exchange and infra-structure building. The UAE emerges at a moment when nations bluster patri-otic while also developing more relationships in this transnational milieu. Already an "anational" society, the UAE evolves, within the legal climates of free trade, a form of governance for which national/democratic structures are mimicked in organizing dynasties.[3] Mixtures of bargains and monarchical decrees are designed to handle global dealings with businesses that have managed to shed what they regard as some of the most cumbersome of those national regulations that the UAE never possessed. In these dealings, ancient kingdoms and contemporary empires recognize and merge with each other to form a world capital of sorts.

The presence of world capitals like Dubai does not support the assumption that transnational sovereignty is waxing as national sovereignty wanes. It may be more accurate to see a historical continuity of global activity within which state and nonstate forces, acting together, craft the most advanta-geous political and economic climates by alternately sheltering, releasing, and laundering their power. Business may, for instance, seek out relaxed, extrajuris-dictional spaces (special economic zones (SEZs), free trade zones (FTZs), export processing zones (EPZs), etc.) while also massaging legislation in the various states they occupy. The stances of any one nation or business are therefore often duplicitous or discrepant reflections of divided loyalties between national and international concerns or citizens and shareholders.

The customary portfolios of political indicators will not always reliably return information about these complex state–nonstate partnerships.

They often create political events that exceed epistemes of war, nation, citizen, and capital. In a contemplation of world capitals, the UAE exposes the limits of the national capital as a self-styled unit of grand historical continuities. With the insulated caprice of petrodollars and free zones, the UAE leads with the increasingly common duplicitous handshake. The triggers and levers of this power may not be easily moralized and analyzed by the left or the right; they may be more venal and evasive as well as more shrewd and innovative. The UAE embodies a transnational extrastatecraft filled with both the dangers and opportunities that rule the world today.

> Dubai. The hot spot where adventurers play the world's most dangerous games of gold, sex, oil, and war.
> Dubai. A wild, seething place in the sunbaked sands of Arabia, where billion-dollar carpetbaggers mix explosive passions with oil. And exotic pleasures pay fabulous dividends.
> Whores, assassins, spies, fortune hunters, diplomats, princes and pimps – all gambling for their lives in a dazzling, billion-dollar game that only the most ruthless and beautiful dare to play.[4]
> (jacket copy from *Dubai*, by Robin Moore, author of *The French Connection*)

In 1976, after *The Green Berets*, *The French Connection* and several other global intrigues, Robin Moore published a novel titled *Dubai*. The novel opens in 1967. Fitz, the monosyllabic hero and American intelligence officer, is fired over his pro-Palestinian/anti-Semitic remarks that appear in the press just as the Six Day War is launched. Dubai, like the not-yet-middle-aged protagonist, is still fluid and unsettled. It is still a place where adventures and deals are flipped and leveraged against each other to propel small syndicates to fame and fortune. Fitz quickly scales a succession of events in the UAE's history during the 1970s. He arrives when a handful of hotels and the new Maktoum Bridge across Dubai Creek are among the few structures that appear in an otherwise ancient landscape, one that has changed very little in the centuries that Dubai has been an entrepôt of gold trade and a site for pearl diving. Just on the brink of Sheikh Rashid's plans for an electrical grid, the air-conditioning in Fitz's Jumeirah beach house must struggle against the 120 degrees and 100 percent humidity by means of an independent generator. The story proceeds by moving in and out of air-conditioning, syndicate meetings, and sex scenes in the palaces of the Sheikh or in hotel cocktail lounges between Tehran, Dubai, and Washington. The tawdry glamour of tinkling ice and Range Rovers is frequently interrupted for a number of rough and tumble adventures that are evenly distributed throughout the book. The discovery of oil has already propelled the development of the Trucial States (states that have made maritime truces with the original oilmen, the British).

Fitz's first escapade uses the old gold economy to capitalize on the new oil and real estate economy. The syndicate's dhow (the traditional vessel on the creek) is souped up with munitions and technology that Fitz has stolen from the American military. Dubai is an old hand at smuggling, or what it likes to call "re-exporting," during embargoes or wars that are always available in the Gulf. Shipping gold to India usually involves armed encounters in international waters. The dhow's US military equipment vaporizes the Indian ships, thus trouncing piracy and resistance to the free market. Fitz plunders enough money to bargain with the sheikh for shares of an oil enterprise in Abu Musa, an island in the Gulf halfway between Dubai and Iran. He has enough money left over to finance a saloon, equipped with old CIA bugging devices and an upstairs office with a one-way viewing window. From this perch Fitz entertains the growing number of foreign businessmen who are laying over in Dubai and the growing number of Arab businessmen who want to see and approach Western women. He continues in his plot to become a diplomat to the new independent federation of Trucial territories, the United Arab Emirates, to be established in 1971.

Fitz (like Dubai) gets things done. With a wink and a nod sheikhs and diplomats reward him. He even manages to single-handedly crush a communist insurgency in the desert. (Most Robin Moore novels fight the old Cold War fight, although his most recent forays take on the new devil: terrorism.) In the novel, America's heroic Cold War deeds in the Gulf have made us simple lovable heroes with both naughtiness and vulnerability. Fitz wisely realizes that most political activities are not vetted through recognized political channels. In Dubai, the "naughty hero" formula even goes one dyspeptic step further in engineering sympathy for the character and happily signaling the end of the novel: Fitz hurts his leg fighting the insurgency. Despite his wounds and even though he has contributed a suitcase full of money in campaign contributions, he doesn't get the ambassadorship. He is unfairly tainted with the centuries of regional piracy and the only too recent hotel-bar intrigues. Nevertheless, Fitz gets the girl in the end, the daughter of a diplomat living on the Main Line in Philadelphia, and they begin to plan their middle-aged life "on the creek" in Dubai.

The novel's oblivious mix of Cold War piety and soft porn is, however fictional, appropriate evidence. Indeed, the novel is strangely more informative than most of what is currently written about the UAE in its own self-produced coffee-table books and marketing copy. The country is currently producing a dazzling story of real estate development for the consumption of an obedient press that reproduces its sound-bytes. Even snide and brainy bloggers of architectural critique have assembled obediently in the trap, printing enthusiastic remarks about hyperbolic development projects. Most accounts are looking for yet another big opener to top the last story about new offshore islands, theme parks, or shopping festivals – another superlative prefix meaning "mega." The Emirates get things done in a fast-forward time lapse of oil wealth. The coffee-table books do not present the complicated history of foreign paternalizing, meddling, and arming that has matured into something very different from what either the US or the UK think they have wrought. Behaving as if the UAE was simply an outcrop of Western real estate techniques, they have occasionally offered condescending praise for their exceptionally good pupil. The UAE is happy to nod as if in gratitude and perfectly happy if the global press bites on that line. It may even be good for the real estate market.

Robin Moore's Dubai ends in 1970, just before federation in 1971. Abu Dhabi and Dubai were sibling territories, offshoots of the Ban Yas tribe that migrated between pearl diving and the interior desert oasis of Al Ain. Abu Dhabi, a coastal archipelago with some fresh water, became the headquarters of the Al Nahyan family. In 1833, Sheikh Maktoum bin Butti led a group that seceded from Abu Dhabi to settle farther east along the coast in Dubai, a small fishing village, and the Maktoum family has ruled in Dubai ever since.[5] Since 1820, the British had entered into agreements with these coastal sheikhdoms to regulate piracy and other maritime concerns. In 1892, the so-called Trucial states signed a joint agreement establishing an exclusive relationship with Britain in exchange for its protection. American and British companies negotiated their first oil concessions in the late 1920s and early 1930s. Still, Abu Dhabi did not begin to drill for oil until after World War II and did not discover commercial quantities of oil until 1958.[6] Soon it would become clear that Abu Dhabi was dominant in not only land area but also oil production. Dubai, endowed with far fewer oil resources, did not export oil until 1969. Even early on, Dubai planned to pursue tourism, finance, and trade as its chief sources of revenue.[7] When the British pulled out of territories east of the Suez in 1968, the UAE was flooded with foreign businessmen from all over the world, and the Range Rovers gave way to Japanese cars.[8] Yet well into the 1960s, the Trucial states were barefoot, with no roads or health care, few clothes, and brackish water.

> We lived in the eighteenth century while the rest of the world, even the rest of our neighbors, had advanced into the twentieth. We had nothing to offer visitors, we had nothing to export, we had no importance to the outside world whatsoever. Poverty, illiteracy, poor health, a high rate of mortality all plagued us well into the 1960s.[9]

> The business of government is manufacturing opportunity.
>
> (Sheikh Mohammad bin Rashid Al Maktoum[10])

When, in 1971, the legendary leaders Sheikh Zayed Bin-Sultan Al Nahyan in Abu Dhabi and Sheikh Rashid bin Saeed Al Maktoum in Dubai established a federation to join the seven coastal sheikhdoms, they essentially created a republic of monarchies. The Federal National Council is composed of the Supreme Council, and the remaining seats of the 40-member representative body are apportioned according to the size of each of the seven emirates and filled by each ruler's appointment.[11] Abu Dhabi's ruler will always be the president of the country, while Dubai's ruler will always be vice-president and prime minister. Laws are made by decree and administered by various ministerial appointees that make up the body of the council. Notably, Dubai and Ras Al Khaimah also have an independent judicial system with civil and criminal divisions and Sharia courts to handle family cases. Since mixtures of English, French, and Egyptian law influenced the UAE's federal structure, it offers some gestures and protocols of a democratic process within an auto-representative government. While the organs of government have a superficial resemblance, not only citizenship and representation but other bedrock principles of democracy, such as free speech, freedom of assembly, and the claim to racial and gender equality, are notably absent. Concerns persist about discrimination against women and non-nationals.

As a kingdom-nation, the UAE produces partial reflections and tinctures of Western governmental institutions, yet it operates with a different set of civil and legal assumptions. Moreover, these structural differences often allow the country to thrive on many of the very complications that trouble Western democracies: the contradiction between citizenship and the need for cheap labor, the curious position of public space within urbanism conceived as a privately themed spatial product, the naturalized state of exception from law in corporate paradigms, and the influence of special interests in official political representation. As if in a state of amnesia for these perennial problems of contemporary participatory democracies, the UAE seems not to perceive them.

UAE nationals are not only a constituency to the representative body, but a beneficiary, conduit, and pivot of much of the country's business; they are at once the wealthy elite and the welfare state. While Dubai is currently pursuing an urbanism that is measured in entries in the Guinness Book of World Records (e.g. the world's tallest building, the world's largest artificial islands, the world's largest shopping mall, and the world's largest underwater hotel), Abu Dhabi also lays claim to a Guinness record made by one of its most legendary leaders. Sheikh Zayed was once offered the largest bribe in history: the Saudis offered him $42 million to relinquish Abu Dhabi's claim to Al Ain. Sheikh Zayed's refusal during a time when even he had only a few hundred rupees was consistent with his commitment to manage Abu Dhabi's ensuing wealth in a way that made its citizens beneficiaries. After becoming ruler in

1966, Sheikh Zayed also issued land grants for each national to ensure that development would benefit the population, and, by 1976, he had also offered 5,000 units of "people's housing."[12] The land grants are similar in principle to the many other laws that stipulate partnerships or enterprises in which UAE nationals are either associates or beneficiaries. "Offsets" are among these structuring devices. Defense contracts with the UAE must first negotiate with the UAE offsets group. The contracts must be profitable, and a UAE national must own 51 percent. Moreover, the contract must seed an offset venture in a non-oil industry. So far, these offset projects have funded a variety of industries including fish farms, air-conditioning, medical services, shipbuilding, and even leisure activities like polo grounds.[13] Since the number of nationals is small, the UAE has managed to convert the typically corrupt relationship between government and private-interest lobbies into a form of hyper-representation.[14] In Dubai, this direct benefit to a manageable handful of constituents is regarded as government welfare and beneficent leadership.

The UAE finds advantage in the notion of laborer, expat, or tourist as a temporary citizen. As a temporary citizen, the tourist arrives to deposit vacation money at shopping festivals, golf tournaments, and theme parks. Having paid their taxes in tourist revenues, they then leave without further demands on the government. Denizens of the Trucial States were themselves the guest workers for foreign oil companies before they became partners in the oil wealth.[15] Today, rules are established for managing and housing labor in groups, and problems are the responsibility of the contracting agent. Laborers and contractors must agree to and abide by certain rules or be deported. Dubai can then even boast that it is one of the most diverse places on Earth as its curates its inhabitants from Africa, India, Pakistan, and elsewhere around the world. All of the arrangements are perhaps more transparent than in those countries where citizenship is the impossible option and the guest worker exists in a zone of denial and secrecy. Yet the arrangements have also yielded a situation devoid of responsibility and consequence, except for the outside contractors. Enforcement applies to the infraction of rules but not to procedures or events that exist outside of them. Human rights concerns continue to center on the trafficking of human beings within a large volume of migratory workers as well as on the networks of domestic workers for whom there is no record-keeping or oversight.

The UAE epitomizes the shadow jurisdictions that reside in transnational exchanges, out-maneuvering some official acts of state, and serving as de facto forms of global governance. Indeed, if that shadow government is loosely defined by the scatter of headquarters and zones around the world, the UAE is something like a parliament of this global headquartering. The "park" or free trade zone is naturalized as the ideal urban growth unit. In recent decades, the FTZ, EPZ, SEZ, or other similar incarnations have evolved to allow businesses immunity from taxes, labor regulation, and environmental restrictions or to streamline the logistics for trans-shipment, materials handling, or duty-free retail.

Like any nation, the UAE publicizes its ennobling dispositions, often embodied by the partnership of Sheikh Zayed and Sheikh Rashid. Deploying a familiar modernist script, the two used technology for nation building. Both Sheikh Zayed and Sheikh Rashid capitalized experimental projects that demonstrated their eagerness to diversify. Dubai sponsored a project that paired aluminum production and desalination. Sheikh Zayed sponsored the planting of millions of palm trees, planning to manage water and wildlife with the help of remote-sensing satellites. Since the modernist script usually comes with equal parts traditionalism, the UAE associated this technological expertise with a native wisdom about environment and natural resources. Accessorized with the perfect mix of modern signals and traditional customs such as falconry, horses, and camel racing, Sheikh Zayed's leadership solicited general adoration, almost deification, until his death in 2004. His face appears everywhere, on billboards and talismans. To traditional music with a new-age beat, the official website celebrating his life follows the silhouette of a falcon across the sands from a silhouetted skyline of barasti mud huts to the silhouetted skyline of Dubai. Moreover, part of the UAE's beguiling formula for government involves generosity to the neediest countries in the world. By the mid-1970s the UAE and Sheikh Zayed had developed a reputation for philanthropy that was to become a permanent ingredient of the country's mystique.[16]

As if in suspended animation or taking a break from the twentieth century, Abu Dhabi and Dubai might have seemed, in the 1990s, like sleepy holiday locations offering a growing number of modern developments, air-conditioned hotels, and office buildings. Both perhaps maintained the peculiar relaxation and freedom of the place where one does not stay for long, but after the 1990s the difference between the two emirates and the two cites accelerated. In 1997, Dubai's fabled developed boom began when it allowed for freehold property for all nations in special development areas. In 2006, the emirate legalized foreign property ownership. Somewhat more sober, Abu Dhabi recently clarified its 2005 freehold laws by allowing only GCC nationals to own freehold property while non-GCC members are required to contract for 99 years.[17] Traveling between the emirates is a jolting journey forward and backward through time – between ancient landscapes, national capitals, and new world capitals.

The earth has a new center.
(billboard advertisement for Dubai Mall on Sheikh Zayed Road)

"Dubai is like someone who owns many horses," he said. "He doesn't just put one horse in the race, he puts many with many chances of success."

(Sultan Ahmed bin Sulayem, adviser to the Dubai's Maktoum family[18])

Take wisdom from the wise – not everyone who rides a horse is a jockey.

(a verse of poetry by Sheikh Mohammed bin Rashid Al Maktoum written in island masses and visible from the air in the proposed Palm Jebel Ali[19])

In 1979, Sheikh Rashid completed two projects in Dubai that established it as a regional capital of the Gulf and the Middle East: the World Trade Center and the Jebel Ali Port.[20] As Moore's novel spins around a corridor between Dubai and Tehran, it accurately reflects alignments of power, influence, and relationship that have caused Dubai to be called "the economic capital of Iran."[21] The World Trade Center signaled a willingness to foster regional partners and reinforced the image of Dubai as a Gulf nexus. Situated at the border between Abu Dhabi and Dubai, the Jebel Ali Port was the largest man-made port in the world. The free trade zone permitted complete foreign ownership of land and no taxes. The stretch of development between the World Trade Center and Jebel Ali Port, comparable to the length of Manhattan, has since been rapidly filling with a corridor of skyscrapers since 1990. This highway, called Sheikh Zayed Road on the Dubai side and Sheikh Rashid Road on the Abu Dhabi side, is a deferential handshake that is perhaps more unevenly extended as development in Dubai outpaces that of any other emirate.

Business practices that have long been familiar to the Gulf entrepôts but that have also emerged as contemporary global business models are the perfect accompaniment to Dubai's overarching approach to trade. A city of warehousing, smuggling, and gold trading, Dubai was on the circuit of the Gulf's Qawasim pirates, brought under control at approximately the same time that the Barbary pirates were defeated in the Mediterranean.[22] More important than product stability has been the movement of a volume of goods. Products are best when they are capable of behaving like fluctuating currency. With more choices, more merchandise, and more labor from around the world, the odds are better for playing currency and wage differentials.

General Sheikh Mohammed bin Rashid Al Maktoum, who succeeded his brother Sheikh Maktoum bin Rashid Al Maktoum, has, for some time, been the mastermind behind the most recent chapters of hyperbolic development going on in Dubai – the petrodollar flush before the 2008 economic downturn. On Sheikh Rashid's watch, Dubai has developed seven-star hotels and mega-projects.

Dubailand, an enormous, two-billion-square-foot tourist installation, projected to include 45 megaprojects and 200 subprojects. Dubai has rehearsed the "park" or zone with almost every imaginable program beginning with Dubai Internet City in 2000, the first IT campus as free trade zone. Calling each new enclave "city," it has planned or built Dubai Health Care City, Dubai Maritime City, Dubai Silicon Oasis, Dubai Knowledge Village, Dubai Techno Park, Dubai Media City, Dubai Outsourcing Zone, Dubai Humanitarian City, Dubai Industrial City, Dubai International Financial Centre free zone, and Dubai Textile City.[23] Similarly, mutations of Portman/Hines/Jerde malls and atrium hotels like Burj Al Arab, Dubai Mall (the largest mall in the world), or Ski Dubai (an indoor ski resort in a 120-degrees desert), were all components of an instant metropolis growing before the world's eyes. The first of Dubai's largest artificial islands, Palm Island, launched in 2001 by the Nakeel, was to be joined by two more palm-frond-shaped formations, the Palm Jebel Ali and the Palm Deira. In the interim, The World, another archipelago, this time in the shape of the world's continents, created a global media sensation. Island properties associated with their position on the globe were sold as private compounds to celebrities like Rod Stewart and Elton John. Since governments like Dubai legally engineer their own status as islands of immunity and exemption in free-trade-zone loopholes, or archipelagos, The World, as an archipelago of archipelagos was an extravagant global witticism that was advertised by its own potential critics. The financial crisis froze Dubai in its state of development euphoria. But in its recent growth spurt, the city became a global urban paradigm as the world's ultimate free zone – keeping everyone's secrets, researching everyone's forbidden products and procedures, and laundering global identities.

> Many journalists have booked rooms in prestigious hotels here, but instead of covering the summit they have gone to Dubai to shop.
> (journalist from the Saudi delegation headquartered in Abu Dhabi for the GCC conference, 2005[24])

> Our long-term goal is to establish Abu Dhabi as a centre for development of new technology in energy ... we are looking forward to see Abu Dhabi as world capital of energy.[25]

Passing across the border on Sheikh Zayed Road to Sheikh Rashid Road, the difference in political disposition is visually clear. The forest of skyscrapers gives way to cultivated palm trees and somewhat dated and earnest public-works buildings. Abu Dhabi's urbanism is more conservative. Tall buildings conform to a grid and regularly offer a very similar retail podium. The emirate invokes gravitas and tradition, playing the role of the more responsible sister, closer to the ecological and philanthropic ethos established by Sheikh Zayed. Sitting on a giant spout of oil, Abu Dhabi has no intention of competing with Dubai's world capital ambitions. Still, it too must deliberately acquire components of culture that craft the correct global profile. While Abu Dhabi borrows from Dubai some world capital techniques for power building, it will also work to strengthen its position as a regional/national capital. If the UAE is to become more than a source of oil, a temporary warehouse for goods, or a stopover for labor and tourists, it must send a variety of special signals to the rest of the world. Sheikha Lubna Al Qasimi, the Minister of Economy and Planning, first female government minister of the UAE and a protégé of Sheikh Mohammed bin Rashid Al Maktoum, is one of these signals. Among the present concerns is the need for jobs and leadership positions for the nationals who either emigrate to jobs elsewhere or have less expertise than foreign candidates.[26] Ailing economies in the larger region threaten stability and present some mutually beneficial opportunities for investment and philanthropy. The UAE must also partner with both national and corporate powers to sponsor innovation and simultaneously appropriate technological expertise. The raft of initiatives is designed to engage economies and power centers around the world.

While tourism is one avenue of growth, Abu Dhabi plans to distinguish itself from Dubai by being a center of culture and education. One new initiative, Saadiyat Island, will serve as demonstration of some of these new initiatives. While it will have a full range of programs, its cultural center will be home to a Guggenheim outpost by Frank Gehry, a performing arts center by Zaha Hadid, a branch of the Louvre by Jean Nouvel, and a Zayed National museum by Norman Foster. Promoting "universal" cultural installations, Saadiyat Island is to become an "international cultural hub for the Middle East on par with the best in the world." While various educational institutions including Yale University and the Sorbonne have been approached, NYU has most recently been promoted as an educational partner for the venture.[27]

Even though located at the epicenter of oil, Abu Dhabi is leading the UAE's sophisticated energy and transportation experiments. Abu Dhabi's Masdar City, established by the Abu Dhabi Future Energy Company, is a free zone for green energy enterprises – something like the free zone as intentional community. Master-planned by Norman Foster, the plan of the town, not unlike a Roman Ideal town, is a square grid. The sectional shape of the city is designed for shading, solar energy collection, and an underground zone for automated personal rapid transit vehicles.[28] The UAE plans to join the Arabian Railway network connecting Abu Dhabi and Dubai with a larger Gulf circuit, making it possible to travel from Dubai to Damascus and Beirut to Cairo by rail.[29] The emirates also have their own internal plans for a railway that would link the coastal ports. While this UAE railway would begin as a freight network, it would eventually service passenger travel. Dubai is also building an automated metro system, and Abu Dhabi plans to follow suit.[30]

> The United Arab Emirates has earned the dubious distinction of having some of the worst labor conditions in the world. Human Rights Watch has cited the country for discrimination, exploitation, and abuse. Many foreign workers, especially women, face intimidation and violence, including sexual assault, at the hands of employers, supervisors, and police and security forces, the rights group said.[31]

> "It's a funny thing about Dubai, the minute people get here they try to figure out how fast they can get out."
>
> (Fitz, in *Dubai*, by Robin Moore)

> [Through Alameen] ... the public can assist and communicate any information related to security matters to law enforcement personnel. The service is considered unique in employing the latest technologies and in not requiring the presence of the caller. The information is dealt with in complete confidence, without focusing on the caller's identity or motives; the focus is on the subject and the authenticity of the information. The service runs 24/7 in complete confidence.
>
> As an indication of its success, Alameen in its first year received 1,178 calls, of which 107 were traffic information, 87 prostitution reports, 30 fraud, 28 illegal immigrants and workers, 20 drug, 15 begging, 12 harassments, and 7 witchcraft, 5 money laundering, in addition to various suggestions.[32]

Both Abu Dhabi and Dubai continue to be sites of labor abuse. Repeatedly cited by the International Labour Organization and Human Rights Watch, the UAE's building projects draw a volume of corruption that corresponds to the volume of construction and occasionally overwhelms regulatory agencies like the Ministry of Labor.[33] Labor problems such as nonpayment are brought before the ministry, which in turn insists on compliance with the rules, exacting fines and administering cures at least in those situations about which it is made aware. The stories are familiar. Laborers, primarily from Asia, are organized in crowded labor camps, with 50–60 immigrants per house and 6–10 workers per room.[34] Human Rights Watch even cited Saadiyat Island, the "island of happiness," for labor abuse, putting on notice the Tourism Development and Investment Company of Abu Dhabi as well as all of the high-profile architecture offices involved in the project.[35] One response in both Dubai and Abu Dhabi has been to create model labor villages like Labour City in Dubai or the Saadiayat Island

Construction Village. These demonstration cities may contain everything from air-conditioned rooms and cafeterias to a cricket pitch.[36] While the labor camps that are legal and partially transparent are largely for men in jobs ranging from taxi drivers to road workers, domestic workers who are largely women are often isolated in individual homes with few avenues for protest or assembly.

The UAE merges traditional, commercial, and civil practices to address a variety of political concerns including the labor issue. For instance, in the absence of familiar forms of citizenship or representation, workers may communicate grievances through a hotline. Just as there is a hotline to report labor abuses, there is also a hotline to report suspicious activity or people for deportation. Dubai is then at once rehearsing new techniques that acknowledge labor contradictions and evading responsibility for labor's alienation from culture.

UAE development companies like Emaar and Nakeel are offering development expertise to other nations in the region and in Africa. King Abdullah Economic City, on the Red Sea, near Jedda, is a free zone world city on the Dubai model. Launched in 2006 by the Saudi government and the Dubai real estate developers, Emaar the city, when complete, will be 168 square kilometers and comparable to the size of Brussels. If techniques for sharing oil wealth (like those used to share oil wealth among UAE nationals) were on offer in the partnerships with African nations, there might be real opportunities to alleviate some of the extreme suffering exacerbated by oil on that continent. In Khartoum, capital of the Sudan, the UAE is reaching out to offer Dubai-style real estate development. Yet, Almogran, 1,660 acres of skyscrapers and residential properties, only underlines the extreme discrepancies between oil wealth and the exploitation of oil resources in mostly black southern Sudan. The overt, even hyperbolic expressions of oil money have been among the chief tools for instigating war and violence within non-Arab populations in the south.[37] Most chilling is the sense that outside the UAE an ethos of using oil for nation building and social welfare need not be deployed for non-Arab populations like those in the Sudan.

> Oh Cloud above all others!
> Oh sea of generosity let nothing bring you harm
> Nourishing rain that brings life to kith and kin
> But denies to your adversaries
> Is pure for your neighbors but not for your foes
> To whom it offers but a bitter draught of woe
> Fearless hand of generosity
> No sacrifice we make for you can be too great
> You ward off all misfortunes

All dangers banished with no efforts spared
In your inscriptions in the book of glory
Every letter betokens honour.

(poem by Sheikh Mohammed bin Rashid Al Maktoum in memory of
Sheikh Zayed)

Kingdoms and brands have a mutual understanding about mythmaking. Both deploy ambitious and comprehensive use of traditional imagery, capitalizing, tabulating, and constantly refreshing the effects of irrational desire and value. Fetish and symbolic capital, no longer merely ineffable enhancements of capital, are themselves fully capitalized as commodities. In the UAE's versions of experience economies, the collapse between architectural language and logistical envelope becomes complete, and it becomes even easier to float more fantastic fictions over a revenue stream. Without introspection, experience economies instantly blend with the natural urges and talents of a dynasty. Like the Burj Al Arab's imagery of sabers, turbans, and billowing *dhow* sails, Sheikhs, more than Jon Jerde or postmodern architects, come by it honestly. But in this sense, the UAE only makes a broad cartoon, a vivid indicator, of the ageless mutually sustaining partnership between power and fiction. There can be no handwringing over the potential power of a totemic marketplace to wipe away meaning. Here, the supposedly tragic, meaningless sign of the spectacle is the meaning – a subtextual indicator of a willingness to be in the game. It may therefore also indicate a willingness to make bargains of all sorts, within which meaninglessness is an instrumental political lubricant.

The UAE has created a global model for development that the entire world wishes to emulate. Now major cities and national capitals that did not have a sister city are engineering their own world city doppelgängers on the Singapore or Dubai model. Navi Mumbai, New Songdo City outside Seoul, or Astana in Kazakhstan are national capitals cum free trade zones perfectly designed to legally legitimize the duplicities of nonstate transactions. The world capital and national capital can shadow each other, alternately exhibiting a regional cultural ethos and a global ambition.

Social critic Mike Davis loads, aims, and fires his bracing message from the left, saying that the future of Dubai "looks like nothing so much as a nightmare of the past: Walt Disney meets Albert Speer on the shores of Araby."[38] Yet the UAE tutors much more than righteous binary opposition. In some sense the UAE is an example of "new/old" or "the new oldness and the old newness," to borrow from the activist group Retort.[39] For Retort, the phrase describes a dyspeptic mixture of primitive power urges accessorized with sophisticated techniques of spectacle, allowing it to float financial sustenance over an even more obdurate ancient script. The emirates have found a number of lubricated techniques for pirating the world that are both primitive and sophisticated. Some of those techniques override the entrenched corruption of national stances to initiate mechanisms of intergovernmental cooperation, while others intensify that corruption in outlaw environments designed to avoid global compacts. The UAE recognizes that aggression, but never violence, keeps the money flowing. Most politics operate through subterfuge and contradiction rather than in environments of conceptual or ethical purity. The new/ancient is at once more resilient and stable than the Western spectacle it absorbs. If the emirates can maintain enough contradictions and the secrets of enough foreign powers, no one can call their bluff.

# Postscript

The Burj Dubai, now called the Burj Khalifa in honor of Sheikh Khalifa of Abu Dhabi, has become a monument of sorts to Dubai's debt crisis and its special relationship with Abu Dhabi. Freighted with some resentment, the wealthier and more sober emirate offered a bail out to its sister city-state in December 2009 by giving $10 billion to Dubai World. Dubai World, Dubai Holding, and Investment Corporation of Dubai are three sprawling investment instruments in which the government and the sovereign Sheikh Mohammed are major stakeholders. In the years since 2009, Dubai has been scrambling to restructure debt and is showing some positive signs of recovery. Yet even in May 2011, the IMF warned Dubai that their total debt would reach 53 percent of their total GDP by 2016.[40]

Dubai World has within its umbrella Nakeel, the developer of The World and the various Palm Island experiments as well as DP World, the global ports company. Nakeel's debts presented the most precarious situation and the one that prompted Abu Dhabi to ride to the rescue. Dubai now hopes to rely less on the floating real estate casino of artificial islands and focus on trade, logistics, and tourism. Its cachet as the Vegas of the emirates is only partially diminished by mimicry from other cities in the Middle East who are hiring starchitects for enclaves of all sorts.[41] Meanwhile the furious pace of building – previously almost as fast as a stop-frame time-lapse – has ground to a halt with over 200 projects on hold or canceled and reports of the artificial islands dissolving back into the sea.[42]

Winds of change from the Arab Spring met with the UAE's characteristic set of duplicitous political gifts. The federation has often appeared to opened its front doors while bolting all of the others or appeared to completely capitulate to demands while simultaneously defanging those demands. They often respond to controversy in a way that preserves both public image and the status quo of power. As mentioned above, the government is always prepared to provide a gift of an airline ticket out of the country. In response to demands for something like universal suffrage in electing the Federal National Council members, the UAE relented, and yet this body is largely a ceremonious demonstration of representation since important decisions about the regime are made elsewhere.[43] Zayed Military City, another of the enclave units of development in Dubai, is reportedly training a private military force for security against both external and internal disruption.[44]

## Acknowledgment

This text is adapted and updated from a text published as "Extrastatecraft" from Perspecta 39, "Re_Urbanism" (2007). Reprinted with the permission of Perspecta, Yale School of Architecture.

Notes

1   Credit might naturally go to Peter Hall and his book *The World Cities* (1971) or to Saskia Sassen's *The Global City: New York, London, Tokyo* (1991). This train of thought is, however, closer to an analysis offered by Marchal, 2003. Marchal uses the term "world cities" in reference to Fernand Braudel's 1992 work on city-states and trading capitals.
2   Ohmae, 2000.
3   Anscombe, 2003.
4   Moore, 1976, frontispiece.
5   Heard-Bey, 2004, pp. 174, 238.
6   Al-Fahim, 1995, pp. 73–74.
7   Heard-Bey, 2004, p. 238.
8   Al-Fahim, 1995, p. 147.
9   Al-Fahim, 1995, p. 88.
10  Al Tamimi, 2003, p. 3.
11  Moving west to northeast, Abu Dhabi, Dubai, and Sharjah are the first three emirates, and they each have a chief city of the same name. Continuing further north, toward the Straits of Hormuz are the smaller emirates of Umm al Qaiwain, Ajman, and Ras al Khaimah. Finally, on the eastern coast of this rocky peninsula is the seventh emirate, Fujairah.
12  Al-Fahim, 1995, p. 140; Heard-Bey, 2004, p. 405.
13  www.state.gov/e/eb/ifd/2005/42194.htm; www.abudhabichamber.ae/user/SectionView. aspx?PNodeId=802.
14  Only 18 percent of the population are UAE nationals. The majority of the population (65 percent) are Asians. See: www.datadubai.com/population.htm.
15  Heard-Bey, 2004, p. 107.
16  Al-Fahim, 1995, p. 163.
17  http://realestate.theemiratesnetwork.com/articles/freehold_property.php; www.ameinfo. com/110401.html.
18  *New York Times*, February 17, 2006, p. C1.

19  www.thepalm.ae/index.html.

20  www.emporis.com/en/wm/bu/?id=107779; www.jafza.ae/jafza; www.dnrd.gov.ae/dnrd/
Profile/JabalAliPort+.htm; www.dpworld.ae/jafz/jafz.htm.

21  See www.datadubai.com/population.htm and Marchal, p. 96. The population of the UAE is
over three million and at least 70,000 UAE nationals have Iranian background. Marchal
quotes Fariba Adelkhah's "Dubaï, capitale économique de l'Iran," in Marchal, 2001,
pp. 39–55.

22  Heard-Bey, 2004, pp. 68–72, 284–286.

23  www.dubaiinternetcity.com; www.arabsat.com/Default/About/OurHistory.aspx; www.
dubaiholding.com/english/index.html.

24  *Gulf News*, December 19, 2005.

25  "Energy 2030 to get underway next Wednesday," *Emirates News Agency*, October 27,
2006.

26  Marchal, 2003, p. 107.

27  www.saadiyat.ae/en.

28  www.masdarcity.ae/en/index.aspx.

29  *MENA Business Reports*, December 13, 2005.

30  *Construction Week*, December 17–23, 2005, p. 1.

31  *Herald Tribune*, September 26, 2005.

32  www.dubai.ae/portal/en.portal?dae_citizen,Article_000214,1,&_nfpb=true&_
pageLabel=view.

33  *Construction Week*, December 17–23, 2005, p. 32.

34  Khalaf and Alkobaisi, 1999, p. 292.

35  www.hrw.org/reports/2009/05/18/island-happiness-0.

36  www.saadiyat.ae/en/project-update/saadiyat-construction-village.html.

37  www.alsunut.com; "Glittering towers in a war zone," *The Economist*, December 7, 2006.
Alsunut Development Company Ltd. is a venture of the Khartoum State, National Social
Insurance, the DAL Group Company Ltd.

38  Davis, 2005.

39  Boal *et al.*, 2005, p. 18 (use of "new/old"); and "An exchange on *Afflicted Powers: Capital
and Spectacle in a New Age of War*," interview with Hal Foster and Retort, *October* 115,
Winter 2006, p. 5.

40  *The Times*, October 12, 2011.

41  *The Economist*, December 29, 2010; *The Guardian*, November 29, 2010.

42  *The Telegraph*, June 12, 2011.

43  *The Economist*, June 30, 2011.

44  *New York Times*, May 14, 2011.

Chapter 2

# Atlanta

*Rem Koolhaas*

Sometimes it is important to find what the city *is* – instead of what it was, or what it should be. That is what drove me to Atlanta – an intuition that the real city at the end of the 20th century could be found there . . .

- Atlanta has CNN and Coca-Cola.
- Atlanta has a black mayor, and it will have the Olympics.
- Atlanta has culture, or at least it has a Richard Meier museum (like Ulm, Barcelona, Frankfurt, The Hague, etc.).
- Atlanta has an airport; actually it has 40 airports. One of them is the biggest airport in the world. Not that everybody wants to be *there*; it's a hub, a spoke, an airport for connections. It could be anywhere.
- Atlanta has history, or rather it had history; now it has history machines that replay the battles of the Civil War every hour on the hour. Its real history has been erased, removed, or artificially resuscitated.
- Atlanta has other elements that provide intensity without physical density: one building looks innocent from the outside – like a regular supermarket – but is actually the largest, most sophisticated food hall in the world. Each day it receives three cargo planes of fresh products from Holland, four from Paris, two from Southeast Asia. It proves that there are hundreds of thousands, maybe millions, of gourmets in Atlanta.
- Atlanta does not have the classical symptoms of city; it is not dense; it is a sparse, thin carpet of habitation, a kind of suprematist composition of little fields. Its strongest contextual givens are

vegetal and infrastructural: forest and roads. Atlanta is not a city; it is a *landscape*.

- Atlanta's basic form – but it is not a form – its basic *formlessness* is generated by the highway system, a stretched X surrounded by an O: branches running across the city connecting to a single perimeter highway. The X brings people in and out; the O – like a turntable – takes them anywhere. They are thinking about projecting a super-O somewhere in the beyond.

- Atlanta has nature, both original and improved – a sparkling, perfect nature where no leaf is ever out of place. Its artificiality sometimes makes it hard to tell whether you are outside or inside; somehow, you're *always* in nature.

- Atlanta does not have planning, exactly, but another process called zoning. Atlanta's zoning law is very interesting; its first line tells you what to do if you want to propose an exception to the regulations. The regulations are so weak that the exception is the norm. Elsewhere, zoning has a bad name – for putting things in their place simplistically: work, sleep, shop, play. Atlanta has a kind of reverse zoning, zoning as instrument of indetermination, making anything possible anywhere.

Atlanta has changed at an unbelievable speed, like in a nature film when a tree grows in five seconds. It reveals some of the most critical shifts in architecture/urbanism[1] of the past 15 years, the most important being the shift from center to periphery, and beyond.

No city illustrates this shift, its reasons and its potentials, better than Atlanta. In fact, Atlanta shifted so quickly and so completely that the center/edge opposition is no longer the point. There *is* no center, therefore no periphery. Atlanta is now a centerless city, or a city with a potentially infinite number of centers. In that way, Atlanta is like LA, but LA is always urban; Atlanta sometimes post-urban.

When I first went there in 1973, the notion of downtown in America was in crisis. Downtown Manhattan, downtown Boston, downtown San Francisco: the cores of most American cities were in total, demonstrative states of disrepair – crime, rotting infrastructures, eroding tax bases, etc. There was an apocalyptic atmosphere of downtown doom, doubt that they could ever be rescued.

But Atlanta was an exception. Construction was resuming in former disaster areas. Block by block, downtown was being recovered (literally, some downtowns looked like accidental checkerboards: half-full, half-empty) and actually rebuilt. Atlanta was the test case for an American renaissance, for the rebirth of the American downtown. And you can't talk about Atlanta's rebirth without talking about John Portman.

John Portman, artist-architect, is said to be a very rich billionaire, his story shrouded in rumors of bankruptcy. He works in offices crowded with his own Pollock-like paintings.

He is undoubtedly a genius in his own mind.

In a book on John Portman by John Portman, John Portman writes, "I consider architecture frozen music."

The lobby of his newest building downtown is a private museum for his own sculptures, gigantic homages to fellow artists such as Dubuffet, Brancusi, and Stella: megalomania as welcome.

John Portman is a hybrid; he is architect *and* developer, two roles in one.

That explains his tremendous power: the combination makes him a myth.

It means, theoretically, that every idea he has can be realized, that he can make money with his architecture, and that the roles of architect and developer can forever fuel each other.

In the early seventies, to a power-starved profession, this synthesis seemed revolutionary, like a self-administered Faustian bargain.

But with these two identities merged in one person, the traditional opposition between client and architect – two stones that create sparks – disappears. The vision of the architect is realized without opposition, without influence, without inhibition.

Portman started with one block, made money, and developed the next block, a cycle that then triggered Atlanta's rebirth. But the new Atlanta was a virgin rebirth: *a city of clones*. It was not enough for Portman to fill block after block with his own architecture (usually without very interesting programs), but as further consolidation, he connected each of his buildings to each of his other buildings with bridges, forming an elaborate spiderweb of skywalks with himself at the center. Once you ventured into the system, there was almost no incentive to visit the rest of downtown, no way to escape.

John Portman is also responsible for single-handedly perfecting a device that spread from Atlanta to the rest of America, and from America to the rest of the world (even Europe): he (re)invented the atrium.

Since the Romans, the atrium had been a hole in a house or a building that injects light and air – the outside – into the center; in Portman's hands it became the opposite: a container of artificiality that allows its occupants to avoid daylight forever – a hermetic interior, sealed against the real. Actually, the evacuation of the center implied by the atrium, the subsequent covering of the hole, the mostly cellular accommodation of its perimeter – hotel rooms, office cubicles –

make it a modern panopticon: the cube hollowed out to create an invasive, all-inclusive, revealing transparency in which everyone becomes everyone else's guard – architectural equivalent of Sartre's *No Exit*, "Hell is other people . . ."

Downtown becomes an accumulation of voided panopticons inviting their own voluntary prisoners: the center as a prison system.

Portman's most outrageous atrium is the Atlanta Marriott, a tour de force transformation of the slab – democratic, neutral, anonymous – which he splits in two halves, then eviscerates to bend its carcass into a sphere – as nearly as concrete permits.

This interior is not "frozen music" but "arrested maelstrom." Its accumulated architectural intensity is beyond a single perceptual grasp. Is the result of this convulsive effort beauty? Does it matter?

The new atrium became a replica as inclusive as downtown itself, an *ersatz* downtown. Downtown's buildings are no longer complementary; they don't need each other; they become hostile; they compete. Downtown disintegrates into multiple downtowns, a cluster of autonomies. The more ambitious these autonomies, the more they undermine the real downtown – its messy conditions, its complexities, its irregularities, its densities, its ethnicities.

With atriums as their private mini-centers, buildings no longer depend on specific locations. They can be anywhere.

And if they can be anywhere, why should they be downtown?

At first the atrium seemed to help rehabilitate and stabilize Atlanta's downtown, but it actually accelerated its demise.

That was Portman's Paradox.

The rediscovery of downtown quickly degenerated into a proliferation of quasi-downtowns that together destroyed the essence of center.

By the eighties, building activity had moved away from Portman's part of the city, north toward the perimeter highway, then beyond . . .

Atlanta was the launching pad of the distributed downtown; downtown had exploded. Once atomized, its autonomous particles could go anywhere; they gravitated opportunistically toward points of freedom, cheapness, easy access, diminished contextual nuisance. Millions of fragments landed in primeval forests sometimes connected to highways, sometimes to nothing at all. Infrastructure seemed almost irrelevant – some splinters flourished in complete isolation – or even counter-productive: in the middle-class imagination, *not* being connected to MARTA, the subway system, meant protection from downtown's unspeakable "problems."

The new program was usually abstract – offices for companies that were no longer tied to geography, fueled by an unlimited demand for insurance (cruel equation: hell for the insured – Elsewhere; paradise for the insurers – Atlanta).

Sometimes an area becomes suddenly popular. Attractors appear: it might be the proximity of a new, or even a rumored highway, beautiful nature, or comfortable neighborhoods. Attraction is translated in building. Sometimes the nature of the attractor remains a mystery; seemingly *nothing* is there (that may be the attraction!) – it might be the building itself. Suddenly clumps of office and residential towers spring up, then a church, a mall, a Hyatt, a cineplex. Another "center" is born, stretching the city to apparent infinity.

North of downtown there is a place where a highway starts to fork, leaving downtown behind. There is an area of nothingness, and beyond the nothingness you see outposts of a new architecture that has the intensity of downtown, but it's not downtown. It's something totally different.

In 1987, somewhere near here, two skyscrapers were built facing each other, one hyper-modern (i.e., clad in mirror-glass), the other almost Stalinist (covered in prefabricated concrete). They were built by the same firm for different corporate entities, each searching for its own elusive identity.

Two buildings, so close together, built by a single firm in opposite languages ... A new esthetic operates in Atlanta: the random juxtaposition of entities that have nothing in common except their coexistence, or – favorite formulation of the surrealists – "the accidental encounter between an umbrella and a sewing machine on a dissecting table."[2]

I wanted to find out what kind of firm could design with such equanimity, what kind of firm could generate the same enthusiasm for such different architectures. So I made a tour of Atlanta's architects' offices.

They were usually located in idyllic situations – dense forests, hills, on lakes. Designed as corporate villas, they were large, sometimes very large: 250–300 people. The typical architect was a southerner, 26, laundered at an Ivy League school, who then returned to Atlanta to produce buildings like these two towers. They could generate an entire oeuvre in one afternoon – receiving instructions over the phone – then have it rejected without pain. They would plan symmetrical projects, then find them distorted overnight by economics – shrunk by failure, inflated by success – and have to perform adaptive amputations or stitch on additional limbs with the urgency of a field hospital: infantry on the frontline of an architectural panic.

The partners were very accessible and eager to talk about Atlanta, their work, the present situation, the dilemmas they faced – a cluster of issues that formed a very plausible argument for the emergence and consolidation of postmodern architecture, the only architecture, it seemed, that could be generated quickly enough to satisfy the needs of the clients.

In a situation where architecture is no longer the construction of city but, like a new branch of physics, the outcome of the dynamics of force fields in perpetual motion, that precious professional alibi of the architect – the mystical "spark" of inspiration – is obviously outdated. No one can wait for it, least of all the architect. His task is truly impossible: to express increasing turbulence in a stable medium.

Architecture has always equated greatness with the breaking of rules.

Now you can be great through their effortless application.

Only a postmodern architect can design building proposals of huge scale and complexity in a day, any day. Postmodernism is not a movement: it is a new form of professionalism, of architectural education, not one that creates knowledge or culture, but a technical training that creates a new unquestioning, a new efficacy in applying new, streamlined dogma.

Post-inspirational, past erudition, intimately connected with speed, a futurism, postmodernism is a mutation that will be from now on part of architectural practice – an architecture of the flight forward.

One of the offices I visited had a room: it was locked. Inside was a model of a large piece of Atlanta – particular features: none. Twelve people were working on four schemes, each as big as the Rockefeller Center, each composition hyper-symmetrical but placed arbitrarily on the huge map, surrounded by single-family homes; there was no sign of highways ... At the last moment the table had been enlarged to make room for one additional Rockefeller Center.

The model was a complete inversion of metropolis as we know it – not the systematic assembly of a critical mass but its systematic dismantlement, a seemingly absurd dispersion of concentration. Alarmingly, it suggested that the elements that had once *made* the city would now cease to work if they got too close together. Spaced out, far apart, they needed the neutral medium of nature or (at the most) the single-family house to ensure further their noninterference.

The reason that the room had to be secret – the only vault in the otherwise open office landscape – was that none of the clients of these five centers knew that the other projects were being prepared. The architects believed that there were probably still other architects working on similar projects, maybe for the same neighborhood – in similar rooms in other offices – but nobody could really be sure.

This deliberate disinformation, lack of adjustment, represents a revolutionary reversal of the role architects traditionally claim. They no longer create order, resist chaos, imagine coherence, fabricate entities. From form givers they have become facilitators. In Atlanta, architects have aligned themselves with the uncontrollable, have become its official agents, instruments of the unpredictable: from imposing to yielding in one generation.

Working on the emergence of new urban configurations, they have discovered a vast new realm of potential and freedom: to go rigorously with the flow, architecture/urbanism as a form of letting go . . .

Atlanta is a creative experiment, but it is not intellectual or critical; it has taken place without argument. It represents current conditions without any imposition of program, manifesto, ideology.

As extrapolation, each site in Atlanta is exposed to a theoretical carpet bombardment of "centers," possibilities hovering somewhere, waiting to be activated by a mysterious process – only vaguely related to money – according to laws not yet identified, at least not by architects.

It is now possible, at any point in Atlanta (and Atlanta is just a metaphor for the world) to create a brutal, often ugly container that accommodates a wide variety of quasi-urban activities and to turn anywhere, with savage competence, into a point of density, a ghost of city.

In the future, a "realistic" frisson[3] about the periphery as a new playground for architects, a field of one-liners, will not be enough. If *the* center no longer exists, it follows that there is no longer a periphery either. The death of the first implies the evaporation of the second. Now *all* is city, a new pervasiveness that includes landscape, park, industry, rust belt, parking lot, housing tract, single-family house, desert, airport, beach, river, ski slope, even downtown.

Atlanta's is a conclusive architecture that will eventually acquire beauty. Sometimes there are prefigurations, occasional schemes that seem to intellectualize the new freedoms: a project by I. M. Pei for a chain of skyscrapers very close to the highway, causing short, stroboscopic sensations for passing cars, even at 55 mph.

Paradoxically, a more convincing premonition of this potential architecture is the prefabricated landscape that is being prepared to receive it. Atlanta has an ideal climate. Because it approximates jungle conditions it was used as training ground for the war in Vietnam. Everything grows there immediately and energetically. Landscaping carries authority, the vegetal sometimes more robust than the built. A thick tapestry of idyll accommodates each architectural appearance and forms its only context; the vegetal is replacing the urban: a panorama of seamless artificiality, so organized, lush, welcoming, that it sometimes seems like another interior, a fluid collective domain, glimpsed through tinted glass, venetian blinds, and the other distancing devices of the alienated architecture – *almost* accessible, like a seductive fairy tale.

Imagine Atlanta as a new imperial Rome – large urban figures no longer held together by small-scale urban cement but by forest, fragments floating in trees.[4]

After John Portman rescued the center, he could only react to its explosion as a developer must – by following the "demand." To outbid its centrifugality he proposed an entirely new city way up north, beyond the periphery even, and named it Northpark.

It is presented in an impressionistic brochure with a conscious fuzziness (derived from recent breakthrough in science?).

"The first of the series symbolizes the gaseous state," says the caption, "beginnings of an idea with only a hint of structure. The second expresses the solidification of ideas into emerging forms. And the last adds shading, form, and structure, bringing Northpark closer to reality."

Looking at the Northpark renderings, you may laugh, but you may also think, "Where have we seen these forms before?" Are they ugly or accidentally, unbelievably beautiful? Is this the reappearance of the sublime? Is it finally possible to identify them as the same shapes that Malevich launched at the beginning of the century – Architectons – abstract pre-architectures, the vacant but *available* volumes that could contain whatever program the century would generate in its ruthless unfolding?

If the forms of Northpark can be traced back to Malevich's Architectons, the most extreme streak of modernism, Atlanta itself can be described as a mixture of the imaginations of Malevich and Frank Lloyd Wright, whose Broadacre City described the American continent as a continuous urban – that is to say, artificial – condition: homogeneous, low intensity, with an occasional high point of visible concentration. In other words: there was advance warning. It did not come as a surprise. Atlanta is a realized prophesy.

Are these inhabited envelopes in their thick forests the final manifestation of modernization? Is this modernity?

Modernity is a radical principle. It is destructive. It has destroyed the city as we know it. We now inhabit "what used to be the city." In a bizarre way, Portman's Northpark – in fact, Atlanta as a whole – comes close to fulfilling that kind of modernity, a post-cataclysmic new beginning that celebrates revolutionary forms in liberated relationships, justified, finally, by no other reason than their appeal to our senses.

Portman lost his nerve with Northpark.

Maybe it was the economy, or maybe he never believed in it. He returned to the center, this time applying the esthetics of the periphery: a singular tower no longer interested in belonging, in being part of his web, but a needle, standing simply on its own.

It is *in* downtown, but not *of* downtown.

Downtown has become anywhere.

Hiding behind it, a private dream: his very last, most secret project is a touching relic – it shows the depth of his own misreading.

Now, maybe as a personal testament, he wants to bring the European city to the heart of Atlanta: arrogance or sentimentality? A rip-off of Leon Krier's "community" emblem: glass pyramid over pedestrian plaza supported on four pylonlike buildings. When I asked in Portman's office whether he was inspired by Krier, I was officially told, "Mr Portman doesn't need inspiration."

Portman has three identities according to Portman: artist, architect, developer. He has yet to discover a fourth: that of the thinker or theoretician. He could assert that *each city is now an Atlanta* – Singapore, Paris – what is the Louvre now if not the ultimate atrium?

He could have been – or maybe is – disurbanist to the world. **1987/1994**

Notes

1 Of course, the word *urbanism* – which somehow suggests a minimum of steering – does not apply. For now, we could adopt the term *disurbanism* which, in the twenties, described a branch of constructivist urban theory aimed at dissolving the city.
2 Comte du Lautréamont, *Les Chants de Maldoror*, 1868–70.
3 During the eighties, critics like Alexander Tzonis and Liane Lefaivre began to suggest that the periphery might be the appropriate territory for a disabused architecture of Dirty Realism, so named after its eponymous literary equivalent.
4 The purity of this contrast may soon be compromised by the extravagant, palatial frenzy of Atlanta's residential architecture, now generating colossal mansions in absurd proximities at the potential expense of the vegetal. But then, that may make the city ultimately even more Roman.

Chapter 3

# Barcelona – Re-thinking Urbanistic Projects

*Joan Busquets*

In the 1980–2000 period, the city of Barcelona developed a series of urbanistic strategies which sought to reinterpret existing urban structures and to restructure primary functional systems in order to face up to the start of the new century. In a description of this process it is vital to bring a new approach to certain of the city's urban planning projects, with a view to including new urban dynamics.

Barcelona's urban planning process over the last two decades led to many reflections on the necessity of disciplinary changes. The spaces of city planning, whether in terms of urban architecture or the urban project, have undergone a highly interesting development and are potential points of reference for future evolutions.

There are a number of important approaches to the issue of city-making that are a part of the recent discussions in Barcelona, as well as Europe as a whole. These include the following.

1 The *existing city* is a point of departure for future planning rather than a passive datum in the long-term project. An understanding of its forms and its capacity for modification and transformation can provide the basis for valuable projects of intervention and urban improvement.

This approach sees the city as an entity comprising *different morphologies*. According to the intrinsic conditions of their historical

**3.1**
**Barcelona region.**
**Compact central**
**town and city**
**system around it**

origins and the way in which their construction materialized, strategies of change can be introduced in the form of specific projects. So morphologies have different forms of organization and act as relatively autonomous urban units. The Italian school of the 1970s, represented by A. Rossi and C. Aymonino, blazed a trail for this kind of disciplinary development.[1]

2    *Infrastructures* are the means to ensuring the functioning of the city, and sometimes explain its origin. Their importance led the Modern Movement to use them as the basis for their propositional structure: Le Corbusier described infrastructures as communicating with seven levels or "ways," corresponding to different levels in their organizational hierarchy. Conventional planning still accords infrastructures a demiurgical value in ensuring the correct functioning of the whole. It was according to these principles that networks of motorways were planned for post-war European cities, sometimes generating greater urban destruction than the war itself. Above all, they established gaps between the infrastructure – the terrain of engineers – and the spaces between the roads to be developed by architects for residence, industry, amenities, etc.

It is true that certain levels of efficiency have to be guaranteed, but we are discovering that there are different ways to ensure sufficient levels of service and a need to evaluate the material, social and cultural costs of transforming infrastructures. The city has to be efficient but also habitable, and the use of infrastructures is more adaptable than we ever imagined. By way of example, the

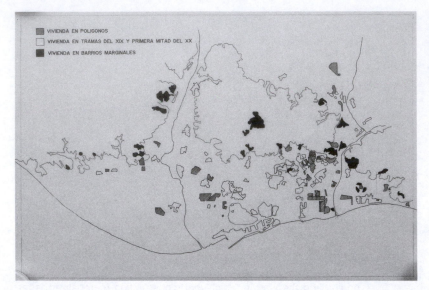

VIVIENDA EN POLIGONOS
VIVIENDA EN TRAMAS DEL XIX Y PRIMERA MITAD DEL XX
VIVIENDA EN BARRIOS MARGINALES

3.2
**Metropolitan Barcelona and housing development in the 1960s: housing estates, row houses and informal sectors**

discussion between public transport and private mobility is, in Europe, finding innovative and exemplary formulas of commitment. At the same time, the evolution of the various infrastructures – communication between parts of the territory – is changing at a dizzying rate.

It seems necessary to reinstate the role of *infrastructure as an integrated element* of the city, which is attributed the power of articulation and the weight of urban significance, rather than being an element of separation between adjacent parts. This is one of the major targets of today's urbanistic discipline, which is recovering the strategic, dynamic value of infrastructures, but also their innovative capacity within the urban and territorial landscape. This leads to the hypothesis that urban systems have to be designed in "networks" that on the one hand ensure their complementary nature, and on the other allow their definition as multipurpose units which are firmly implanted in their territory.

3  A new understanding of the *city's fit within its macrogeography* – to apply a similar interpretation to that of F. Braudel[2] – seems to be the motive behind the orientation of major urban projects in Europe. The issues of the greater landscape and the relationship with the territory are, once again, basic: this explains the force behind the recovery of the line between cities and water (the famous waterfronts), the connection of ports with historic cities, and the reservation of

3.3
**Aerial view, 1998**

valleys and watercourses, etc. These are themes which appear as leitmotifs in strategic operations in Barcelona, Lisbon, Lyons and many other European cities.

4   Recognition that the complexity of the project in the city calls for the intervention of *various actors*, including the public and private sectors but also associative and cultural sectors. It is only on the basis of the judicious involvement of these agents that the urban project can achieve the revitalizing effects in economic and social terms that are so often pursued. This explains its importance for the communicative action that is so relevant in the Anglo-Saxon context, as represented in the work of John Forester, Patsy Healey or Jordi Borja.[3] This capacity for dialogue of the projects does not

signify the propositional negation that occasionally confounded advocacy planning in the 1970s, as "consensus" is only effective if there is a prior proposal which can be submitted for critical discussion. This is also the root of the force of image to which urban projects are subjected, on occasion succumbing to the temptations of the media and overlooking the rigor that is vital to their disciplinary argumentation.

3.4
**Suburban fabrics, made of different types of urban projects**

5   The evolution of projects in the city is subject to an ever-increasing *multicultural tension*. The "ideas of force" in each context vary very quickly. The discussion between global innovation conveyed by the international media, sometimes acting as leader culture, and the intrinsic value of that which is local, contextual and unique is a central issue. Writers such as François Ascher[4] seek to distinguish the consequences for the urban planning model, while others such as Joel Garreau advocate the innovative strength of this tension, which, in keeping with its argument, takes place outside the city in the form of "edge cities" where "the new" seeks the best space.

Yet it is true that the city today is more than ever a "multicultural" place, due both to the composition and origin of its residents, and to

3.5
**Urban park, placed within the
suburban fabric**

the variety of people who visit and use it in very different ways. This leads to the need to recover in projects a capacity for symbiosis – in other words, an active state of these situations seeking recognition of their values in their differences.

6   The general objective of projects with the most progressive ambitions is to seek a *rebalance* between the various parts of the city, according to which a fair city is not one that is equal in form but one that offers a fairly homogeneous level of service and use. These principles of "social justice" advocated among others by David Harvey[5] on the basis of a Marxist interpretation of urban evolution are based on more general strategies as to the indexes of land or the rates of urban development and socialization of the surplus value, etc. This is where the legal framework has to back the plan and the urban project in order for these aims to be achieved.

It might be said that, in our context, the legal framework is defined by laws which happen to take their name from "land," giving us an idea of how important this factor is in urban development. It has on occasion been these laws which have dictated the formal structure of plans and projects for the city, but we need to reinterpret them as the framework according to which more rational and balanced development can come about without overlooking other variables.

7    Recognition of the seminal value of cities' "historic" planning projects, which act as distinguishing references but also as models for their modern-day development. This is the case of the influence of Cerdà's project on the Barcelona of 1855, or Wagner's for Vienna at the turn of the century.[6]

The interpretation of some of these projects will be key to the interventions described below.

# Recovering the city

These salient factors or dimensions go to explain the theoretical "framework" in which urbanistic projects are taking place. We are, then, a long way from having a single, precise, well-defined "theory," and are working in a context which is multidimensional and above all "non-linear," as it was thought after the war, to produce proposals for urban transformation and rehabilitation.

3.6
**Plaza intervention
to recover left
over spaces**

It is important to realize that among these factors, the project or the plan for the city and its parts revived a concern with the physical aspect which two-dimensional "planning" had practically forgotten. Today the urban project seeks to discern, within this complexity, criteria of physical coherence, urban composition and spatial priority that suggest a rebirth of the practice of "urban urbanism"[7] and "urban architecture." This direction, not without its difficulties, centers the discussion of the project for our cities on the turn of this century. The recovery of a degree of protagonism of the physical dimension of the project or the urban strategy to a large extent involves emphasis on the development of the public space as a privileged space in the urban event, be it in the city center or on the suburban outskirts. Its recomposition answers the above-mentioned criteria of integration and symbiosis, more than the criterion of order in urban composition in the second half of the nineteenth and early twentieth centuries, Multidimensionality, a differential use of spaces and their adaptability oblige us to consider other criteria in the composition of spaces of this kind.

## The different scales of the urban project

Recent urbanistic practice has been based on proposals which correspond to fields of a different scale and different levels of definition according to the needs of the brief. While we describe the factor of context, plans and projects are subject to their individual times of development. We might almost say that a city works with *"visions" of its future in the mid-term*, which are linked to fairly precise proposals for some elements – infrastructure, landscape, macrogeography, etc. – and on the basis of which a general "consensus" can be established, such as, for example, the opening up to the seafront of Barcelona, which then went on to take the form of plans and projects with more specific briefs.[8] However the city works at the same time with *strategies of improvement* and rehabilitation, which are based on *the internal logic* of the existing construction of its fabrics and neighborhoods.

## An interpretation of the contemporary urban planning experience of Barcelona

This chapter now goes on to describe a series of actions on the fabrics and empty interstices of today's Barcelona in an attempt to explain how it can operate on different levels: projects to improve and renovate neighborhoods, programs to improve mobility, and areas of new centrality supported by large obsolete spaces left between districts.

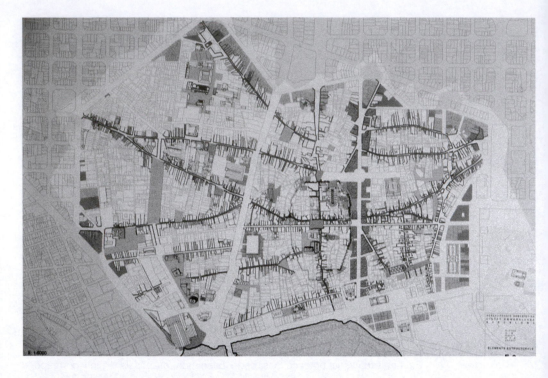

## Suburban fabrics and the residential periphery

Barcelona, like most cities, can be considered on the basis of the construction of its various districts. In 1981, at a seminar at the School of Architecture,[9] we worked on an interpretation of Barcelona on the basis of its main morphologies: the old town, the Eixample, the suburban fabrics and the residential periphery. The "suburban Barcelona reading" stands out in particular: in the second half of the nineteenth century the old boroughs around central Barcelona (Poblenou, Sagrera, Sant Andreu, Horta, Gràcia, Sarrià, Sant Gervasi, Sants, Poble Sec, etc.) mainly developed a series of interesting urban planning parts, constituting the base which is sometimes referred to as "other Barcelonas." The work shows the many latent or explicit projects and plans on which the traditional Barcelona, comprising its present-day Districts, was built, modified and transformed,[10] with the urbanization of streets and roads, projects for squares, the creation of new streets through districts, drawn-back facades, avenues to connect the entire city, housing projects with squares, major amenities or residential complexes, etc. It explains the continual propositional capacity which is so often based on a conflicting logic but which, finally, after differing periods of time, produces and renovates the city. These projects are sometimes considered "minor" in comparison with large urban planning proposals, such as the expansion of the Eixample across the plain, but together they represent a projectual articulation of comparable entity which should perhaps not be seen

3.7
**Old City**
**reinterpretation**

as exclusive. In this way a fundamental part of Barcelona was woven from medium-density housing with shops, amenities and production and industrial centers on the same scale.

It is on the basis of this logic that we have to reinterpret the PERIs (Internal Renovation Plans) of the city districts carried out in the eighties with the idea of "adding" new elements to the existing city in order to ensure its rehabilitation and renovation.[11] The specific aims vary a great deal: from the rationalization of the existing street layout to the reuse of unoccupied land within these districts for amenities and gardens.

## Interventions in squares, parks and gardens

The planning logic and legal framework for a hundred or so squares, parks and gardens throughout these districts in *the internal process* of this suburban Barcelona constitute an updating of its original structure, conforming a metropolitan whole with the central city. This process judiciously pieces together a puzzle in which we can highlight the following types.

### Urban parks

These parks, set in the urban fabric, with dimensions of between six and ten hectares, correspond to the re-use of industrial and service enclosures. Obvious examples include the Escorxador (a former abattoir), España Industrial, El Clot, Pegaso and Renfe-Meridiana.

The foremost purpose of these parks was to turn a situation of "urban backs" – historically created by the walls of these enclosures – into a permeable urban element capable of offering a new service to the surrounding neighborhoods.[12]

### Squares and gardens

These are small operations totally integrated into the city's various residential fabrics. The sheer quantity of works carried out – over 150 – and their quality supposes a thorough-going rehabilitation of the urban space of Barcelona.

Despite their limited size, their central positions in each district fragment has the quite remarkable effect of generating increased urbanity. The squares respond to clear functional needs to systematize traffic and overground car parking, and set out very varied spaces.

Most of the projects manifest a particular concern with restoring the symbolic values of the square, such as the incorporation of especially significant elements like sculptures, which had previously disappeared with excess functionality of design.

*Gardens with amenities*

These include a series of old private properties which are now re-used as public spaces in the city. The old buildings are converted for use as communal amenities. The specific theme of the project is the adaptation of a garden that was designed for exclusive use to new functional and urban requirements.

*Urban axes*

These interventions systematize the intermediate street layout in order to increase the protagonism of pedestrian space in some principal elements of the urban form. They are predominantly linear projects whose most significant decisions involve the design of the cross section. In turn, the project always tables a new discussion with the general street layout and public transport; and with parking opportunities and the tangential uses of the commercial ground floors. It is, then, easy to see how this introduces a degree of complexity into the management process.

Particular mention should also be made of Via Julia and Carrer de Prim, two newly designed urban axes on Barcelona's periphery. Their construction has turned abandoned spaces between building into civic axes, which give a new lease of life to the areas of Nou Barris and El Besòs, respectively.

*Large-scale parks*

These larger interventions change Barcelona's overall proportion of green. They include: the seafront, with its conversion into a great linear park and public access to the new beaches; the western side of Montjuïc overlooking the Llobregat delta, where the Olympic sports amenities were installed; the Vall d'Hebron in the northern part of the city, where residential land has been used to build a great park with amenities in one of the most built-up sectors; and the Diagonal park in the western extreme, which completes one of the city's large sports areas.

**The restructuring of Ciutat Vella**

The strategy of recovering the suburban districts and peripheral areas was to find a special complement in Ciutat Vella and the Eixample.

Urban areas such as the district of Ciutat Vella (the old town) called for more resolute action, in view of the fact that they were in a very advanced state of decline. Here the "projects" sought "internal reform," which consisted of evacuating strategic blocks to improve living conditions (the sunlighting and ventilation of houses that J. L. Sert and the GATCPAC had called for in the 1930s for these very same sectors), based on the theory that this was the only way to bring about a change in the process. In the face of the disinterest of proprietors, who considered these districts to have no future and to be destined

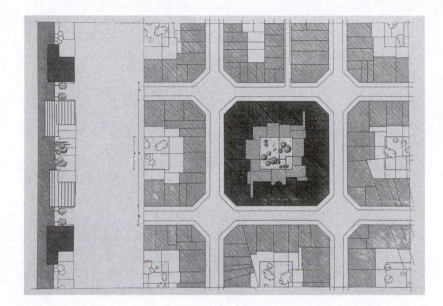

3.8
**Building code to green internal courtyards for Barcelona's Eixample**

to become ghettos, reorganization meant major public investment. These interventions led to others which reinforced the historically central functions based there. To this end, new cultural functions were developed, like the Centre de Cultura Contemporània and the Museu d'Art Contemporani in the old Casa de Caritat hospice buildings, and agreements were promoted to encourage the universities to relocate faculties there to attract students and lecturers to these spaces. Reconversion has reached an advanced stage, yet it is a project which still needs time to become irreversible.[13]

"Rehabilitation strategies" were also undertaken in the famous Eixample, the city extension designed by Cerdà in the mid-nineteenth century, which was the point of reference of a seminal "urban plan" for Barcelona. The Eixample had its own economic dynamic in which, like so many modern downtowns, residents were tending to get pushed out by the pressures of more powerful tertiary activities. Intervention in interior spaces, turning inner courtyards into mainly private gardens with a dozen or so for public use, gave a new incentive to residence, the strategy being accompanied by other means of support for housing and detaining the tertiary sector – which was later to find more convenient premises in the new downtowns.

### From the Cerdà Plan to Barcelona's Eixample
The value of the area of the Eixample in the formation of contemporary Barcelona requires attention to both the dimensions of the project and the present-day urbanistic result. Let's compare the plan to the built city.

Ildefons Cerdà devoted over twenty years to generating the ideas in his project and making its implementation viable. It is beyond doubt a fundamental project in the formalization of contemporary Barcelona, but it is also a pioneering work in modern urban planning theory.

Cerdà planned a thorough reworking of Barcelona, on the scale and dimension expressed in his powerful concept of city. At the same time he was introducing the first set of modern urban planning instruments, where the project for the new city involved an analytical approach to reality and cities which was neither deterministic nor univocal.

The advances made by Cerdà have recently been discussed in the light of documents discovered in various archives.[14] These prove that he was a singular figure in European urban planning, and one who has been underestimated to date – due perhaps to the difficult gestation of his project.

We have to bear in mind the fact that the "founders" of modern urban planning generally mentioned in the history books – R. Baumeister (1874), J. Stübben (1890), R. Unwin (1909) etc. – carried out their work after Cerdà and probably did not have information about Barcelona's urbanistic process.

The theory of urban development on which Cerdà was working regarded prior conceptual formulation as being vital to the drafting of a city project.[15] His theory included the 1859 *Teoría para la Construcción de la Ciudad* (Theory for the Construction of the City) and the 1879 *Teoría General de la Urbanización* (General Theory of Urbanization).

For Cerdà, each work of "theory on" required its "application to" a specific case, and his theoretical approaches in turn had to be proved to be viable; in his own words, "the best idea is useless unless the means to carry it out are presented at the same time."

He developed his theory according to three principles:

1   Hygiene, based on the critique of the existing urban situation, with sound precedents. Cerdà wrote the *Monografía estadística de la clase obrera* (Statistical report on the working class) which accompanies the description of the preliminary project in which he minutely studies living conditions in the walled city. In addition, the description of the preliminary project presupposes an in-depth geographical analysis of the position and siting of the city, as well as its climatology and sunlighting. His ultimate purpose was to produce a thorough-going urban analysis to help him make propositional decisions. This concern with information based on disciplinary research led him to a further study of other cities such as Paris, and to interpreting maps of such far-flung cities as Boston, Turin, Stockholm, Buenos Aires and Saint Petersburg, among others.

2 The second component of Cerdà's theory was traffic flow. The profound impression of the steam train, with which he became acquainted on its introduction in Barcelona, led him to think about how to prepare the city for this great instrument of mechanical mobility.

3 Finally, Cerdà introduced a new idea of city which saw it spread right across the Barcelona plain: the already constructed and the yet to be built. We might say that his project involved the refounding of Barcelona.

This idea of a hygienic, functional city was, according to Cerdà, to produce conditions of equality among the residents using it; his proposal was therefore to cover the entire territory so that all the forms of settlement would fit into this homogeneous fabric.

Cerdà's proposal for the natural space consisted of organizing the city by means of street layout and regulations:

1 The basic layout comprised a system of street blocks situated between axes of 113.3 meters and streets of 20 meters. Its directrices correspond to the dominant lines of the plain, and are turned through 45° from the north, repeating the Roman orientation. The general or regional layout comprised a greater breadth of layout – 50 meters – to establish the main functional relations: Gran Via, Diagonal, Meridiana and Paral·lel. These two latter layouts correspond, as their names indicate, to their geographical position, and explicitly manifest the idea of bringing a global design to the city by integrating the different scales of interpretation.

2 When finally passed in 1860, Cerdà's proposal included a series of construction regulations that differed from those established by the urban police, which had traditionally formed part of a single juridical *habeas*. At the same time, he purported to guarantee good hygienic conditions, and proposed that only 50 per cent of the plot in the center of the block be developed. Cerdà trusted that the scope of the great Eixample would introduce large tracts of land into the market, thereby making cheap land available for affordable housing.

3 Economic thought aimed to put into practice Cerdà's constant idea that projects should be viable. The distinguished engineer's concern with this issue had been revived by his visits to Paris, where he had been a privileged observer of the fundamental changes that Baron Hausmann was carrying out in the French capital. Here, there were two interesting extremes. The first was the need for property-owners

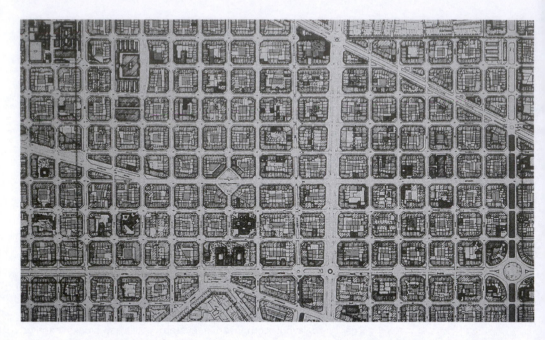

to contribute to the development scheme – a bold and highly socializing proposal for the time. The second controversial idea was his determination to make the renovation of Ciutat Vella economically viable by associating it with the dynamics and benefits of the extension of the city over the plain. The very ambitious scope of this proposal came up against an overwhelming reaction on the part of property-owners in the old town, who finally vetoed the situation, and the "Renovation" part of the Cerdà project was never passed.

3.9
**Intervention on existing blocks to improve residential quality**

This was one of the great urban planning projects in nineteenth-century Europe, which, having been approved in 1860, after 140 years of construction has now produced an admirable complex known as "Barcelona's Eixample." However, during the process of development, the complex became built up beyond the limits originally planned, and some of the principal ideas of the project lost definition.

As it stands today, the central Eixample covers half the area planned by Cerdà; however, in terms of building and activity it has multiplied by four. It covers 880 hectares, or 550 street blocks, and in the order of 125 kilometers of street; there is a resident population of about 350,000 inhabitants, and 300,000 people are employed there. Another indicator of use, activity and structure is traffic: some 600,000 cars pass through this area. This highlights the importance of this center, and the major presence of both residential and work functions.[16]

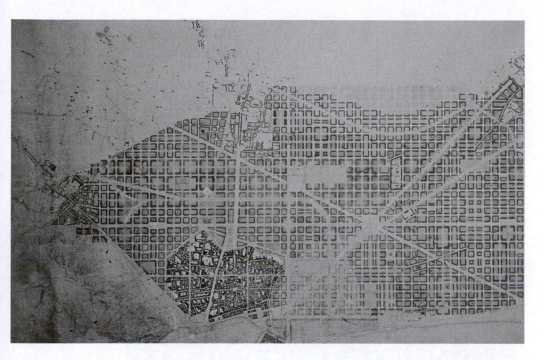

3.10
**Cerdà Plan,
designed in 1855**

The significance of this major project and the different reality it actually produced illustrates the importance of this urbanistic episode, and also explains other elements of the rehabilitation of Barcelona. Its protagonism in the urban form and second its influence on the morphological transformation were effected by the large-scale projects described below.

## Large-scale urbanistic projects

We must also look at the situation from the reverse or complementary point of view. The urban form can be understood by its empty spaces, and we must bear in mind the problems of function or brief arising in each situation. Let's take a look.

The empty spaces between "urban pieces" usually comprise vast tracts of land which are unused or have an obsolete function – industries that have fallen into disuse, dismantled railway spaces, old port land, and so on. Here we have spaces of opportunity, providing potential for endogenous development in the city. However, in Barcelona there were also problems of traffic access and a shortage of public transport between different areas of the city. Through-traffic was still using the Eixample to the extent that it attracted commerce and services, and spoiled its residential quality.

A series of large-scale projects were drawn up, endeavoring to combine increased connectivity of traffic and public transport between districts with the development of a series of new downtowns in empty or obsolete

3.11
**Barcelona, plain
designed by Cerdà
as preparation for
the Plan**

central areas. A system of large connector roads (the Ronda) was also to provide a means of bypassing the city.

This program of multiple "centrality" meant that the increase in value of interstitial areas as a result of new accessibility was not totally privatized. Each new downtown would offer facilities and parks in the newly introduced areas and decentralize the overcrowded tertiary sector.

The program meant that the waterfront – previously occupied by nineteenth-century industry – was now brought into use, and development included new residential areas and the necessary infrastructures to provide access to the city's beaches.

These projects were all furthered by these: election of Barcelona as the 1992 Olympic host city, which served to concentrate a great many of the strategies of the various public and private operators.

A highlight among these schemes was the recovery of the city's port and seafront. Barcelona is proud of its role in the development of Mediterranean urban civilization, yet any possible relation with the sea was blocked by the old railway line, the port and the old warehouses, and the drainage system emptied straight out into the sea. This question had for decades been the center of ideas aspirations, but the problems of infrastructure and land ownership were difficult ones to solve.

The Barcelona of the 1980s threw itself into the task with a series of successive projects. First of all, the project for the Moll de la Fusta wharf created a new link between Ciutat Vella and the port, through-traffic was taken to a semi-underground level, and work was started on a model which was later extended to the Ronda ring roads: separating through-traffic from urban traffic heading for neighboring sectors. This urban project was the basis for the reform of the port, which was completed in 1995 by the Viaplana-Piñón team with a leisure and recreation complex called Port Vell.

Meanwhile, by 1985 work had started on designing the infrastructure ready for the construction of the Olympic Village and regeneration of the city's beaches. The project team, headed by O. Bohigas, systematized the route of the Rondas, the rail tracks were taken underground, a sewage plant beside the river Besòs freed the beaches of pollution, and its geometry was drawn out on the basis of a series of dikes which followed the rhythm of the Eixample. The construction of the Olympic Village involved the collaboration of a dozen teams of architects, and the different buildings follow Cerdà's urban scale, reducing density and producing a housing district which incorporates the services of the present-day central residential area.

At the same time, other new downtowns were developed in empty interstices such as Glòries, Carrer Tarragona and in Diagonal, with the project for L'Illa by M. Solà-Morales and R. Moneo. Each project worked with specific functional briefs in which the objective requirements of the development were common to certain urbanistic conditions of this new "urban piece" in relation to others surrounding it. This was perhaps the way to promote a public–private partnership in which the quality of spaces and buildings was not an incidental component. In the case of L'Illa, the building became a landmark in the city's most important avenue, and, as part of the development, the project includes two public schools, a new street underpass connection, and a huge public garden in a dense residential area that needed opening up.

The experience of Barcelona reveals the need to bring together the solution of major infrastructures (traffic, drainage, etc.) and services (parks, schools, etc.) with the urban space that surrounds them, not merely as a condition of context, but also, and above all, because it is these spaces that can give them their real urban meaning.

This premise leads to new relationships, such as the one between built artefacts and environment in the case of Foster's Communications Tower set in the midst of the Parc de Collserola, justifying the effort of creating a 268-meter high element at the top of the hill with a minimum shaft of 4.5 meters in diameter to reduce its environmental impact.

## Barcelona's experience in the framework of Europe

In Barcelona, as in other major European urban development projects, we would seem to be looking at operations with one singular characteristic. One of them is infill of the existing city to increase its value by placing particular emphasis on improving the urban space. If at other times the dynamics of cities found expression in what happened beyond them, such as the huge urban expansions outside the cities during the 1960s and 1970s, the central theme now is reorganization of the city in itself. This does not mean that there are no processes of suburbanization on the edges of the metropolis, though they are, for the moment, complementary.

As a working hypothesis, we might suggest that these "urbanistic projects" concentrate their efforts on providing a strong projectual content, with attention to at least four components:

1   Public space is becoming the *leitmotif* of urban composition, be it in the city center or on the outskirts. It is acknowledged as the element which can voice the city's cultural capacities and respond to its functional and esthetic requirements. Here, the use of other urban spaces or the city's own historical projects serves as a point of reference for planners who have to propose layouts in their designs which may require time to take shape. Think of green and environmental systems in the city.

2   Urbanistic projects have to move around the most complex network of public and private agents ever. The present-day situation, with the superposition of various levels of government (state, regional,

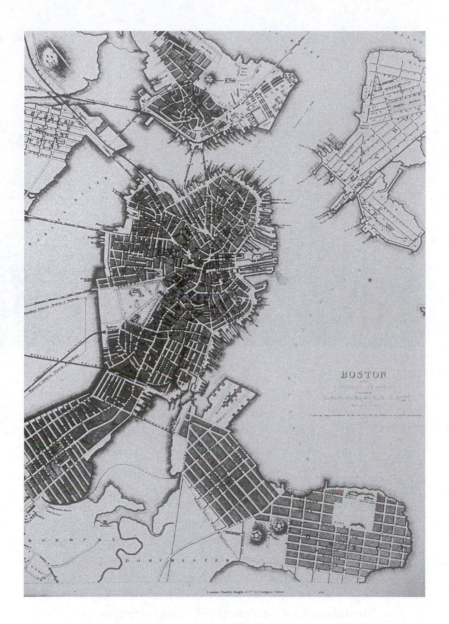

3.12
**Boston, mid-nineteenth century, as incorporated on Cerdà research for Barcelona's expansion**

provincial, municipal, district, etc.), makes unitary administration of the urban project very complicated, but only by launching the project into this arena can possible efforts be catalyzed. The case is similar for private investors at various levels, who, with forms of partnership, have to try and go beyond the programmatic requirements of each developer.

3   Time also becomes an important factor. Urbanistic projects need time, as we all know, but if they are to last, the project has to

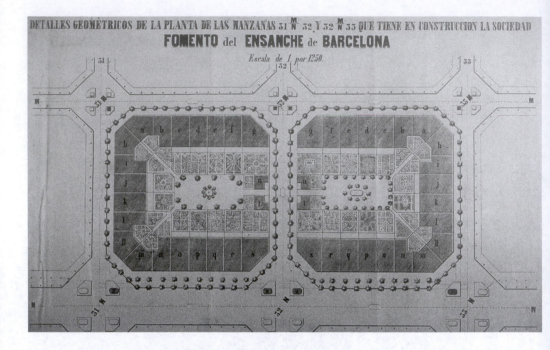

DETALLES GEOMÉTRICOS DE LA PLANTA DE LAS MANZANAS 51 $\stackrel{M}{N}$ 52 Y 52 $\stackrel{M}{N}$ 53 QUE TIENE EN CONSTRUCCION LA SOCIEDAD

## FOMENTO del ENSANCHE de BARCELONA

Escala de 1 por 1250.

channel its efforts towards "strong" elements of the urban form. We know that our thoughts and forms of action on the city often change; for "long-term" projects we have to go back to basics in the terms J. D. Burnham referred to at the beginning of the twentieth century, while our projects for intervention have to be well delimited and contextualized. This dimension has to be taken into account in urban projects, not so much to "think small" as to be aware of their capacities for implementation.

4  On the other hand, the "urban form" is once again the central element in the urbanistic project. We are coming to recognize its power of synthesis to express the urban process and make for a field of negotiation between technical, social and development agencies. But the urban form is now benefiting from the wide repertory of methodological disciplinary instruments developed in recent decades, which help to combine the discourse of the project with relevant analyses, describe morphological realities, and gauge the impact of the proposals – in short, to understand the form not so much as a final result but as a guide in an urban transformation process which is full of uncertainties that sometimes serve to cover up mediocre projects.

3.13
**Block development, as proposed by Cerdà**

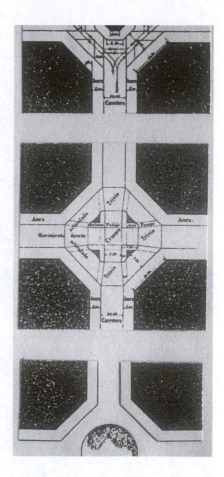

3.14
**Crossing, as proposed on Cerdà (Plan)**

This is where work on the "intermediate scale" comes in very useful: this means that while we establish the project on the basis of its own scale and autonomy, we force ourselves to look up to its wider context and down in a refusal to validate the project unless we are sure that it is reasonable in its viability. This exercise in planning brings us closer to the discussion concerning the traditional terms of the space of the Plan and the space of the Project.

To return to the recent Barcelona experience, there were two singular conditions: the major political capacity of the municipality, and the fact that the city's Olympic candidature for 1992 was accepted in 1986. We can see how many other cities have sought to take advantage of the spin-off of a set date: Lisbon in 1998 with its Expo, Rome in 2000 with its Jubilee, Berlin and the new capital projects, and so on. Yet we also see other major projects in Europe which have produced satisfactory results, such as K + Z in Rotterdam, or the cases of rehabilitation in Lyons, which have not had the advantage of a set date (which, on the other hand, has the disadvantage of unduly pressurizing some

3.15
**Barcelona's Eixample as it is
now after Cerdà Plan and 140
years of development**

3.16
**Fragment of large-scale
project on mobility**

3.17
**New "centrality"
programe.
Olympic sites
were placed on
four of its poles**

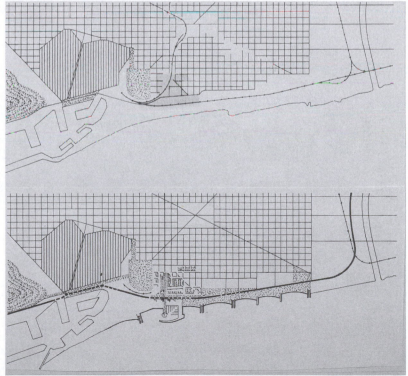

3.18
**Waterfront
infrastructures.
Diagram
representing
the situation
before and after
the urbanistic
intervention**

parts of the project and of forcing a double course of simultaneous projects, one for the event and, another for the future city).

In these projects, too, we see a search for specific objectives, attention to harmonic formulas based on well contextualized "pieces" of urban form and urban infrastructure. The logistics of these operations tend to differ from the classical bureaucratic services, and task forces are created with well-defined objectives – partly by government agencies, but also with a great many external private services.

In any case, here we have a great many of the ingredients of the discussion regarding the urban project today. These lead us to think of the vast field of work in cities, with, very different specific situations, though starting with the logic of mobilization of efforts – where existing opportunities allow us to turn some problematic points in cities into innovative, dynamic spaces.

This is a moment of far-reaching change of our urban systems in which we can appreciate the phenomena of change in their main functions and the appearance of new infrastructures almost without fixed channels which, with limited issuing centers, make for city development with unprecedented forms. Here we come up against more marked situations of discontinuity, as well as examples of heterogeneity between urban areas of different orders. We think we can understand this new territory without denying the efforts to revalue the existing city covered above, but it undoubtedly forces us to validate these new instruments of intervention in the light of new realities. This is

3.19
**Waterfront view in 1985. Access to the edge blocked by old railway line and drainage emptied**

3.20
**Waterfront rebuilt
for 1992**

where we have to be aware of the complexity of this new situation, which is so open in terms of decision-making mechanisms, and urban and market forces. Yet a major effort would seem to be in order on the part of the design disciplines to come up with rules of play that allow interesting urban results, and also the endogenous development which is characteristic of every city. This new urban culture will force us to discover the values of the city in the mutation surrounding every urban building or space, and concentrate our efforts on the "strong points" of form of these new territories – which doubtless offer other stimuli and charms. In short, each generation has to come to a new understanding of the "basic" problems of the urban territory and ambitiously articulate the proposals it can put into effect. This is the only way to see the new waterfront in Barcelona; as the carrying out of a long-range idea, with the means and skills brought to bear by the generation of the 1990s. In Barcelona and in every city, this is the starting point for new potentials and new themes for the beginning of this century.

## Notes

1 See, among others, Rossi, 1982 (1st edn, 1966); Caniggia and Maffei, 1979.
2 Braudel, 1976.
3 See, for example, Borja, 2001; Healey, 1989.
4 Ascher, 1999.
5 See the recent work by Harvey, 2000.
6 Various authors; also Cerdà, 1995; Blau and Platzer, 2000.
7 Terms which are covered in detail in issues 5 and 6 of the *UR* magazine of the Laboratori d'Urbanisme, Barcelona 1988. See principally the article by M. Solà-Morales.
8 Busquets, 1992.
9 See Busquets and Parcerisa, 1983.
10 The present-day Districts were defined in 1985 within the municipality of Barcelona in order to facilitate administrative decentralization and broadly to reproduce the perimeters of the old nineteenth-century municipalities before they were annexed to Barcelona at the turn of the twentieth century.
11 A more precise description can be found in *Barcelona. Plans cap al 92* (Ajuntament de Barcelona, 1987) and, more recently, *Barcelona. La segona renovació* (Ajuntament de Barcelona, 1997).
12 Many books have been written both here and abroad about these projects. For a more complete version, see *Barcelona espais i escultures* (Ajuntament de Barcelona, 1987); *Plans i Projectes 1981–82* (Ajuntament de Barcelona, 1983).
13 Further explanation of this process can be seen in Busquets, 2002.
14 The relatively large bibliography devoted to Cerdà and his work includes: Estapé 1971, 1977; LUB, 1978; Cerdà, 1992.
15 Cerdà himself, in *Despojos* (Facsímil, Madrid, 1991) tells us at the end of his life: "I did not merely content myself with solving questions by casuistry, which is the common and most convenient procedure; instead, when I needed a theory to apply to the issue in hand, I invented it, in most cases, not to say always, with the most laborious effort."
16 Data taken from the detailed study of the evolution and present state of the Eixample, produced by a team directed by Busquets and Ordóñez, 1983.

## Chapter 4

# Brasilia – City as Park Forever

*Farès el-Dahdah*

Beneath Brasilia's Three Powers Plaza is an underground gallery called Espaço Lucio Costa, suggested by Oscar Niemeyer in 1989 to memorialize the winning entry of the 1957 design competition as well as its author, Costa. Niemeyer suggested this space in response to an inquiry from the Minister of Culture, José Aparecido de Oliveira, regarding eventual locations where a 50′ × 50′ model of Brasilia could be housed.[1] The model had been built as an exact replica of what Brazil's modern capital looked like in 1987 when UNESCO added it to its World Heritage list. Where to house this model prompted Niemeyer to find a solution that would give Costa "the tribute owed to him by the city" and be so discrete as to neither offend his modesty nor "inconveniently" compete with the plaza's principal monuments.[2] Niemeyer's proposal, presented in a letter and a few sketches, was for an underground space that would house both the model and a copy of Costa's design competition winning entry boards.

Inaugurated on Lucio Costa's ninetieth birthday, i.e. February 27, 1992, the subterranean room is equipped with a marble plaque next to its entrance, whereon Niemeyer dedicates the space to "Lucio Costa, Creator of the Brasilia Pilot Plan 1957–1992." What is noteworthy about this dedication and the space itself is that they were, in fact, both written and detailed by Costa, not Niemeyer. The two architects are often mistaken for each other in terms of Brasilia's authorship, yet their collaboration in this case reveals Costa's apparently "modest" participation in anything related to his creation, his words all the while tending to not only end up being written in stone but also become law. Another illustration of such all powerful, yet modest, control of the Brasilia project occurs in Costa's *Memória Descritiva*, the 1957 competition report that begins with an apology to the jury, claiming that it was not his intention even to enter the competition.[3] Some 30 years later, however, the same text becomes the standard against which the urbanism of Brazil's capital is legally protected. Costa may have initially proposed his Brasilia project hesitantly yet he simultaneously conceptualized, as will be shown below, the means by which his creation would survive in perpetuity.

Represented in the giant model is the usual image one has of Brasilia, a dragonfly-shaped plan commonly referred to as "Plano Piloto" or "Pilot Plan." The origin of such nomenclature dates back at least to 1955, when Brazil's Commission for the Location of the New Federal Capital attempted to invite Le Corbusier himself to supervise the planning of the new Brazilian capital.[4] Even though the commission's president eventually vetoed the participation of a "foreign urbanist," Le Corbusier did go so far as to propose a five-stage process in which he would be responsible for the city's schematic design, or "Plan Pilote" as he called it and had previously used for his 1951 project for Bogotá.[5] The expression "Pilot Plan" also serves today to distinguish the city's original form from subsequent peripheral developments, known as satellite cities. Even road signs refer to Brasilia as Pilot Plan, as if to suggest that once in Brasilia, one theoretically lives in a "project" rather than in a city. This

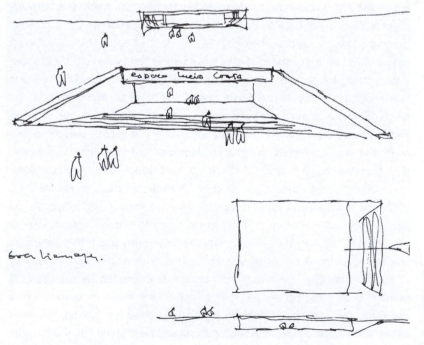

4.1
**Oscar Niemeyer, sketches for the Espaço Lucio Costa, 1989**

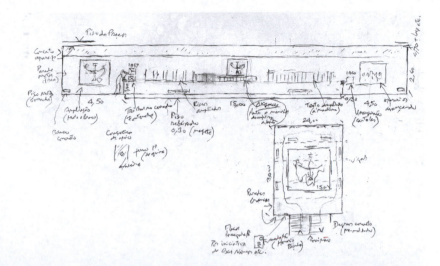

4.2
**Lucio Costa,
sketches for the
Espaço Lucio
Costa, c.1991**

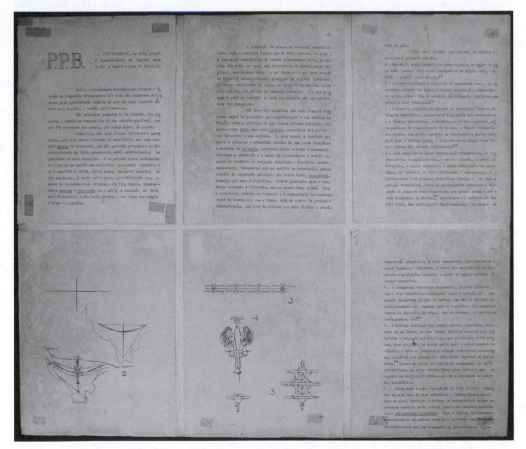

4.3
**Lucio Costa, Brasilia Pilot Plan, first six pages of the competion report, 1957**

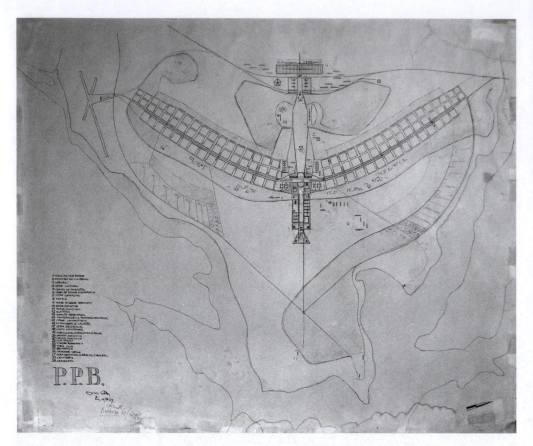

4.4
**Lucio Costa,
Brasilia Pilot Plan,
competition entry
board, 1957**

semantic slippage between the name of a city and the title of its masterplan is also borrowed by the city's critics, who use the metonym to prove that living in Brasilia is like living in an architectural model. What is nonetheless telling about the recurrent labeling of Brasilia as Pilot Plan is how Brazil's new capital ever since its inauguration has always been identified with the project described by Costa in his report.

Filling almost the entire room, the giant model also makes it possible to understand what Costa means when he uses another peculiar nomenclature to describe his project: "cidade parque" or "park city."[6] The expression is used not only in the competition report but also in subsequent correspondence urging Oscar Niemeyer, for example, to speak with Israel Pinheiro – president of the development company in charge of executing the Brasilia project – in order to have Roberto Burle Marx hired as the landscape architect of Brazil's new capital. Given the stature of Burle Marx's international reputation, it was not understandable, in Costa's opinion, "that a capital be built without someone responsible for the proper treatment of its natural environment, especially when in the Pilot Plan's competition report the city was already identified as a park city."[7]

The use of the expression "park city" is significant inasmuch as it reveals the degree to which Brasilia was, in fact, conceived as a landscape architectural project, making Burle Marx's absence from the construction process all the more critical. In his choice of words, Costa avoided using the obvious and more common term of "garden city," which as an urban design strategy had, in fact, been criticized by Le Corbusier during the lectures conducted at Rio de Janeiro's National Music Institute back in 1936.[8] Le Corbusier's own expression "Ville verte" was another possible and predictable choice but it would have indicated only that a city should be equipped with trees rather than necessarily be considered a park as such.

For Costa, Brasilia is a park in the strict sense of the word and it is this park that qualifies its urban form. Brasilia is therefore to be understood as a constructed nature, one that requires terraces, terrepleins, embankments, and retaining walls to distinguish it from the surrounding savannah-like cerrado vegetation. The language Costa often chose to describe many elements of his "park city" – high atop Brazil's Central Plateau – is particularly landscape architectural, especially when referring to such important areas of the Pilot Plan as the Three Powers Plaza, the Ministries Esplanade, the Cultural Sector, or the housing schemed termed Superquadra.

When, for example, Costa describes his Three Powers Plaza as "the Versailles of the people," he is obviously not referring to the architecture of Louis XIV's palace but rather to the latter's relation with the surrounding complex of deep axes and grand vistas.[9] The Pilot Plan's competition report

4.5
**Lucio Costa, Brasilia Pilot Plan, detail of the Three Powers Plaza and the Monumental Axis, competion report, 1957**

gives particular emphasis to the governmental plaza as being elevated off the natural ground by relying "in contemporary terms" on an "ancient eastern ter-replein technique" that would ensure "the cohesion of the project as a whole and lend it unexpected monumental emphasis."[10] This technique is extended along the Ministries Esplanade, which Costa fittingly compares to the English "lawns" of his childhood, in addition to which, French perspectives, Chinese terraces, and American cloverleaf interchanges were retroactively chosen as the landscape architectural "ingredients" of his project.[11] The competition report is itself written in such a way as to organize a visitor's promenade through the city much like the park at Versailles was to be visited according to a prescribed itinerary.[12] Having gone through the Three Powers Plaza and the Ministries Esplanade, the promenade Costa describes proceeds through the bus station platform and continues along the monumental axis before coming back to the Superquadras and ending on the lake's bucolic shore.

Many years later, in 1986, when Niemeyer made his first proposal for completing Brasilia's Cultural Sector, Costa sent him a note reminding him that the area in question had always been imagined as "duly wooded in order to contrast with the vast and empty lawns, and where great clearings would be left open."[13] Costa's suggestion went so far as to indicate the diameters of these clearings. The purpose of the note was to remind Niemeyer of the original intention behind the Pilot Plan, which consisted of landscape architec-tural devices that, in this case, would frame the lawns of the Ministries Espla-nade rather than have them extend beyond preconceived limits. Brasilia's vast "malls," as Costa called them, would, therefore, extend from the Three Powers

4.6
**Lucio Costa,
Sketch for
Brasilia's Cultural
Sectors, c.1986**

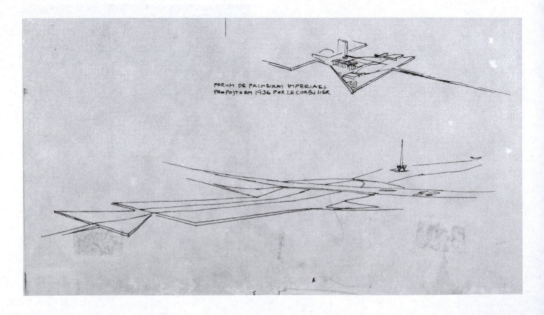

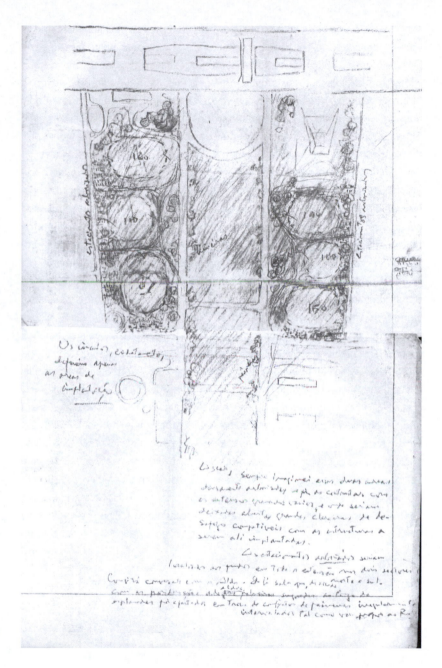

**4.7**

**Oscar Niemeyer, Sketch for Brasilia's Cultural Sectors, c. 1986**

Plaza all the way up to a wooded barrier that would, in turn, define the North and South Cultural Sectors. Niemeyer subsequently proposed many versions for the Cultural Sectors, all Giacometti-esque with platonic shapes strewn about in a landscape void of vegetation.[14]

The Superquadra is yet another element in the Pilot Plan that is entirely described in landscape architectural terms. The architecture itself is given almost no specifications other than the fact that it ought be elevated on pilotis and be limited to six stories in height. The natural setting, however, is "framed" by a "wide" and "densely wooded belt" that can be interrupted only once for vehicular access but is otherwise permeable to pedestrians.[15] In each Superquadra, Costa determined that only one particular type of tree would predominate, the ground would be carpeted with grass, and there would also be "an additional and intermittent curtain of shrubs and foliage always in the background and as if blended in the landscape in order to better identify, irrespective of viewpoints, the content of each quadra."[16] The percentage of land occupancy (equivalent to 15 percent) was derived from one of the vignettes that illustrated the *Memória* and no other architectural requirements was suggested in order, on the one hand, to favor innovation while, on the other hand, insuring uniformity along the Residential–Highway Axis by surrounding all Superquadras with the compulsory tree canopy suggested in another of Costa's vignettes. The green belt is essentially there to visually outline city blocks where residential slab buildings can "hover" on their pilotis above a continuous ground. The resulting skyline is therefore always underscored with trees in the foreground, which all together act as an interface between the city's residential scale, necessarily attenuated, and its monumental scale, deliberately vast.

It is ultimately the project of this "park city" as a whole that state and federal laws today protect by preserving the voids between buildings, which for the most part can be torn down and rebuilt according to a given "scale."[17] The question of how to protect Brasilia was originally posed by Juscelino Kubitschek himself, soon after the city's inauguration, in a note written to Rodrigo Mello Franco de Andrade, then director of the SPHAN, the agency in charge of protecting Brazil's historic and artistic heritage.[18] This, however, only became a pressing issue in 1985 when the then governor, José Aparecido de

4.8
**Lucio Costa, Brasilia Pilot Plan, detail of a Superquadra, competion report, 1957**

Oliveira, invited Costa, Niemeyer, and Burle Marx to complete (and rectify) the project as it had been intended. The governor's strategy for protecting the city against local real-estate development forces also included the pursuit of international recognition, which is why he proposed to UNESCO that contemporary monuments such as Brasilia should also be added to the World Heritage list. UNESCO, in turn, commissioned a report that described Brasilia as one of the greatest achievements in the history of urbanism, yet it nonetheless dismissed the governor's petition, arguing that he could not make such a request when Brazil's own preservation laws regarding Brasilia were so abstract and ill-defined.[19]

Two sets of preservation measures were subsequently undertaken on state and federal levels in Brazil, and in both cases Costa's opinion was not far away. At the state level, the governor's decree included the addendum "Brasília Revisitada," written by Costa himself, which explained how the four "scales" of his "park city" ought to be protected.[20] Federal District Government Decree Law #10.829/1987 begins by stating accordingly that the protection of Brasilia's "Pilot Plan" will be guaranteed by the preservation of the essential characteristics of its four distinct monumental, residential, aggregation, and bucolic scales. The Federal District Law is the legal instrument that ultimately convinced UNESCO to confer the title of World Heritage Site on Brasilia. At the federal level, the Instituto Brasileiro do Patrimônio Cultural (Brazilian Institute of Cultural Heritage), or IBPC, and the former Secretária do Patrimônio Histórico e Artístico Nacional (Secretariat of Historical and Artistic National Heritage), or SPHAN, passed Ministerial Directive #314/1992, which afforded the city a level of national protection. The directive replicates the language of Costa's "Brasília Revisitada" and ratifies the notion that in Brasilia voids are protected yet buildings are not – only their outline and the ratio of their building/land occupancy are maintained. Another common denominator between the two laws is Ítalo Campofiorito, who had astutely suggested to Costa that the four scales in question could very well become themselves an "object" worthy of legal protection.[21] In 1987 Campofiorito was the research coordinator at the Fundação Nacional Pró-Memória (FNPM) who was, at Governor Aparecido de Oliveira's request, in charge of putting together the legal case for Brasilia's preservation. Campofiorito subsequently headed both the FNPM and the SPHAN, and in 1990 he drafted the first version of the Federal District Law that was enacted two years later.

In terms of historic preservation, an unprecedented condition in Brasilia therefore permits most buildings to be destroyed as long as their scale is somehow reconstituted (the exception is those buildings that are specifically protected, such as the cathedral and the Catetinho). It is the project – the "Pilot Plan" as "park city" – rather than the city itself that is to ultimately survive.

What the two federal and state laws seek to protect is not Brasilia's urban fabric, but its grammar as dictated in the competition report. This means that, thanks to Lucio Costa, a modern city in Brazil is not protected in the same way as an eighteenth-century town. The difference being that in colonial Ouro Preto, for example (which is also on UNESCO's list of World Heritage Sites), buildings are physically frozen in time, while in Brasilia they remain forever new … and open areas are to remain park-like, in perpetuity.

## Notes

1   Letter, Oscar Niemeyer to José Aparecido, October 4, 1989.
2   Letter, Oscar Niemeyer to José Aparecido, October 4, 1989.
3   Lucio Costa, "Memória Descritiva do Plano Piloto" [1957], in *Registro de uma vivência*, 1995, pp. 283–297.
4   Telegram, Hugo Gontier to Le Corbusier, June 2, 1955.
5   Cavalcanti de Albuquerque, 1958, p. 189.
6   On Costa's use of the term "*cidade parque*" in a comparative study between the *Memória Descritiva* and the *Athens Charter*, see also Tattara, 2011.
7   Letter, Lucio Costa to Oscar Niemeyer, undated, VI.A.01.
8   Le Corbusier, 2006.
9   Costa, "Saudação aos críticos de arte" [1959], in *Registro de uma vivência*, p. 299.
10  Costa, "Memória Descritiva do Plano Piloto," p. 289.
11  Costa, "Ingredientes da concepção urbanística de Brasília," in *Registro de uma vivência*, p. 282.
12  See Berger and Hedin, 2008.
13  Letter, Lucio Costa to Oscar Niemeyer, undated, III.B.04–03362.
14  See Alberto Giacometti, *Model for a Public Square (Projet pour une place)*, 1931–1932, Peggy Guggenheim Collection, Venice, 76.2553 PG 130.
15  Costa, "Memória Descritiva do Plano Piloto," p. 292.
16  Costa, "Memória Descritiva do Plano Piloto," p. 292.
17  Federal District Government Decree Law #10.892, October 14, 1987 and IPHAN *Portaria* #314, October 8, 1992.
18  Letter, Juscelino Kubitschek to Rodrigo Mello Franco de Andrade, June 15, 1960.
19  See Peralva, 1988, pp. 105–110.
20  Costa, 1987.
21  Campofiorito, 1989, p. 36–41.

Chapter 5

# Chicago – Superblockism: Chicago's Elastic Grid

*Sarah Whiting*

The September 11, 2001 destruction of Minoru Yamasaki's World Trade Center rapidly rekindled the long-standing debate over the viability and desirability of the superblock as an urban type. Condemnations forcefully outnumbered endorsements: "Break up the 16-acre Trade Center superblock" was the dismissive refrain of many a newspaper editorial. "Restore the traditional street grid so as to restore neighborhoods [. . . and] espouse community"[1] and other such suggestions directly echoed the urban critiques penned by urban advocate Jane Jacobs 43 years ago when she took on Lewis Mumford, Clarence Stein, Henry Wright, and the rest of the Garden City movement in *The Death and Life of Great American Cities*: "The Garden City planners and their ever increasing following among housing reformers, students and architects," Jacobs complained, "were indefatigably popularizing the ideas of the super-block, the project neighborhood, the unchangeable plan, and grass, grass, grass; what is more they were successfully establishing such attributes as the hallmarks of humane, socially responsible, functional high-minded planning."[2]

That one can draw a ring around bucolic suburban Garden Cities – such as Stein and Wright's Radburn, New Jersey of 1929 – and the extremely metropolitan World Trade Center and then label the entire lot of it "superblocks" reveals the Houdini-esque quality of this term, which eludes hard definition despite its extensive use throughout the world during the twentieth century. As an urban strategy – more specifically, as a platting strategy – the term "superblock" is used to describe three completely different organizational paradigms: the park-like configurations belonging to the Garden City; the enormous slabs or perimeter blocks of housing and other programs that emerged in Red Vienna, the Amsterdam School and the Soviet Union in the early twentieth century; and the superscaled plats embedded within Modernism's gridded orthogonality. If the former is associated with Mumford and Stein (and eventually with the pastoral pretense of suburban subdivisions), the second invokes de Klerk, Karl Ehn, and Mosei Ginzburg, and the third is firmly wed to Le Corbusier, whose "towers in the park" sprouted in city centers around the world throughout the 1950s and 1960s.

Enter Chicago and its particular perpendicular proliferation of the superblock. How does Chicago fit into the superblock's multifarious genealogical tree? Simple: it doesn't. Offering examples of all types of superblocks *avant la lettre* and then some, it exposes the weak spots of this system of classification. This is not to suggest that Chicago offers the *origin* of the superblock or an especially atypical form (or forms) of this urban type. Instead, it is to highlight the special case of Chicago as a city where the superblock is more a norm than an anomaly, due to the city's settlement history as well as certain economic and political histories. The value of Chicago as a case study for the superblock emerges especially from the particularities of its grid – a grid that marks the coincidence of urban and agricultural logics as they intersected at what was once the gateway to the American west. The historically threaded textual blocks below offer a verbal corollary to the urban superblocks of the Chicago metropolis: different in scope, scale and import, each offers a freeze-frame image of the elastic grid that makes up this city.

## Long division

The Chicago plain, in common with most of the Western United States, was surveyed in mile-square sections, which in turn were cut into four square quarter-sections and thus sold to settlers. Subdividers found it convenient to adopt a rectangular block plan in cutting up these quarter-sections, and such a layout was virtually forced upon them when the one-hundred-and-sixty-acre tracts were divided into four square "forties," or into sixteen square ten-acre parcels.[3]

Platted in 1830, Chicago, Illinois was squarely set within the gridiron tradition systematized by Thomas Jefferson's 1785 Northwest Ordinance, which subdivided the Western Territories into townships of 36 square miles. This gridded system divided the landscape into commodifiable parcels, thereby facilitating rapid (and rampant) land speculation. The grid homogenized the landscape in such a way that the cityscape was liberated, unanchored from its ground. Whereas earlier examples of landownership turned a deed or a title into a metaphoric stake in the earth, in Chicago and other Western cities land became paper thin, as if each plot were but randomly dealt chances in an endless game of seven-card draw. James Silk Buckingham's hyperbolic description from the early 1830s provides a telling glimpse of the city's speculative whirlwind: "some lots changed hands ten times in a single day and the 'evening purchaser' paid at least 'ten times as much as the price paid by the morning buyer for the same spot!' "[4] Land division multiplies economies. This redundant, repetitive exchange of plots depended upon the assumption that the city's platted rectangles were both easily identifiable and interchangeable. Accordingly, the plots were numbered and, throughout the city's first real estate boom of 1836, were sold sight-unseen in auction houses in New York, oftentimes offering surprises to the owners when they eventually made their way to the city named by the Indians for its unpleasant smells.[5]

## Usually . . .

The blocks may be made 300 feet square, and *usually* not over 320 feet by 400 feet, with a 20-foot alley running the long dimension of the block. The principal streets are *usually* made 80 feet in width, though frequently as much as 100 feet where the greater width appears to be needed or desirable, and the less important intersecting streets are seldom given a width of less than 60 feet. An alley is *usually* placed in each block, 20 feet in width and paralleling the principal street system. . . .Unless planned differently, the whole system is laid out on cardinal directions . . .[6]

Despite the implied rigor of the Ordinance grid's mathematical definition, Chicago's blocks are not entirely homogeneous. The phrase "usually," oft repeated within the pages of *The Manual of Surveying Instructions* of 1947, props up the image of a uniform grid like a broomstick holding a scarecrow against the wind: the term suggests regularity but admits aberration. If New York's unyielding grid "forces Manhattan's builders to develop a new system of formal values, to invent strategies for the distinction of one block from another,"[7] Chicago's is essentially the opposite: the grid itself is manipulated in order to distinguish one project from another. Because Chicago emerged from a territorial organization (unlike Manhattan, whose organization is limited by its island configuration), the city's logic lies at a scale much greater than its urbanism. Jefferson's original Ordinance divided the Northwest Territories into a grid of squares of 100 miles; subsequent amendments reduced the township scale to grids of 36 miles, 6 miles square on each side. Townships that were sold whole alternated in a checkerboard pattern with townships that were divided into 640 acre lots (1 square mile) or "sections."[8] Only when divided do these sizes become viable for agriculture or urbanism. Forty acres, one-sixteenth of a section, became the standard module size for farms, which would thereafter appear as 40 acres or multiples thereof (hence the saying, "forty acres and a mule"). Even if cities were divided into smaller parcels, urban subdivisions to this day continue to reveal the importance of the 40-acre module. Homer Hoyt's *One Hundred Years of Land Values* of 1933 illustrates the various ways in which a 40-acre tract can be divided into urban lots (Figure 5.1). It was this practice of subdivision that led to Chicago's "usually" blocks: some areas of the city were developed and therefore subdivided at the same time, leading to homogenous block sizes for entire zones. While it was only speculation that determined such continuity, lengths of streets such as Western Avenue reveal the scale of Chicago's real estate ventures: at 24.5 miles, Western remains the

5.1
**Various Methods
of Subdividing
a 40 Acre Tract,
1320 Feet Square.
In Homer Hoyt,
1933.** *One
Hundred Years
of Land Values,*
**p. 431, Figure
103, University of
Chicago Press**

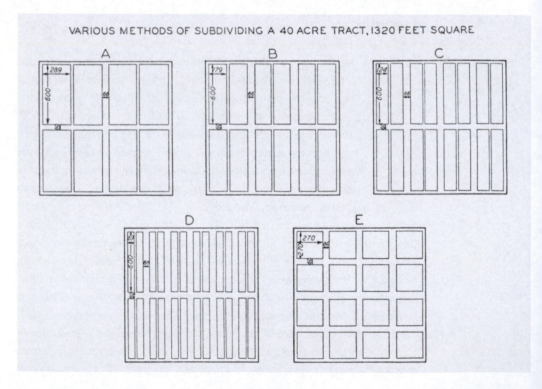

VARIOUS METHODS OF SUBDIVIDING A 40 ACRE TRACT, 1320 FEET SQUARE

longest continuous street within city limits in the world.[9] Chicago block sizes range from 218 by 341 feet to 320 by 360 feet to what became, during the real estate boom from 1866 to 1873, the standard (or *usual*) Chicago block of 266 by 600 feet.[3]

## Quarter-sections

> The site comprises a quarter-section of land assumed to be located on the level prairie about 8 miles distant from the business district of the City of Chicago. The tract is without trees or buildings and is not subdivided. The surrounding property is subdivided in the prevailing gridiron fashion . . .[10]

It was only in 1832 that Congress permitted the sale of the quarter-quarter-section, or the "forty." Until then, the primary module of land sale had been the quarter-section, or 160 acres.[11] Although the forty quickly became the favored unit for individual sales, the quarter-section remained firmly established as the module for subdivisions, as demonstrated by the City Club of Chicago's competition of 1913 for subdividing a typical quarter-section of land in the outskirts of Chicago.[10] While many of the 39 submitted entries can be considered "superblocks" in that they offer grids greater than the surrounding contextual grid of 272.5 by 610.5 blocks, one entry in particular constitutes an innovative superblock: Frank Lloyd Wright's non-competitive quarter-section plan[12] (Figures 5.2, 5.3). Wright's design maintained the overriding orthogonality of the Chicago grid system, but eschewed monotony by introducing what Wright called "picturesque variety." Wright's innovation for developing the residential section was the "quadruple block plan," which he had developed for an article that appeared in the *Ladies' Home Journal* in 1901.[13] The Quadruple Block Plan adopts not a rectangular but a square block subdivision (equivalent to Option E in Hoyt's diagram, Figure 5.1). By placing only four houses on a single small block, Wright was able to offer each house its own orientation. He pinwheeled the four around an inner core of shared utilities, thereby guaranteeing a degree of privacy while also ensuring visual variety: "[Each] building," Wright argued, "is in unconscious but necessary grouping with three of his neighbors', looking out upon harmonious groups of other neighbors, no two of which would present to him the same elevation even were they all cast in one mould. A succession of buildings of any given length by this arrangement presents the aspect of well-grouped buildings in a park, *of greater picturesque variety than is possible where façade follows façade.*"[14]

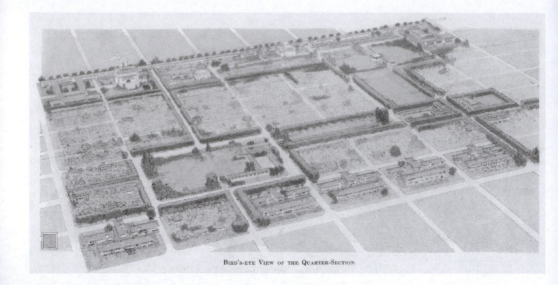

BIRD'S-EYE VIEW OF THE QUARTER-SECTION

Indeed Wright created a picturesque relationship between buildings and park, but without either sacrificing the orthogonality of the grid or reducing the park to the role of mere spatial buffer. Financed by the sale of the residential property, the internalized park system weaves through the subdivision, ordering recreation features such as playgrounds, athletic fields, and a music pavilion. Balanced, although not entirely symmetrically, around a diagonal axis across the site, the park subtly segregates the residential from the civic and commercial sections of the subdivision in addition to differentiating residential zones of seven- or eight-room houses, two-flat buildings, workmen's houses, and women's and men's apartment buildings. It is this park that makes Wright's proposal a superblock prototype: the project foreshadows the two superblock types of the tower in the park and the garden city. The park reaches to the edges of the superblock but unlike the green carpets that Le Corbusier would design a decade later, this one is strategically programed: it combines low-rise and medium-rise densities with non-residential programming to animate the entire subdivision perpetually. While the park system blocks some through streets, it never creates cul de sacs like garden city superblocks would do, and thereby does not turn its back on Chicago by asphyxiating the larger urban grid.[15] While architect Albert Pope's book *Ladders* offers a provocative tableau of how the superblock can be read as a closed system, inverting the grid's centrifugal spatial field by introducing centripetal points of gravity within it, I would argue that certain developments in Chicago stem from the original platting patterns of this region and that, rather than shutting down the grid, these developments reveal this particular grid's ability to absorb and promote different scales and uses. While Wright's Quarter-Section Plan for the 1916 Competition was never executed, it illustrates the relationship between the dominant

5.2
**Bird's-Eye View of the Quarter-Section," Frank Lloyd Wright, in Alfred B. Yeomans, 1916, *City Residential Land Development: Studies in Planning*, p. 97. University of Chicago Press**

5.3
**Plan by Frank Lloyd Wright, in Alfred B. Yeomans, 1916, *City Residential Land Development: Studies in Planning*, p. 98. University of Chicago Press**

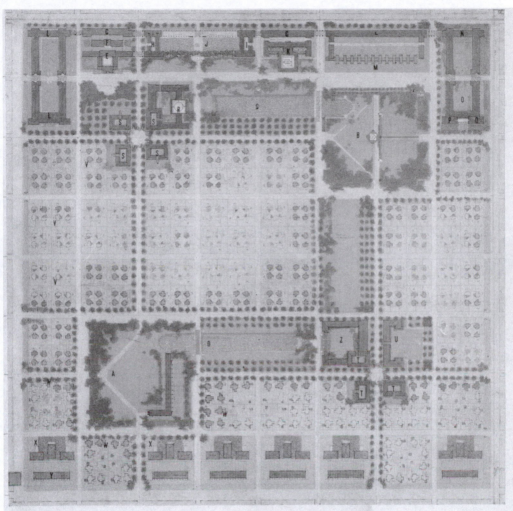

PLAN BY FRANK LLOYD WRIGHT

## KEY TO PLAN

A. Park for children and adults. Zoölogical gardens.
B. Park for young people. Bandstand, refectory, etc. Athletic field.
C. Lagoon for aquatic sports.
D. Lagoon for skating and swimming.
E. Theater.
F. Heating, lighting, and garbage reduction plant. Fire department.
G. Stores, 3 and 4 room apartments over.
H. Gymnasium.
I. Natatorium.

J. Produce market.
K. Universal temple of worship, non-sectarian.
L. Apartment building.
M. Workmen's semi-detached dwellings.
N. Four and five room apartments.
O. Stores with arcade.
P. Post Office branch.
Q. Bank branch.
R. Branch library, art galleries, museum, and moving picture building.

S. Two and three room apartments for men.
T. Two and three room apartments for women.
U. Public school.
V. Seven and eight room houses, better class.
W. Two-flat buildings.
X. Two-family houses.
Y. Workmen's house groups.
Z. Domestic science group. Kindergarten.

### STATISTICAL DATA

304 Seven and eight room houses.
120 Two-flat buildings, five and six rooms.
18 Four-flat buildings, four and five rooms.
6 Fourteen-family workmen's house groups.
12 Seven-room semi-detached workmen's houses.

6 Apartment buildings, accommodating 320 families in all.
4 Two and three room apartment buildings for women, accommodating 250 to 300.
Total, 1032 families and 1550 individuals (minimum).

quarter-section subdivision land package and the superblock as a Chicago type. Additionally, it offers a more appropriate prototype for Chicago's boom period of superblock development during the 1940s than do the three typical models of superblock, for it demonstrates how development can work within the logic of the Chicago grid (that is, by prioritizing the most efficient sale of property) without being entirely subsumed by that same grid: Wright's superblock offers an urbanism of its own that emerges from the larger-gridded urbanism of its surroundings.

## Centering the civic

A civic center to serve Chicago where governmental and other related functions could be grouped, would promote greater efficiency in the conduct of the public's business. Its location should be readily accessible to all Chicagoans and at the same time tend to reduce congestion within the Loop.[16]

In 1943, the mayor of Chicago, Edward Kelly, was so confident that the United States would win the war he asked the Chicago Plan Commission to coordinate the city's envisioned public works projects so as to establish a Master Plan for a long-term improvement campaign. Like Daniel Burnham's famous Chicago Plan of 1909, the 1943 preliminary study included a proposal for a civic center. However, where Burnham's Civic Center interrupted the city grid – providing a Haussmannian focal point for his Plan's diagonal axes – the 1943 schematic proposal made a superblock (Figure 5.4). The whole Center occupied approximately eleven city blocks, straddling the Chicago River and Wacker Drive, both which were bridged by the project's gardens.

Six years later the Chicago Plan Commission submitted to the city a more complete proposal for the Civic Center. Covering the same eleven blocks and still a superblock, the project reveals modernism's impact on America at the war's end (Figure 5.5). The classical axes of the previous scheme were abandoned in favor of modernist slabs in a park, with each building corresponding to one part of government: Federal, State, County, and City. Additionally, there was one building for the Board of Education and another for all levels of judicial courts. The project was characterized by open siting, accessibility, efficiency, spaciousness, and diverse, flexible programming, including private as well as government offices. Sited along the river, the Civic Center foretells a new beginning, a renewal of Chicago's downtown in light of burgeoning suburban flight. The green carpet of the project deliberately offers a striking contrast to the Loop's three-dimensional density, and the Center's similar but not

5.4
**Civic Center. In Chicago Plan Commission, 1943, *Chicago Looks Ahead: Design for Public Improvements*, p. 30**

# CIVIC CENTER

A CIVIC CENTER TO SERVE CHICAGO WHERE GOVERNMENTAL AND OTHER RELATED FUNCTIONS COULD BE GROUPED, WOULD PROMOTE GREATER EFFICIENCY IN THE CONDUCT OF THE PUBLIC'S BUSINESS. ITS LOCATION SHOULD BE READILY ACCESSIBLE TO ALL CHICAGOANS AND AT THE SAME TIME TEND TO REDUCE CONGESTION WITHIN THE LOOP.

The most feasible location, involving the demolition of only outmoded structures and where adequate space could be secured, is at the Chicago River west of the Loop. The potentials of such a river front development are thus revealed. It is set apart from, yet is readily accessible to the Loop and to local transit facilities.

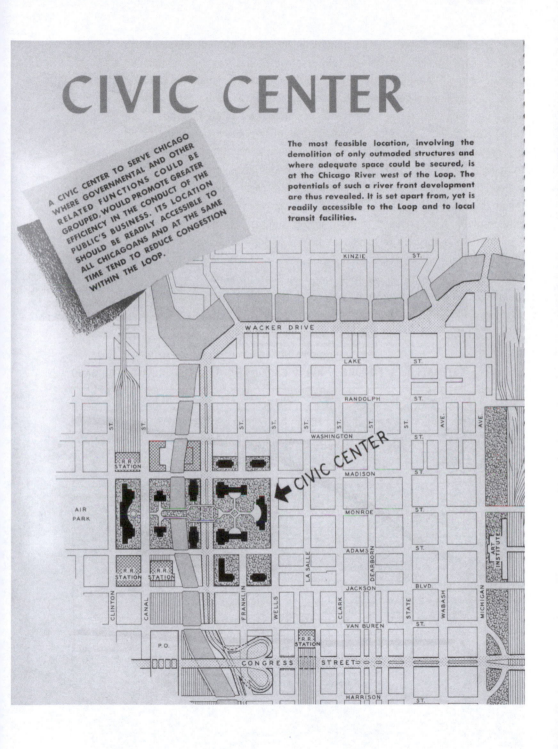

identical buildings suggest a continuity of government without compromising the autonomy of each branch – a "proper atmosphere," as the presentation booklet notes. Modernist forms – maximal in size and minimal in articulation – were asymmetrically arranged like objects placed on a coffee table, and the space between and around these forms was as formed as the buildings themselves. The project's presentation emphasized these public spaces, suggesting that spectacles could take place in the expansive plaza and that more personal exchanges would result within the project's various social arenas, such as its restaurant and shops. The twelfth floor was a public concourse, like a street in the sky that joined all the slabs where its social and commercial amenities were concentrated. The openness of the planning, the reliance on spectacles and leisure, and the absence of traditional ornamental references were part of an effort to foster and symbolize what Sigfried Giedion had referred to as "communities of experience" in his 1944 argument for a redefined modern monumentality.[17] Indeed, underlying the project's openness and emphasis on public space was a desire to concretize post-war democracy.

5.5
**Chicago Civic Center. In Chicago Plan Commission, 1949, *Chicago Civic Center*, p. 17**

Looking at the scheme, it would be easy to claim that its superblock configuration was as influenced by European modernism as its building forms were; however, the classical Civic Center proposal from 1943 reveals that the superblock urbanism preceded the architecture. And it was the urbanism that remained constant even as the project underwent several more incarnations before Chicago was to get a Civic Center in the 1960s. It is not insignificant that when the Chicago Civic Center project went dormant after failing to secure the land east of the river, it was revived five years later for a site north of the river under the auspices of a privately funded business venture led by developer Arthur Rubiloff. Business was in a stronger position to design post-war democracy than government. "The Fort Dearborn Project" (even its name shed the legislative emphasis implied by "civic center") formally resembled the 1949 project (Figure 5.6). Programmatically, this version maintained the Civic Center's municipal and juridical functions, but also included significant additional programs, such as a Chicago campus for the University of Illinois. (As an aside, that campus was eventually realized west of the river in the 1960s. Remarkably, the University of Illinois Chicago campus site is exactly that of Burnham's 1909 Civic Center.) Like the 1949 project, Fort Dearborn was also never built because Rubiloff could not acquire the necessary land. Ultimately, the realized

**5.6**
**A vision of Hope and Promise: How the Ft. Dearborn Project would appear in a view looking west from Dearborn St. Building in rear would be Federal building. Round building would be Hall of Justice. Building at right would be State building. Reflecting pool would be ice rink in winter. From** The Chicago Daily News, **Wednesday March 17, 1954, p. 60**

EWS, Wednesday, March 17, '54

FT. DEARBORN PROJECT AND HOW IT WOULD TRANSFORM THE NEAR NORTH SIDE

*A Vision of Hope and Promise*

Federal Center and Civic Center, designed by Mies van der Rohe and C.F. Murphy respectively, which were built in the 1960s, dropped much of the programmatic complexity and "event-potential" of these previous schemes, but maintained the superblock configuration, albeit at a much smaller scale. Mies's Federal Center, for example, combines three buildings – an office building, courtroom building and post office – that cover a block and a half of the city. While Dearborn Street cuts the project in two, the Federal Center nevertheless reads as a single superblock of civic programming.

The conflation of public and private in these projects – most evident in the Fort Dearborn project, but even visible in the Civic Center proposal of 1949, which included shopping and restaurant facilities – was almost obligatory in the face of the large urban scale of these schemes. Like the Rockefeller Center, they were "cities within the city." While this designation may imply a fortress-like condition, these large campus-like insertions necessarily included the larger city within their borders – or, to put it differently, the boundary between the city and the city within was rarely exclusionary, particularly in the case of these primarily public institutions.

## Inner-city landfill

> So I think it was a matter of passing through a space, spaces that were varying in dimension and varying in scale of height between buildings, length ... You have a different psychological feeling when you come into a space with a high vis-à-vis a low, and vice-versa, building. So I think [Mies] was very careful, just in studying these things abstractly in blocks, cut pieces of wood ... I was aware, yes, of what kind of space he was creating and what the effect was going to be by being in it.[18]

In 1937, after four years of trying to purchase property somewhere other than the Near South Side, the Armour Institute of Technology (later renamed the Illinois Institute of Technology or IIT) Board of Trustees concluded that the school could not afford to leave the area. With resigned optimism (tinged with a stiff shot of Manifest Destiny), President Willard Hotchkiss proclaimed that "now is the time to move forward and possess the land."[19] The 100-acre campus designed by Mies van der Rohe between 1939 and 1958 that ultimately emerged from this fortuitous decision has been recognized for its structural integrity and elegance, as well as for its innovative approach to American campus design, but it has yet to be read as a productive urban model (Figure 5.7). When studied in the context of Chicago's Near South Side of the 1940s,

5.7
**Mies van der
Rohe, "IIT campus,
photomontage
aerial view
showing model
within Near South
Side" (detail),
1947.
Hedrich-Blessing,
photographer.
Chicago Historical
Society HB 26823B**

however, another, more effective reading of IIT emerges: rather than forming just a set of innovative buildings, the campus forms an integral component of a larger, more complex and multifarious field. Mies's plan for IIT initiated a new form of modern urbanism that represents an epitome of the Chicago super-block that is at once figural and abstract, figure *and* ground. An inner-city landfill of green carpet, the campus offers an example of how the superblock reconfigures the urban grid in order to *figure space*.[20]

Even fans of the campus describe it as an autonomous island that disregards its physical and social context. Such an interpretation is only reinforced by Mies's presentation collages, which ruthlessly eliminated 100 acres of the city's dense urban fabric in order to make way for the expansive, low-density campus. But both the size of the campus and the strategy of dispersing buildings on the site were decisions that predated Mies's arrival on the scene. IIT was one of a network of superblocks that emerged in unison on the Chicago South Side during this period (Figure 5.8). Beginning with IIT, and later including Michael Reese Hospital, the Chicago Housing Authority, Mercy Hospital, and several private-housing developments, a group of institutions collaborated to plan and execute one of the first large-scale modern urban plans in the United States. This seven-mile-square plan paved the way for federal slum clearance, redevelopment, and urban renewal legislation, including the Housing Acts of 1949 and 1954. In addition to Mies and Ludwig Hilberseimer from IIT, key figures involved in the promotion of the Near South Side Plan included Walter Gropius, planners Reginald Isaacs and Walter Blucher, real-estate developer Ferd Kramer, IIT President Henry Heald, and University of Chicago sociologist Louis Wirth, among others.

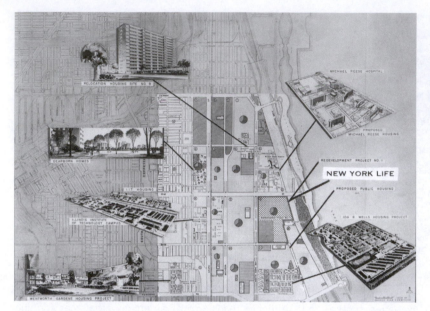

5.8
South Side
Planning Board
Redevelopment
Plan for the
Near South
Side. In John
McKinlay, 1950,
*Redevelopment
Project No. 1: A
Second Report*,
The New York
Life Insurance
Company
Redevelopment
Plan, p. 8

Contrary to what one might assume, once Mies was officially asked to design the campus, he did not start by designing the plan. Instead he began by studying the program, which was just being developed (and which would continue to be developed over the twenty years that Mies directed the project). After considering and testing various alternatives, he determined that a 24-foot-square module could be used to accommodate the programs of classroom buildings, lab buildings, and office spaces. Rough volumes were established and wooden blocks were cut, with gridded elevations pasted on, and then Mies and his associates played with the blocks on the "site": a large piece of paper, gridded with the same 24-foot module.[21] Although Mies once claimed that he did not think that site was "that important,"[22] the combination of the gridded background and the gridded blocks gives the impression that the blocks protrude from the paper – that the figures of the buildings emerge from the field of the Chicago grid, flipping it up 90 degrees from a horizontal to a vertical surface. Although the decision to divide the school's program into several individual buildings predated Mies's arrival at IIT, and although this choice was probably driven largely by economic concerns (it was easier to raise money for individual departments and to proceed slowly if the process was broken down into pieces), this decision was also the mechanism that allowed the design of IIT to be as much the design of a campus (or quasi-urban) space as it was a design of buildings. Mies's method of moving blocks about rather than working only in plan demonstrates to what extent he recognized the problem of the campus design to be a three-dimensional spatial issue.

At the scale of the campus, the "ceremonial" or communal pro-grams (the library and the student union) are given significant sites, but do not serve to centralize or focus the campus as they would had they been conceived along the lines of a traditional city plan. Rather than occupying the center of the central courtyard space these programs define its edge, as well as the edge of what is referred to as Mies Alley. Presentation drawings also reveal the campus's accessible institutional identity, or new monumentality. Rather than con-verging onto one significant point or feature, Mies's perspectival views tend to draw the outsider into the campus; their multiple side axes promise endless possibilities lying just around the corners of the drawn buildings. When the perspectives do focus upon a building's entry, the ground plane slips through the door into the lobby, suggesting a continuum rather than a boundary. In the earliest schemes, many of the buildings were on pilotis; it was Mies's dream that the entire ground plane could be one surface, interrupted only by the glass walls of the lobby spaces and stairs, smoothly taking people up into the build-ings above. Each building would then have a transitional, public/private space between the exterior public world and the interior private or academic world. Even if budget considerations eventually forced the elimination of the pilotis, the continuum was stressed: once the decision was made to put the buildings on the ground, Mies put them directly onto the ground, aligning the ground floor slab with the ground itself.[23] Even the detailing of the doors does not interrupt the flow of space between outdoors and indoors, as demonstrated by the centered, pivot-hinge doors to Lewis (now Perlstein) Hall: the door handles are kept vertical and in alignment with the doorframe, avoiding any interruption of the view. Given that the campus plan was designed as if the field and the figures were one and the same – the gridded blocks emerging from the grid of the ground plane – it was not necessary for the "ground level" of the buildings and of the landscape to remain level zero: the "ground" is sometimes at grade and sometimes raised above grade, as with Crown Hall, where the main level is half a level above street level. Even the lower levels that get used – Crown, the Commons, and Alumni Memorial Hall – are more like a ground plane that has dipped downwards rather than a basement. The use of half-levels, high clere-story windows, ramps, and shallow, wide, and unenclosed stairways turn the experience of this modulated ground plane into that of a continuous topographi-cal surface.

In 1942, then IIT President Henry Heald wrote a letter to Mies sug-gesting that, for esthetic and security reasons, a wall be erected around the perimeter of the campus. In a particularly insensitive gesture toward those dis-placed by the demolition, Heald even suggested building the wall of recycled materials culled from former homes: "It has been suggested that a brick wall might be used, built from brick salvaged from some of our wrecking operations."[24] While no reply is documented, Mies's answer lies in the campus's permeability.[25] Just as the courtyards are not closed off with four walls, the campus as a whole is open. The field upon which IIT's buildings sit extends out from the centermost courtyards to the very edges of the campus. With such moves, Mies deliberately redirected the city grid in a positive way and at two scales: that of IIT itself, where he replaced the *tabula rasa* of the land-clearance program with a modulated abstraction, and that of the entire Near South Side, which would follow Mies's design lead.

## Superscale

> Marina City was the first mixed use city center complex in the United States to include housing ... The Marina City towers were the tallest apartment buildings in the world and the highest concrete buildings in the world at the time of construction ... Marina City remains the densest modern residential plan in the United States, and possibly in the world, with 635 dwellings per acre.[26]

America's Midwest is the land of big vistas, Big Gulps™, and big buildings. Not surprisingly, Chicago is no stranger to superlatives. It is the home of the first mail-order company (Montgomery Ward), the largest commercial building (the Merchandize Mart), and, until recently, the world's busiest airport (O'Hare) and the world's tallest building (the Sears Tower). Bertrand Goldberg's Marina City is perhaps best known for its formal and structural innovation: the primary components of the project are two concrete residential towers shaped like corncobs (Figure 5.9). Goldberg himself underscored the project's superlative achievements: "At 588 feet, these towers were the tallest concrete buildings in the world and also the highest apartment buildings; at $10 per square foot, they were also the most economical. They were also the first American mixed-use urban complex to include housing."[27] Each tower's core carries the majority of the building's structural load: a concrete tube houses the elevators and stairs with the apartments ringing it like flower petals on a daisy. As a superblock, it maxes out a three-and-a-half acre block of the city grid. In comparison to IIT's 100 acres this size may not seem very superblock-esque, but Marina City qualifies because, like Frank Lloyd Wright's Quarter Section Competition entry, it offers a city within a city – a residential enclave with commercial, communal and recreation amenities.

As a *type*, Marina City might be compared to the Socialist super-blocks of Mosei Ginzburg and others – for few people realize that the complex includes other buildings than the superscaled, iconic residential towers and

5.9
**Marina City.** In
Ira J. Bach, 1965,
1980, *Chicago's
Famous Buildings,*
p. 82. University
of Chicago Press

marina base. But Marina City presents the Narkomfin's resolutely capitalist cousin: its communal living occurs only at the level of recreation, rather than dining or laundry or other aspects of personal life. The apartments were envisioned for singles or childless couples, and the lifestyle of what was advertised as a "twenty-four hour city block" (to heighten the contrast with the bedroom communities surrounding Chicago) was tailored for this particular demographic. The complex includes housing, parking, an office block, commercial space, four theaters, and a restaurant, bowling alley, swimming pool, skating rink, and marina. Conceived as a city within a city, the recreation and office facilities ensured that it would *participate in* rather than *isolate itself from* the city, for the project's programs deliberately reach beyond its own constituency to draw people in from all of Chicago. As a prescient solution to both urban sprawl and urban fiscal crises, Goldberg imagined entire cities composed of such complexes. These urban complexes would increase the city's density, thereby providing the population needed to support the costs of public transportation, culture, and other urban amenities. Goldberg's initial proposal for River City in Chicago was a linear city of tower triads which, reminiscent of the Civic Center's twelfth-floor public concourse, would be connected at every eighteenth floor by bridges offering communal amenities, such as post offices, health care, and daycare facilities, in addition to having commercial and other support programs at their base. This triad scheme takes the city within a city one scale further: different identities (and amenities) are provided at the scale of the single tower, the joined triad, and the 750 residents across the three towers who define a bridge community (there are three such horizontal communities in each triad).

# Superminiurbanism

> The superblock is more (and less) than a building. It has implications of size and complexity but also of the lowering of architectural voltage, because, unlike the representational buildings of the past, it is unable to acquire the status of a metaphor.[28]

Alan Colquhoun has argued that a superblock can never play a representational role within the city and that these are "rapidly destroying the traditional city." In the context of Chicago, however, the superblocks that stretch the city's original grid, causing it to absorb ever-variable, ever-evolving programs, are on the contrary constantly constructing the city, *figuring* it. The combination of grid and superblocks of all kinds works to redefine the urban understanding of background versus foreground: here the background is the grid, an ever present datum that is consistent enough to be understood, even if in reality it varies considerably. Read against this background, each superblock offers its own mini-urbanism – each constructs its own version of a different kind of Chicago grid. Colquhoun is right to say that superblocks cannot operate as metaphors, but that does not mean that they are not read or representational. Each superblock in Chicago contains an urban vision, an urban representation or snapshot of one part of Chicago. Like a tartan plaid, each one can read as a specific block unto itself, but each block also connects into the city via the grid. While the superblock has been condemned as a large-scale totalizing vision, the totalization that is Chicago is – because of the superblock's agglomeration – the most heterogeneous homogeneity of urban tableaus.

## Acknowledgments

I would like to thank Albert Pope for provoking my interest in the superblock and Ron Witte, R. E. Somol and Cécile Whiting for their helpful suggestions regarding this text. Thanks also to Ed Robbins and Rodolphe el-Khoury for their generous patience and perseverance.

## Notes

1  See Shiffman, 2002.
2  Jacobs, 1961, p. 22.
3  Hoyt, 1933, p. 428.
4  Buckingham, 1842 (cited in Reps, 1965, p. 302).
5  "Historians still argue over the origin of the name, some maintaining it comes from the Indian *Chicagou*, 'garlic,' while others hold that it was derived from *Shegagh*, or 'skunk.' There is general agreement, however, that the odors of the place were dreadful and that the Indians were correct in referring to it as "the place of the evil smell." Reps, 1965, p. 300.
6  Bureau of Land Management, 1947, p. 352 (emphasis added).
7  Koolhaas, 1984, pp. 20–21.
8  Johnson, 1976, pp. 42–44.
9  Condit, 1973, pp. 52–53.
10  Yeomans, 1916, p. 2.
11  Johnson, 1976, pp. 60–61. An 1804 Act of Congress established the section, half section and quarter section as units of land sale; an 1832 Amendment included the quarter-quarter section, or "forty."
12  According to Frank Lloyd Wright specialist Neil Levine, the plan is "non-competitive" (as Yeomans labels it in the competition book) because it was most likely submitted to the City Club after the competition deadline, after Wright had been solicited to offer a scheme. Wright did not participate in competitions.
13  My thanks to Neil Levine for this reference. Levine has an article forthcoming on the quadruple block plan.
14  Yeomans, 1916, p. 99 (emphasis Frank Lloyd Wright's).
15  Pope, 1996.
16  Chicago Plan Commission, 1945, p. 30.
17  Giedion, 1944, p. 568.
18  George Danforth in conversation with Kevin Harrington, Canadian Centre for Architecture Oral History Project, unpublished transcript: 96–100.
19  Willard E. Hotchkiss in *Armour Institute Board of Trustees Minutes* (1934–40), addendum 2 (May 17, 1937), 11.
20  A longer version of this section appears in Lambert, 2001, pp. 642–691. This version, which concentrates less on the policies that enabled this superblock than on the figuring of space within the superblock, owes thanks to Robert McAnulty for perceptively suggesting that the thing to pay attention to in the "tower in the park" is the park, not the tower.
21  "We then also, as Mies got the program from the various departments of the school, we

made wood blocks of the volume of the building, and on a plot of the whole site I drew up, he would work those out in some arrangement within the spaces of the buildings, having had that plot from – what was it? – 31st Street down to 35th, State Street over to the tracks to the west, drawn up in a modular system that he had found workable for the contents of the program." George Danforth in conversation with Kevin Harrington, CCA Oral History Project.

22  Interview with Katherine Kuh, in Kuh, 1971, p. 35.

23  Safety considerations were an issue as well: as George Danforth notes, had the buildings been built in this manner, the stairwells would have been filled with a dangerously crushed crowd of students at the beginning and end of each class. (George Danforth in conversation with Kevin Harrington, April 9, 1996, CCA Oral History Project.

24  Letter from Henry Heald to MvdR, July 30, 1942, Heald papers, Box 17, folder 4, IIT Archives, Paul V. Galvin Library. Thank you to Phyllis Lambert for kindly pointing me to this reference.

25  It has been argued that Mies's open perimeter depended upon an urban "wall" of poché, formed by the context around the campus; see Pierce, 1998, p. 5. Given that Mies was cognizant of IIT's expansionist desires and land-purchasing efforts, I would be surprised that he would base his logic upon the campus's immediate context. Second, given that the landscape of the campus deliberately extends to the public realm, I hold to my reading that Mies envisioned it extending as far as it could.

26  Goldberg, 1985a, p. 33.

27  Goldberg, 1985b, p. 192.

28  Colquhoun, 1981, p. 98.

# Chapter 6

# Detroit – Motor City

*Charles Waldheim*

> The belief that an industrial country must concentrate its industry is, in my opinion, unfounded. That is only an intermediate phase in the development. Industry will decentralize itself. If the city were to decline, no one would rebuild it according to its present plan. That alone discloses our own judgment on our cities.[1]

In the second half of the twentieth century, the city of Detroit, once the fourth largest city in the US, lost over half its population.[2] The *motor city*, once an international model for industrialized urban development, began the process of decentralization as early as the 1920s, catalyzed by Henry Ford's decision to relocate production outside the city to reduce production costs. While similar conditions can be found in virtually every industrial city in North America, Detroit recommends itself as the clearest, most legible example of these trends evidenced in the spatial and social conditions of the post-war American city (Figure 6.1).

> Forget what you think you know about this place. Detroit is the most relevant city in the United States for the simple reason that it is the most unequivocally modern and therefore distinctive of our national culture: in other words, a total success. Nowhere else has American modernity had its way with people and place alike.[3]

In August 1990, Detroit's City Planning Commission authored a remarkable and virtually unprecedented report.[4] This immodest document proposed the decommissioning and abandonment of the most vacant areas of what had

been the fourth largest city in the US. With this publication, uninspiringly titled the *Detroit Vacant Land Survey*, the city planners documented a process of depopulation and disinvestment that had been under way in Detroit since the 1950s.[5] With an incendiary 1993 press release based on the City Planning Commission's recommendations of three years previously, the City Ombudsman, Marie Farrell-Donaldson, publicly called for the discontinuation of services to, and the relocation of vestigial populations from, the most vacant portions of the city (Figure 6.2):

6.1
**Downtown Detroit figure-ground diagrams, Richard Plunz, "Detroit is Everywhere,"** *Architecture Magazine*, 85(4), 55–61

6.2
**Brush Park, aerial photograph courtesy Alex MacLean/ Landslides**

The city's ombudsman ... is essentially suggesting that the most blighted bits of the city should be closed down. Residents would be relocated from dying areas to those that still had life in them. The empty houses would be demolished and empty areas fenced off; they would either be landscaped, or allowed to return to "nature."[6]

Until the public release of the survey, the depopulation of Detroit was largely accomplished without the endorsement of, or meaningful acknowledgment by, the architectural and planning professions. What was remarkable about Detroit's 1990 *Vacant Land Survey* was its unsentimental and surprisingly clear-sighted acknowledgment of a process of post-industrial de-densification that continues to this day in cities produced by modern industrialization. Equally striking was how quickly the report's recommendations were angrily dismissed in spite of the fact that they corroborated a practice of urban erasure that was already well under way (Figures 6.3–6.6).

While European proponents of modernist planning had originally imported Fordism and Taylorism from American industry and applied them to city planning, it was the American city (and Detroit in particular) that offered the fullest embodiment of those principles in spatial terms. Ironically, while the American planning profession ultimately embraced the virtues of Fordist

urbanism in the middle of the twentieth century, it was ill-prepared for the impact those ongoing processes would have on forms of urban arrangement as evidenced by the condition of Detroit at the end of that century. Among those impacts were the utter abandonment of traditional European models of urban density in favor of impermanent, ad hoc arrangements of temporary utility and steadily decreasing density.

While flexibility, mobility, and speed made Detroit an international model for industrial urbanism, those very qualities rendered the city disposable. Traditional models of dense urban arrangement were quite literally abandoned

6.3
**Motor City,
photographs
courtesy Jordi
Bernado**

6.4
**Motor City,
photographs
courtesy Jordi
Bernado**

6.5
**Motor City,
photographs
courtesy Jordi
Bernado**

6.6
**Detroit's Vacancy,
photographs
courtesy Jordi
Bernado**

in favor of escalating profits, accelerating accumulation and a culture of consumption. This of course was the genius of Ford's conception: a culture that consumes the products of its own labor while consistently creating a surplus of demand, ensuring a nomadic, operational, and ceaselessly reiterated model of ex-urban arrangement. That ongoing provisional work of rearrangement is the very model of American urbanism that Detroit offers.

Typical of their peers in other American cities, Detroit's city planners, architects, and urban design professionals clinicalized the dying industrial city to the extent that Detroit came to represent an urban failure, as though

the responsibility for its viability rested with the techniques of modernist urbanism that shaped its development. This was to mistake effect for cause. As a product of mobile capital and speculative development practices in the service of evolving models of production, Detroit was a clear and unmistakable success. As promoted internationally by the proponents of Fordism, Detroit served as a model of urbanism placed in the service of optimized industrial pro- duction. With each successive transformation in production paradigms, Detroit re-tooled itself more completely and more quickly than virtually any other city in history.

What was remarkable about the Detroit Vacant Land Survey and the City of Detroit's plan to decommission parts of itself was not its impossibility, but rather the simple fact that it dared articulate for public consumption the fact that the city was already abandoning itself. This fact alone did not make Detroit unique. In the 1990s, Detroit ranked a distant twenty-second nationally in the percentage of its population lost compared with other metropolitan centers, having already surrendered the majority of its citizenry over the previous four decades.[7] The original abandonment and subsequent suburban annexation of central Detroit began well before similar conditions emerged in other major cities. Unlike other cities, however, Detroit began its process of decentraliza- tion and urban abandonment sooner and pursued it more completely than any other city in the modern world. Perhaps more importantly, Detroit was the only city that dared publicly to articulate a plan for its own abandonment and conceive of organizing the process of decommissioning itself as a legitimate problem requiring the attention of design professionals. In a graphically spare document featuring maps blacked-out with marker to indicate areas of vacant land, Detroit's planners rendered an image of a previously unimaginable urban- ism of erasure that was already a material fact (Figure 6.7).[4]

One last question must now be asked: during a crisis period, will the demolition of cities replace the major public works of traditional politics? If so, it would no longer be possible to distinguish between the nature of recessions (economic, industrial) and the nature of war.[8]

Over the course of the 1990s, the City of Detroit lost approximately 1 percent of its housing stock annually to arson, primarily due to "Devil's Night" vandalism.[9] Publicly, the city administration decried this astonishingly direct and specific critique of the city's rapidly deteriorating social conditions. Simultan- eously, the city privately corroborated the arsonists' illegal intent by developing, funding, and implementing one of the largest and most sweeping demolition programs in the history of American urbanism. This program continued through- out the 1990s, largely supported by the city's real estate, business, and civic

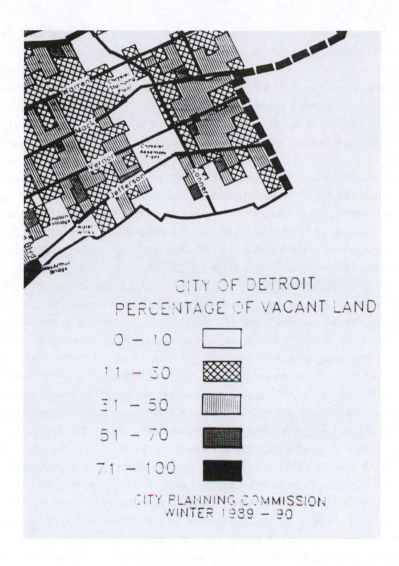

6.7
**City of Detroit
City Planning
Commission
Vacant Land
Survey**

communities. This curious arrangement allowed both the disenfranchised and the propertied interests publicly to blame each other for the city's problems while providing a legal and economic framework within which to carry out an ongoing process of urban erasure. Ironically, this "solution" to Detroit's image problems completed the unsanctioned process of erasure begun illegally by the populations left in the wake of de-industrialization. Vast portions of Detroit were erased through this combination of unsanctioned burning and subsequently legitimized demolition.[10] The combined impact of these two activities, each deemed illicit by differing interests, was to coordinate the public display of social unrest with administration attempts to erase the visual residue of Detroit's ongoing demise.

In The Practice of Everyday Life, Michel de Certeau describes the limits of disciplinary relevance absent the human subjects demanded by professional authority: "the dying man falls outside the thinkable, which is identified with what one can do. In leaving the field circumscribed by the possibilities of treatment, it enters a region of meaninglessness."[11] For the architectural profession, the city of Detroit in the 1990s entered a similar condition of meaninglessness precisely because it no longer required the techniques of growth and development that had become the modus operandi of the discipline. Absent the need for these tools, Detroit became a "non-site" for the architect in the same sense that de Certeau's dead body ceased to operate as a "site" for the physician's attention.[11] As the city decommissioned itself, it entered a condition that could not be thought by the architectural and planning disciplines. As Dan Hoffman put it, in the early 1990s "unbuilding surpassed building as the city's primary architectural activity" (Figures 6.8, 6.9).[12]

The fact that American cities began to dissolve as a result of the pressures of mature Fordist decentralization came as a surprise only to those disciplines with a vested interest in the ongoing viability of a nineteenth-century model of urbanism based on increasing density. Free of that prejudice, the development of American industrial cities can more easily be understood as a temporary, ad hoc arrangement based on the momentary optimization of industrial production. The astonishing pliability of industrial arrangement and the increasing pace of change in production paradigms suggest that any understanding of American cities must acknowledge their temporary, provisional nature. The explosive growth of Detroit over the first half of the twentieth century, rather than constructing an expectation of enduring urbanism, must be understood as one-half of an ongoing process of urban arrangement that ultimately rendered its previous forms redundant.[13] Detroit can be seen as nothing more than the most recent idea about production as manifest in spatial terms. The fact that American industrial urbanism would decreasingly resemble its European and pre-Fordist precedents should come as no surprise. Rather than a permanent construction, one must take American urbanism as an essentially temporary, provisional, and continuously revised articulation of property ownership, speculative development, and mobile capital.[14]

Especially for those modernists interested in mobility and new models of social arrangement, the flexibility and increasing pace of technological change associated with Fordist production served as models for an increasingly temporary urbanism. The most obvious model for this iterative and responsive urbanism could be found at the intersection of industrial production and military infrastructure.[15] For Le Corbusier, the origins of the city itself could be found in the urbanism of the military encampment.

6.8
*Erasing Detroit,*
courtesy Dan
Hoffman

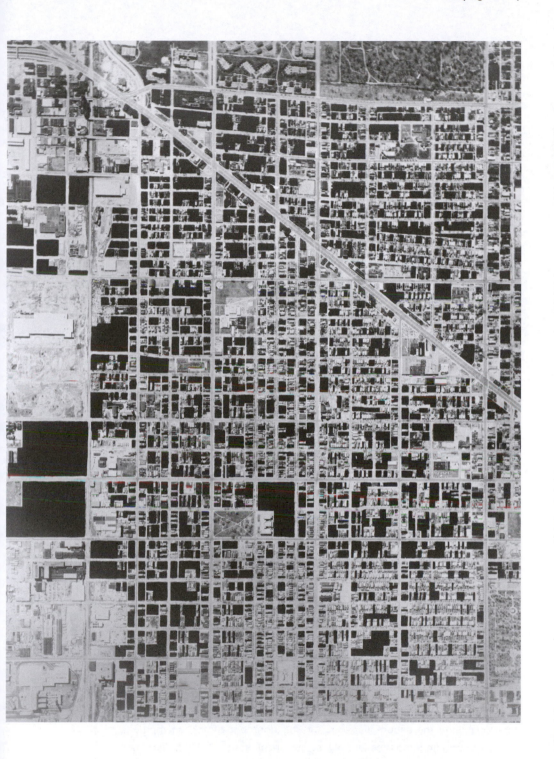

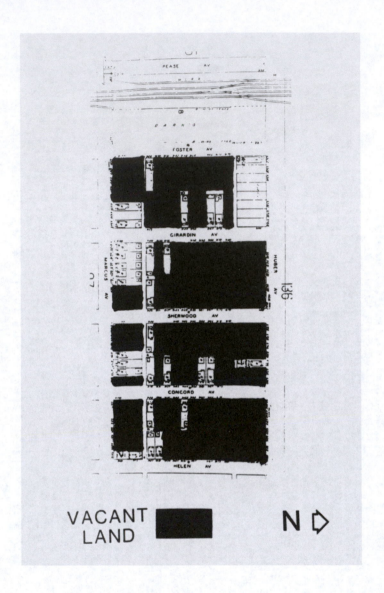

VACANT LAND

N ▷

6.9
**Detroit Vacant Land Maps, City of Detroit**

Commenting on the architectural myths of the primitive hut, this drawing of a circumscribed martial precinct reveals the essentially nomadic pre-history of urban arrangement in European culture (Figure 6.10). Ancient rites for the founding of Roman cities were essentially symmetrical with those for the founding of military encampments. In The Idea of a Town, Joseph Rykwert describes how performing the precise reverse of those founding rites was used to signify the decommissioning or abandonment of an encampment, thus corroborating their essentially symmetrical status.[16] With his Coop Zimmer project, Hannes Meyer commented on the collusion between the

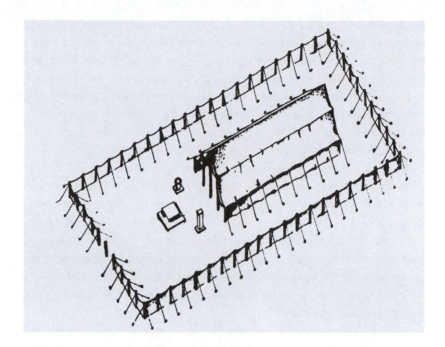

6.10
**Military
Encampment as
Primitive Hut**

mass consumer products of Fordist production and their replication in the miscellany of modern military nomadism.[17] Meyer's project arranged a petit-bourgeois domestic ensemble of semi-disposable consumer furnishings as the interior of an equally transportable military accommodation (Figure 6.11).

The most direct critique of modern urbanism as informed by twentieth-century military techniques can be found in the projects of Ludwig

6.11
**Hannes Meyer's**
*Coop Zimmer*

Hilberseimer.[18] Hilberseimer's proposals for a radically decentralized pattern of regional infrastructure for post-war America simultaneously optimized Fordist models of decentralized industrial production and dispersed large population concentrations that had become increasingly obvious targets for aerial attack in the atomic age. Hilberseimer's drawing of an atomic blast in central Illinois renders a clear imperative for the construction of a civil defense infrastructure capable of transporting dense urban populations away from the dangers of the city and toward the relative security of suburban dissolution. This model of the highway as a military infrastructure afforded a form of civil defense through camouflage. Not coincidentally, the depopulation of urban centers in response to the Cold War argues quite effectively for precisely the kind of decreasing density that his previous work had been predicated on in the name of efficient industrial production and optimized arrangement. In both modalities, as military encampment and industrial ensemble, the vision of a nationally scaled infrastructure of transportation and communication networks revealed a fundamental sympathy between Fordist models of industrial production and military models of spatial projection.

Much has been written on the military origins of the modern interstate highway system in the US, and the impact of military policy on post-war American settlement patterns has been well documented. While the highway is arguably the clearest evidence of Fordism's impact on post-war urban arrangement in America, it is also clear that this most Fordist network is itself an essentially military technology. Given Ford's well-documented sympathy to Nazism, the infrastructural and logistical logics of the German war machine provided an essential case study in the virtues of Fordist mobility.[19] Not simply a model of production, but an essential Fordist precept, mobilization was understood as a preparation for not only the projection of military power but also the retooling of the very industrial process itself toward martial ends. It should come as no surprise that the modern interstate highway, the very invention Ford's success postulated, was itself first proven necessary through German military engineering. By witnessing the logistical superiority and civil defense potential of the autobahns, the American military industrial complex was able to articulate the need for the highway as an increasingly urgent matter of national security.

Not coincidentally, Detroit has the dubious honor of being the only American city to be occupied three times by Federal troops.[20] Another evidence of the parallels to be drawn between military encampments and Detroit's temporary urbanism can be found in the symmetrical techniques employed to enforce social order amid the dense concentration of heterogeneous populations. The history of Detroit's labor unrest documents the various quasi-military techniques employed to render a suitably compliant labor pool to serve the needs of the production line. Detroit's social history has oscillated between periods of peacefully coerced consumption (fueled by advertising and increasing wages) and periods of profound social unrest, largely based on the desire for collective bargaining, improvements in economic conditions, and to redress racial and ethnic inequities.[21]

Ford's famous five-dollar day and five-day workweek were quite calculated levers intended to fuel the consumption of mass products by the working classes themselves. The volatile concentration of diverse populations of laborers in dense urban centers was among the factors that led Ford to begin decentralizing production as early as the 1920s.[14] The combination of decentralized pools of workers each with sufficient income to consume the products of their own labors produced a new economic paradigm in the twentieth century, and also helped to fuel the rapid depopulation of post-industrial urban centers in post-war America.

In 1955, at the height of post-war emigration from the city, a uniquely talented team was assembled to renovate one of the city's "failing" downtown neighborhoods.[22] A federally underwritten Title I FHA urban renewal project, which would come to be known as Lafayette Park, the work of this interdisciplinary team offers a unique case study in a continuously viable and vibrant mixed income community occupying a modernist superblock scheme. In light of recently renewed interest in the problems of modernist planning principles, and the continual demolition of many publicly subsidized modernist housing projects nationally, Lafayette Park offers a unique counterpoint, arguing precisely in favor of modern principles of urban planning and recommending a thoughtful revision of the perceived failures of modern architecture and planning vis-à-vis the city (Figures 6.12–6.14).

Led by the developer Herbert Greenwald (until his untimely death in a 1959 airplane crash) and a team of real-estate professionals, the financial underpinnings of the project included $7.5 million in FHA loan guarantees (out of a total construction budget of $35 million) as well as a substantial federal subsidy toward the cost of the land. Originally planned as a mixed-income and mixed-race development, Lafayette Park continues to this day to enjoy multiple original family residents, high relative market value, and greater racial, ethnic, and class diversity than both the city and suburbs that surround it. Greenwald's original conception of the neighborhood remains remarkably viable today, as the site continues to provide central city housing to a middle-class group of residents with the perceived amenities of the suburbs, including decreased density, extensive landscaping and public parks, easy access by automobile, and safe places for children to play.

Greenwald enlisted the professional services of architect Ludwig Mies van der Rohe for the design of the project, with whom he had previously

6.12
**Lafayette Park,
Hedrich Blessing
Photographs
courtesy Chicago
Historical Society**

6.13
**Lafayette Park,
Hedrich Blessing
Photographs
courtesy Chicago
Historical Society**

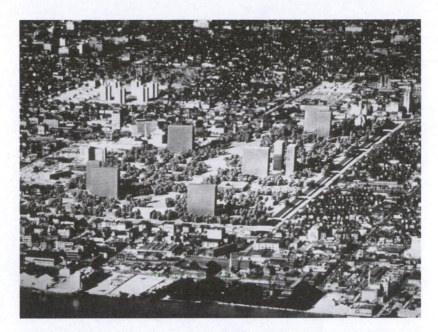

6.14
**Lafayette Park,
Hedrich Blessing
Photographs
courtesy Chicago
Historical Society**

worked on the development of the 860–880 Lake Shore Drive Apartments in Chicago. Mies brought to the team Ludwig Hilberseimer, to plan the site, and Alfred Caldwell, to execute the landscape design. Based largely on his previous academic projects in Germany and the US, Lafayette Park provided the most significant application of Hilberseimer's conception of the "settlement unit" as well as the most important commission of his career. Hilbs's settlement unit was particularly apt as an aggregation of planning principles and types appropriate to the decentralizing North American city.[22] Best known for his unbuilt urban design projects from the 1920s (e.g. Hochhausstadt, 1924), Hilbs began to work on the notion of landscape as the primary medium for a horizontal and radically decentralized post-urban landscape as early as the 1930s. First evidenced in mid-1930s projects for mixed-height housing schemes and the University of Berlin campus, these tendencies toward an idea of landscape as urbanism are immediately evident in Hilb's plans for the Lafayette Park site, a portion of the city of Detroit that decentralized first, fastest, and most fully.

Hilberseimer's plans for the site proposed landscape as its primary material element, the commission offering both sufficient acreage as well as budget for what could have otherwise been an uninspired urban void. Central to this was Greenwald's finance and marketing scheme, which positioned landscape as the central amenity in the form of an 18-acre park bisecting the site and providing a much sought-after social and environmental amenity in the midst of Detroit. Lafayette Park removed the vestiges of the obsolete nineteenth-century street grid, in favor of a lush verdant and extensive green tabula verde. By doing this, Hilberseimer accommodated the automobile completely at Lafayette Park yet rendered it secondary to the primary exterior spaces of the site, as the parking is in proximity to units while zoned to the perimeter of the site and dropped by approximately one meter below grade. To the extent that landscape can be seen as a primary ordering element (in lieu of architecture) for the urbanization of the site, Hilbs's collaboration with Mies at Lafayette Park provides a unique case study for examining the role of landscape in post-war modernist planning more generally.

At the end of the twentieth century, at least 70 urban centers in the US were engaged in an ongoing process of abandonment, disinvestment, and decay.[23] While most Americans for the first time in history now live in suburban proximity to a metropolitan center, this fact is mitigated by the steadily decreasing physical density in most North American cities. Rather than taking the abandonment of these previously industrial urban centers as an indicator of the so-called "failure" of the design disciplines to create a meaningful or coherent public realm, these trends must be understood as the rational end game of industrial urbanism itself, rendering legible a mobility of capital and dispersion of infrastructure that characterize mature Fordist urbanism as prophesied by Ford himself.[14] In spite of a decade-long attempt to "revitalize" the city of Detroit with the construction of theaters, sports stadia, casinos, and other publicly subsidized, privately owned, for-profit destination entertainment, Detroit continues steadily to lose population and building stock. These latest architectural attempts to proclaim Detroit "back" have effectively committed the city to a future as a destination entertainment theme park for its wealthy suburban expatriates. Rather than signaling a renewed "vitality" or life for the postindustrial city, these projects continue to mine the brand name of Detroit, while the city continues to abandon itself to a decentralized post-industrial future. In spite of a massive federally funded advertising campaign and a small army of census takers, the 2000 US census showed Detroit's population continuing to shrink (Figure 6.15).[24]

As Detroit decamps it constructs immense empty spaces – tracts of land that are essentially void spaces. These areas are not being "returned to nature," but are curious landscapes of indeterminate status. In this context, landscape is the only medium capable of dealing with simultaneously decreasing densities and indeterminate futures. The conditions recommending an urbanism of landscape can be found both in the abandoned central city and on the periphery of the still spreading suburbs. Ironically, the ongoing process of greenfield development at the perimeter of Detroit's metropolitan region brings up similar questions posed by the incursion of

6.15
**The infrastructure of the automobile and the city it emptied, aerial photograph courtesy Alex MacLean/ Landslides**

opportunistic natural environmental systems into areas of post-urban abandonment. For these sites, both brownfield and greenfield, what is demanded is a strategy of landscape as urbanism, a landscape urbanism for Detroit's post-industrial territories.[25]

## Acknowledgments

Work on this chapter has benefited greatly from the support and advice of others, particularly Rodolphe el-Khoury, whose generosity and insight were abundantly apparent at all stages of the work. This work has particularly been informed by numerous conversations with Jason Young and Georgia Daskalakis, with whom I co-edited Stalking Detroit (Barcelona: ACTAR, 2001). Contributors to that anthology, Jerry Herron, Patrick Schumacher, Dan Hoffman, and Kent Kleinman, have each helped to clarify my interests in Detroit in particular ways. The origins of this chapter can be found in the research and design project "Decamping Detroit," co-authored with Marili Santos-Munne in Stalking Detroit, pp. 104–121.

6.16
**Andrey Tarkovsky's** *Stalker*

6.17
**Andrey
Tarkovsky's**
*Stalker*

6.18
**Andrey
Tarkovsky's**
*Stalker*

## Notes

1  Henry Ford as quoted in Ludwig Hilberseimer, 1945, pp. 89–93.
2  In the first half of the twentieth century, the population of Detroit grew from under 285,700 in 1900 to over 1,849,500 in 1950. That number dropped steadily in the second half of the century to 951,270 at the 2000 census. For more on Detroit's declining population, see Rybczynski, 1995, pp. 14–17, 19.
3  See Herron, 1993.
4  *Detroit Vacant Land Survey*, 1990.
5  *Detroit Vacant Land Survey*, 1990, pp. 3–5.
6  *The Economist*, 1993, pp. 33–34.
7  US Census Bureau figures for Detroit indicate that the populations of 21 metropolitan areas in the US, including St Louis, Washington, DC, and Philadelphia, were shrinking at a faster rate than Detroit's during the decade of the 1990s.
8  Virilio, 1986. In 1998, Detroit's Mayor Dennis Archer secured $60 million in loan guarantees from the US Department of Housing and Urban Development to finance the demolition of every abandoned residential building in the city. See *Metropolis*, 1998, p. 33.
9  See Chafets, 1990, pp. 3–16. While precise numbers of houses lost to arson are hard to quantify, local myth places the figure at a conservative 1 percent annually. On media coverage of arson in Detroit, see Herron, 1993.
10  On the urban impact of Detroit's massive demolition program, see Hoffman, 2001a, 2001b.
11  De Certeau, 1984, p. 190.
12  See Hoffman, 2001a. According to research by Sanford Kwinter and Daniela Fabricius, between 1978 and 1998 approximately 9000 building permits were issued for new houses in Detroit, while over 108,000 demolition permits were issued. See Kwinter and Fabricius, 2000, p. 600.
13  Hoffman, 2001b.
14  Schumacher and Rogner, 2001.
15  Paul Virilio has commented on the fundamentally warlike conditions of Fordist urbanism. See Virilio, 1986.
16  Rykwert, 1988.
17  Hays, 1995, pp. 54–81.
18  Hilberseimer, 1949; Pommer *et al.*, 1988.
19  For a discussion of the military imperatives of modernist urbanism, see Kwinter, 1994, pp. 84–95.
20  For a description of the martial enforcement of civil order in the context of race relations in Detroit, see Sugrue, 1996.
21  Sugrue, 1996, pp. 259–271.
22  For an excellent overview of Lafayette Park, see Pommer *et al.*, 1988, pp. 89–93.
23  Alan Plattus, "Undercrowding and the American City: A Position Paper and a Proposal for Action," unpublished manuscript, pp. 1–8.
24  The aggressive and unsuccessful federally funded campaign to count Detroit's citizens for the 2000 census was aimed in part at maintaining Detroit's eligibility for certain federally funded programs available only to cities with a population of one million or more. See *Chicago Tribune*, 2000.
25  Waldheim coined the term "landscape urbanism" in 1996 to describe the emergence of landscape as the most relevant medium for the production and representation of contemporary urbanism.

Chapter 7

# Hong Kong – Aformal Urbanism

*Jonathan D. Solomon*

Hong Kong is an advanced form of the spatial logic of late capitalism; a shopping mall, a theme park or atrium hotel elaborated to the complexity of a city. Characterized by a three-dimensional publicly accessible network that facilitates propinquity and integration of diverse sectors, the city's unique take on a generic urbanism complicates understandings of the postmodern city and suggests exciting futures.

More than any site save Disneyland, John Portman's 1976 Bonaventure Hotel in Los Angeles established the spatial grammar of postmodernism. With its outwardly opaque spaces of international capital, its thoroughly disorienting interiors, its wholesale dismantling of any sense of exteriority in the city, and its lack of visual hierarchy and traditional urbanity, the building was characterized by Fredric Jameson as a "Postmodern Hyperspace."[1] In Hong Kong, Hyperspace is the norm, for there was never truly any traditional space in the city for it to supersede. If the Bonaventure, in Jameson's eyes, "aspires to being a total space, a complete world, a kind of miniature city,"[2] then Hong Kong succeeds. If the Bonaventure aspired to miniaturize the city in a building, in Hong Kong the city has coalesced into a single enlarged building.

The origins of this fascinating urban complex are unlikely: the shopping mall in Hong Kong serves as the medium both for pedestrian connectivity and of civic culture.[3] Typically located over busy public transit nodes, these malls are a development of the 1950s American dumb-bell mall, with two anchor department stores linked by 600-foot arcades of smaller shops. Hong Kong malls advance this model by adopting an inclusive approach to anchors, which can include office or hotel lobbies, transit stations, and residential estates; these malls also expand the network of anchors and arcades into three dimensions. At the International Financial Center (IFC), developed on landfill in the late 1990s, systems of interlinked publicly accessible passageways coalesce in three dimensions around the IFC Mall, a continuous medium of pedestrian traffic between ferry piers, underground rail stations, bus terminals, taxi stands, and the city beyond that renders not just the streets but the very ground of the city irrelevant.[4] At the same time, the IFC and other sites like it across the city generate a unique culture. The density, connectivity, and redundancy of these networks generate new forms of public space that, to function, require neither the images of classical European or Chinese urbanity to signify a street, a courtyard, a square, nor the underlying guarantees they suggest.[5]

While lacking traditional legibility, Hong Kong's pedestrian networks, when mapped as a seamless continuum uninterrupted by ownership, management, function, or vertical position, and describe a perceptible spatial logic. In the case of the IFC, the mall is at the center of a network of connective

**7.1
Footbridges in
Central, 2001,
photograph by
Adam Frampton**

passages that link diverse populations and activities through transit. Knockoff goods are sold meters from the real thing. Amateur musicians perform just steps away from professionals. Tourists, expat bankers, foreign domestic workers, and local commuters converge.

Networks such as these are common in the city: in Mong Kok East, a footbridge runs from Mong Kok Station through the Mong Kok East Station, the Grand Century Plaza mall and the lobby of the adjacent Royal Plaza Hotel, down two flights of escalators and across a bridge over Prince Edward Road West, then through a street of local flower markets and a bird market on an elevated park before crossing the historic border between Hong Kong and Qing Dynasty China. In Lam Tin, a transit hub spans the highway below Sceneway Gardens Estate, and connects to older residential estates and a bus terminal through eight stories of escalators and two shopping malls, the Sceneway Plaza and the Kai Tin Shopping Center.

Aformal urbanism refers to a form of decision-making and design process in cities that falls between traditional understandings of the formal and the informal. Evidence of aformal urbanism can be found by examining the organizational structures it produces, which reject traditional form-based hierarchies that rely on visual legibility, such as solid-void or figure–ground relationships.

**7.2**

**Publicly accessible pedestrian access networks in and around IFC Mall and Exchange Square, Central, drawing by Adam Frampton, Jonathan D. Solomon, and Clara Wong**

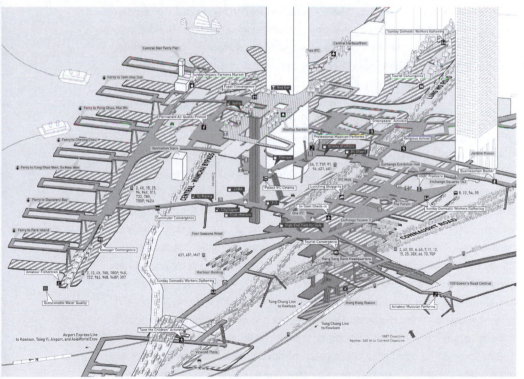

"Aformal" thus has two meanings, one referring to the city's organization, the other to its spatial products.

## Aformal logics

Discussions of the formal and the informal in architecture and urbanism, and particularly in areas experiencing rapid urbanization, tend toward polarization. On the one hand, the formal tends to be equated with the legal and specifically with the state apparatus either directly or through the application of codification or regulation to market forces. On the other hand, the informal, as explored by critic Mike Davis and others, tends to be equated with the illegal, or at least with the extra-legal solution-based results typical of less empowered operators.[6]

At the same time, the formal tends to be equated with the legible, and specifically with the kind of state-modernist visual legibility described by James C. Scott and others as ultimately ill-fated attempts to reduce complexity and unpredictability into models that better suit bureaucratic administration, while the informal tends to be equated with the illegible, and specifically with the express lack of precisely that type of bureaucratic clarity.[7]

In Hong Kong the impression of this dualism can be reinforced by other assumptions that rest on binary oversimplifications – residues of a colonial past neatly incorporated in the city's official slogan, "Asia's World City": East and West, rich and poor, fast and slow, old and new. In fact, all these assumptions are outdated. Hong Kong resists simple dualisms with surprising levels of integration in its spatial products. Its intense pedestrian connectivity is a result of a combination of top-down planning and bottom-up solutions, a unique collaboration between pragmatic thinking and comprehensive master-planning, played out in three-dimensional space.

Take, for example, the footbridge over Chater Road, built in the early 1960s to join second-level pedestrian shopping arcades in Prince's building with the Mandarin Hotel. While the continuous elevated deck has an extended modernist pedigree, most notably in this case through the work of Colin Buchanan, whose Traffic in Towns (1963) influenced Hong Kong planners at this time, it is hard to see Chater Road as anything other than a pragmatic solution to the needs of the developer to maximize profitability of space; an expression of the city's so-called laissez-faire urbanism.[8] Once the Chater Road Bridge, and others like it in a network joining properties owned by the developer Hong Kong Land proved successful, the Highways Department began building footbridges too. It is hard to see the network of bridges erected along Connaught Road in the 1980s as anything other than the product of government bureaucracy exercising top-down planning. The resulting complex, the network of public and private

7.3
**A footbridge on Chater Road, 1965, photograph courtesy the Government of Hong Kong SAR**

7.4
**Footbridges along Connaught Road, 1982, photograph courtesy the Government of Hong Kong SAR**

7.5
**Aformal urbanism
of Central, 2001,
photograph
CS01235
reproduced with
permission of the
Director of Lands.**
© The Government
of Hong Kong SAR.
License No.
64/2011

armatures, falls into neither category. The Highways Department owns bridges between privately developed properties and public transportation interchanges. If either party shut their portions, the system breaks down. This network is generated by the pressures and constraints of Hong Kong's context, not imported as an abstract idea. It is the result of neither top-down planning nor self-organizing systems. It is some new thing: an aformal urbanism.

Examples of aformal urbanism abound in Hong Kong, and not all of them are entirely anonymous. The Central and Midlevels escalator was envisaged by the Highways Department as a kind of pedestrian flyover linking the Central business district with residential neighborhoods in the Midlevels of

Victoria Peak; it was proposed as a means to alleviate traffic on the region's narrow roads. By making the steep hills behind Central easier to access, the escalator had the unexpected effect of transforming a formerly sleepy neighborhood into a premier entertainment district, raising property values, and bringing new congestion. New escalators are under construction and several more are in planning on the west side of Hong Kong Island, pushed now not by the Highways Department, but by developers and local politicians seeking to emulate the effects seen in Central. Resistance to the projects from residents is based on a desire to avoid precisely the same effects.[9]

Times Square, a mall in Causeway Bay, was built on the model of the American atrium mall, multiple levels linked by elevator banks and sequential escalators organized around a central open space. As pedestrian flows in the upper floors of the mall decreased, it became clear they were too isolated. So the atrium was filled. New escalators, or "Expresscalators" make the nine-storey journey in a few quick jumps, skipping floors in an ascending spiral. Like shortcuts taken across a formal quad that eventually create informal paths that the college paves, the Central and Midlevels Escalator and the Times Square Expresscalators formalize informal patterns and generate aformal urbanism.

The easy fluidity of public passage through diverse and apparently contradictory spatial and social complexes is a symptom of a more general and more fundamentally unlikely condition in Hong Kong with its origins in the city's

7.6
**The Central and Midlevels Escalator, shortly after its opening in 1994, photograph courtesy the Government of Hong Kong SAR**

extremes of geography and climate and unique historical circumstances. A closer study of three Hong Kong buildings, which, while radical, fall somewhat outside the city's mainstream architectural narrative, reveals why aformal urbanism flourishes in the city. Shun Tak Center in Sheung Wan is an example of Hong Kong's rejection of both a physical and a cultural ground and its embrace of connectivity. Queensway Plaza in Admiralty is an example of how the lack of a ground prevents visual hierarchies from developing by precluding figure–ground relationships. The Lockhart Road Municipal Services Building is an example of how in place of legible formal rules other sensorial atmospheres, like temperature, smell, sound and touch, develop new ordering systems.

# A city without ground

Ground is a continuous plane and a stable reference point for the public life of the city. It is the surface on which the conflicts of urban propinquity – public and private, planned and impromptu, privileged and disadvantaged – are worked out. This stable reference point is what Hong Kong lacks.

A city built on steep slopes and vast areas of landfill at incredible density, Hong Kong's physical ground is equal parts elusive and irrelevant. Ground is never where you expect it. Nor is it often what it seems. What appears to be terra firma was likely water or air not so long ago. What appears to be a natural outcropping of rock is more likely a formed concrete retaining wall or even the side of a building. Often times a glance over a curb reveals not a gutter but several stories of descending platforms, drainage channels, and forested slopes, with no clear indication of datum. Even when a ground can be identified, such as the few blocks of urban grid in older areas of the city, it is often remarkably obfuscated, immersed in clouds of exhaust, or obstructed by major infrastructural programs like bus terminals or electrical substations.[10]

In place of a physical ground, Hong Kong has connectivity. On the North Shore of Hong Kong Island it is possible to walk from Sheung Wan through Central and Admiralty to Pacific Place 3 on the edge of Wanchai without ever having to leave a continuous network of elevated or submerged pedestrian passageways and interconnected malls, lobbies, and gardens.[11]

Shun Tak Center, completed on the site of the Macau Ferry in 1984 by the architects Spence Robinson, illustrates this substitution perfectly. The new development replaced a broad and open pier, diverse and congested; a single surface was the space of commerce, tourism, industry, transportation, and leisure; substituting a complex that separates various transit modes and functional zones, including the ferry terminal, bus station, taxi stands, parking, connections to the Sheung Wan Station of the Mass Transit Rail (MTR), a

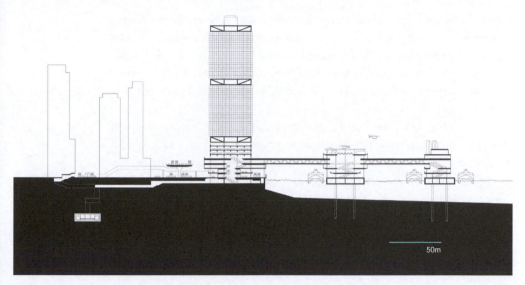

7.7
**Shun Tak Center, Section, drawing by Adam Frampton, Jonathan D. Solomon, and Clara Wong**

7.8
**Shun Tak Center,
Sheung Wan,
1999, photograph
CN23237
reproduced with
permission of the
Director of Lands.**
© The Government
of Hong Kong SAR.
License No.
64/2011

helipad, shopping mall, office tower, and, originally, a hotel. At the former ground level, a sliproad formation for taxi and coach circulation precludes access for pedestrians. Pedestrians enter at level three, where elevated walkways from the city connect to a shopping arcade and lobbies for the towers, and escalators lead down to trains, taxis, and buses or up to bridges to the ferry piers and helipad.

Shun Tak Center cedes ground to connectivity. It is not seen so much as it envelops, not entered so much as moved through, on your way from a bus to a train. An elegant intermodal switch between land, sea, and air, it is an almost primordial modernism – futurist in its ambitions. The scale of Shun Tak's coordination and efficiency require legality, coordination between government agencies and private transit operators, not to mention customs and immigration, demand it. Legibility, however, is absent. Spatial experiences like the sea approach to Hong Kong's edge are replaced by interior connective sequences that insure continuity of flow. Symmetry, centrality, axiality – the legible visual order that characterizes transit hubs envisaged by Garnier, St. Elia and Le Corbusier turns out to be unnecessary.

## Figure-to-figure

Without a ground Hong Kong can have no figure–ground relationships. Rather, the city is a dense mass of figures abutting each other directly in three dimensions. In this dense mass, even circulation becomes figural. Queensway Plaza in Admiralty, developed by the MTR Corporation and designed by the architects

7.9
**Queensway Plaza, 2012, photograph by Jonathan D. Solomon**

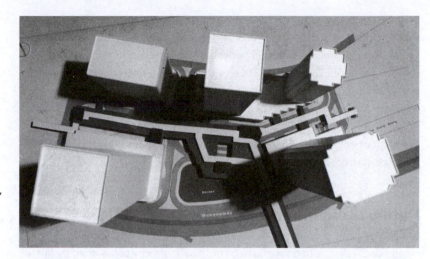

7.10
Queensway Plaza,
Model, image
courtesy Chung
Wah Nan
Architects Ltd.

Fitch and Chung, opened in 1980.[12] The complex serves as an ideal illustration of figure-to-figure spatial relationships.

Queensway Plaza sits amid a group of towers developed in the late 1970s above the then newly opened MTR station, on a narrow strip of land formerly reserved for the British Navy. A shopping mall housed within an elevated walkway, it was intended to connect the train station and new bus terminals to the surrounding towers and over Cotton Tree drive, a high-speed artery west of the site, to a new parking structure.

Instead of the classical modernist solution, a continuous ground or plaza from which the figures of the six asymmetrically arranged towers would form a void from which they could be read and appreciated, figural connectivity fills the void with another figure. This has the effect of eliminating figure–ground relationships on the site, an architectural move that is reinforced by narrow and opaque reveals between the elevated shopping mall and the surrounding buildings, just wide enough to differentiate the various figures but too slim to allow their relationships to be read.

Pedestrians crossing into the site on elevated walkways from Central encounter an artificially lit and ventilated double-loaded corridor lined with shops. The interiority is extreme, an environment that could be replicated anywhere, floating above the ground or burrowed beneath it. Intermittent breaks in the retail façade lead over short bridges to the podiums of the surrounding towers, past more shopping or directly into elevator lobbies. On the east side of the site the corridor splits, one arm leading to a narrow bank of escalators serving the bus terminal directly under the platform, the other to a similar escalator serving the Admiralty MTR station.

New connections from the site to the rapidly developing neighborhood have been provided since the project's completion, notably elevated bridges south over Queensway to the shopping mall and hotel complex at Pacific Place and north over Harcourt Road to the new government campus at Tamar. Now serving as a critical pedestrian link, the Hong Kong government recently described Queensway Plaza as a "unique" property, "both a commercial retail centre and an important public thoroughfare in a prominent location,"[13] a conflation frequently bestowed upon streets but rarely seen attributed to interiors. Queensway Plaza is unique precisely because it is able to perform like a street without the figure–ground relationships that signify it or the underlying social structures it is meant to guarantee.

## Public atmospheres

Hong Kong lacks the traditional lexicon of visual hierarchy established by figure–ground relationships. It has no perceivable edge, no axis, no center, no ground. Rather, diverse sequence of atmospheres generates urban hierarchy.

Microclimates of temperature, humidity, noise, and smell organize Hong Kong. Order appears in the juxtaposition of climates. The domestic workers that gather under the HSBC Main Building in Central do so for a number of complex reasons. But they are doubtless also attracted by the shade and swell of cool air that plunges down in summer months from the atrium above. Profit-generating space tends to be air-conditioned, while smokers gather at covered walkways open to bus terminals or heavily trafficked roads. The smell of streetside cooking or a waste transfer point, the sound of street vendors or expat bars, create equally as potent ordering systems.

The Lockhart Road Municipal Services Building, completed in 1984 by Fitch and Chung, is an extreme example. Programs that elsewhere would be figural, a market, a library, a gymnasium, are packed together so tightly that they become a single building. Radically diverse atmospheres organize space that cannot be ordered visually: the smell of meat or fish, the quiet sounds of rustling pages under fluorescent light, a cool dry blast of air.

The origins of Lockhart Road lie in state-modernist legibility. Starting in the 1970s, the Hong Kong government began to clear its informal street markets; often referred to as wet markets, their main trade was in fruits and vegetables, fish and meat, but also sold dry goods. Indoor centralized markets had already been introduced in Hong Kong as early as 1844, but the new initiative proposed to combine markets with other facilities to form neighborhood centers. What were informal street markets moved indoors, where they were reordered into a legible plan, conveniently drained, and consistently lit and ventilated.

Lockhart Road was the first centralized market to hybridize the wet market with diverse community programs. The building includes major breaks

7.11
**Lockhart Road Municipal Services Building, Interior, 2012, photograph by Jonathan D. Solomon**

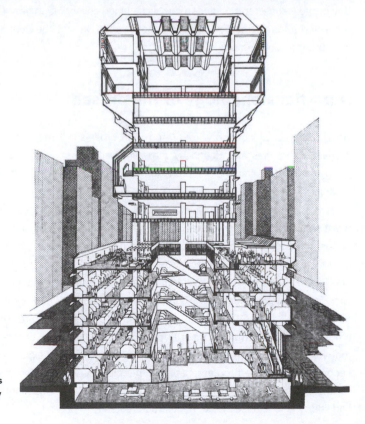

7.12
**Lockhart Road Municipal Services Building, Section, image courtesy Chung Wah Nan Architects Ltd.**

in section and diverse circulatory sequences in order to accommodate very different uses. An open-air atrium leads from the street through the multi-level market to a food court on an outdoor deck. Linked by escalators, smooth connectivity and continuity of climate with the street is reinforced. The library, government offices, and sports hall require isolation and climate control. Each is accessed by a separate elevator bank. Heterogeneity of plan layout extends to massing, as the double-loaded corridor of the government offices slims down to allow natural lighting to penetrate the plan and the sports hall again projects out. Even building services are planned separately as each use requires specific drainage, lighting, and ventilation solutions.

Lockhart Road is a multipurpose tower. Unlike the Downtown Athletic Club, with which Rem Koolhaas illustrated the potential for the skyscraper to accommodate radical heterogeneity, it is public. This is a critical difference: it achieves continuity with the public armature of the street and structures diversity with atmosphere. The market, envisaged as a legible cell in an organized hierarchy, developed over 25 years into an extension of the informal streets, complete with the heterogeneous and unpredictable clutter that modernization was supposed to reduce. Lockhart Road, like the Expresscalators in Causeway Bay or the Central footbridge network, is a unique collaboration between legible order and informal solution-finding, inconceivable without the contributions of both but reducible to neither.

# A partial archeology of the present

Hong Kong is a laboratory for a form of urbanism largely ignored since megastructure was abandoned by the avant-garde over 30 years ago.[14] The struggles of that era and its promise of reconciliation foreshadow aformal urbanism.

In his 1976 book Megastructure, Reyner Banham credits the movement's original appeal with its ability to reconcile the designed and the spontaneous, the large and the small, the permanent and the transient; and he locates its downfall in its inability to reconcile the avant-garde and the establishment.[15] The failure of megastructure falls in the same place from which aformal urbanism grows: between formal "comprehensible design" and informal "self-determining" systems. In the first case, the megastructure proved too amenable to the formal, as seen in projects for socialist governments, urban redevelopment authorities, state expositions, and university expansions. In the second case it proved too amenable to the informal: leaving "so much liberty for the self-housing and self-determining intentions of the inhabitants that they had liberty also to destroy the megastructure itself."[16]

7.13
**Construction of
Olympic Station,
West Kowloon,
1999, photograph
CN23316
reproduced with
permission of the
Director of Lands.**

By the 1970s, "[m]egastructure," Banham writes, "deserted by the avant garde, was left to the despised establishment as a conventional method for maximizing the returns of urban development."[17]

It is perhaps not coincidental that the history of aformal architecture begins in Hong Kong at the same time Banham is chronicling megastructure's demise. While megastructure's eventual collapse as a viable political or intellectual movement in architecture, according to Banham, came about as a result of establishment organization and avant-garde expression, the cryptomegastructures that accompany aformal urbanism in Hong Kong and elsewhere exhibit avant-garde organization and establishment expression. John Portman's Peachtree Center in Atlanta, begun in the 1960s and under continual development since, illustrates this moment perfectly; operating like megastructure without looking like it.

Peachtree Center is a vast aformal network joining 30 individual projects and 16 city blocks developed over 50 years on a site in Downtown Atlanta. Joining private developments to public transit infrastructure, its hallmark is a continuous publicly accessible pedestrian interior. Conceived as a matrix of "coordinate units" and "supporting structures," the development grew organically according to the needs of each new program. A successful

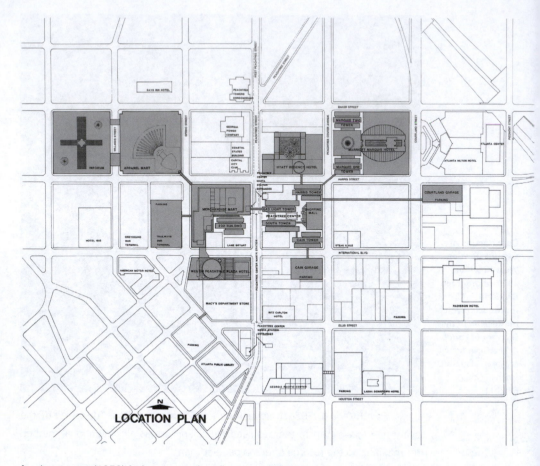

LOCATION PLAN

furniture mart (1956) led to a merchandise mart (1961) then to an office tower and subsequently a hotel (1967), links to mass transit (beginning 1975), a shopping mall (1973, expanded 1979), and more. Peachtree Center's process-based organization and entrepreneurial growth breaks radically from modernist compositional masterplanning, but its comparatively mainstream architectural expression and business model rendered it invisible to the eyes of the contemporary avant-garde. Peachtree Center is an example of aformal urbanism at work.[18]

7.14
**Peachtree Center, John Portman & Associates, site plan, image courtesy John Portman & Associates**

The same aformal logics can be observed in the development of the new district surrounding Tokyo's Shinjuku Station. Long a subcenter of the city's urban rail network, the undeveloped west of the neighborhood was a site for intense speculation in the post-war period, yielding a 1960 proposal by Fumiko Maki and Masato Otaka for an elevated pedestrian platform linking a complex of urban activities in various formally distinct clusters. The west of the district was eventually developed in the 1970s according to a plan by Kenzo Tange calling for tall towers offset from the street by large plazas, while the

7.15
**John Portman, flanked by U.S. Secretary of Transportation John Volpe and President of Central Atlanta Progress William Calloway, beside a model of Peachtree Center, 1972, image courtesy John Portman & Associates**

east continued to grow on small urban building plots. An underground network of passageways leading from the station, the world's busiest, gradually spread to surrounding developments. Property owners, who saw profitability in connection to the network, financed portions of its later growth. With establishment expression and avant-garde organization, Shinjuku Station aformally provides the publicly accessible pedestrian network and process-based development model Maki and Otaka proposed.

Hong Kong's aformal architecture holds out the promise of reconciling the formal and the informal both in the city's decision-making process and its spatial products, yielding a unique urbanism with broad implications worldwide. Of particular interest are the possibilities for the aformal to generate civic

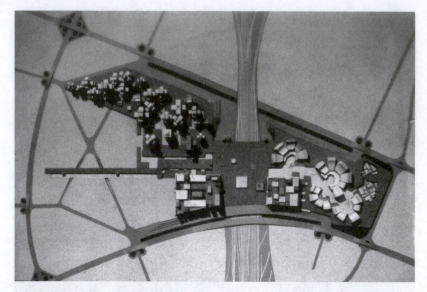

7.16
Project for
Shinjuku,
Fumihiko Maki,
and Masato
Otaka, 1960,
image courtesy
Maki and
Associates

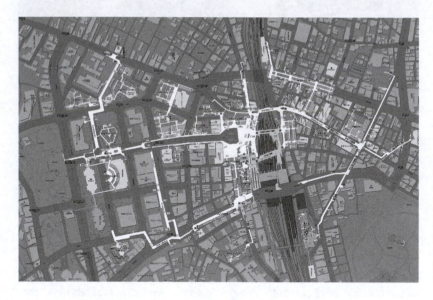

7.17
The aformal
urbanism of
publicly accessible
access networks
in Shinjuku,
Tokyo, 2012,
image courtesy
Yahoo Japan.

**7.18**
**The Central and Midlevels Escalator, 2012, photograph by Adam Frampton**

culture, a goal that was famously elusive to modernism and megastructure alike. Hong Kong's aformal spaces – its shopping malls and footbridges – do just this. Art exhibitions and political protests occur in shopping malls, domestic workers gather on footbridges on their day off, sidewalks become salons or workshops, and streets become restaurants or dance halls. Hong Kong demonstrates the viability and even robustness of public spaces that do not resemble a street, a courtyard, a square.

The following design proposals exacerbate Hong Kong's aformal architecture by testing the interplay between the city's formal and informal decision-making processes, by accentuating the acuity of its atmospheric imbalances, and by generally exploring the freedom of design without ground.

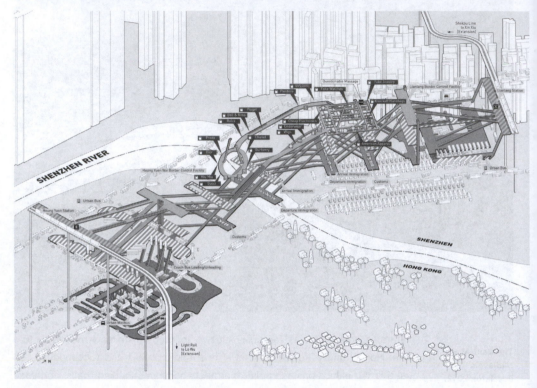

7.19

Heung Yuen Wai Border Crossing Facility, 2011. Adam Frampton, Jonathan D. Solomon, and Clara Wong.

The proposal for Heung Yuen Wai Border Crossing Facility explores connectivity in the context of Hong Kong's border dynamics. The control points between Hong Kong and its northern neighbor, Shenzhen, are the busiest land ports in the world, a kind of Maxwell's Demon for preserving the region's productive cultural and economic disequilibrium. At the same time, the smooth and efficient connectivity that characterizes other facilities like Chek Lap Kok airport is designed to erase distinctions between the city and distant points around the globe.

Heung Yuen Wai Crossing provides spatial solutions for satisfying cross-border desire. Two malls reach out from either side, each allowing shoppers to avail themselves of transgressive opportunities without transgressing the border. From Shenzhen, cross directly into a climate-controlled and super-cooled atrium mall where global luxury brands are available without import tax. From Hong Kong, cross to a poorly ventilated labyrinthine market where illicit goods and cheap or questionable services can be found. The project is a vision of the logical extremes of hyper-connectivity in a region that continues to derive enormous energy from inequality

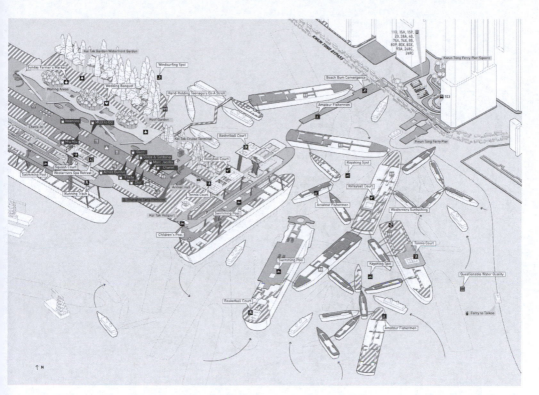

7.20

Kai Tak Park, 2011. Adam Frampton, Jonathan D. Solomon, and Clara Wong.

The proposal for Kai Tak Park explores direct figure-to-figure relationships by exacerbating the city's groundlessness. At Hong Kong's Sai Kung Fish Market, fishing boats lashed to a series of piers form a floating market. The literal dynamics of the physical urbanism of the market reflect the dynamics of development over time in older areas of the city such as Central, where gradual evolution of the pedestrian network generated unpredictable and productively redundant results.

Kai Tak Park includes a sports and leisure district on various craft joined together between the new Kai Tak Cruise Terminal and the Kwun Tong boardwalk. The project explores the opportunities of more literal dynamism applied at the scale of the Central network. Imagined as a series of linked cruise ships, yachts, fishing boats, ferries, and tugs that already ply Victoria Harbour, the project takes the notion of a city without ground quite literally, proposing directly abutting figures that lack any stable reference points

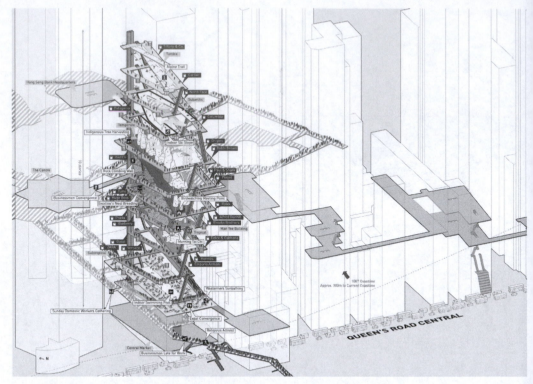

7.21

**Central Market Oasis, 2011. Adam Frampton, Jonathan D. Solomon, and Clara Wong.**

The proposal for Central Market Oasis explores vertical atmospheric hierarchies by exacerbating the manipulation of climate in the city's interiors. Atmosphere is already used as a vertical ordering system in the Lockhart Road Municipal Services Building. Other models of continuous vertical space in the city offer expanded possibility. Langham Place in Mong Kok provides an ideal reference. A nine-story spiral of shopping, the Jon Jerde-designed mall is imagined as a street in the sky, but the heterogeneity of its interior design is belied by a homogeneity of atmosphere.

Central Market Oasis tops a historic market structure with a 20-story spiral of interior recreation facilities: an equatorial beach, a tropical rainforest, a temperate forest, a ski slope, and an alpine peak. Shopping opportunities and informal activities that organize around these diverse climates cling to an outer loop that also provides connections to the upper levels of adjacent office towers, creating a three-dimensional network. The project introduces levels of climate management that while extreme and perhaps unusual in Hong Kong are hardly uncommon in contemporary urbanism

## Notes

1  Jameson, 1984.
2  Jameson, 1984.
3  Solomon, 2010, pp. 67–70.
4  For a deeper analysis of the IFC Mall and its role in the city of Hong Kong's access networks, see Solomon, 2012.
5  Portions of this text appeared previously in Frampton *et al.*, 2012.
6  See Davis, 2004.
7  See Scott, 1998, for a complete review of this position.
8  Zhang *et al.*, 1997, pp. 13–16.
9  DeWolf, 2011.
10  For an alternative analysis of Hong Kong's "multiple" grounds, see Shelton *et al.*, 2010.
11  For an early analysis of the elevated walkways in Central Hong Kong, see Ohno, 1992, pp. 55–77. For a more contemporary analysis, see Frampton *et al.*, 2012.
12  Alan Fitch, the firm's founding partner, was the architect of Hong Kong's City Hall, and the firm continues to operate today as Chung Wah Nan Architects.
13  Government Property Agency, 2008.
14  Portions of this text appeared previously in Solomon, 2011.
15  Banham, 1976, p. 10.
16  Banham, 1976, p. 218.
17  Banham, 1976, p. 10.
18  Portman, 2010.

## Chapter 8

# Los Angeles – Between Cognitive Mapping and Dirty Realism

*Paulette Singley*

The Los Angeles region is increasingly held up as a prototype (for good or ill) of our collective urban future. Yet it is probably the least understood, most understudied major city in the United States.[1]

A Metropolis that exists in semidesert, imports water three hundred miles, has inveterate flash floods, is at the grinding edges of two tectonic plates, and has a microclimate tenacious of noxious oxides will have its priorities among the aspects of its environment that it attempts to control.[2]

Define *postmodernism*. Or more specifically, define *Los Angeles*. These two terms – which resist the limitations of conventional definition – act as accomplices in discussions about the contemporary city. If postmodernism (PM) in architecture and urban design implies the indiscriminant application of historical references to the production of space, resulting in superficial layers of pastiche, then the stylistic diversity and commercial noise of Los Angeles – a city of back lots within an urbanism of set design – certainly fits this model *avant la lettre*. If postmodernism, conversely, works within literary theory as a set of operations that expand upon and transform the canons of high modernism into an empty chain of signifiers, imploding vertiginously upon an illegible hyperreality, then again Los Angeles – and its postindustrial landscape of late capitalism – might offer a different model of this same term.[3] The unclean alliance between PM and LA begs the following questions. Is Los Angeles superficial or is postmodernism? If the city cannot be read is this because it is illegible or because many of its interpreters are casual readers? We know that a frontal attack on the slippery practices of postmodern theory and its concomitant libidinal freedoms proves unwise and that nostalgia – worse yet – contaminates any possible return to history. Wresting an image of the city, therefore, from the mythology that has placed it within the crosshairs of such theorizing, proves challenging if not entirely Utopian. In other words, Los Angeles is bigger than *postmodernism* and yet, has been defined by it.

Admittedly, several other pivotal moments in Los Angeles's urban history and theory would provide rewarding areas of inquiry to the extent that focusing on the so-called postmodern moment of the city, at a certain level, risks further shoring up the same rhetoric. Regarding in particular the impact of what has come to be known as the "LA School" of thought on configuring the city, Kazys Varnelis writes the obituary for this phase of Los Angeles's urban history, arguing that:

> the 1992 riots and 1994 Northridge Earthquake validated the L.A. School's predictions, but, they were also the end of its relevance. Unable to propose any intervention and unable to offer an insight into the recovery of the late 1990's, the L.A. School seems spent, the fatalism of the program having inevitably undermined it.[4]

Varnelis's indictment likewise verifies a need to examine the city with different criteria and to focus our attention on different sites. Included in such research might be approaching the city as it has been rendered in film, beyond the discussion of *noir* and the later interpretations of this genre, such as Roman Polanski's *Chinatown* (1974) or Ridley Scott's *Bladerunner* (1982). The influence of various waves of European immigration upon the city, ranging from the arrival of Rudolf Schindler and Richard Neutra to Theodor Adorno and Bertolt Brecht, might form another locus of inquiry. Another compelling study of the city might consider shifting patterns of diversity, density, and ethnicity through an analysis of emigration and demography that examines physical rather than cultural geography. Or one might explicate Los Angeles with equal success by examining infrastructural matrices such as those formed by the Pacific Electric Railway, oil wells, freeways, the Metro Transit Authority, the Department of Transportation, or the Department of Water and Power.

Although a number of scholars have initiated or completed some of the projects outlined above, establishing a substantial bibliography about Los Angeles, the work of contemporary theorists has absorbed this often conventional research into a larger and more exciting fiction of postmodernism that reaches a wider audience than that of a simple architecture or urban design readership.[5] As proffered by Jean Baudrillard in "The Precession of the Simulacra" (1983), Fredric Jameson in "Postmodernism or, The Cultural Logic of Late Capitalism" (1984), Umberto Eco in *Travels in Hyperreality* (1986), Edward Soja in *Postmodern Geographies: The Reassertion of Space in Critical Social Theory* (1989), and Mike Davis in *City of Quartz: Excavating the Future in Los Angeles* (1990) – to name the most conspicuous examples – the geopolitical imaginary of Los Angeles remains coincident with the writings of these thinkers. Soja summarizes Jameson's take on the Westin Bonaventure Hotel in downtown Los Angeles as emblematic of the larger city:

> For Jameson, this "populist insertion into the city's fabric" has become a "hyperspace" of both illusion and compensation, a new kind of cultural colony and brothel (my combining of Foucault's separate allusions) that exposes many of the archetypal "performative" conditions of contemporary postmodernity: depthlessness, fragmentation, the reduction of history to nostalgia, and, underlying it all, the programmatic decentering of the subordinated subject and the rattling awareness that the individual human body has been losing the capacity "to locate itself, to organize its immediate surroundings perceptually, and cognitively map its position . . ."[6]

Back and forth, these scholars have invested a certain amount of intellectual capital debating whose interpretation of John Portman's design for this hotel is the most prescient to the extent that ever since Baudrillard, Jameson, Soja, and Davis have had their way with the city, little, one might think, is left to be said about LA.

Jameson's essay, both for its clarity and its chronological position in the debate, is the definitive starting point for explicating the conditions of postmodernity. He outlines the following attributes that Soja began to enumerate above: (1) a lack of depth, center, or thematic coherence; (2) the death of the author, the subject, and the grand narrative; (3) history as pastiche, *la mode rétro* (4) "the spatial logic of the simulacra"; and (5) fragmentation or random heterogeneity – terms that he conveniently exports into LA urbanism. If, as Jameson asserts, architecture remains "the privileged esthetic language" of postmodernist culture, then Los Angeles, too, remains the privileged city for describing such an urbanism.[7] In the approximate decade spanning from the early 1980s to the early

1990s, Los Angeles served as a model site for discussions surrounding the loss of a center, fragmentation, uncritical paranoia, the lack of a master narrative, etc., that collectively stood in for a larger notion of postmodern urbanism.

However, rather than serving as an exemplar of these terms, Los Angeles has been buried, somewhat paradoxically, under the weight of a surplus of the rhetoric that initially made this city a subject of interest. One method – to borrow a phrase from Davis – for "excavating the future" of Los Angeles involves reinterpreting the past with the very terms that provoked its inhumation. Or to put it in yet another way, and borrow instead from Catherine Ingraham in *Architecture and the Burdens of Linearity*, is to claim:

> What is not so clear – what is here in a state of suspension and suggestion – is how architecture and cities are built at the crossroads of their own lines (urban and architectural) and the lines of writing. This is ultimately related to the question of how the violence of spacing (urbanism and architecture) occurs before or at the same time as the violence of writing.[8]

Ingraham offers an understanding of urbanism wherein metropolitan parietals emerge from a drive toward a singular, pre-Euclidean assessment of space and from a point of view that acknowledges the violence of the critical project as much as that of the design of cities – a warning against the hypostatization of research into urban design.

Instead of dismissing either historical research or postmodern theory *tout court*, conjoining these unwilling twins allows students of the city to return to the scene of the crime with the same tools, applied to different subjects, and yielding – one might suppose – alternative results. Given that *Heterotopia* or its feeble counterpart of *Heteropolis* is a compelling yet dangerous (or compelling because it is dangerous) condition to which any city might aspire, the proximity of these terms to the contemporary condition of Los Angeles should be treated neither as fact nor as fiction but certainly as both.[9] Thus it is that occasionally approbative words such as fragmentation, heterogeneity or incommensurability become positive when examined with the slightly different critical view of multiplicity, diversity, or even sublimity. A subtle shift in emphasis portrays Los Angeles as a diverse urban milieu of intense and, at times, profound spatial experiences, instead of as a city where generic spaces produce bland experiences.

In what follows I will arrest Los Angeles through the flipside of these terms, through "Lefebvre's concept of abstract space as what is simultaneously homogeneous and fragmented."[10] I will respond to Jameson's challenge that it is impossible "to draw the boundary lines in which we ourselves are contained" and argue that, unlike the Bonaventure Hotel, it is possible to produce a cognitive map of the city by using the very critical tools implemented to congeal it in an unmappable state.[11] Based upon Jameson's idea of the "cognitive map," Los Angeles emerges through a series of archaeological sondages – or probes – as sharply delineated by borders, centers, lines, and networks etched upon the landscape of Southern California and brought into relief by the most ordinary of analytical tools – plan, section, and perspective. Based upon Jameson's explication of "dirty realism," these maps ultimately play upon a critical field of urbanity described by the factual, if at times brutal, exigencies of the city.

In this discussion about cognitive cartographies, one of the more lasting perceptions of Los Angeles is that it lacks a center – hence the neat lamination of postmodern theory onto this supposed urban prototype. But where lacking a center certainly implies that the center is lacking – as with LA's rather anemic downtown core – we cannot claim that the city lacks centers.[12] Even the most orthodox studies of Los Angeles conclude that its growth followed the pattern of mulitcentered or polynucleated cities, of villages loosely grouped around a downtown core. Perhaps the indefinite center suggests instead a deeper lack, a more problematic loss, or a similar absence of any attributes with which either to identify or to empathize. In response to this, one could convincingly argue that the various centers dotted throughout the city define specific urban territories that offer mythological, psychological, and libidinal pressure points. Such is the organization of the balance of this chapter in which I will examine the quasi-mythological origins and psychological trajectories of the city at Olvera Street, the La Brea tar pits, and Griffith Park. Taking one small step at a time, my strategy here is modestly to add more dimension to debates about the city by examining three specific sites as they might relate to the research of Elizabeth Moule and Stefanos Polyzoides, Mario Gandelsonas, Douglas Suisman, William Fain, and Dagmar Richter. That the earth is moving under the city while I write is one of the more reliable determinates of the city, adding to the discussion of an unstable and shifting terrain where fault lines lie hidden both below and above ground.

## Cognitive map

Where Jameson will mention urban cartography In "Postmodernism or, The Cultural Logic of Late Capitalism," asserting that Los Angeles is an unmappable product of postmodernity, indeed of the "dirty realism" he eventually will describe in *The Seeds of Time*, he sets forth the principles of his psychological geography in a later, 1988 essay titled "Cognitive Mapping" – explaining that this "slogan," as he calls it, is a "synthesis between Althusser and Kevin Lynch."[13] Jameson proposes that the processes Lynch describes in constructing a mental map of the city might also apply to the construction of a mental map of the "social and global totalities we all carry in our heads." As Jameson puts it, "Lynch suggests that urban alienation is directly proportional to the mental unmappability of local landscapes."[14] Jameson's earlier visit to the Bonaventure – with its vertical elevators accelerating spectacularly upward through a glass atrium, jetting along the exterior mirrored skin, and finally landing its captive audience next to a rotating cocktail lounge – provoked him to argue that:

> this latest mutation in space – postmodern hyperspace – has finally succeeded in transcending the capacities of the individual human body to locate itself, to organize its immediate surroundings perceptually, and cognitively to map its position in a mappable external world.[15]

Despite Jameson's forceful erudition and the depth of his analysis, the more interesting question is not whether it is possible to produce a map of the city cognitively – we all navigate to a greater or lesser extent through some crude understanding of our geopolitical coordinates – but instead, to interrogate the quality of that map, to ask what the map indicates *vis-à-vis* the subject's apprehension of ideological and representational space.

The publications from the 1980s and 1990s succeeded in reducing Los Angeles's image into that of an urban *enfant terrible* thrashing about destructively, and in telescoping its history into a timeline beginning with the 1965 riots, concluding with 1992 rebellion, and leaving the 1781 Spanish foundation, the 1848 USA conquest, or even the 1943 Zoot Suit Riots to mere historical miscellany.[16] For a theory seeking a subject without a history, without depth, Los Angeles's own history had to be erased in order to tell the story. Likewise, its unique silhouette necessarily disappeared into an amorphous layer of form-eradicating smog that dispersed itself uncontrollably into an arid infinity of sprawl. Yes, marathon commutes occur in the larger metropolitan area, and the city, especially around late August, appears as vast and as ugly as Adorno described the products of the culture industry "whose monuments are a mass of gloomy houses and business premises in grimy, spiritless cities."[17] As with Richter, who clearly understands the aerial view of "Euclidian fields woven together by threads of moving red and white lights, the larger metropolitan area of Los Angeles should be measured by the speed of jet planes descending into LAX" (Figure 8.1).[18] This, alas, is to agree with Suisman and others who claim that Los Angeles is "the manifestation of forty years of investment in suburbanization, sustained by the automobile industry."[19]

8.1
**Study of arrival and departure
patterns of planes above Los Angeles
by Dagmar Richter**

Where Los Angeles does not exhibit the rigid boundaries of Manhattan, the strict planning of Savannah, or the scenic texture of New Orleans, it does display definitive and unimpeachable geographies that both enable navigation and fix the city's physiognomy within a precise cartographic imaginary (Figure 8.2). To the north, the Angeles National Forest and the San Gabriel Mountains separate the city from the desert and form a natural boundary of open space set against expansion in this direction. These mountains delimit a symbolic section in which it is possible, quite literally, to stand above the refreshing (though highly polluted) ocean surf in 80-degree weather while looking directly at snowcapped peaks that, at Mount Baldy, rise to a height of more than 10,000 feet above sea level. When the city does leak between the San Gabriels and the eastern edge of the Santa Monica Mountains into the San Fernando Valley, the Santa Susanna Mountains ultimately bound this edge. Expansion to the east is more vulnerable to the encroachment of sprawl, with the first formidable natural boundaries located as far out as Palm Springs and the San Andreas fault line, the Joshua Tree National Park and, ultimately, the Mojave Desert. Where Los Angeles struggles to engulf the city of San Diego to the south, the naval base of Camp Pendelton separates these two metropolises with 28 miles of raw coastline and scattered war games. The Inland Empire, a euphemism for an area of unplanned expansion and rampant growth, accommodates the momentum growing between San Diego and LA to merge with development sneaking behind Camp Pendelton.

And further south still to the definitive Mexican–American border, if any distinction between these two cities will perhaps blur with reciprocal growth, more permeable walls, and the progressive urbanization of Tijuana, it will remain nonetheless a symbolic separation between Los Angeles, North America, and Mexico. To the west, where the Pacific Ocean functions as

**8.2**
**Satellite view of**
**Los Angeles**

another permeable boundary for Asian immigration, it nonetheless forms an acute physical edge to the city as well as to the United States. In comparison with the size of other metropolitan areas – such as New York City – Los Angeles's urban dimensions and concomitant tensions dwarf Manhattan and the combined other four boroughs of Brooklyn, Queens, Staten Island, and the Bronx (see Figure 8.3). A comparative view of Los Angeles might place it in proximity to a reverse Manhattan; an oasis surrounded by desert, rather than an island bounded by water; a city wrestling with an expansive and irregular natural terrain, rather than a city boxing a highly regular park; a city where rabid land speculation promoted horizontal rather than vertical expansion. The city's physical geography alone offers striking coordinates with which to begin constructing a cognitive map.

## Rotated grid

In their important essay "The Five Los Angeleses," Elizabeth Moule and Stefanos Polyzoides document the urban history of the city from its origins to their prognosis for its future. "The Five Los Angeleses," for these authors, are "The Pueblo" (1781–1880; Figure 8.4) and its siting near the river; "The Town" (1880–1900; Figure 8.5) which coincides with the transcontinental railroad reaching LA in 1876; "The City" (1900–1940; Figure 8.6) which expanded

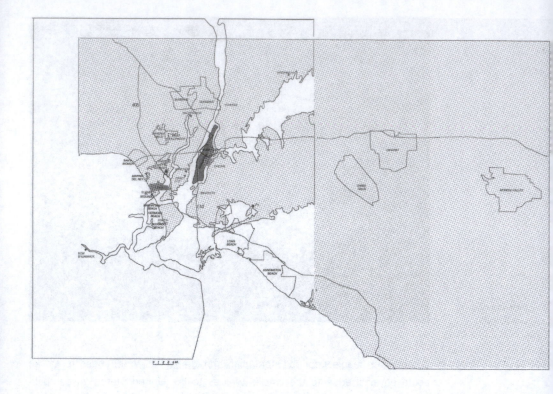

proportionally with the 1913 aqueduct importing water from the Owen's river valley, "The Metropolis" (1940–1990; Figure 8.7) which emerged with the ground breaking of the Pasadena Freeway in 1938; and finally "Region/State" (1990–), a Los Angeles that dominates an increasingly expansive geopolitical position and faces numerous but not necessarily abject circumstances.[20] Along with analyzing and diagramming the growth of the city in a series of diachronic maps of the first four Los Angeleses, Moule and Polyzoides also rail against the pernicious topos that the city has no history. They present a compelling critique of the more renowned interpreters of the city for having set agendas that disadvantaged the development of Los Angeles to the extent that "the romance of a *tabula rasa* to be redeemed through modern form was irresistible to the cultural protagonists of the last era and still persists today."[21] Moule and Polyzoides point out that Reyner Banham – author of *Los Angeles: The Architecture of Four Ecologies* – exhibits a "particular fixation on freeways," and indulges his desire to promote the agenda of the post-CIAM generation that "caricatured Southern California as the epitome of a futurist paradise in our midst." "The gap between the myth and the facts," according to the authors, may be explained by: (1) a rapid speed of building that promoted urban clearance and "collective memory lapses"; (2) a cultural heterogeneity and mass immigration that underestimated the traditions of a "common, native past"

8.3
**New York City superimposed upon Los Angeles by Paul Wysocan**

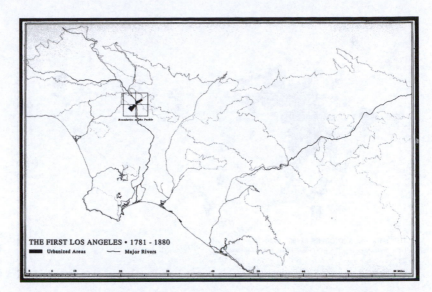

**8.4**
**First Los Angeles by Moule and Polyzoides**

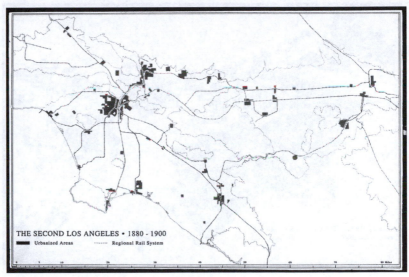

**8.5**
**Second Los Angeles by Moule and Polyzoides**

and; (3) an emphasis on progress that deprecated the "value of the existing city and its natural setting."[21]

As they describe the 1781 foundation of *El Pueblo de Nuestra Señora La Reina de Los Angeles de Porciuncula*, Los Angeles

> was afforded the rare civic destiny of being settled by decree of the Spanish Crown. On September 4, 1781 Governor Felipe de Neve, having laid out the pueblo based on the guidelines for site selection and urbanization coded in the Laws of the Indies, led a procession

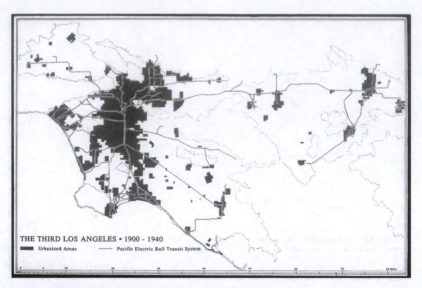

8.6
**Third Los Angeles by Moule and Polyzoides**

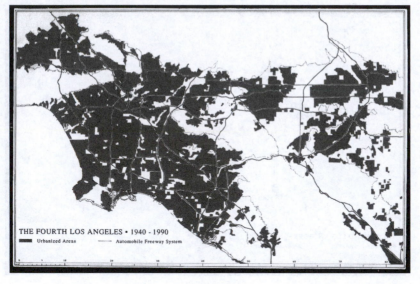

8.7
**Fourth Los Angeles by Moule and Polyzoides**

of other soldiers, eleven families of forty-four individual settlers, mission priests and some natives marching slowly around the pueblo site. They invoked the blessing of the new community. Los Angeles became one of the few cities in the North American continent deliberately planned in advance and ceremoniously inaugurated for and by its new settlers.[22]

What is most significant about their description of the city's inauguration, for the purposes of this discussion, is the tenacity of this story and its replication at the site of Olvera Street – a "colorful Mexican-style marketplace" and "part of the city-owned *Pueblo de Los Angeles* Historic Monument."[23] As Moule, Polyzoides, and others have written, the original pueblo was founded on a site closer to the river, but owing to flooding was relocated to the higher site of the present plaza, the legendary location of the city's founding. Not unlike the supposed hut of Romulus on the Palatine in Rome, the Olvera Street plaza and its little rustic shops provide physical evidence for the equivalent of Los Angeles's *roma quadrata* – a cosmic urban axis established by locating polar coordinates of the city through the use of a templum. Where the 1573 Laws of the Indies required the pueblo grid to be rotated at the compass corner points rather than on a strict north–south axis as in ancient Rome, the precedence of such a rotation nonetheless refers to Roman planning techniques.

The plaza has been constructed and reconstructed as an idealized reflection of the ranchero life of Spanish aristocracy and the pastoral landscape Helen Hunt Jackson extolled in her novel *Ramona*.[24] Even more than Pershing Square, the putative heart of the central business district, Olvera Street functions as an active and vital component of public life. The visual corridor created by the Hollywood Freeway makes visible an important urban twist in José Rafael Moneo's design of the Cathedral of Our Lady of the Angels (see Figure 7.8). If only by the accident of Los Angeles's grid shifts and the architect's overt gesture to the 101 freeway that borders the site, the cathedral's façade faces east toward the Plaza of Olvera Street, turns its back on the cultural corridor of Bunker Hill, and shifts the urban focus from downtown to the pueblo – from the last cathedral to the first church of the city. More than a tourist attraction for those unwilling or unable actually to travel to Mexico, more than a state park preserving the pseudohistory of Los Angeles, Olvera Street provides physical space (albeit severed from downtown by the 101) for the city's Hispanic

8.8
**The Cathedral of Our Lady of the Angels by Nicholas Roberts**

community to congregate in proximity to the governmental center. Considering Olvera Street's inclusion in the cultural menagerie created by its proximity on the east side to Chinatown, and on the west to Little Tokyo, it nonetheless performs successfully as part of a series of cultural centers dedicated to LA's diverse ethnic communities.

In spite of (or perhaps because of) the overly scripted narrative of the Spanish revival architecture, the street and plaza preserve, mark, and provide a center for the original geometry of the city, the point where the Spanish grid begins its 45-degree rotation off of true north to eventually collide – after one or two significant metamorphoses developed through the surveying of Ord (1848) and Hancock (1853) – with Jefferson's mile-by-mile grid on Hoover Boulevard (Figure 8.9). These laws required a church and a government house to be built at the edge of a central plaza. The Laws also established sophisticated parameters for expansion so that "a roughly orthogonal grid of streets" could spread, as Suisman explains, "outward from the plaza and a square pueblo boundary of two leagues (=5.25 miles) per side." Outward further from the Pueblo, the Ranchos established a system of land division that allowed the Spanish to "carve up and distribute the lands of greater Los Angeles under a system of public and private land ownership," the traces of

**1781**
*Pueblo Founding*

**1848**
*Ord's Survey*

**1853**
*Hancock's Survey*

8.9
**Douglas Suisman's diagrams of the Ord and Hancock surveys**

which may be seen in many of the city's boulevards.[25] Finally, Suisman writes, in an argument that places Los Angeles once again upon a rotated *roma quad-rata*, "the original plaza's diagonal orientation – prescribed by the 1573 Laws as a Vitruvian technique for breaking prevailing winds – set into motion the sequence of diagonal grid planning efforts."[25]

In contrast to Moule and Polyzoides, who generate a series of diachronic studies of the city, in *X-Urbanism* Mario Gandelsonas draws a self-described "synchronic cut" through Los Angeles.[26] Such a move from chronological to formal analysis works well with Richard Lehan's understanding of postmodern literature as a kind of writing wherein "synchronic time replaces diachronic time."[27] Gandelsonas's postmodern cut through Los Angeles asserts a combined reading of the "specific *formal armature* of the city" with the "local *sociopolitical* and *economic* forces."[28] In "Plan 1: The Territorial Grid" he describes this work as documenting "the perceived chaos of the Los Angeles plan" which "obscures a complex system combining city grids as colossal city fabrics as objects (laid out at different angles) with the one-mile grid as background (acting as a "glue" between the different cities)" (see Figure 8.10).[31]

Gandelsonas analyzes the geometries of Santa Monica, Beverly Hills, the megacity, the boulevards, intersections, grids shifts and more in a cartography that, in fact, describes an architectural cognition of the city (see Figure 8.11). Indeed Gandelsonas specifically contextualizes his work in opposition to the *Image of the City*, explaining that his "object is the architecture of the city," which he describes with "two- or three-dimensional drawings based upon plans, as opposed to the phenomenological mapping suggested by Kevin Lynch." Gandelsonas defends this position by arguing that "the urban drawings

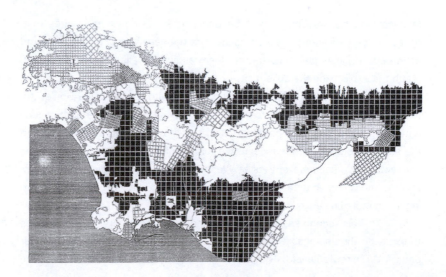

8.10
**Mario
Gandelsonas's
"Territorial Grid"
of Los Angeles**

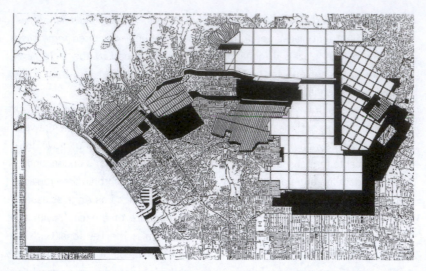

are conceived as part of a practice with the potential to transform or mutate the city and not the city as a place for the development of everyday tactics."[28] That Lynch attempts to test the urban alienation of a region as a direct index of its mental mappabililty by no means suggests that Gandelsonas's cartography is any less cognitive, but rather that it is a form of mapping that might be included in a more ecumenical or even more precise understanding of the techniques available in such an exercise.

# Linear city

In describing his drawing titled "The Boulevards," Gandelsonas writes that, because flows of energy "act as connectors between the different elements of the Los Angeles plan," he depicts them as linear walls channeled through "both the explicit and the absent city grids" (Figure 8.12).[30]

Here Gandelsonas draws upon the armature of Wilshire Boulevard, the single most dominant and forceful street in Los Angeles, created by a seventeen-mile-long business corridor linking downtown with Santa Monica and the sea. Gaylord Wilshire is responsible for completing the four-block-long link connecting two separate streets at Westlake Park – one leading from downtown to the ocean, and the other from the ocean to downtown – thereby creating a complete boulevard.

This second sondage into Los Angeles's "deep structure" proposes to excavate the undiggable terrain of the archaeological site at the La Brea tar pits on Wilshire Boulevard. The largest of the pits is an open lake of bitumen,

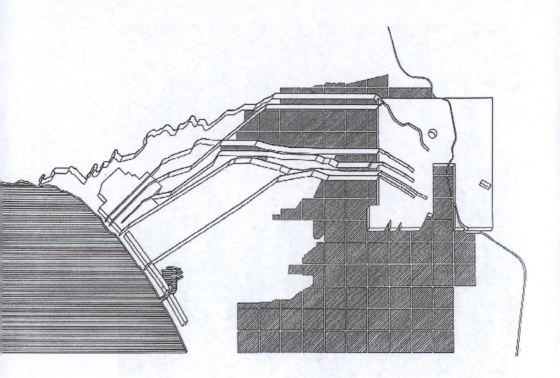

8.12
**Mario
Gandelsonas's
The Boulevards**

mistakenly referred to as tar, out of which bubbles up the bones of mastodons, saber-toothed tigers, and other fossils dating back 40,000 years (Figure 8.13). Between the destabilizing tar and the promised demolition of the museum to make way for Rem Koolhaas's winning design for an extension to Los Angeles County Museum of Art, Ed Rushca's 1965–1968 painting, titled "The Los Angeles County Museum on Fire," is more than a vivid portrait of the city's cultural center, it is also portentous of the museum's proposed demise (see Figure 8.14). The gaseous, viscous liquid of ur-suppe underneath the surface is a reminder of the hundreds of oil wells that once dotted the city and the vestiges of these landmarks found at sites such as the Beverly Hills High School and the Beverly Center. The conflation of such images was not lost on Mick Jackson, who directed *Volcano* (1997), or Steve De Jarnatt, who directed *Miracle Mile* (1989) – films that portray the mass urban destruction of Los Angeles either with lava flowing through shopping malls (The Beverly Center in fact) or the ubiquitous helicopter (also see *Boys N the Hood*) sinking into the tar pits after a nuclear attack destroys the city.

8.13
View of La
Brea tar pits
and the Los
Angeles County
Museum of Art
photographed by
author

In Jackson's film:

A volcano appears in Los Angeles and sends lava flowing towards houses. There are minor complications, such as a stranded subway car, but essentially this one situation sustains the movie. In 1991, Jackson directed Steve Martin's hilarious *L.A. Story*, a film that

8.14
**Ed Ruscha, the Los Angeles County Museum on fire 1965–1968**

painted (admittedly with some sense of irony) a picture of L.A. as an idyllic wonderland for the rich. Riots, fires and mudslides dated that one fast, and Jackson seems intent on making amends with this slow motion L.A. demolition job. As the sky rains fireballs and the ground spouts flame and molten rock, it's hard not to read a judgement day subtext to the whole thing.[31]

As Mike Davis points out, Los Angeles is one of those cities that cinema takes pleasure in destroying. While Park La Brea contains a version of the "psychological lava" that Colin Rowe finds bubbling underneath the contemporary city, it locates Los Angeles's cultural center at the County Museum of Art.[32] The museum, the mastodons, and the ongoing excavation fuse the urbane and the fantastic, the cultural and the prehistorical. While the staged prehistory undoubtedly bears a striking resemblance to Baudrillard's concept of the *simulacra*, "the generation of models of a real without origin or reality," this site also describes a deeper umbilicus leading from Los Angeles, quite allegorically, to the center of the earth.[33]

Inscribed, then, on an infinite "Y" axis of the city, the tar pits operate on an infinite "X" axis as the symbolic midpoint along Wilshire between downtown LA and the Pacific Ocean. In *Los Angeles Boulevard: Eight X-rays of the Body Public*, Suisman (1989) researches the symbolic and spatial implications of linear public spaces such as Wilshire Boulevard and Sunset Boulevard, concluding that, in Los Angeles, a boulevard "makes arterial connections on a metropolitan scale," "provides a framework for civic and commercial destinations," and "acts as a filter to adjacent residential neighborhoods."[34] We might note, as a compelling aside, Suisman reported on a panorama built on Main Street that depicted the 1870 Battle of Paris. He speculates that "through the smoke and the cannon fire," this attraction presented to the populace "a vivid

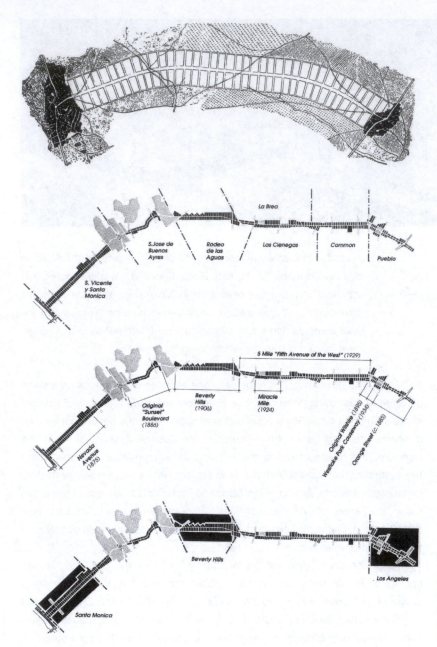

La Brea

S.Jose de
Buenos
Ayres

Rodeo
de las
Aguas

Las Cienegas

Common

Pueblo

S. Vicente
y Santa
Monica

5 Mile "Fifth Avenue of the West" (1929)

Beverly
Hills
(1906)

Miracle
Mile
(1924)

Original
"Sunset"
Boulevard
(1886)

Nevada
Avenue
(1875)

Original Wilshire (1895)

Westlake Park Causeway (1934)

Orange street (c. 1885)

Beverly Hills

Los Angeles

Santa Monica

8.15
**Douglas
Suisman's
"Comparison
between Wilshire
Boulevard and the
Linear City"**

image of Haussmann's Paris."[35] The density and urban disposition of Wilshire
supports Suisman's explication of this boulevard as a nascent "linear city" after
Arturo Soria y Mata's 1886 plans for Madrid (Figure 8.15).[36] Indeed, Suisman
tells us that "Reyner Banham would dub it the world's first linear downtown."[37]

Wilshire, of course, is not a linear city and although the many other satellite downtowns that have sprung up throughout LA – in places like Glendale, Century City, and Universal City – have rendered this morphology a remote possibility, they do not take away from the significance of Suisman's perceptual cartography.

As listed in his table of contents, Suisman's eight "X-rays" divide the city into the colorful allegorical sections of: (1) Suture: The Pueblo/Rancho Landscars; (2) Umbilical: The Spawning of Sunset Boulevards; (3) Spine: Piecemeal Grandeur on Wilshire Boulevard; (4) Girdle: The Studios Face the Boulevards; (5) Phosphors: Day for Night on Hollywood Boulevard; (6) Torrent: The Boulevards Accelerate; (7) Pathogen: Signs and Symbols on the Boulevards; and (8) Fuselage: Cross-sections of the Public Realm. His work contributes to a larger understanding of the city both through his careful analyses and through the visual imagery he deploys to elicit meaning from the maps he describes. His mapping, while perhaps more playful than Moule, Polyzoides, or Gandelsonas, arrives at a cognition of the city based upon highly imagistic formal comparisons that serve as visual shifters whose value it is to explain the city through comprehensible analogies. Thus, where his comparison between the Discobolus and the boulevard is glib, it also serves visually to reinforce the notion that Wilshire is the city's spine – bending and flexing at the will of its burden to link downtown with the ocean (Figure 8.16). For this comparison alone, Suisman has created a lyrical cartography of Los Angeles's geopolitical form.

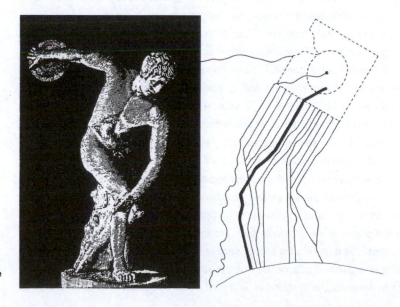

8.16
**Douglas Suisman's comparison of Wilshire Boulevard and the Discobolus**

# An urban wilderness

A third and final site for probing the city centers on the observatory, an astronomical museum located in Griffith Park that offers a panoramic view of LA from the San Gabriel to the Santa Monica Mountains. Built in 1935 according to the designs of John C. Austin and F. M. Ashley, the various domes shelter a solar telescope, a refractor telescope, and a planetarium – equipment dedicated to surveying and studying the universe. The most facile reading of the observatory would be to interpret it as a Panopticon, as a structuring system of surveillance that the Scottish social engineer Jeremy Bentham designed and that Michel Foucault made indelible in the memory of architects and urban designers with his publication of *Discipline and Punish: The Birth of the Prison*. Wim Wender's depicted this site as a remarkably similar space of social reform in his 1997 film *The End of Violence*, by transforming the observatory into the headquarters for a secret government plot to eliminate criminal activity through satellite surveillance and instant execution.[38] Under the large rotunda that some might describe as Foucault's Panoptican we find not a gaoler but, instead, Foucault's Pendulum, a moving sphere that swings reliably from a suspending cable, marks the earth's rotation, and acts as a metronome, keeping time with the urban pulse.

The observatory – inhabited by the citizenry of the city rather than by prison wardens – is the single most pivotal location from which to comprehend and observe Los Angeles (Figure 8.17). On a necessary but not infrequent clear day it is possible to absorb the city, see the 45-degree rotation of downtown in comparison with the Jeffersonian grid, witness the geographic boundaries of the mountains and the ocean, see the saucer-shaped outline of the Santa Monica bay extend from Point Dume to Palos Verdes, and understand the arching movements of the boulevards – scar tissue from the ranchos acting as subcutaneous ripples beneath the more recent surface of the mile-wide grid. For those who do not respond well to a printed map, the Griffith Park Observatory transforms Los Angeles into a version of Jorge Luis Borges's "Map of the Empire," a map that is drawn at the same scale and is coexistent with the city it describes. Conversely, the observatory also works as a focal point for navigation in which, from distant points and among random hills, the white domes appear and disappear with the curves and swells of the urban topography.

One of the paradoxes of urbanity is its reliance upon its opposite, the condition of coarse activity in unprogramed spaces that approximates Foucault's idea of *heterotopia*. Such are the pleasures of tracking and hunting in a dangerous built domain as if it were raw wilderness. Contrary to the expectations of order and culture, part of the *jouissance* of urbanism is the proximity to lawlessness, wild abandon, and illicit behavior. Undomesticated and feral,

8.17
**View of the
Griffith Park
Observatory at
night**

a large part of urbanity derives from those pockets of space that provide for these desires – such as *Club Silencio*, a locus of sortilege and sexuality in David Lynch's 2001 film *Mulholland Drive*. These terms are more than "desires" in Los Angeles; they are physical components of the city that drives its unconscious narrative.

Griffith Park dominates the center of the larger metropolitan area stretching from the San Pedro Harbor to the San Fernando Valley sprawl: a 4,000 acre parcel of land – "the largest municipal park in the nation" – donated to the city in 1896 by Mr. Griffith J. Griffith as a "place of recreation and rest for the masses, a resort for the rank and file."[39] According to Greg Hise and William Deverell, Mr. Griffith – "a Progressive reformer interested in issues of social hygiene and the influence of the environment over the individual" – believed that integrated parks and boulevards could "do the work of deep reform." For Griffith, "park space could be the lungs of the city; parks would relieve class tensions; parks could be tied directly to Comprehensive City planning."[40] Griffith Park features 53 miles of hiking trails, two open-air theaters (the Greek Theater and the Hollywood Bowl), tennis courts, golf courses, and the Los Angeles Zoo – caged animals dwelling within a larger field of liberated predators. As the literature warns, "hikers should approach the park with caution; Griffith Park is a wilderness area with wild quail, rodents, foxes, coyotes, rattlesnakes and deer."[41]

In Los Angeles, the ever-present markers of the park, the observatory, Mt. Hollywood, and the Hollywood sign stand as reminders that wild abandon and atavistic urges dwell in the heart of the city. The Griffith Park acreage provides pathways for imagined and real predators to find their way from the wilderness directly into the city proper. In Los Angeles, the presence of lions on city hall – Terry Gilliam's image of Philadelphia in *12 Monkeys* (1995) – is something of a possibility. Mike Davis has made much of the predatory persona of Los Angeles in his *Ecology of Fear: Los Angeles and the Imagination of Disaster* (1998), writing a series of essays which also portray wild fires, liquefaction zones, drought, and earthquakes with such convincing detail that he provokes even semi-rational citizens to question the sanity of living in Los Angeles.[42] Ten years earlier, John McPhee's "Los Angeles Against the Mountains," in *The Control of Nature* (1989), similarly terrified readers learning about the near-death experiences caused by flows of rock and mud trapping people perilously in their homes. As McPhee demonstrates, to understand Los Angeles is to know its precise geography; the natural environment provides the significant window onto the urban landscape.

Mulholland Drive runs through Griffith Park as a narrow, winding artery of fairly high-speed traffic that Lynch fuses into the opening scenes of his film as a ribbon of road slipping up and down, in and around the crest of the Hollywood Hills and the Santa Monica Mountains. Operating as a boundary between the Los Angeles basin and the San Fernando Valley, the 21-mile-long highway connects the Cahuenga Pass in Hollywood with Leo Carillo State Beach at the Venture–Los Angeles county line. The name of the highway, of course, memorializes William Mulholland (1855–1935), the founder and head of Los Angeles's Department of Water and Power, who in 1913 and with a 233-mile-long network of channels and aqueduct, brought water to the arid ground of the valley and, with it, the possibility of suburban morass. Mulholland Drive, less for the lore that surrounds car chases and more for its physical condition as a hinge between the city and the valley, dwells in the work of David Hockney, an avid interpreter of both the city and complex visual fields. In his 1980 painting "Mulholland Drive: The Road to the Studio," Hockney develops a definitive cognitive cartography based upon shifting perspectives and simultaneous spatial moments, offering specific strategies for documenting the city that merge plan and perspective into an interpretive and analytical representation of space (Figure 8.18). The tools Hockney develops offer a unique understanding of the city, one that he spatializes as the interpenetration of flat grids and curving mountain roads in order to reveal a cognitive map created by the superimposition of perspectival vignettes upon a city map.

In fact, Richter documents the area of Century City as a series of cartographic exercises that offer an architectural response to Hockney's spatial lesson of hybrid drawing. Richter "studied and overlapped maps from various

**8.18**
**David Hockney**
**Mulholland Drive:**
**The Road to the**
**Studio**

moments in the history of Century city" producing documents that marked "forgotten landscapes" and displayed the "apparatus of dislocated film towns, as well as oil fields, orange groves, and single-family bungalows." She then, in a second reading of the city, transformed the shadows cast by the skyscrapers into an "axonometrical collapse of the vertical object onto the projection screen," and in a third, studied the skyscraper façades as folded and layered surfaces.[43] Richter's analyses, in which she ultimately collapses these various cartographies upon each other, emerges as a simultaneous map, urban analysis, and building design (Figures 8.19, 8.20).

      The views from Griffith Park evoke such cartographic potential. The park also serves as a gigantic, almost incomprehensible example of the many smaller open spaces that can be found throughout the city with the major difference being less about size than about a persistent state of dilapidation. Much of Los Angeles is filled with what Norman Klein refers to as empty dirt patches – patches of raw nature filled with the foundations of recently demolished homes or the debris of illicit activities.[44] As far back as the early 1930s,

**8.19**
**Collected Traces**
**and Shadows of**
**Century City**

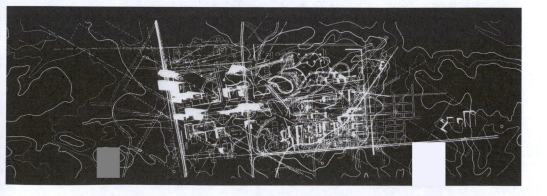

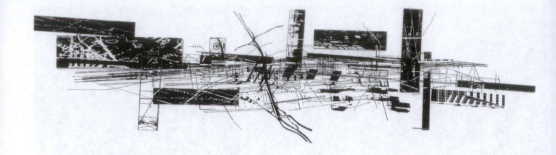

8.20
**Working Diagram
A: Layered Traces
and Shadows**

when members of the Los Angeles business community observed that a short-age of open space in the city would act as a possible hindrance to tourism, citizens employed the firms of Olmsted Brothers in Brookline Massachusetts and Harland Bartholomew and Associates of St. Louis to propose a solution to the problem. Through this initiative emerged the "178-page, clothbound docu-ment, *Parks, Playgrounds and Beaches for the Los Angeles Region*" (1930). The Olmsted–Bartholomew plan demonstrates the significance the authors placed on the natural environment of the city. As Hise and Deverell also write, their "focus is resolutely on systems – the robust but ultimately endangered systems of nature in the mountains, high desert, the basin, and the Pacific coastline – and the ways these might be integrated with urban systems, espe-cially the infrastructure necessary for expanding the metropolitan region."[45] Conflicting interests would see to it that little direct transformation of the city based upon the recommendations of the report would occur, given that it "garnered almost no public attention" and the response was a "resounding silence."[46]

Many of the neglected patches of open space that can be found in the contemporary city run along abandoned rights of way or next to property owned by governmental services. In 1994 the architectural firm of Johnson Fain Partners, in collaboration with Beth Rogers of Pacific Earth Resources (California's largest grower of turf), addressed the problem of open space in the city when William Fain observed that Los Angeles devotes only 4 percent of its area to open space – in contrast to Boston and New York, which main-tain 9 percent and 17 percent respectively. Fain devoted unreimbursed office time to creating the award-winning "Greenway Plan for Metropolitan Los Angeles."[47] He and his team of architects and urban designers completed a series of close analyses of the city, drawing layer upon mylar layer of separ-ate infrastructures, systems, networks, and demographics in order to arrive at the last map, the "closest to a polemic," they developed into a plan for open space that takes advantage of these overlapping systems and networks.[48] Given that this was primarily a self-sponsored project, the Johnson–Fain research remains an attempt to offer guidelines for the city's development, some of which are being realized with plans to transform the Los Angeles river from a concrete-lined flood control basin filled with waste water into a viable riparian landscape. The firm describes this research with the following words:

> The Los Angeles Open Space concept provides a substantial increase in public open space by using available land resources such as transit lines, bikeways, rail rights-of-way, rivers, flood control channels, and powerline encasements. The plan links a number of these land resources to existing town centers, schools, libraries, post offices, and senior centers while providing new sites for other uses. The concept can be the catalyst for the establishment of additional public parks, squares, and plazas, increasing the amount of open space available for public use and enjoyment.[49]

The design team attempted to study the "unnoticed network of connective tissue" that forms the city of Los Angeles and derives from rights of way, interstices, networks, and parallel activities.[48] The various layers include: (1) an analysis of the over 50 various "centers" that can be identified throughout the metropolitan area; (2) independent jurisdictions with their own city halls; and (3) an existing greenways map (Figures 8.21, 8.22). As with the Olmsted–Bartholomew report, the Johnson–Fain analysis focuses on open space, geography, infrastructure and demographic data in order to form a stratified but nonetheless cognitive map of the city wherein nature and natural elements frame and define Los Angeles.

## The dirty real

Writing in his 1965 novel, *The Crying of Lot 49*, Thomas Pynchon delineates what could be the landscape of LA:

> Like many name places in California it was less an identifiable city than a grouping of concepts – census tracts, special purpose bond-issue districts, shopping nuclei, all over laid with access roads to its own freeway. . . . She [Oedipa Maas] looked down a slope, needing to squint for the sunlight, onto a vast sprawl of houses which had grown up all together, like a well-tended crop, from the dull brown earth; and she thought of the time she'd opened a transistor radio to replace a battery and seen her first printed circuit. The ordered swirl of houses and streets, from this high angle, sprang at her now with

8.21
**Johnson Fain,
Los Angeles Open
Space**

the same unexpected, astonishing clarity as the circuit card had. Though she knew even less about radios than about Southern Californians, there were to both outward patterns a hieroglyphic sense of concealed meaning, of an intent to communicate.[50]

An urban *roman à clef* in which both real and fictional place names merge into a composite portrait of LA urbanism, Pynchon weaves a detective story concerning the spatial narratives of paranoia, entropy, and aporia into Southern California's physiognomy. Pynchon's novel serves as a pivotal location for concluding this discussion about Los Angeles as a quintessential PM city. Underscoring this assessment of LA, Lehan summarizes the conclusion to *The Crying of Lot 49* with the following observation:

**8.22
Johnson Fain,
Greenway
Developments**

At the end of the novel, she is left at the edge of the ocean, a rented car between her and the lifeless continent, holding a dead phone. She has come to land's end in the machine society, dependent on technological forms of communication that constantly fail her. What she gets back, as with a computer, is what she brings to it. All of Los Angeles has become an Echo Court, as the motel where she is staying is called. By the end of the novel the world is breaking down into solipsism.[51]

In Lehan's distinction between modern and postmodern writing about the city, once urban signification breaks down into an unstable system of signs, into solipsism, then the city no longer holds claim to being "real."[27] Lehan's use of the term *real*, in specific connection with a more recent kind of fashioning of this term – see, for example, Rodolfo Machado and Jorge Silvetti's *Unprecedented Realism*, Hal Foster's *Return of the Real*, Baudrillard's and Eco's "Hyperreal," or the spate of publications on the "Surreal," – when taken in combination with Jameson's deployment of "dirty realism," marks a moment of potential insight into the enigmatic and shifting cartographies that constitute Los Angeles.

For Baudrillard it is not that, in "the precession of the simulacra" the map "engenders the territory" rather than the other way around, but that "it is no longer a question of maps and territory" – hence the insignificance of cognitive navigation when faced with a more overwhelming inability to break free from ideological constructs. "Something has disappeared" and this is the possibility of perceiving reality:

> Disneyland is there to conceal the fact that it is the "real" country, of all "real" America, which *is* Disneyland (just as prisons are there to conceal the fact that it is the social in its entirety, in its banal omnipresence, which is carceral). Disneyland is presented as imaginary in order to make us believe that the rest is real, when in fact all of Los Angeles and the America surrounding it are no longer real, but of the order of the hyperreal and of simulation. It is no longer a question of a false representation of reality (ideology), but of concealing the fact that the real is no longer real, and thus of saving the reality principle.[52]

While an initial rejoinder to Baudrillard's assessment of LA might be to suggest a similar comparison with, say, Paris, Norman Klein would argue that indeed postmodernism hazards superficial and casual readings of LA, that this "theory has probably devoted too much energy to looking at corporate simulation – engaged too much disengaged gawking at expensive hyper-real spaces, and not done enough digging into the political contradictions of local culture step by step."[53] Step-by-step, Disneyland offers a peek at the evil genius behind its curtains, step-by-step LA is neither monolithic nor homogeneous, and step-by-step the notion of the *simulacra* has been displaced by the actuality of the "pure event," to pit Baudrillard against himself, "an event that can no longer be manipulated, interpreted, or deciphered by any historical subjectivity" – earthquakes, fires, floods, uprisings, terrorism.[54] Any reading of LA must go beyond Baudrillard's idea of an "operational negativity" in which the fake serves the utilitarian purpose of making real.

As a cautionary note, the notion of *realism* pulls upon certain semantic threads that become Gordian knots when placed in an urban or architectural context. Unlike literature, cinema, or painting, that arguably maintain an explicitly representational modality in contrast to an external or "real" space, architecture and urbanism exist as both representational and inhabited domains. Thus when we describe a city such as Los Angeles through a term such as *realism*, this critique necessarily suggests that other stylistic motifs – "Noir," "Tech," "Futuristic," "Jungle," "Frontier," or "Glam," for example – may apply. My interest here, instead, is to examine *realism* in opposition to *idealism* as a philosophical construct that critiques the Utopian with the quotidian, and the theoretical with the absurd. As the sondage into Griffith Park presupposes, Los Angeles's urbanity dwells in both the real and ideal, the planned and accidental, the cultivated and fallow; it exists as much in the topiary, the floral, and the perfumed as in the patches of dirt, the dirty, the trashy, the seamy, and the real. Thus, in addition to Lehan's tempting assertion that the postmodern city ceases to be real, the other way of looking at this is that the city also becomes all too real, "dirty real." If a city ceases to be understood as artificial, that is, as a construct, then is it part of the natural order, a brute fact of some deterministic principle, lacking design and, most necessary of all, artifice?

Jameson takes the idea of "dirty realism" from Liane Lefaivre, who in turn appropriates it from the literary critic, Bill Buford. Buford's realism concerns the "unadorned, unfurnished, low-rent tragedies about people who watch day-time television, read cheap romances, or listen to country and western music," focusing on "drifters in a world cluttered with junk food and the oppressive details of modern consumerism."[55] The condition of dirty realism describes a world in which mass culture penetrates the "utmost recesses and crannies" of everyday life, with a resulting colonization of any "residual enclaves that had hitherto remained exempt," enclaves as diverse as those instituted through farming, high culture, ghettos, traditional villages, or "classical urban forms of collective living." Finally, Jameson presents this concept as "the passage from the amusement park to the mall," a world in which a "new type of closure simulates all the chaotic libidinal freedom of the now dangerous world outside."[56] In order to exemplify this condition of the "fallen real," he seeks allegories of the "intestinal necessity of the modern building." He finds them in Rem Koolhaas's Zeebrugge Terminal, which includes "whole former structures, such as a hotel and an office building" along with on- and off-ramps, which he compares to the "delicately interlaced" ramps at the "Figueroa grade crossing in downtown Los Angeles"[57] If not precisely the Phalanstery Jameson alludes to in his description of this "new type of closure," then at least LA appears to be the archetypal city for this anti-urban urban form. And while comparing the landscape of Los Angeles to the detritus of consumer culture unleashed within these novels may further liberate a field of reductive cliches into the city, it also brackets the infrastructure of transportation, complex spaces, hybrid programs, and parasitical structures proliferating LA as significant conditions of urbanity.

Jameson turns to *Blade Runner* and cyberpunk, to megastructures and OMA's Piranesian spaces, spaces that blur the distinction between inside and outside. But the more recent depiction of Los Angeles in films such as *Pulp Fiction* (1994, Quentin Tarantino) or *Boogie Nights* (1997, Paul Thomas Anderson) more closely approximates Buford's original thesis – the Big Mac cum *Royale* with cheese and the beverage choice of beer, the blandness of the San Fernando Valley and the malaise of living on the extremity of the so-called city of LA. This is the genre that compels Roemer Van Toorn to question and to answer:

> To what extent does Tarantino enable us to read reality more per-
> ceptively? In *Pulp Fiction*, it is not so much the filmic montage of
> sound and image, but the *mise en scène* that induces us to compre-
> hend everyday reality as a "dirty realism." The film is set in the city
> periphery. It is a pulp movie with an architecture without architects.
> It tells strange stories that come across as completely realistic.[58]

Ironically or pathetically, Tarantino's filmic perspective reterritorializes the grim condition, the infinite acreage of sheer architectural sludge in Los Angeles that so depressed Adorno, through the very medium of mass culture that Adorno condemned. This is the aspect of the dirty real found in "supermarkets, road-side cafes, cheap hotels."[55] It is the sectional cut through the city described by Michael Douglas's walk through the film *Falling Down*, or by the sectional slice of Sunset Boulevard as it winds its way from downtown, past flop houses, bill-boards, cafes, hotels, motels, mansions and murders in the neighborhoods of Echo Park, Silverlake, West Hollywood, Westwood, Brentwood, and the Pacific Palisades, only to end unceremoniously at the sea. Through cinema these sub-genres of LA's urban milieu proliferate, reframed and distilled into a series of infinite jump cuts. In this respect, cinema operates in Los Angeles at the inter-section of the cognitive map and the dirty real. If it anticipates its subject, as Baudrillard argues, the deformations and excrescencies of its subject anticipate cinema.

While eschewing any ethical imperative, the postmodern sublime successfully colonizes the uncultured, feral, filthy, and raw as viable design terrain responding to the libidinal play of city pleasures. The "dirty real" clearly differs from "popular culture and the everyday," as an urbanism predicated upon conditions in the city that, while undesigned, is also incomplete, ruinous, fragmented, or unsupervised. As the title of Michael Sorkin's collection of essays verifies – *Variations on a Theme Park: The New American City and the*

*End of Public Space* – Jameson's trajectory from amusement park to mall is an apt description of LA, but one that should not exclude the city's omnipresent and equally apt persona of a working town.

While the socioeconomic axis from Malibu Beach to Beverly Hills describes one dimension of the city, other dimensions pertain to the axes from Central America to MacArthur Park, the Greyhound bus terminal to skid row, or San Pedro to the sweatshops of downtown. Each manicured lawn presupposes the dirt lots and hovels that occupy much of the city. From the depths of despair to the height of affluence, the dirt of LA provides fertile ground not only for prosperous residents within the city, but also for the rest of the United States. To place the possibility of the cognitive map onto the field of the real, the fallen, or even the execrable is to adopt what the editors of the *Assemblage* understand to be Richter's approach to LA, "a belief in the transmutative effect of formal operations and a conviction that a critical reading of the negative characteristics of Los Angeles might generate new, constructive principles."[59] All of this protective apparati I have marshaled in depicting the city ultimately has very little to do with realism – a Hollywood term after all – but does attempt to displace the rather uninteresting "precession of the simulacra" from its position of authority in defining LA as a theme park. Which all goes to say that Los Angeles is a living breathing entity, an organism, an object of love and hate, a serpent of highways, an ocean of asphalt, a monster, a war zone, a playground, a flowering garden, a map – a city.

# Epilogue

Walking in LA
Look ahead as we pass, try to focus on it
I won't be fooled by a cheap cinematic trick
It must have been just cardboard cut out of a man
Top forty cast off from a record stand
Walkin' in LA
Walkin' in LA
Nobody walks in LA
I don't know, could've been a lame jogger maybe
Or someone just about to do the freeway strangler baby
Shopping cart pusher or maybe someone groovie
One thing's for sure he isn't starring in the movies
'Cause he's walkin' in LA
Walkin' in LA
Only a nobody walks in LA

You won't see a cop walkin' on the beat
You only see 'em drivin' cars out on the street
You won't see a kid walkin' home from school
Their mothers pick 'em up in a car pool
Could it be that smog's playing tricks on my eyes
Or it's a rollerskater in some kind of headphone disguise
Maybe somebody who just ran out of gas, making his way
Back to the pumps the best way he can

Missing Persons
Spring Session M
1982 One Way Records Inc.

## Notes

1   Dew *et al.*, 1996, p. ix.

2   McPhee, 1989, p. 191.

3   See Jameson, 1991, p. 3, originally published in the *New Left Review* (1984) 146, 53–92.
I have, in this phrase, conflated two terms Jameson discusses in this essay: Daniel Bell's
"postindustrial society" and Ernest Mandel's book title of *Late Capitalism*. "Postindustrial
society" refers to consumer, media, information, electronic, or high-tech societies, while
"late capitalism" refers to a "third stage or movement in the evolution of capital." Later
in this essay Jameson further explains that, according to Mandel, the three phases of
capitalism are: "market capitalism, the monopoly stage or the stage of imperialism, and our
own, wrongly called postindustrial, but what might be better termed multinational capital"
(p. 35). Also see Lyotard (1984), where Jameson explains that Daniel Bell and others have
argued in for the concept of a "postindustrial society" in which "science, knowledge,
technological research, rather than industrial production and the extraction of surplus
value," are the determining factors.

4   See Varnelis, 2003. Special thanks are owed to Dr. Varnelis for his generosity in sharing
his unpublished manuscript with me as well as several bibliographical references. On the
ascendancy of the LA School see Marco Cenzatti, 2003. According to Cenzatti "the name
'Los Angeles School' identifies the work of a group of local researchers who, from the early
'80's onwards, discovered in Los Angeles a series of social, economic, and spatial trends
symptomatic of a general transformation currently taking place in the entire U.S. urban and
social structure" (p. 5). The inherent assumption in this loose collection of thinkers from UC
Irvine, UCLA, USC, and SCIARC is that "Los Angeles is exemplary of the new urban model
currently emerging from a new round of economic and social changes taking place across
the country" (p. 6).

5   Along with the authors mentioned in elsewhere throughout this text the following
publications have contributed substantially to the bibliography on Los Angeles: McWilliams,
1946; Fogelson, 1967; Hayden, 1995; Barron and Eckmann, 1997; Hall, 1998; Heilbut, 1998;
Cuff, 2000; Fulton, 2001; Salas and Roth, 2001.

6   Soja, 1996, p. 196. Soja writes the following about Jameson's essay "Postmodernism or,
the Logic of Late Capitalism": "In 1984, while the article was in press, Jameson, Lefebvre,
and I wandered through the Bonaventure, rode its glass-encased elevators, and had some
refreshments in the rooftop revolving restaurant overlooking downtown. In 1989, I took

much the same trip with Robert Manaquis and Jean Baudrillard, when Baudrillard was participating in the revolutionary bicentennial."

7   Jameson, 1991, p. 37. For alternative interpretations of postmodern cities, see Ellin, 1999.

8   Ingraham, 1998, p. 86.

9   My reference to *heterotopia* alludes to Michel Foucault's nomenclature (see Foucault, 1993, pp. 420–426). *Heteropolis* refers to Jencks, 1993.

10  Jameson, 1988, p. 351.

11  Jameson, 1994, p. 130. I am indebted to Michael Speaks for directing me to the publication where Jameson outlines his idea of "dirty realism." On "dirty realism" also see Office for Metropolitan Architecture, Rem Koolhaas, and Bruce Mau, 1995.

12  We might recall that Gertrude Stein's famous 1935 quip that "there is no there there," refers not to Los Angeles, but rather to Oakland, California.

13  Jameson, 1998, p. 353. While the *psychogeography* of Situationism comes to mind here, this act of urbanism is perhaps too vague and imprecise a term upon which to develop an apprehension of LA.

14  Fredric Jameson, 1998, p. 353. Jameson explains these authors with the following: "you know that Kevin Lynch is the author of the classic work, *The Image of the City*, which in its turn spawned a whole low-level subdiscipline that today takes the phrase 'cognitive mapping' as its own designation" and Althusser's "great formulation of ideology itself" as "the Imaginary representation of the subject's relationship to his or her Real conditions of existence."

15  Jameson, 1991, p. 44.

16  For example, Suisman (1992, pp. 586–587) writes: "Per come appariva dopo la seconda guerra mondiale, Los Angeles fu a lungo trattat da *enfant terrible* delle città americane."

17  Adorno and Horkheimer, 1994, p. 120.

18  Richter, p. 69. Her description merits quoting at length:

> "When one arrives in Los Angeles by plane at night, the city appears as fragments of Euclidian fields woven together by threads of moving red and white lights. From the air, these threads, interconnected at geometrically unpredictable points, superimpose a fluid order over a basin of pixels. They sponsor the illusion of effortless movement from point to point on this urban screen of light. But the lack of congruity among the different layers of spatial orders in Los Angeles in fact emphasizes a reading of fragmentation, rupture, and localization. On closer inspection, the nighttime city reveals itself to be a giant shantytown on a desert ground; the lights illuminate the spaces in between, a no-man's land of parking lots, roads, and industrial yards."

Also see Dagmar Richter *XYZ: The Architecture of Dagmar Richter* (New York: Princeton Architectural Press, 2001).

19  Suisman (1992, p. 52) writes: "Questa città è la manifestazione estrema d'una quarantina d'anni di investimenti nazionali nella suburbanizzazione, sostenuta dalle industrie automobilistiche, bancarie, ed edilizie, e dalle linee programmatiche governative."

20  Soja and Scott (1996) similarly divide LA's history into chronological "surges." Surge I (1870 to 1900) "created a regional economy based in agriculture, land speculation, real estate boosterism, and the provision of specialized health and leisure services particularly to white retirees" (p. 5). During Surge II (1900–1920) "the private and public promoters of Los Angeles turned increasingly to industrial development and succeeded in plugging the city into the dynamo of the American manufacturing belt in the northeastern states" (p. 5). Surge III (1920–1940) experienced a "renewed land boom, petroleum production and refining experienced a

resurgences," as well as growth of the motion picture and the air craft industries. During Surge IV (1940–1970) the region tripled in size to nearly 10 million, mass suburbanization emerged "on a scale never before encountered" (p. 8). Finally, Surge V (1970–1990) led to the development of an "extremely varied economy based on a diversity of high- and low-technology industries, as well as a thriving business and financial services sector" (p. 12).

21  Moule and Polyzoides, 1994, p. 9.

22  Moule and Polyzoides (1994, p. 10) also explain that "the *Laws of the Indies* was a very sophisticated set of urbanizing rules propagated by decree of King Philip II in 1573 and used extensively in the process of Spanish colonization in America. The Pueblo's location near a river and not near the ocean was deliberate, protecting the settlement from the unhealthy effects of swamps and from pirating. Two separate precincts were delineated for each settler: a lot for the construction of an urban house and a plot of land in the adjacent countryside for farming. The residences encircled the plaza along with royal public buildings, the granary and a guardhouse lining the southern edge. The plaza was rectangular with corner streets heading straight into the square. It was oriented at the compass quarter-points in order to protect the streets from the wind . . . in 1815 the pueblo was washed away by floods and its site was subsequently moved to its present location."

23  Pitt and Pitt (1997, p. 366). The authors also write:

> A powerful tourist magnet since its opening in 1930, Olvera Street now attracts 2 million visitors yearly. The street's original name, Winde Street, reflected the vineyards and wineries one located nearby. It was renamed in honor of Mexican judge Agustín Olvera, a prominent Mexican who once lived there. In the 1920's when Christine Sterling organized a campaign to save its brick and adobe structures from destruction, the street was a back alley for machine shops. Out of whole cloth she created a lively Mexican *mercado*, closed to cars and open to tourists . . . counts among its other attractions the Avila Adobe and the Sepulveda House . . ."

24  Thanks to Diane Ghirardo and a lecture she gave at the regional ACSA conference in St. Louis, Missouri for directing my attention to the staging of Olvera Street. Pitt and Pitt (1997, p. 227) note:

> Although Jackson's novel, about a part-Indian orphan raised in Spanish society and her Indian husband, achieved almost instant success, it failed to arouse public concern for the treatment of local Native Americans. Instead, readers accepted the sentimentalized Spanish aristocracy that was portrayed, and the Ramona myth was born. Jackson died a year after her novel was published, never knowing the impact her book made on the Southern California heritage. The novel *Ramona* has inspired films [the first directed by D. W. Griffith], songs [the 1920s hit "Ramona"], and a long-running pageant in Hemet . . .

25  Suisman (1989, p. 12) also mentions that the colonists "generally ignored the territorial claims of the Native American tribes."

26  From a telephone interview with Mario Gandelsonas conducted during the writing of this essay.

27  Lehan, 1998, p. 266.

28  Gandelsonas, 1996, p. 6.

29  Gandelsonas, 1996, p. 101.

30  Gandelsonas, 1996, p. 104.

31  Stephen Rowley, from http://home.mira.net/~satadaca/v.htm.

32  Rowe and Koetter, 1975, p. 11.

33  Baudrillard, 1984, p. 253.

34  Suisman, 1989, p. 6.

35  Suisman, 1989, p. 21.

36  Suisman, 1989, p. 23.

37  Suisman, 1989, p. 29.

38  Conversely Baudrillard (1984, p. 273) claims that "We are witnessing the end of perspective and panoptic space . . ." A perhaps more noteworthy film that features this site is the 1955 *Rebel Without a Cause*, with performances by James Dean and Natalie Wood.

39  Pitt and Pitt, 1997, p. 183.

40  Hise and Deverell, 2000.

41  See: http://www.laparks.org/grifmet/gp/test/main_hiking.htm.

42  Davis, 1998, pp. 1, 2, 108.

43  Richter, 74–75. Joshua Levine, Theodore Zoumboulakis, Anna Bolneset, Mark Donnahue, Rick Mascia, Cordell Steinmetz, and Robert Thibodeau assisted Richter on this project.

44  Klein, 1997, p. 1.

45  Hise and Deverell, 2000, p. 8.

46  Hise and Deverell, 2000, p. 4.

47  The firm received a citation in the January, 1994 41st Annual P/A Awards. The office team consisted of William H. Fain Jr., Robert P. Shaffer, Patric B. Dawe, Donna L. Vaccarino, John C. Begazo, Neil Kritzinger, Mark R. Gershen, Katherine W. Rinne, and Lori Gates. Cf. *Progressive Architecture* (January 1994). Thanks to Alan Loomis and Vinayak Bharne of Moule and Polyzoides for pointing this work out to me.

48  From an interview Mr. Robert P. Shaffer, Senior Associate at the Johnson–Fain Partnership, generously offered me during the course of writing this chapter.

49  Dobney, 1997, p. 88.

50  Pynchon, 1965, p. 49.

51  Lehan, 1998, p. 273.

52  Baudrillard, 1984, p. 262. He continues:

> Los Angeles is encircled by these "imaginary stations" which feed reality, reality-energy, to a town whose mystery is precisely that it is nothing more than a network of endless, unreal circulation – a town of fabulous proportions, but without space or dimensions. As much as electrical and nuclear power stations, as much as film studios, this town, which is nothing more than an immense script and a perpetual motion picture, needs the old imaginary made up of childhood signals and faked phantasms for its synthetic nervous system.

53  Klein, 1997, p. 140.

54  Baudrillard, 1987, p. 70.

55  Jameson, 1994, p. 145.

56  Jameson, 1994, p. 144.

57  Jameson, 1994, p. 138.

58  Van Toorn, 1997.

59  Preface to *Assemblage* 14, p. 68.

## Chapter 9

# New Orleans – Ecological Urbanism

*Victor J. Jones*

Urban discourse recognizes the role that social and economic forces play in shaping the form and substance of a city – the continental grid as the instrument for mapping territory and stimulating land speculation, and the axial plan as the device that delineates social order and maximizes circulation. In practice, however, such abstract and "totalizing" urban operations have proven to be vulnerable to both human and natural forces at work in cities, particularly those located in geographically challenged areas. This chapter examines alternative "ecological" urban operations and assesses their potential effect on the rebuilding of post-Katrina New Orleans. Among the many initiatives that have been launched in the wake of the hurricane, three case studies in particular represent the broad agenda of ecological urbanism as they lay the groundwork for a symbiosis between the natural conditions of the city's site, human activity, and cultural identity.

In the mid-1990s, landscape architects began expanding the idea of "landscape" to include human interventions in the urban fabric of cities. In so doing, they enlarged their sphere of operation to engage the unnatural ecologies as well as the natural environment – the topography of the territory, the natural substrates, and the creatures and the plant life that inhabit it. Rather than being relegated to a secondary and often purely ornamental role in the urban domain, landscape (now including unnatural landscapes and unnatural ecologies of all kinds) was elevated to a primary place.[1] More recently, the term "ecological urbanism" has enlarged this domain yet again, describing an approach to cities that is not only more sensitive to the natural environment and issues of sustainability, but also less ideologically driven and more socially inclusive.[2] In many ways, ecological urbanism is an evolution of, and a critique of, "landscape urbanism," inasmuch as it advocates a more holistic approach to the design and management of cities.

Ecological urbanism argues for "new ethics and aesthetics of the urban." It recognizes and articulates the need for a systems-based design approach that integrates and expresses complex systems and social processes in ways that are fundamentally humane. This shift of emphasis radically alters the dynamics that have determined how urban environments are conceived, designed, built, and maintained up until relatively recently. At the same time, the notion of ecology, having moved beyond the mere notion of environmental sustainability, has gained new agency in the lexicon of urban theory and planning.

## Deluge and disaster

In parallel with this renewal of traditional disciplinary recognition with respect to natural settings and ecosystems,[3] dramatic effects of climate change and extraordinary weather events have begun to be felt in cities around the world. As a consequence, the notion of ecology has gone from being considered "relevant" to being a determining factor in the discourse on cities. Take as just one example the extraordinary case of New Orleans. When Hurricane Katrina struck in late August 2005, one of America's worst environmental disasters exposed the fact that the city was already poised at the threshold of oblivion before the hurricane overwhelmed it. The incapacity of human artifice to impede natural forces was bluntly demonstrated. The extreme event was, in part, a human disaster resulting from three centuries of urbanization supported by an unflinching confidence in aggressive infrastructural practices. With land uses attuned only to economic agendas, traditional urban patterns portrayed a city as it had been dreamed, rather than as it actually existed in relation to the landscape and the sea. The legacy of the ancien régime, with its blind eye to the practical and the specifics of a site, bolstered by invasive infrastructure, never acknowledged the environmental threat that urbanism posed in this sensitive domain.

## Not urban but policy renewal

In the course of reconstructing New Orleans, conventional urban planning practices have been suspended in recognition of the precarious ecological conditions of the site, which for centuries went unheeded. With the expressed mandate of establishing more resilient forms of urban organization in the city, nature itself has been invited to participate in the redefinition of territory and boundaries based upon new logics of organization. Rather than turning the landscape against itself by mounting heroic feats of engineering to compensate for the city's unfortunate topography, proponents of ecological urbanism have begun to elicit from the design fields of landscape architecture, architecture, and urban design alternative approaches based on the notion of cooperation with and adaptation to natural forces. This points to a reshaping of the urban realm that is based on something other than formalist or economic premises.

The following case studies represent reflective ecological urbanism practices – a macro-scale comprehensive planning analysis by the Urban Land Institute (ULI); a micro-scale design proposition located in one the hardest-hit areas of New Orleans, Viet Village Urban Farm; and a meso-scale proposal paradoxically located on high ground, New Orleans Waterfront: Reinventing the Crescent. While the ULI report underscored the importance of ecologically "sensible" redevelopment in New Orleans, the two design proposals, both recipients of several national design awards, advocate ecologically "responsive" approaches to urban development, expressing sensitivity not only to the natural environment, but also to the complex social and cultural dimensions of New Orleans. The case studies serve as pointed examples that call into question the feasibility of "sustainable" and "ecologically based" approaches for a post-Katrina New Orleans.

## Past as foreword

American geographer Peirce F. Lewis described New Orleans as "the impossible but inevitable city."[4] Surrounded by swamps, threatened by floods, and graced with little solid ground, New Orleans was always the site of a struggle between human intentions and the natural tendencies of the place. Establishing their city at the very mouth of the Mississippi River Delta, French colonialists favored the flat and below-sea-level terrain, speculating that the logistical advantages outweighed the less than hospitable geographic and climatic conditions.

In 1718, Jean-Baptiste Le Moyne de Bienville founded a French outpost on the site of the future city. Situated on high ground running along the Mississippi River, what would become the French Quarter was laid out in 1728 by engineer Pierre Le Blond de la Tour. The plan consisted of a gridiron with 14 square blocks flanking the river and six squares inland from the river's edge. Each square block was surrounded by a ditch, and the whole ensemble was bordered by a canal. Rainwater and raw sewage together would flow from the

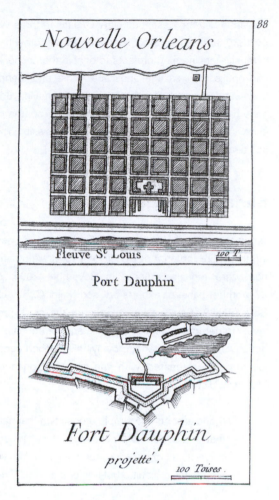

88

9.1
**Engraving of Le Vieux Carré (upper) envisioned by engineer Pierre Le Blond de la Tour. Private collection of Alain Fièvre**

ditches around the squares, and then were funneled into two large ditches that emptied into the canal. The canal, in turn, emptied into the swamp lying behind the city and stretching to the natural levee of Lake Pontchartrain. During heavy rainstorms, the streets were completely flooded, and each square block became an island.

Fur trading sparked a burgeoning economy, and by the end of the eighteenth century, sugar-cane plantations occupied the natural levees along the banks of the Mississippi. The striking difference between the gridiron of the French Quarter and the settlement patterns of the plantations is that the latter followed the winding geography of the Mississippi rather than the hardline geometry of the French Quarter. As New Orleans weathered its unsavory environmental circumstances, robust commerce and trade effected the city's transformation from languid, topographically challenged backwater town to thriving and boisterous hub. Still, water haunted the fate of the city. In 1819, architect

Benjamin Latrobe described New Orleans in three words: "mud, mud, mud."[5] By 1830, efforts to protect America's fastest growing city from flooding ignited extensive engineering projects to enable the unchecked expansion of the new metropolis into a savage landscape. Those engineering feats, together with the later subdivision of the plantations into smaller, urban-scaled parcels, determined the foundational organization of the contemporary city. By the 1960s, every inch of land nested between the Mississippi River and Lake Ponchetrane had been slated for development.

## Shrinking the footprint

When the levees gave way in 2005, it was widely assumed that neither restoring the entire footprint of the city nor full-scale urban abandonment and relocation were tenable options. In November 2005, on behalf of the ULI, a 37-member panel of experts advised Major C. Ray Nagin's Bring New Orleans Back (BNOB) Commission to refigure the city's footprint using natural flood levels to determine new boundaries and territories of occupation. In theory, the notion of conceding certain low-lying neighborhoods to nature seemed sensible. It also resonated with the gist of pioneering ecological planner Ian McHarg's dictum:

> If one accepts the simple proposition that nature is the arena of life and that a modicum of knowledge of her processes is indispensable for survival and rather more for existence, health and delight, it is amazing how many difficult problems present ready resolution.[6]

The ULI report submitted to the BNOB Commission was a carefully crafted narrative that sensitively and rationally outlined guidelines for rebuilding. The recommendations included creating an economic development corporation to manage and dispense the billions of dollars expected to flow into the region, establishing mixed-income neighborhoods that could incorporate affordable housing with market-rate homes, developing more dense, walkable neighborhoods on higher ground using mid-rise residential buildings interspersed with commercial and retail facilities, and introducing a light-rail system that would run from the airport to the CBD, along which new neighborhoods could be built.

However, what caught the attention of most citizens and the press was the re-zoning map of the city that dictated development prescriptions for three "conditions": Minimal or Moderate Damage (should be repopulated immediately and services restored to current needs); Hardest Hit (should receive environmental testing and flood protection surveys to determine which neighborhoods should be redeveloped); and Flood Control (should include levees, parks, neutral grounds, and water reservoirs). Hardest Hit and Flood Control areas represented over 50 percent of the city's landmass, which would be refigured either through radical restructuring plans or abandonment. In any case, whole neighborhoods of families and businesses would be expected to find "solid ground" elsewhere.

Negative public reaction may have been the consequence of poor graphic judgment, or more likely, failure on the part of ULI to take into account the limitations of top-down strategies in the wake of urban disasters – a time when the most ambitious and revolutionary rebuilding plans are subject to the greatest likelihood of failure. The ecologically driven zoning map omitted any concrete solutions to crucial cultural and social issues that troubled the rebuilding process. Not even after ULI panel member, Jeffery Gardere officially acknowledged that "we need to address the social injustices, and the psychological damage that has been done to generations of African-Americans. We have to be able to speak about it," were citizens willing to support shrinking the city's footprint.

Cultural layers composed of family lineages, social networks, and sentimental attachments collided with the environmental realities of the site. Before long, citizens and neighborhood community groups pushed local politicians into guaranteeing that the city's footprint would remain unchanged. Residents suspected that officials did not respect every citizen's right to return to his or her home, pointing to a foreseeable outcome in which stakeholders and policy makers would seize the opportunity to permanently banish the poor and disenfranchised from New Orleans. This derailed any hope that the longstanding struggle between the bayou habitat and humanity could find common ground. Skeptics feared that New Orleans's great debate over shrinking the footprint officially ended in a political quid pro quo: citizens could return home at their own risk, while politicians and policy makers could pursue recovery on their own terms.

Regardless of the political outcome, the ULI's recommendation to shrink the city's footprint provoked design discussions that took environmental assessment as the starting point for the recovery of New Orleans. Design professionals and academics eager to understand the implications of this approach began working directly with grassroots neighborhood associations and civic groups.

# Viet Village Urban Farm

Working collaboratively with the Tulane City Center, the Urban Landscape Lab at Louisiana State University, and the University of Montana Environmental Studies Program, the landscape architecture firm of Spackman, Mossop and Michaels designed the Viet Village Urban Farm – a project that embraced the challenge of achieving environmental as well as cultural sustainability through an ecologically based approach to remediation of an irreparable part of the city. It opened up a conversation that had been suppressed by interest groups with political, financial, social, and aesthetic agendas – notably the BNOB Commission. Accepting the city's fluid and mutable terrain, figuratively and literally, SM+M jettisoned the fiction of occupying stable, solid, dry land in New Orleans. Their proposal advocates newly constructed ground that creates topographies and corridors linking existing ecologies and ecosystems with specific site conditions.

The first Vietnamese immigrants arrived in Village de l'Est in 1975. Developed extensively during the 1960s onwards, Village de l'Est, situated east of the Industrial Canal, is part of the Ninth Ward, a zone labeled "Hardest Hit" by the ULI report. Early on, the Vietnamese community established kitchen gardens where traditional fruits and vegetables were grown. Following Katrina, when these residents began to re-imagine their community, the idea of an urban farm emerged and took hold. Located on 28 acres, the urban farm combines small gardens for families with larger commercial plots focused on supplying food to local restaurants and grocery stores throughout the region. There is also a livestock area for raising chickens and goats using traditional Vietnamese methods. Situated in the heart of the community, Viet Village Urban Farm is supported by green infrastructure and is founded on sustainable irrigation and organic agricultural practices: energy is renewable, water is managed on-site, and kitchen waste is composted.

> The goal is to make the Viet Village Urban Farm an exemplar of sustainable technology.... We combined a system of low-tech drainage canals with a high-tech system of recycling that water for irrigation. A green-waste facility for composting was developed. The design for the structures is driven by the technology involved – collecting and recycling water, a passive solar design – and the look is modern.[7]

The entire site, consisting of land donations from the City of New Orleans and Mary Queen of Vietnam Community Development Corporation, is riddled with water and soil obstacles. Located in a high-water-table area subject to frequent flooding during storms, the site is essentially flat and lacks positive drainage. The soil is the notorious Kenner Muck, a dense and deep, and consequently very poor draining, organic soil fundamentally unsuitable for farming or raising live-stock, or even for urban development – though it exists throughout the entire area of New Orleans. Given the impenetrable character of the soil, the most sig-nificant environmental issue is, not surprisingly, the movement of water. Crops need multiple access points to water, especially in the small community garden plots where 40–50 individual access points are required and the runoff from irri-gation must be drained back to a central location through a series of bio-swales to aid in water remediation. A secondary system for storm-water runoff during heavy rains must be established to prevent the farm plots from flooding and the crops from being ruined.

The plan is organized to make most efficient use of the area, maxi-mize productivity, and create inviting and attractive spaces for community use. The different uses are located to take advantage of site features. The design strategy was developed as a series of fully functional sub-watersheds that could be established incrementally, yet come together to create a comprehen-sive system to deal with the programmatic and water/soil challenges. Water would be distributed to the farm plots for irrigation, and post-irrigation water would return to a central reservoir through a series of bio-swales. Each of the discrete watersheds could supply water for irrigation independently. If there were a break in the larger system, portable pumps powered by a windmill/water tower system would maintain water circulation.

While design for the Viet Village Urban Farm works hand in hand with ecological, social, and economic enterprises, funding remains the biggest challenge, along with the administrative concerns that consume even the

**9.2**
**Aerial view of the Viet Village Urban Farm. Provided by Spackman Mossop and Michaels, Landscape Architects**

9.3
**Perspective view of the Viet Village Urban Farm boardwalk. Provided by Spackman Mossop and Michaels, Landscape Architects**

simplest projects in a city where recovery is a labyrinthine process. The resistance that thwarted ULI's ecotopian vision for the city and similarly plagues the realization of the Viet Village Urban Farm are systemic. Many citizens in New Orleans have participated in what has become an endless series of public discussions and debates that have thus far produced little. More strangely, these open forums resemble what Ila Berman calls a "form of psycho-social therapy."[8] The topics and issues – racial, political, economic, and ethical – reflect deep societal divisions that indicate the absence of common sense, the inability to generate collective reasoning.

# New Orleans Waterfront: Reinventing the Crescent

The project site consists of a continuous six-mile stretch comprising 15 zones along the East Bank of the city's central riverfront. The crescent-shaped East Bank of the Mississippi River is part of New Orleans's natural high ground. Paradoxically, most of this land is currently inaccessible to the public. Littered with abandoned industrial wharves and railroad lines, it is also where significant maritime structures, earthen levees, and floodwalls render the river invisible from the city. Reinventing the Crescent was a direct response to what Alan Berger has called the drosscape or "waste landscape," an urban phenomenon emerging out of two primary processes: first, rapid horizontal urbanization (urban "sprawl"), and second, the leaving behind of land and detritus after economic and production regimes have ended.[9]

Collaboratively designed by the landscape architecture firm Hargreaves Associates, the planning firm Chan Krieger Sieniewicz, and the architectural firms Eskew + Dumez + Ripple and TEN Arquitectos, the project sets out to restore naturalized shoreline, produce new public open spaces interspersed with architectural interventions, and make the river's edge accessible to pedestrians. Defined by a horizontal landscape strategy, the scheme deploys a series of basic open space typologies: gardens, batture/rip-rap, green roofs, parks, plazas, streetscapes, and pier/bridges. Decayed piers no longer in use, much less providing good habitat for vegetation or wildlife, will be replaced with a naturalized edge that will facilitate the return of shoreline wildlife. The replacement of acres of impervious surfaces all along the river will further enhance the environment as well as allocating more than 85 percent of the river's edge to public open space. Connective streetscapes are extended from the city to the riverfront, frequently ending at piers and bridges surrounded by parks, and naturalized shoreline areas of batture (ecological zones formed in the alluvial lands between the Mississippi and the levee) are restored. New areas of batture will be formed with rip-rap, sediment, and vegetation accruing over time. These areas will act to restore wildlife to the original riparian edge.

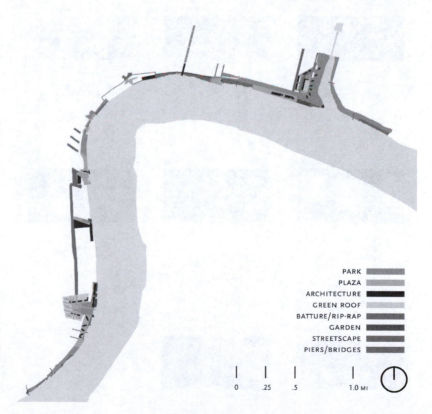

PARK
PLAZA
ARCHITECTURE
GREEN ROOF
BATTURE/RIP-RAP
GARDEN
STREETSCAPE
PIERS/BRIDGES

0    .25    .5    1.0 MI

9.4
**Reinventing the Crescent, six miles of public space plan. Provided by Hargreaves Associates**

The diverse landscape typologies along the riverfront construct a "terra fluxus" by taking into account the temporal qualities of the site – challenging climatic conditions and incorporating the unpredictable ecological future by avoiding over-determined programming of the spaces. A layered composition of open spaces also creates the potential for public space to expand and contract with the economic ebb and flow of the city as it evolves into the future.

Some of these places reinforce and enhance existing public domains, such as improving the riverfront's Moonwalk by creating a better pedestrian connection between it and Jackson Square. Others constitute new urban nodes, allowing the city to reconnect with the river's edge. Each of the new development nodes is strategically located to facilitate the mitigation of

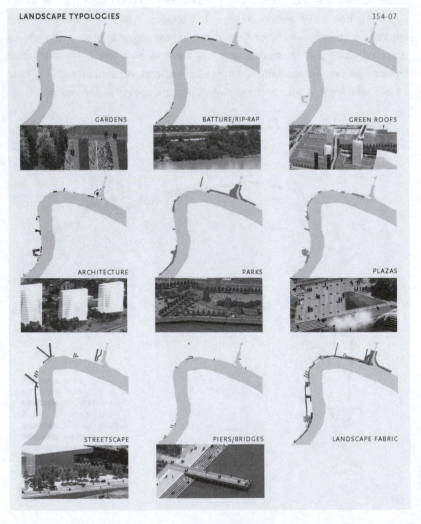

LANDSCAPE TYPOLOGIES                                           354-07

GARDENS          BATTURE/RIP-RAP          GREEN ROOFS

ARCHITECTURE          PARKS          PLAZAS

STREETSCAPE          PIERS/BRIDGES          LANDSCAPE FABRIC

9.5
**Reinventing the Crescent, six miles of public space typologies. Provided by Hargreaves Associates**

9.6
**Reinventing the Crescent, aerial view of Celeste Park from Jackson Avenue to Market Street. Provided by Hargreaves Associates**

physical barriers that have kept citizens at an "urban arm's length" from their river.

This proposal offers a range of ecological solutions, for example, the possibility that all future roofs – including the many acres of flat industrial roofs throughout New Orleans – be designed green. Consider the possibility of harvesting some of the 60 inches of rainfall that New Orleans endures each year, or greater local reliance on solar-powered hot-water heaters, by now a staple of many subtropical regions in the developing world. The scheme also advocates alternative energy sources, including wind and solar; expanding planted areas; reducing impervious surfaces; improving storm-water mitigation and reusing gray water for irrigation and sanitary applications. These are but a few of the many ways in which the proposal represents ecological aspirations to tread more lightly on the planet.

## Conclusion

In his introduction to Ecological Urbanism (2010), Mohsen Mostafavi posed the question, "Why Ecological Urbanism?" His response was:

Increased numbers of people and cities go hand in hand with a greater exploitation of the world's limited resources. Every year, more cities are feeling the devastating impacts of this situation. What are we to do? What means do we have as designers to address this challenging reality?[10]

As New Orleans approaches its 300th anniversary, projects such as those discussed here concretely illustrate the *feasibility* of bridging the divide between natural systems, human activity, and cultural identity. Defined by highly specific ecological objectives, each one adumbrates a unique proposition for a newer New Orleans. Conventional wisdom dictates the selection of a site for human settlement with *favorable natural conditions* – elevation, topography, water, air, risk of exposure to the sea and harsh weather. This wisdom – already expounded by Alberti in the fifteenth century, based on texts dating back to ancient Greece – was tacitly ignored by the founders of New Orleans, who willfully occupied and developed a place that many still believe should had never been developed. Clearly the only way forward is to recast urbanism itself with a restored emphasis on both the natural aspects of a city's site and the human dimensions of settlement.

The ULI report spurred the Viet Village Urban Farm and Reinventing the Crescent plan, which in turn tested projective ideas drawn from the general platform of ecological urbanism, invoking an emergent agenda that is attuned to the myriad species – human, plant, and animal – that share the diverse and sometimes conflicting habitats of New Orleans's fragile ecosystem. These studies and projects witness the transformative powers of urban and design collaborations as landscape architects, architects, urban planners, and urban designers blur disciplinary boundaries to respond to problems that afflict our cities today. As global climate change triggers even harsher weather and natural disasters, the nearly 200 million people worldwide who live in high-risk coastal flooding zones will be faced with challenges for which conventional urban planning currently has no response. The case studies presented here are evidence of fresh thinking about the ecological means at our disposal to reconfigure the urban realm. It is imperative to use these means to foster greater understanding of the value of the natural substrates, biodiversity, and cultural diversity, and to allow new conclusions to be drawn about where we humans, as a civilization, fit into the planetary ecosystem.

© Victor J. Jones

## Notes

1 Charles Waldheim coined the term "landscape urbanism." As he explained, "Landscape Urbanism describes a disciplinary realignment," in which "landscape replaces architecture as the basic building block of contemporary urbanism"; Waldheim, 2006, p. 11. Waldheim attributes this "realignment" to two main factors: first, a response to changing urban conditions from dense spatial concentration and a departure from the architectural fabric of the traditional city to a more contemporary urban organization of sparse horizontal surfaces and infrastructure across extensive land areas; second, a reaction to the wounds caused by the deindustrialization of city centers.

2 The term "ecological urbanism" had emerged at least by 2006, when it appeared in the title of a paper by Jeffrey Hou delivered to the 94th annual ACSA conference in Salt Lake City (March 30–April 3); see Hou, 2006. Mohsen Mostafavi elaborated on the idea in 2007 in his chapter on "Ecological Urbanism" (see Mostafavi, 2007) and in a talk he presented at an international colloquium at the Canadian Centre for Architecture in Montréal, entitled "Sustainable?" (June 16–17, 2007). As dean of the Graduate School of Design at Harvard University, he mounted a more extensive project on the subject, a conference and exhibition, and eventually the multi-authored volume he edited with Gareth Doherty, 2010. See also "ecology," in Williams, 1976.

3 In book 1, chapter 3 of *De re aedificatoria*, Leon Battista Alberti reflected on the requirements of the site – the *regio* or locality, as it has been translated – of a city, asserting almost immediately:

> For while there is no doubt that any defect of land or water could be remedied by skill and ingenuity, no device of the mind or exertion of the hand may ever improve climate appreciably; or so it is said.

As usual, he harks back to ancient writers on the subject as he develops the details of his argument. See Alberti, 1988, p. 9ff.

4 Lewis, 1976, p. 17.

5 Sublette, 2008, p. 8.

6 McHarg, 1969, p. 7.

7 Mossop, 2011.

8 Berman and el Khafif, 2008, p. 17.

9 Berger, 2006, p. 12.

10 Mostafavi and Doherty, 2010, p. 12.

Chapter 10

# Oslo – The Triumph of Zombie Urbanism

*Jonny Aspen*

Contemporary discourses on urban redevelopment and design are, at least as seen from the perspective of Northern Europe, surprisingly alike and homogeneous. They all subscribe to the idea that the future lies in building some version of "the creative city." It is a city being rebuilt based on the happy mix of creativity and knowledge with culture and urban consumption. In this chapter I examine the odd and striking consensus that drives many urban redevelopment projects and processes, especially the fact that overall attention seems to be given to the task of staging and marketing the city as vibrant and vital: cultural institutions, architecture and public spaces are ascribed new roles and meaning in urban policies and redevelopment.

The point of departure for discussing these development trends is that cities are different, often extremely so. Cities contain historical trajectories that point, inevitably, to different futures. It is therefore peculiar that architects, planners, and politicians, in the name of creativity, look for one and the same future city. The overall focus of the chapter is to figure out how such a situation has come about and with what effects. The argument is grounded on case study material from Oslo, Norway, and especially the large Fjord City project that is in the making.

# Entrepreneurial city development

Throughout the history of modern urban planning, planners have often been accused, especially by social scientists, of having a poor and restricted understanding of urban ways of life. The simple zoning principles of modernist planning were for a long time considered as emblematic of the planning profession's preoccupation with rigidity and order.[1] Even though time has changed and more flexible regimes of urban planning have been established, I still believe that the core concepts of urban planning and design can be accused of being stiff, rigid, and imprecise, maybe even more so than during the heroic modernist period. This may seem paradoxical, especially since planners and urban designers today claim to be more informed by "social" and "cultural" interests and values than before.

Increased inter-urban competition, due to deregulated political economies and global competition, seems to have effected a shift in the urban planning agenda of many cities.[2] This shift is most clearly reflected and celebrated in notions of "the creative city" and variations on culture-led urban redevelopment strategies. Cities and regions compete against each other in attracting investors, tourists, and the most qualified workforce, and in positioning themselves in the global agenda. Important assets in this competition are related to establishing institutions and amenities of culture, knowledge production, and urban consumption, besides mandatory factors such as good housing standards and a well-functioning infrastructure system.[3] Even though there are different voices in this narrative and slightly different factors that are given priority between cities, it seems that both the vocabulary used to describe challenges, ambitions, means, and assets, as well as the strategies and plans that are prescribed for regenerating the city, are surprisingly formulaic and increasingly similar.[4]

In a famous article on the transformation of urban governance in late capitalism, the urban geographer David Harvey describes a radical shift in urban politics starting in the 1970s, which he portrays as a change from managerialism to entrepreneurialism. The change marks a shift from managerial practices providing urban populations with local services, facilities, and benefits to a form of governance increasingly preoccupied with promoting and encouraging local development and employment growth; that is, an entrepreneurialism with an overall focus of making the city more attractive to the outside world. Harvey points out that this shift happens at different spatial scales, involves actors and stakeholders in public–private partnerships, and is directed at creating an attractive urban imagery through strategies of physical upgrading and selling places.[5]

The shift that Harvey describes can be considered a still ongoing process that increasingly informs strategies of urban development and design.

It's a shift that carries different names and has many eloquent proponents. Within urban policy and planning a common denominator seems to revolve around efforts to interconnect ideas about creativity, cultural strategies, and place making through architecture and design – as reflected in strategies of cultural planning and culture-led urban regeneration, as propagated in manifesto-like publications on the creative city (Charles Landry) and the creative class (Richard Florida), and as promoted by consultancies like Comedia and networks such as Knowledge Cities.[6] As Miles and Paddison put it: "What is remarkable here is not just the speed with which culture-driven strategies have become advocated by governments and local development agencies as means of bolstering the urban economy, but also how their diffusion has globalised."[7] My contribution to this volume will be to scrutinize some important features in the development here sketched out by focusing on a contemporary Norwegian planning situation and examining more closely the specific role and meanings of cultural institutions and public place production in a large, and in an international context fairly typical, urban waterfront redevelopment project.

## Zombie concepts

The core concepts in the increasingly homogeneous discourse on "the creative city" and the importance of culture in urban planning and redevelopment – the strategic goals they point out and the main ingredients and features that the discourse lays out as most important for redevelopment and urban design – resemble what the German sociologist Ulrich Beck has labeled zombie concepts. Zombie concepts are concepts that are still much in use, but no longer fit the reality they were intended to describe. They are concepts that are living dead, alive in our heads and our language, but not any longer useful for making precise propositions about what the world looks like and how it might be improved.[8] The perspective is that there are new kinds of driving forces in society and new types of complexity, all of which requires that we rethink and reconceptualize the basic notions of what constitutes society.

Even though Beck's perspective on zombie concepts derives from a more general theorizing about modernity, it also sheds light on contemporary discourses on "the creative city" and culture-led urban regeneration strategies in general and how they are translated in practice. It is especially interesting, and also worrying, to see that zombie discourses on urban redevelopment seem to run forward and spread on their own terms, apparently independent of what characteristics and challenges the cities adopting them have. As such there seems to be a mismatch between the words and concepts that are used, that is the planning discourse on "the creative city," and the actual state and challenges that many cities face. What makes this situation even more disturbing is the fact that the discourses concerned are not solely descriptive or analytical, but first and foremost prescriptive. One therefore not only runs the risk of operating with an inadequate understanding of the urban situation, but of actually building the new city on the basis of zombie concepts – of building zombie cities.

# Oslo's Fjord City plan

In what follows I shall examine more closely how discourses and strategies of urban regeneration and design are playing themselves out in Oslo. Special attention will be given to the city's Fjord City plan and the related planning of public urban places in the new harborfront areas. The argument is that urban design is given a new role both in terms of legitimizing large-scale urban redevelopment projects and in staging public places that are putatively vibrant and diverse.

The Fjord City plan for Oslo, which after many years of preparation and planning was finally approved by the City Council in February 2008, is an overall strategy for the urban development of the city's waterfront. As in many other cities throughout the world, removal of infrastructural functions and barriers along the central city coastal line, especially related to harbor activities, roads and industry, open up for massive urban redevelopment. Though the present plan for Oslo's new waterfront is neither especially typical nor that explicit in invoking creative city claims, it plays upon many of the same features and ingredients that one can find in the international discourse on creative cities and culture-led urban regeneration. This is most evident in the role prescribed for cultural institutions and in plans and strategies for creating public places.

This said, the most conventional and stereotypical aspect of the plan is related to what stands out as fairly rigid zoning principles and layout of roads and public areas. All blocks, roads, and public places are planned in detail in order to give predictability and sense of security. In the many illustrations that follow the actual Fjord City plan, and in the more specific plans for each of the 13 project areas, one can see pictures of vibrant new waterfront areas with all the ingredients from the international creative city discourse in place: iconic modern architecture, clean and tidy environments, the right amount of happy and smart-looking people occupying streets and public places, and glimpses of urban or natural scenery to indicate that the surrounding context is nice and enticing. The images are exceedingly seductive and compelling. All of this makes me quite suspicious. Not necessary because the new waterfront won't look as depicted when finished (the conventional mode of depicting future situations in architectural drawing allows for quite a degree of glorification), but precisely because it just might become what is imagined! What we can see is a kind of staged urbanism in which there is no room for irregularity and the unexpected, a neat and tedious urbanism based on a simplified understanding of the urban combined with more ideal aspirations – a kind of zombie urbanism.

The development areas along Oslo's waterfront constitute 225 hectares and cover more than 10 kilometers of the central shoreline (see Figure 10.1). It is divided into 13 project areas, all of them planned as comprehensive development projects. Some of these areas have already been subject to redevelopment, such as Aker Brygge and parts of Bjørvika (with the already famous new National Opera and Ballet building by Snøhetta) and Tjuvholmen. The Fjord City plan can be considered partly an overall strategy toward developing the whole of the waterfront, partly a guideline for the planning and assessment of the remaining areas to be redeveloped: "The idea of The Fjord City is to create better connections between the City Centre and the fjord, providing unique physical surroundings for living and leisure."[9] Instead of going in detail into all

10.1
**The Fjord City plan. Bjørvika is located in the eastern bay of the inner city.**
Source: City of Oslo and ViaNova

aspects of the plan, I will comment upon the plan for what is to become a new cultural institution axis along the waterfront, and, thereafter, examine how public spaces are to be planned, especially in Bjørvika.

The Bjørvika area is positioned between the sea and Oslo's main public transport hub (see Figure 10.2). The local development plan for the area was approved as early as in 2003. One million square meters of building is planned in an area of 70 hectares, for residential, commercial, and public purposes. A road tunnel was opened in 2010, relieving the area of much heavy road traffic. The already mentioned opera building was finished in 2008. It has developed into an architectural spectacle; the roof of the building has been taken into use as a public walking space, and the opera has become one of Norway's most visited tourist destinations. A more disputed development is the Barcode project, situated between the railway lines and what is to become the district's new main boulevard, Dronning Eufemias Street (replacing the existing motorway). The project, which involves a cluster of 12 more or less slim high-rise buildings placed side by side as in the pattern of a barcode, all designed by renowned Norwegian and international architects, has been criticized for both building heights and densities. The Barcode is said to become a wall that rather than opening the new waterfront district up to the existing city in fact closes it off. Another important development in Bjørvika is the Sørenga Pier, a former container port that is to be transformed into a new housing district interspersed with public functions such as a park and a waterfront promenade.

**10.2**
**The Fjord City plan – Bjøvika development area.**
Source: Oslo Waterfront Planning Office, City Of Oslo

# New cultural axis

It is, however, in terms of new cultural institutions that the district of Bjørvika recently has gained most attention and spurred much debate. In addition to the Opera House a new central library, Deichmanske Library (designed by Lund Hagem and Atelier Oslo Architects), and a new art museum, the Munch Museum and Stenersen Museum Collections, are being planned. The winning proposal for the latter project is a tall building of 12 floors named Lambda, designed by the Spanish architectural firm Herreros, which has been the subject of much dispute.[10] There are also plans for a new Museum of Cultural History in the area of the Medieval Park. All the new cultural institutions make deliberate use of state-of-the-art architecture and design features for purposes of identity building and branding. As Herreros says it: "we are consciously designing the postcard that everybody wants."[11] As such both the star architects involved and the signature buildings themselves play an important role in creating an image of a new and vibrant urban waterfront district. This is, of course, also how the politicians have reasoned it.

The prestigious new cultural institutions in Bjørvika, of which only the Opera House is yet completed, have in fact just recently been presented as components in what is to be seen as a new "National Axis of Culture" along Oslo's redeveloping waterfront. The intention is, as it is said in the city of Oslo's new architectural policy, to make the cultural axis "the capital city's most important factor for identity-building and marketing."[12] The cultural axis stretches from the new neighborhood of Tjuvholmen in the west, where Astrup Fearnley Museum of Modern Art is being built (designed by the famous Italian architect Renzo Piano), via the Vestbanen area just beside the Town Hall, where a new National Museum is to be built (designed by the German office Kleihues + Schuwerk), toward Bjørvika in the east, where, in addition to the already mentioned Opera House, Deichmanske Library, and Munch and Stenersen Museum, a new Museum of Cultural History, which possibly might also include a new Viking Ships Museum, is planned in the Medieval Park area at the eastern side of the bay.

Cities all over the world strive for a distinctive image that could be used for international branding, but surprisingly often they seem to rely on the same means. In Oslo the insertion of some of the nation's most important flagship cultural institutions as a strategy for regenerating the urban harborfront stands out as an explicit and consistent policy. The question that remains to be answered is whether such heavy cultural investments will pay off in terms of regeneration and branding profits. And even if it will become a success on such terms, one should take into consideration the total relocation costs. This includes the risk of the emptying out of places and buildings that today function well (as do most of the cultural institutions that are to be relocated to the harborfront), and the general danger of ignoring more prosaic amenity planning for the city's local residents.

## Public places in Oslo's Fjord City

Besides the cultural axis and prestigious cultural institution architecture, the most important aspect of the Fjord City plan when it comes to public benefits and attractions are the plans for public places and what is to become a continuous harbor promenade along the whole seafront development area. In their presentation of the Bjørvika plan, Oslo's Agency for Planning and Building Services says that "the town plan concept in the development plan is the seven public commons."[13] Thereby it becomes clear that it is first and foremost the public commons themselves that are to give the new district its specific urban character. Furthermore, the agency underlines that the public commons are "pedestrian urban spaces, which graphically resemble an open hand where the fingers stretch from the sea into the existing city." As such, the "public spaces will make the seafront accessible to the residents of the urban area behind the development area." The report is surprisingly defensive in its way of presenting the more public aspects of the plan: "The development will not be a barrier; on the contrary, it will open the area up and provide good accessibility which currently does not exist."[14] The impression one gets is that the main role of the new public places in the area is to legitimize the overall plan as such, including controversial issues related to what many criticize as high building heights and floor area ratios.

This is also clearly reflected in the prevailing plans and strategies of the landowners in Bjørvika.[15] The public space program for Bjørvika consists of seven public commons that are to be laid out in Bjørvika as an intersecting pattern stretching from west to east: the Fortress Common, the Opera Common, the Akerselva Common, the Station Common, Bispekilen, Kongsbakken, and the Lo Common. Their main function is to connect the existing city to the new developments in Bjørvika and to make the seafront more accessible. All the commons have an elongated form as they are laid out along a walkway, a riverbed, a greenbelt, or as a more open public area in order to bridge the existing city with the new harborfront (Figure 10.3). The commons are described in very insistent and assertive ways, as if there has been an urgent need to convince the public about the plan's good intentions and the bright and lively future that is to come. In describing the Opera Common, the developer, Bjørvika Development, finds it necessary to highlight that it will become "a great gathering place for events that will create liveliness and activity."

Furthermore,

> The common is an open space that will shift between active and passive conditions, and a hub for movements in many directions and speeds. The common will be given a simple design, and the presence of water in combination with places to sit down and rest, will be like an oasis in the modern city.[16]

The same strange combination of insistency and approximation is found in the description of the Station Common. The common, which will become the most central urban space in Bjørvika, will have "urban life and activity both throughout the day and over the year," and "it'll be facilitated both for places to stay and close interaction between urban spaces and adjacent buildings."[17] How such facilitation will take place is apparently in no need of further explanation or validation.

The descriptions of the other five commons in Bjørvika continue in much the same manner. The commons are to be built according to comprehensive design principles and considerations, in which all relevant design aspects, including lighting, sun and wind conditions, and sightlines to historical landmarks in the city, have been the object of thorough analysis by the winning team of the architectural competition, the Danish urban design office Gehl Architects.[18] The striking thing when it comes to how the commons are described is, however, that, as shown in the example of the Opera Common and the Station Common, the whole discourse on the social functions and cultural meanings of the new

10.3
**Ice on the pond at the future south side of the Opera Common.**
Source: Bjørvika Infrastructure Ltd./ SLA Landscape Architects

public places seems so forced and distended. The language about public spaces is overtly promotional and legitimizing: "Opportunities for activities to invite life into the new public spaces have been maximized to reconnect the new development areas to the existing city fabric."[19]

All of the written assertions are supported by colorful illustrations, many of them hyper-realistic perspective drawings, of what the public places will look like when completed (Figure 10.4). The illustrations add texture and substance to the written descriptions and make the public urban design solutions look even more attractive and credible. Furthermore, they show urban places that either are lively and vibrant, with an urban scenography representing a civilized feel or atmosphere, or have a kind of calm and sensuous quality, for example in terms of architectural and spatial articulation. The latter can be said to add dimensions of picturesque and even pastoral meaning to the depicted scenery. The pictures show public places that are used in meaningful and decent ways, there is no mess or conflict, there are no obstacles or fenced-off footpaths, no people bumping into each other or tiresome congestion, no threatening drug addicts or annoying beggars, no icy and slippery pavements, no muddy water drops or dirty snowdrifts, nor any cold wind or pouring rain.

10.4
**The future Station Common.**
Source: Oslo S Utvikling/Placebo

Neither is there any dust or offensive smoke, garbage or pollution, noise or obtrusive smell. All in all there is nothing frightening, strange, or discomforting about the scenery displayed, it is all pleasant and appealing. Thus the illustrations tell us that there are no reasons to believe that the new public places in Bjørvika will be anything but nice and pleasant places to be in. As such the seductiveness of the illustrations play an important role in making the public believe that there are serious plans for truly public places. They play a major role as a legitimizing authority for the whole waterfront redevelopment.

The soft and poetic reference world of the illustrations stands out as a salutary and radical contrast to the harsher pragmatics and politics of urban redevelopment in this area in general, as well as to the more hardcore economic logic and rhetoric of landowners and real estate developers more specifically. Even though the illustrations are based on fairly conventional ways of representing urban scenery and iconography, they function as a vision for future Oslo (Figure 10.5). As such the illustrations refer both to a known past, in terms of urban ways of life and conduct that people know and like, and to an enticing near future; they inform both the Fjord City plan's historical legitimacy and its overall aim.

There obviously has been an urgent need to cover up both the fact that the existing plans are purely based on fairly traditional design solutions and aesthetic considerations (even though the design language is more contemporary in terms of formal vocabulary, materials, and so on) and that one has very little knowledge about how the places will actually function and be put into use when completed. All the social functions and cultural meanings that the public

10.5
**The future Opera Common at night.**
Source: Bjørvika Infrastructure Ltd./ SLA Landscape Architects

places are assumed to live up to in the future, are based on fairly simple and stereotypical assumptions about what constitutes vibrant urban public places. These assumptions have strong resemblance with zombie concepts. They play up to ideas that most people would subscribe to regarding the attractiveness of inclusive and vibrant public places, while at the same time cover up the fact that the actual challenges of creating such places are not really confronted (Figures 10. 4 and 10.5). Let me take as an example the plans for the harbor promenade. Apparently all relevant factors seem to have been researched and planned for in detail. In this way zombie modes of thinking are disguised behind curtains of thorough surveying and planning.

## The harbor promenade

The harbor promenade will, when completed, stretch through the entire Fjord City development area, but I will restrict my comments to the Bjørvika section of the promenade. The promenade is described very much in the same way as the public commons, but may be even more eloquent and verbose:

> The Harbor Promenade will link together the various commons and generally make the area a recreational space. The Promenade will act as a link between the existing city and the fjord and cater for the variety of identities and functions that are to be found in Bjørvika.

Furthermore, the planning agency states that

> In order for The Promenade to provide the city with unique experiences and activities, it will offer a very varied urban life, making it attractive to a wide range of people both from all over the city and locally from the area. Here, recreation and activities will be offered for young and old, families, office workers and children. Both large- and small-scale activities will be offered, in addition to places that are both vibrant and intensive.[20]

Since the promenade will stretch along the entire waterfront of Bjørvika, issues of diversity and functional mix are highlighted far more than in the plans for the public commons.

Just as with the latter, it becomes clear that the promenade, considered as a public space, is assigned overall important functions in redeveloping the city's harborfront. One such function is to safeguard and provide access to the waterfront as such, for people living and working in the area, and for people from other parts of the city and for visitors. A second important function is to connect the different parts of both the Bjørvika waterfront area and the entire Fjord City development. It is tempting to see such functions as an undeniable good. They add new features and qualities to the city, both in terms of providing better access to one of the city's main natural and recreational resources, namely the fjord and the waterfront, and in providing the city with new public and recreational places. However, as for the public commons, much of the rhetoric around developing the harbor promenade, when it comes to both written statements and visual representations, seems quite overstated and overdone. In an information leaflet from the Agency for Planning and Building Services the harbor promenade is presented in the following way:

> Various cultural and recreational amenities will lie like pearls on a string along the course of the waterfront promenade. The waterfront promenade will be open to all and attract a broad group of users thanks to its universal design and rich range of activities and recreational facilities.[21]

As the quotation indicates, the entire project of making a harbor promenade becomes both overloaded with symbolic meanings and overburdened with claims and expectations. The promenade is given the overall role of providing and safeguarding a whole range of social and cultural values related to urban living and public space use, in terms of attractiveness, multitude, safety, openness, and inclusiveness. This is not to say that the existing plans totally lack contextual consideration or analysis. In fact, the contrary is very much the case. Almost everything seems to be studied and planned in detail. Gehl Architects, the urban design office that won the open international competition for designing the public spaces in Bjørvika, has made a detailed program report for the promenade, as for each of the seven public commons.

The report from the jury of the competition on public places in Bjørvika gives some clues about what priorities such urban design thinking revolves around. The jury says that the winning proposal's "consistent strong forms and aesthetic coherent solution accommodates for experiences and social life."[22] The jury's statement about the winning proposal, called "New urban life," reflects the fact that overall emphasis is put on physical design solutions and related aspects of materials and natural elements.

Both in the jury's deliberations and in Gehl Architects' public space program overall priority is given to features and factors that can be quantified and mapped, such as sightlines at different points along the promenade, distribution of destinations and attractions, water qualities and wind conditions, and shifting sun conditions.[23] In the program for the promenade, all possible factors and features seem to have been accounted for, however with a bias toward factors and features that the urban designers can control and manipulate, either on paper or, at a later stage, on site. As soon as more simple social issues are touched upon, that is, how the promenade will be used and what kind of activities people are assumed to be involved in, the statements are much looser and less binding. According to Gehl Architects, the promenade will, when completed, "offer a broad fan of variations and differences when it comes to atmospheres, characters, and identities." Furthermore, "there will be room for activities both in the small and large scale, and provided for living and intensive places."[24]

In their public space program, Gehl Architects even presents a set of "diagrams of life" that are to guarantee, it seems, that all important features of a rich social life will be provided for, such as activities for all kinds of users and a mixed distribution of attractions and destinations along the promenade. To make sure that no one misses the point, it is said that the overall intention is to guarantee "great variation in activities and spatial experiences."[25] Still, the program statements and the diagrammatic representations stand out as fairly general and without obligation; they seem to mean everything and nothing. The program plays up to notions about variety and multitude, but is undeniably generic when it comes to approach and content. Thus the language used is full of non-binding phrases like "one should provide varying activities and experiences" and "attractive and fluctuating destinations must be established."[26] This is why such modes of urban design thought, despite thorough analysis and detailed programming, and despite all good intentions and aims, end up simplifying the whole notion of public place production.

My argument is that the current way of conceptualizing, reasoning about, and designing urban public places – and the zombie-like concepts and understandings of what such places are, what they mean, and how they are used that such thinking and practice is based on – represents a barrier toward more creative and experimental ways of working. The challenges involved in creating inviting, inclusive, and exciting public places are underestimated. The designers and planners rely too much on physical design solutions and established aesthetic preferences (and of course all features that can be measured and calculated, such as weather conditions and sightlines). And they pay too little attention to the whereabouts, preferences, and aspirations of actual and potential users, not to mention all the uncertainties, unpredictability, and dynamics that impact upon how people use the city in general and its public places in particular. What appears to be missing in the design and planning of public places is a more thorough understanding of the dynamics of social encounters and uses of public places in urban settings. Herein lies the missing link. But it is not a link that is easily reintroduced into urban planning and design, especially since it will presuppose an entirely different approach and way of thinking. Disturbingly enough, the more specific urban design strategies for the Fjord City that have been the object of our inquiry can be said to be a clear reflection of more overall city policies for urban development and the role of architecture and urban design in such a context.

# Architectural policy for Oslo

The general plans for the Fjord City and its different redevelopment areas and the more specific plans for public places and a harbor promenade all reflect the fact that qualities of architecture and urban environments are ascribed greater importance in urban politics than before (Figure 10.6). Increasing inter-urban competition and the happy news of city branding has made architecture and urban design more important in both urban politics and the economy. The architectural discipline clearly seems to have increased its status, but there are also some quite serious disadvantages in this development. One problematic aspect is that since urban environments, as in the case of Bjørvika, are ascribed with new symbolic meaning and function, the practice of producing and regenerating urban environments has become much more infused with politics, commercial interests, and branding strategies (and as such also with many of the zombie concepts that flourish in such disciplines). Another misfortune is that many architects appear to be concerned more with their new role as makers of urban scenography and symbols than in doing serious examination and experimentation with what makes buildings and places interesting and exciting in terms of social exchange and public functions.

Many of these developments are reflected in a white paper on the overall policy for Oslo's architecture, produced by the planning agency in 2009. Already in the introduction it is emphasized that "conscious use of architecture and urban development in marketing Oslo" is an important task.[27] The overall vision of the new architectural policy is to facilitate for sustainability and growth. In a future situation the capital city will "by way of its innovative everyday and

10.6
**The Bjørvika development area, fall 2011. Photo by Jonny Aspen**

monumental architecture [be] a model both inland and abroad for Norwegian quality of life, democracy, and sustainability."[28] The white paper then accounts for seven areas of priority in the proposal for a new architectural policy for the city. Even though many of the suggestions can be said to be reasonable and well-thought-out, such as emphasizing that the public should act as good role models in construction and urban policy and the insistence on, for example, infrastructure as place-constructing structures of major importance, the document is, as is usual in such policy papers, full of overall and ideal statements and abstract description of strategic goals. What is missing is a notion of everyday life. There is no engagement with the quotidian, with people's lived experiences, aspirations, and hopes. Many of the statements are well meant and important, but put in very general language: in the priority area of public construction, for instance, the aim is to develop prototype projects emphasizing "inclusive, beautiful and accessible squares, parks and urban spaces."[29] Such language, even though it is probably hard totally to avoid in an overall strategic document, has the negative effect that it easily makes a reader mistrust what is being said. The reason for this lies in the discrepancy between the complexities of the issue at hand, that is how to make genuine public places, and the generality of the language being used, which is of a kind that undermines and levels out all controversies and contradictions in such an endeavor. There is, for example, no reflection upon the challenge of translating people's needs and aspirations, different, shifting and contradictory as they often are, into inclusive and well-functioning public places. Neither are issues of unpredictability or the transformative potentials of urban living and conduct touched upon. The language involved is zombie-like in that it resonates with what many people consider as overall important values in genuine public places, for instance that they are nice-looking and welcoming, but has little correspondence with urban reality as we know it or as we have reason to believe it will become in the future. Urban living is characterized by ambiguity and contradictions. It is both exciting and tedious, delightful and stressful, enriching and exhausting, comprehensible and bewildering. So instead of treating the public features of urban living as a coherent quantity that can easily be manipulated, issues of complexity and difference and of, for example, future uncertainty, should be taken far more seriously in discussions around the making of public places.

The dangers of using a zombie-like language are of two kinds. One risk is that all kinds of complexity, controversy, and resistance are excluded from the challenging discussion of how to make public places proper. Therefore one very often ends up with simplified discussions and, consequently, very simplified proposals and solutions. The second danger is that what eventually is constructed, be it a public square, a promenade, or the like, very likely will become just as zombie-like as the language used to describe and resonate about it. Zombie concepts make for zombie urbanism. All of this is, of course, triggered and reinforced by the fact that most people, after all, will be tempted to believe in the proclamations that are made, ideal in content and therefore hard to refuse as they are.

## Toward a more grounded urbanism

What seems to be missing in the contemporary discourse on urban harborfront redevelopment in Oslo, which in essence is a replication of an international discourse on "the creative city," is first and foremost openness to and dialogue with existing urban realities. There are at least three dimensions of urban reality that seem to have no or little resonance in the way planners and urban designers conceptualize new public places. First, there are few traces of how the city's existing social and cultural diversity will inform the programming and design of public places in the new waterfront. Second, there seems to be no reflection upon the fact that Oslo during the last decades has developed into a multicultural city in which more than one in four of the city's inhabitants originate outside Norway. That different ethnic minority groups might use and perceive public places in multiple ways, and that such a multitude of uses and perceptions might represent vital and new potentials, seems to be of no interest for the planners and urban designers creating the city's new harborfront. Third, issues related to digitalization of cities and urban living, and in what way it will affect how public places are used and conceived, has yet to inform our way of urban thinking and reasoning.

The three sets of deficiencies that are mentioned here indicate that the redevelopment strategies are weakly grounded. Even though the Fjord City plan pleads to be "an adventurous urban renewal project" that will "provide for new and improved living conditions for Oslo's inhabitants and visitors," there are essential forces of urban development that are not taken into account.[30] Such omissions and blind spots reflect that there are vibrant urban realities that planners and urban designers are not seeing. One aspect that is surprisingly often overlooked consists of the needs and desires that constitute many people's longing for urbanity and urban ways of life. People are attracted to cities that are more than neat and nice, safe and tidy. People also value excitement and challenge, they want to explore and experience things unknown and unexpected, they long for places where multiple desires can be played out. No other places are better suited for enabling such pursuits than urban environments that allow for some complexity and disorder.[31] The reason such issues are neglected could very well be of a similar kind as the one Ulrich Beck raises against mainstream social scientists: as for social scientists, the minds of planners and urban designers seem to be "haunted and clouded by dead ideas that make [them] look in the wrong places and miss what's new."[32] In the same way as many social scientists have a weak understanding of how forces of globalization and transnationalism are shaping contemporary society, many planners and urban designers have a weak understanding of the forces shaping cities and informing urban living. As such the planners and urban designers' concept of urbanity is fairly restricted. In the Fjord City, public places and neighborhood qualities are obviously not to be seen as something that will develop over time as a more or less unpredictable result of a complex set of interactions and interrelations between built-up areas, functional characteristics, open spaces (of very diverse kinds), human uses, needs and aspirations, and a range of factors related to appropriation, attractiveness and cultural meaning. Rather than taking on the exciting but demanding venture of examining the complexities and ambiguities of contemporary urban development and urban ways of life, not to say the even more demanding task of figuring out how such features could be translated into urban design strategies or used as an inspiration for such, the planners and urban designers resort to stereotypical notions of social life and urban public places.

The rhetoric about the creative city has, as I have endeavored to show in this chapter, damaging effects for the reasoning about and design of public spaces in urban redevelopment areas such as Oslo's Fjord City. There is a great irony in this since urban theorists have for so long complained about urban planners and designers' neglect of the city's social and cultural qualities. So when such issues finally are put on planners and urban designers' agendas, they just seem to end up as yet another set of instrumental concerns that makes the designer, more than ever, a kind of universal stage designer for a play that is yet to be written. Thus what we still need are yet more critical perspectives on contemporary urban development strategies, as well as more theoretically and empirically informed discourses on the local specifics of cities. Because cities are not only different in comparison to each other, they are in themselves also containers of difference. Both such perspectives must be taken into consideration in order to establish a richer and more vital discourse on future cities.

Furthermore, we need to remind ourselves that urban living is full of ambiguities and contradictions, and must be so in order to sustain its vibrancy and vitality. It seems to me that it is in relation to just this point that the narrative on the creative city, and its translation into urban design strategies, falls short. Not everything urban can or should be controlled. Especially not when one aspires to make truly public places. Therefore we will have to look in the dark shadows of the discourse on the creative city, and the many zombie concepts it is based on, to get in touch with the inherent tensions that make urban living at one and the same time attractive and repulsive.

## Notes

1  Sandercock, 1998.
2  Miles and Paddison, 2005.
3  Miles and Paddison, 2005.
4  Evans, 2006; Miles, 2010.
5  Harvey, 1989.
6  Landry, 2000; Florida, 2002.
7  Miles and Paddison, 2005, p. 833.
8  Ulrich Beck's argument is that the key concepts within the social sciences have gone out of date, i.e. the basic concepts of classical or foundational social theories. Zombie categories "haunt our thinking," he says, and "focus our attention on realities that are steadily disappearing" (Beck and Willms, 2004, p. 19). This goes especially for categories connected with nationalism and social-class movements, and more generally for ethnocentric Western perspectives on societal evolution (Gane, 2004). All such key concepts have their origin in what Beck sees as the period of *first modernity*. Since then society has moved on to a new phase of *second modernity*, characterized by massive globalization and individualization.
9  Agency for Planning and Building Services, information leaflet, August 2008 (my translation).
10  The Lambda project is not yet approved by the City Council of Oslo. Due to shifting political alliances the project as it now stands (November 2012) seems not to have acquired political support.
11  www.arcspace.com/architects/herreros/munch_museum/munch_museum.html (accessed October 5, 2011).
12  Agency for Planning and Building Services, 2009, p. 23 (my translation).
13  Agency for Planning and Building Services, 2007, p. 4 (my translation).
14  All citations Agency for Planning and Building Services, 2007, p. 4 (my translation).
15  The landowners of Bjørvika are organized as Bjørvika Development Ltd. Bjørvika Development Ltd., again, has established Bjørvika Infrastructure Ltd., which was formed with the purpose of having overall responsibility for all technical infrastructure in Bjørvika, including public areas such as the designated seven public commons. For more information, see handout from Bjørvika Development Ltd./Bjørvika Infrastructure Ltd., 2011.
16  Bjørvika Development Ltd., 2011a (my translation).
17  Bjørvika Development Ltd., 2011b (my translation).
18  Gehl Architects has developed specific public space programs for all of the seven public commons in Bjørvika. All of them are available at the homepage of Bjørvika Development: www.bjorvikautvikling.no/Byromsprogram/53EBBE5D-6CCE-47FF-B63C-90F9D8DC902E/1.
19  Gehl Architects, information leaflet, 2005.
20  Agency for Planning and Building Services, 2007, p. 12 (my translation).
21  Agency for Planning and Building Services, 2008 (my translation).
22  Oslo Waterfront Planning Office, 2005, p. 3 (my translation).
23  Bjørvika Infrastructure Ltd./Gehl Architects ApS, 2006.
24  Bjørvika Infrastructure Ltd./Gehl Architects ApS, 2006, pp. 20–21 (my translation).
25  Bjørvika Infrastructure Ltd./Gehl Architects ApS, 2006, p. 24 (my translation).
26  Bjørvika Infrastructure Ltd./Gehl Architects ApS, 2006, pp. 24–25 (my translation).
27  Agency for Planning and Building Services, 2009, p. 5 (my translation).
28  Agency for Planning and Building Services, 2009, p. 14 (my translation).
29  Agency for Planning and Building Services, 2009, p. 14 (my translation).
30  Agency for Planning and Building Services, 2008 (my translation).
31  See also Evans, 2006; Miles, 2010.
32  Beck and Willms, 2004, p. 52.

Chapter 11

# Philadelphia – The Urban Design of Philadelphia: Taking the Towne for the City

*Richard M. Sommer*

William Penn developed the plan of what is now known as center-city Philadelphia in the middle of the seventeenth century. Penn's plan for Philadelphia, an alloy of Quaker Utopianism and colonial real-estate speculation, is distinguished not only for its influence as a prototype in the founding of subsequent American cities, but for the ways in which its basic outlines have continued to endure in the form of the city's historical center. Although not unique among North American cities for having been established with a deliberate plan, Philadelphia's evolution over the past three centuries presents an singularly important case through which to examine the interplay between the concepts embodied in an originating plan, the material characteristics of the plan itself, and the historical circumstances that transform, usurp or supersede that plan.

Prescribing a precise layout of streets, squares and boundaries, Penn's scheme sought, but fell short of achieving, an ideal combination of the pastoral order of a seventeenth-century English gentleman's country farm with the market and communal functions of a town. The anomalies and omissions found in Penn's plan may be explained by the conflicts of use and spatial incompatibilities that arise from this somewhat unique attempt at a hybrid urban settlement. In what follows, the fate of both the ideas and the forms that have endured from Penn's plan are taken as a synecdoche for the larger conditions and urban geographies that have come to characterize Philadelphia today. Several issues are at play in such a reading. Foremost among these are questions concerning the interplay between so-called planned and un-planned aspects of cities; that is to say, the very usefulness of distinguishing between conscious, comprehensive efforts to project or reform the layout of a city, and the effects of more piecemeal forms of land development. Also at play is the recurring appeal, within American culture, of a pre-industrial, pastoral vision of the city.

Two moments stand out as examples of deliberate planning and design in Philadelphia: the crafting of Penn's original plan, and planning efforts undertaken three centuries later that came to fruition in redevelopment projects led by the city planner Edmund Bacon. In between these two moments, and during the period of its greatest expansion, Philadelphia grew primarily by means of *laissez-faire* commercial development. Along with the extension of existing suburban patterns, new territories were surveyed and platted in an entirely perfunctory way. Pressure to plan and manage unbridled growth built up towards the end of the nineteenth century, following the city's incorporation of all of the surrounding county's townships in 1854. This incorporation made Penn's "walking city" just one-tenth of an emerging metropolis.

This study of Philadelphia will concentrate on the symbolic and functional role that its historical core has come to play within a city whose physical extents have grown well beyond its original boundaries. For aging industrial cities such as Philadelphia, whose populations and economic fortunes have been in steadily decline since the 1950s, the fate of the historical core is especially important. Such a reading of Philadelphia necessitates retracing the assumptions and critically accessing the planning and urban design efforts led by Edmund Bacon during three decades of major transformations in the middle of the twentieth century. Harking back to the authority of William Penn's vision for the city – and the city's colonial prominence as the "cradle of liberty" – Bacon's efforts focused on reinvigorating the historical core by using new projects and infrastructure to recast implicitly the original figures and boundaries of William Penn's plan.

In weighing the hegemony of schemes orchestrated by Bacon in Philadelphia against both Penn's founding principles and 250 intervening years of "un-planned" changes to the form of the city, I hope to explore two interconnected dilemmas which generally plague the professional practice of urban design. The first concerns how the goals of urban design are established relative to the question of what distinguishes a metropolis from a town.[1] The second concerns the analytical means used to establish a methodological ground to justify such goals, including the ways in which a city's historical and contemporary form are framed, evaluated and characterized in the urban design process. To examine Philadelphia in this context will require a short historical survey of its founding plan and evolution, an analysis of some of the projects that prefigured Bacon's work in the early twentieth century and a rehearsal of the background, intentions and outcome of Bacon's work itself.

## Philadelphia's propitious beginning: William Penn's plan

In exchange for the settlement of a debt with the estate of Admiral Penn, in 1670 Charles II of England established a charter granting his son William Penn as proprietor and governor of 26,000,000 acres in the American Colonies. Named Pennsylvania, the territories granted were in the mid-Atlantic region of the colonies bordered by Delaware and New Jersey on the eastern coast. Penn had already gained experience in the planning, development and governance of colonial cities in the region, having participated in establishing the provincial capitals of Burlington and Amboy (later Perth-Amboy) in New Jersey.[2] The plan of Burlington presages the general disposition of Philadelphia, but without its innovations or distinct gridiron. At Burlington Penn employed the most fundamental of town-making devices, which he would later repeat at Philadelphia; the establishment of two main crossing roads – in this case a "high" street and a "broad" street.

While the form of these earlier cities in which Penn participated provides some insight into the later planning of Philadelphia, they are perhaps more indicative of Penn's entrepreneurial skill. He was adroit at establishing colonial settlements that would attract his fellow Quakers with the combined promise of commercial opportunity and freedom from religious persecution in England.

Seven months after he received the charter from Charles II, Penn selected three commissioners to accompany the first group of settlers to Pennsylvania. Drawing on his previous experience with colonial towns, Penn drew up an elaborate memorandum for the commissioners that included detailed and pragmatic directives on how to select a site for the city, taking into consideration the acreage needed. Penn asked that a site be chosen along the Delaware River where the rivers and creeks are "sounded" (long and broad) on his side and where "it is most navigable, high, dry, and healthy; that is, where most ships may best ride, of deepest draught of water . . ."[3]

He then instructed that (my italics):

> 3d: Such a place being found out, for navigation, healthy situation and good soil for provision, *lay out ten thousand acres contiguous to*

*it in the best manner you can, as the bounds and extent of the liberties of the said town.*[4]

After the selection of a proper site, Penn also specified the uniform way in which the streets, parcels and buildings would need to be disposed, asking the commissioners to "12th: Be sure to settle the figure of the town so as that the streets hereafter may be uniform down to the water from the country bounds . . ."[5]

Penn's instructions concerning the placement of houses is perhaps the most revealing of his intentions for the character of the town:

> 15th: Let every house be placed, if the person pleases, in the middle of it plat, as to the breadth way of it, so that there may be ground on each side for gardens or orchards, or fields, that it may be a green county town, which will never be burnt, and always be wholesome."[6]

Following Penn's instructions, the commissioners selected a "high and dry" site where the bank of the Delaware River ran closest and parallel to the banks of Skulkill River, the main inland tributary in the area. A few Dutch and Swedish settlers had already established themselves in the area. There is some ambiguity as to the sequence of events that led up to the completion of a formal plan for the city in 1683. Penn appointed Captain Thomas Holme as surveyor general, but he did not arrive until June of 1682, after the site for the city had already been selected. Holme worked with the commissioners on a plan, of which no record survives, but it is understood to have only covered an area extending halfway from the Delaware Bank towards the banks of the Skulkill. What is now understood as the original plan did not emerge until Penn joined Holme four months later. Anticipating the success of Philadelphia and "future comers," Penn had the city extended to the banks of the Skulkill, allowing for a front on each river. In a short time Penn and Holme finalized the plans. A survey was prepared and lots were sold. A year later Holmes published *A Portraiture of the City of Philadelphia* with a written narrative and "Plat-form" meant to draw new settlers (Figure 11.1). Holme's drawing and narrative describes the pattern of streets and public squares that still define central Philadelphia:

> the City of Philadelphia now extends in Length from River to River, two Miles and in Breadth near a Mile . . .
> The City (as the model shews) consists of a large Front-street to each River and a High-street (near the middle) from Front (or River)

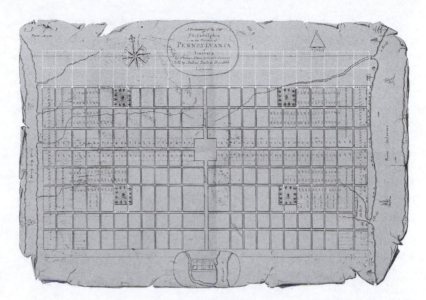

**11.1**
**Plat-form (plan)**
**of Philadelphia**
**in 1682, after**
**Thomas Holme,**
**surveyor (Olin**
**Library, Cornell**
**University)**
Source: As
published in John
W. Reps, *The
Making of Urban
America: A History
of City Planning in
the United States*
(Princeton, NJ:
Princeton University
Press, 1965)

to front, of one hundred Foot broad, and a Broad-street in the middle of the City, form side to side, of the like breadth. In the center of the City is a Square of ten Acres; at each Angle there are to be Houses for Public Affairs, as a Meeting House, Assembly or State-House, Market-House and several other buildings for Publick Concerns. There is also in each Quarter of the city a Square of eight Acres, to be for like Uses, as the Moore-fields in London; and eight Streets, (besides the High-street), that run from Front to Front, and twenty Streets, (besides the Broad-street) that run cross the City, from side to side; all these Streets are of Fifty Foot breadth[7]

The creation of a great "city or town" was central to Penn's plans for a "Holy experiment" in the colonies. "Holy experiment" refers to the then novel idea that adherents of differing religious faiths and political convictions would be free to settle and live side by side in these new territories. Thus the use of the name Philadelphia, borrowed from the name of the ancient city in Asia Minor and the Greek term for "city of brotherly love."

Penn's scheme for Philadelphia was founded on the proposition that each investor in a large rural parcel in Pennsylvania would also receive a "bonus" plot within a large, new capital city.

"I.: That as soon as it pleaseth God ... a certain quantity of land shall be laid out for a large town or city ... and every purchaser shall, by lot, have so much land therein as will answer to the

proportion which he hath bought or taken up upon rent. But it is
to be noted that the surveyor shall consider what roads or highways will be necessary to the cities, towns, or through the lands
... and V.: That the proportion of lands that shall be laid out in the
first great city or town, for every purchaser, shall be after the proportion of ten acres for every five hundred acres purchased, if the
place will allow it."[8]

The linking of large rural tracts to plots in a planned town quickly – and artificially – established European settlement patterns in Pennsylvania that might
have otherwise taken a century or more to achieve. Unlike earlier (and some
later) colonial settlers, who had to build homes, locate ports, and found markets
in essentially wilderness conditions, investors in Pennsylvania could anticipate
a settlement plot in a well-planned community.

# The fate of Penn's colonial plan

Foreshadowing Thomas Jefferson's agrarian vision for the United States, Penn
sought to create, through a highly speculative real-estate venture, a pastoral
yet culturally and economically pluralistic town that would balance the effects
of trade with the civilizing effects of a landed gentry. Philadelphia would be a
"wholesome," "green country town," serving the ideals of religious freedom
while tempering the barbarous effects of trade. Although many of Penn's investors were involved in maritime-based trade, and his instructions for the selection of a site gave priority to the founding of a port, Penn believed that profits
made from the ownership and management of land were morally more defens-
ible than those made from trade.

Penn's original 1683 Plan is consistent with this desire, as it fluctu-
ates between an ideal "checkerboard" geometry, the accommodation of local
geographic circumstance and the anticipation of future extensions into, and
annexations of, the surrounding countryside.

The city's gridiron layout, subdivided into four quadrants by a
"broad" and a "high" street, was fairly typical for colonial towns and had
numerous Spanish and English precedents. Penn and Holmes' subtle innovation was the placement of a large, open public square at the crossing of the two
main streets, and one additional square within each of the four quadrants. John
Reps has conjectured that Penn or Holme may have been inspired by Richard
Newcourt's 1666 plan for the reconstruction of London, which also contains
an equal distribution of five open spaces within a field of regular, rectangular
blocks.[9] Yet the difference between these two plans may be as illuminating

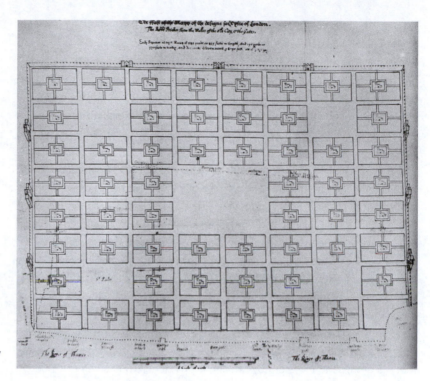

**11.2**
**Design for the**
**rebuilding of**
**London, Richard**
**Newcourt, 1666**
**(retouched**
**by John W.**
**Reps, from a**
**reproduction in**
**Towne Planning**
**Review, Vol. 18,**
**No. 3 (1939))**
Source: As
published in John
W. Reps, *The*
*Making of Urban*
*America: A History*
*of City Planning in*
*the United States*
(Princeton, NJ:
Princeton University
Press, 1965)

as their similarities. Despite being conceived to reorganize both existing areas and the parts of London destroyed by the great fire in 1666, the Newcourt plan is entirely symmetrical, with an equal number of blocks emanating from the central square in each direction. Newcourt also maximized the value of each of the quadrant's public squares by surrounding them on all sides with developable frontage (Figure 11.2).

In contrast to Newcourt's London plan, the Philadelphia plan exhibits some striking anomalies. The southern half of the Philadelphia plan is similar to the London plan: platting five blocks to the south of the east–west High (now Market) Street divide allowed public squares to be positioned at roughly the center of their quadrants. Yet only three blocks to north of High Street were platted, leaving the northern boundary of the public squares exposed. There was also great variation in the size of the rectangular blocks, and their geometry was at odds with that of the squares. The plan pragmatically places rectangular blocks with their long face oriented along the north–south streets, maximizing potential access to daylight. Yet despite the prevailing rectangular geometry, the public squares are projected as absolutely "square." The mismatch between the geometry of the squares and the blocks produces a set of irregular spaces around more than half the frontages of the squares, without planning for any public streets between the squares and the parcels (see dashed overlay on Figure 11.1).

The anomalies in the Philadelphia plan aptly illustrate Penn's struggle to balance Utopian ideals with the exigencies of real estate and land governance. At stake was a legal and symbolic connection between the city and its outlying districts, and the authority of the plan itself to maintain the projected boundaries and disposition of blocks, parcels and set-aside public squares.

A vast amount of Pennsylvania land was already under contract prior to the platting of Philadelphia. The promise of a 2 percent bonus city plot would have been impossible to accommodate within the scale of a sixteenth-century colonial city (or any city at that time). The planned city, at 1,280 acres, would have provided roughly less than one-fifth of the needed parcels, all of which would have exceeded the average seven-acre size of the city blocks. Penn's first ideas for Philadelphia included surrounding a compact rectangular town between the rivers with gentlemanly estates of 80 acres, with the house at the center of each plot separated by at least 800 feet (Figure 11.3). When the geography of the surrounding areas made this pattern of development a difficult prospect, Penn instead, through a questionably legal sleight-of-hand, met his promise to investors by offering land in the 10,000 acres of "Liberty" lands laid out by his surveyors adjacent to the city's northern border. Penn then

11.3
**Map of the improved part of Pennsylvania, including Philadelphia and vicinity, with an inset plan of Philadelphia. Drawn by Thomas Holme, published 1720 (US Library of Congress, Map Division)**
Source: As published in John W. Reps, *The Making of Urban America: A History of City Planning in the United States* (Princeton, NJ: Princeton University Press, 1965)

attempted to incorporate some of the estate planning principles planned for the outskirts into the city center, showing many of the blocks as subdivided into regular acre or half-acre parcels.[10] As the recent history of Philadelphia reveals, the perceived northern boundary of the city continued to be in play well into the twentieth century. By leaving the northern edge of the city incomplete, it is likely that Penn sought ambiguously to associate the undeveloped areas of the Liberty lands with the city proper.[11]

The platting of the parcels in 1683 plan reflects Penn's belief that the city would grow simultaneously from its two river frontages in towards the center. The city did not comply. Rather, following convention, the city grew into unplanned areas to the north and south, extending in a low-slung, crowded pattern parallel to its busy eastern port on the Delaware. During Philadelphia's storied period as the American Revolution's "cradle of liberty," Penn's checkerboard plan could in fact hardly be discerned (Figure 11.4). The broad city blocks with large parcels that were meant to accommodate large, free-standing town homes in a green, leafy setting also succumbed to the conventions of the colonial period. The original 425 by 570 (or 675) foot blocks were subdivided with narrow alleys within which emerged a dense city fabric of rowhouses.

11.4
**Plan of the city and suburbs of Philadelphia, drawn by A. P. Folie in 1994 (US Library of Congress, Map Division)**
As published in John W. Reps, *The Making of Urban America: A History of City Planning in the United States* (Princeton, NJ: Princeton University Press, 1965)

The planned public squares suffered a better fate, and bear out the utility of Penn's scheme. After being obscured by eighteenth-century surveys which document the shifting of Broad Street two blocks west, better to straddle the highest ridge between the two rivers, the central and two western squares reappear in altered locations by the early nineteenth century. All five squares were made subject to new city ordinances, banning their use as dumping grounds. These new ordinances designated the squares as civic open spaces in perpetuity, providing financial support for their improvement.[12]

What logic can be gleaned from the uncoupling, by means of geometry and placement, of the idealized public squares from the rectangular gridiron of private development? Perhaps, because of their ideal geometry, the squares were able to endure (or at least recover) as an idea uncontaminated by the evolving, speculative form of the grid. The recovered squares were eventually able to provide relief from a scale and density of development never anticipated by William Penn. Philadelphia is credited – and blamed – for introducing the gridiron plan with a main square at its center as a model for establishing cities throughout the United States. The scheme was duplicated *ad infinitum*, often on hilly, less appropriate sites. Nevertheless, the public squares establish an important precedent for the concept of neighborhood parks taken up by city planners more than two centuries later. Likewise, the annexing of the northern liberties, as a semi-planned green buffer zone, anticipated the greenbelt and garden city concepts.

# Nineteenth-century expansion: from town to metropolis

Philadelphia's premiere status during the revolutionary period grew out of its dominance of the political and commercial activities of the day. The city hosted the Continental Congress, it was the site of both the signing of the Declaration of Independence and the drafting of the Constitution, and served as the nation's first capital after independence was won. During the latter half of the eighteenth century Philadelphia contained the largest port in the western hemisphere; it was the largest city in the English-speaking world after London, to which it was often compared. Penn's vision of the city as a marketplace and symbolic center for the vast agricultural production of Pennsylvania, Southern New Jersey and Delaware had been achieved.

Yet the city did not achieve its iconic form until the middle of the nineteenth century. Paradoxically, the full realization of the city platted by Penn, stretching from river to river, coincided with a consolidation of the various townships in Philadelphia County under one municipality in 1854. Though still the core, "Old" Philadelphia was now just one-tenth of a vast, expanding metropolis. Until that time the city had been steadily increasing in population by an average of 25 percent per decade, growing from 41,000 inhabitants in 1800 to 121,000 in 1850. The incorporation increased the city's official population fivefold, to about a half-a-million residents. By 1900 the population had increased another two-and-a-half times, to 1.25 million.

If the explosive growth spurred by the industrial revolution had multiplied Philadelphia's population by 30 times over the course of the nineteenth century, New York City had grown at twice that rate. Upon the completion of the Erie Canal in 1825, New York City became the dominant port and commercial center on the eastern seaboard. In addition to New York City's geographic advantage for trade, Manhattan's linear form, clearly delimited boundaries and industrial-scale grid all helped to organize and discipline new growth, making it a highly propitious site for the formation of a distinctive, modern city. The Philadelphia gridiron laid out by Penn, on the other hand, was not large enough to contain the amount of new growth in the city. Moreover there was little impetus to physically integrate, by means of planning, the various adjacent townships that had been legally consolidated in 1854. In Philadelphia, as in much of the US during this period, the rush of industrial expansion and the *laissez-faire* attitude towards commerce allowed little municipal control over – or even reflection on – civic planning and land development.

In the period of Philadelphia's greatest growth and expansion, from the years 1850 to 1950, existing suburban patterns were extended, roadways were improved, and new turnpikes and train lines were built. Outside the center, a robust, but haphazard gridiron pattern of industrial plants and speculative residential blocks eroded formerly agricultural tracts. Though often containing the ubiquitous Philadelphia rowhouse, most of these new areas possessed neither the grandeur of the old downtown, nor its pedestrian scale (Figure 11.5). Though still prosperous, by 1900 Philadelphia trailed New York and Chicago in size. New York, by virtue of its physical layout, and Chicago, by virtue of the "The Great Fire" of 1871, had had the opportunity to expand the physical plan and profile of their central areas.

The form of Philadelphia's center continued to evolve well into the early decades of the twentieth century. At the turn of the century, projects were undertaken to update the downtown. But it was not until faced with loss of population and the decaying of historic districts as the city declined in the wake of the Second World War that the city's leaders and citizens attempted a wholesale remaking of was by then simply referred to as "Center-City."

11.5
Philadelphia,
aerial photograph
looking north,
1951

# The declining fate of the central city

The narrative of stagnation and decline that defines the recent history of Philadelphia is shared by a number of other aging industrial cities in the United States, including Baltimore, Detroit, St Louis and Pittsburgh. Maritime trade and, later, the railroads necessitated compact, concentrated cities during the period in which these cities were established and grew. With the advent of the automobile, mass suburbanization became a possible and often preferred form of land development. The very highways that planners and engineers promised would make physical travel between the old city centers and their outlying regions faster and more convenient facilitated the creation of whole new urban sub-centers that replaced the goods and services formerly only available in the old centers. Via FHA mortgages and highway construction, a new, federally subsidized suburban arcadia of single-family homes also drew business and industry, eager to shed their old plants and avoid the costs of organized labor and higher taxes that faced them in the old city centers.

Industrial plants built to support the war effort during the 1940s temporarily stayed the rates of decline in cities like Philadelphia. These facilities stimulated, for a time, the city's economies, levels of employment and population that had already begun to drop in the 1930s, but following the War the downward trend resumed. By the 1960s, the desegregation of ethnic minorities within the city also played a decisive role in the decline of urban centers such as Philadelphia. Large segments of the white middle-class population had already left the city. Threatened by the changing (read: "ethnic") public face of the city they fled further, a phenomenon that came to be known as "white flight." Once ensconced in new, more homogeneous communities, their xenophobia only increased, further reducing their desire to interact with the old centers.

Although the events that caused a decline in the fortunes of many American cities in the post-industrial era can be generalized as above, the effects of these commonly-shared events upon the physical form of the city in each case varied. Corresponding attempts at redevelopment and revitalization often met with limited success. Unlike many of the other US cities that have suffered decline, Philadelphia eventually managed to reinvent its downtown. The very area platted by William Penn was arguably more vital at the beginning of the twenty-first century than it was before the loss of population and industry began 50 years previously. What actions, if any, on the part of citizens, politicians and designers, contributed to the revitalization of the historic core? How was the transformation achieved, and at what cost to the rest of the city?

# Three phases in the remaking of Philadelphia

## I. Public works inspired by the City Beautiful movement

Anticipating the sesquicentennial of the American Revolution in 1926, and spurred on by the Columbian Worlds Exposition and the City Beautiful movement, Philadelphia undertook a series of ambitious plans beginning in about 1904. These included two major projects, the Fairmont (now Benjamin Franklin) Parkway and the Delaware (now Benjamin Franklin) Bridge. These projects, while essentially transportation-driven, had the effect of creating two new monumental entries into the city. Located to the northwest of the city along the Skulkill River and containing the city's nineteenth-century quasi-Greek Revival waterworks at its base, the promontory at Fairmount was already noted on Penn's 1683 plan.[13] The new parkway was to function as both a traffic artery and a civic center, with a plaza at its southern edge acting as a gateway from Fairmount Park and the expanding northern and western suburbs to the heart of the city. Fairmount itself was to be occupied by an elaborate art museum complex and linked by a grand diagonal axis slashing through one of the city's original squares (now Logan Circle) to Center Square, where the city had built a new, gargantuan, Second Empire style City Hall, completed in 1901.

The Benjamin Franklin Parkway and Philadelphia Art Museum were complete by the 1930s. As with many City Beautiful schemes, the full realization of the Parkway as a civic center was primarily undermined by the lack of centralized authority to plan, finance and develop urban land. The economic challenges of the Great Depression and then the Second World War contributed as well. The *beaux arts* parkway scheme had been part of a larger study by Jacques Greber, a French landscape architect. Greber was the primary designer in charge of the Parkway and the urban planning related to it. He proposed a network of diagonal avenues bisecting the city's original squares, attempting to conjoin them with the city's new train stations, cultural institutions and government buildings in the Parisian manner made popular in the nineteenth century.

While Greber's city-wide proposal was not as visionary or comprehensive as Burnham's plans for San Francisco and Chicago, it does propose a reading and layout of the city that is provocative in the light of urban design and planning projects implemented several decades later. Greber's 1917 "Partial Plan of the City Shewing the New Civic Centre . . ." played down the original northern and southern borders of Penn's plan, placing particular emphasis on integrating built-out areas of the Northern Liberties and Spring Garden Districts into the old downtown (Figure 11.6). The plan projected new development

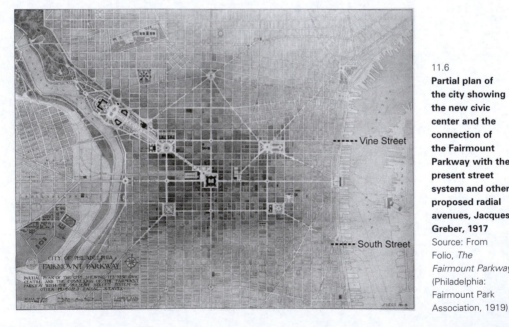

11.6
**Partial plan of the city showing the new civic center and the connection of the Fairmount Parkway with the present street system and other proposed radial avenues, Jacques Greber, 1917**
Source: From Folio, *The Fairmount Parkway* (Philadelphia: Fairmount Park Association, 1919)

around the two northern squares, Franklin Square to the east and Logan Square to the west, fulfilling their potential as open spaces central to their quadrants. Vine Street was no longer understood as the edge of the city, but as another main east–west avenue running between Squares, akin to Locust Street on the south side. The way in which the plan was framed suggested that the city's center was shifting north towards Vine Street, a reorientation confirmed shortly after by the building of the Benjamin Franklin Bridge, the second monumental entry into the city.

After more than 100 years of failed attempts to build a bridge that would span the Delaware River from Camden, New Jersey to Philadelphia, the growing use of the automobile precipitated the construction of the Benjamin Franklin Bridge, completed in 1928. Drawing twice as much traffic as anticipated, the suspension bridge created a sweeping panorama into the early, eastern districts of the city. The Bridge's massive landing fell between Race and Vine Street, ending in a plaza fronting Franklin Square.

Although a movement devoted to the stewardship of the city's colonial past had begun to emerge almost 100 years prior to the construction of the Benjamin Franklin Bridge, completion of the bridge and the celebration of the sesquicentennial in 1926 brought a new set of concerns to light about the "Old (re: eastern, colonial) City." Commercial and business interests that had once thrived in these areas began to move westward with the construction of the new city hall at Center Square. The area experienced a slow but steady decline. Although there were still many buildings of historical value from the Philadelphia's colonial period, much of the built fabric had been transformed during the nineteenth century. Recognition of past and possible future losses promoted the appreciation of older structures from the colonial period, and in particular the veneration of the Old Pennsylvania State House. The State House became the catalyst for a series of projects and studies that eventually led to the construction of the Independence National Park – and, arguably, to the wholesale transformation of the "Old City."

## II. Independence Mall: William Penn's greene country towne writ large

The most hallowed shrine in Philadelphia, perhaps in the United States, is the site of what has come to be known as Independence Hall and Independence Square (not one of the original squares laid out by Penn). Originally the Pennsylvania State House, Independence Hall is the site where the terms of the American Revolution were forged. The first Continental Congress met at the State House in 1776, and subsequently drafted, signed and publicly read the American Declaration of Independence there. Upon winning the War for Independence, the Second Continental Congress met again there and framed the Constitution of the United States. Philadelphia and its State House served as the United States Capitol in the first, formative decade of the county's existence, during which the Bill of Rights was amended to the Constitution. Following the move of the federal government to Washington, DC and the simultaneous transfer of Pennsylvania's capital to Harrisburg, the State House housed a changing series of functions throughout the nineteenth century. These included Philadelphia's city government, federal courts and, from 1802 to 1828, the first public museum of natural history in the United States, formed by the painter Charles Willson Peale.[14] Already in the early 1800s, Peale stated that Independence Hall would be "a building more interesting in the history of the world, than any of the celebrated fabrics of Greece and Rome!"[15]

Only after the much-heralded visit of the Marquis de Lafayette to Philadelphia in 1824, during which he was received in the State House's assembly room redecorated as a "Hall of Independence," did the site emerge as a shrine. The re-naming of the State House as Independence Hall precipitated a series of projects to "restore" the Hall, along with its outbuildings and Square, to their condition at the time of the American Revolution. The first of these projects began to mark the centennial of American Independence in 1876. The Daughters of the American Revolution and the American Institute of Architects undertook later renovation projects.[16]

The veneration of the Hall was furthered by the enshrinement of another relic of perhaps greater symbolic value than the building itself: the old state house bell, inscribed with the Old Testament words "proclaim liberty throughout the land, unto all the inhabitants thereof." While no historical records exist to confirm the Bell's connection with any of the great events surrounding the Revolution, its value as a symbol was nonetheless taken up by the abolitionists, who first coined the term "The Liberty Bell" in the title of an anti-slavery pamphlet. Only later, through popular songs, children's books, and extensive national railroad tours, was the Liberty Bell appropriated as a more generalized patriotic symbol.

Following the First World War, the surge in patriotism only increased the status and veneration of the Independence Hall complex and the Liberty Bell enshrined therein. Temporary viewing stands were often constructed adjacent to Independence Hall on Chestnut Street to serve the frequent patriotic parades, pageants and rallies held there. Many found the eclectic language, workaday uses and decaying condition of the older buildings facing the hall on Chestnut Street distasteful, and hoped to replace them with a plaza that would more permanently serve patriotic events.[17] Jacques Greber, the designer of the Parkway, and many of his collaborators and professional colleagues that taught at the University of Pennsylvania (including the prominent architect Paul Cret) made proposals for the site over a 30-year period.[18]

The scheme that most influenced the remaking of this area was not conceived by an architect, politician or civic leader, but rather by a Professor of Hygiene at the University of Pennsylvania named Dr Seneca Egbert. His 1928 proposal was apparently a response to a 1925 Philadelphia City Council proposal to abate traffic congestion at the Benjamin Franklin Bridge Plaza by diverting traffic from the Plaza to Market Street, through the creation of a grand boulevard mid-block between Fifth and Sixth Streets. Egbert instead proposed "the development of a Concourse or Esplanade between Independence Hall and the plaza at the west end of the Delaware bridge that should serve as a permanent and impressive Sesquicentennial memorial of the historic events incident to the founding of the nation."[19]

No drawing is known to exist of this scheme, but Egbert did draft an elaborate report outlining his proposals. Several aspects of the scheme he outlined were present in the plan finally implemented in the late 1940s. Egbert justified his boldest proposition, the demolishing of three city blocks stretching from Independence Hall on Chestnut Street to the Bridge plaza on Race Street – over 20 acres – by citing a widely-held fear that a fire could at any time consume one of the area's abandoned or dilapidated buildings and spread to Independence Hall or another cherished colonial edifice. His other influential proposals included the widening of Fifth and Sixth Streets to accommodate increased traffic from the Bridge, the creation of a central pedestrian esplanade "possibly as broad as Broad Street," the creation of a plaza for events fronting Independence Hall, the accommodation of underground parking, and the building of a new subway stop.

Most of his proposals for the surface development of individual blocks were not adopted. Egbert envisioned a scheme in which a building representing the Pennsylvania Commonwealth would cap the first block at the far end of the Mall at the bridge plaza. The Pennsylvania building was to be symmetrically flanked on the next block south by replicas of colonial buildings representing the other original twelve states of the union. The final block fronting Independence Hall was to house memorials and a plaza for celebrations.

Perhaps even more influential than the physical proposals made was Egbert's supposition that the new Mall would increase tax revenues by increasing the assessed value of the three cleared blocks – and, ultimately, increase the perceived value of adjacent properties and the district as a whole. Egbert chided the city for narrowly promoting development around Center (now Penn) Square to the west at the expense of the area of the city most associated with its illustrious history. He also implied that the historical value of the Old City could be mined to commercial advantage. To achieve a project of this magnitude, Egbert also foresaw the need for a structure of cooperation between various federal, city and state agencies. Egbert's scheme remained unrealized until world events prompted a reconsideration of his proposal for the Mall.

The bombing of Pearl Harbor and the outbreak of the Second World War brought a renewed resolve to protect Independence Hall and the Liberty Bell. Starting in 1941, Edwin O'Lewis, a charismatic, highly persuasive and well-connected judge, and president of the Pennsylvania Society of the Sons of the Revolution, mounted a campaign to build the three-block long Independence Mall. Mindful of the potential for federal support for the construction and management of the Mall, the project was conceived as a National Park that would eventually include the entire complex of buildings associated with Independence Hall. Roy Larson, a partner of Paul Cret's who made a proposal for the site in 1937, prior to the war, which drew liberally on Egbert's scheme, was asked to develop a plan for the Mall. It was Larson's revised plan from 1937, extending three blocks north of Independence Square and two partial blocks to the east, that was eventually implemented after the National Park was approved by the US Congress in 1949[20] (Figure 11.7).

11.7a
**Looking east from "Independence Hall" towards the future site of Independence Mall**

11.7b
**Adopted proposal for Independence Mall, Roy Larson, 1937**
Source: From pamphlet, *Independence Hall and Adjacent Buildings, A Plan for their Preservation and the Improvement of their Surroundings* (Philadelphia: Fairmount Park Art Association in collaboration with the Independence Hall Association, 1944)

The construction of the Mall, eventually part of a larger entity known as Independence National Park, did not proceed without resistance and controversy. Three blocks of businesses, many of which were (despite statements to the contrary) still active, were taken by eminent domain. Many fine nineteenth-century buildings were destroyed, including Frank Furness's magnificent polychrome Guarantee Trust Company and the Provident Life & Trust Company Bank and Office Building. Gaining governmental approval for the project hinged on the landmark status of the colonial buildings, and having the Park Service manage the site. Nevertheless, architects, preservationists and historians associated with the Park Service were critical of the effect the wholesale clearance of the site would have on the colonial monuments entrusted to them.[21]

Linking a memorial dedicated to a patriotic theme to an infrastructure-driven urban renewal project was not unique in the early decades of the twentieth century, or in previous eras; the roughly concurrent Jefferson National Expansion Memorial in St Louis was a prime example of the type. However, the sheer degree to which the Independence Mall and National Historic Park of which it is part combined an anachronistic, if not reactionary, esthetic project with a somewhat progressive economic planning model warrants further examination.

One could simply reduce the esthetic proposition of Independence Mall to a matter of stylistic fashion, expressive of its historical moment, but this reading would not fully embrace the profound irony and implications of the project. Here a crude imitation of eighteenth-century European classicism was deployed in a plan to transform a once discreet set of colonial buildings and artifacts, prized for the way their modest form and casual arrangement connoted the humble beginnings of the American democracy, into a National Historic Park. In the process, a large piece of the city's actual history, a dense but often architecturally rich urban fabric built up over three centuries, was destroyed.

The Mall itself was considered a failure almost from the start. Too vast to frame the diminutive Independence Hall and too formal to serve as an active city park, the Mall's most lauded purpose was as an underground garage serving the adjacent businesses and institutions in the bureaucratically designed office buildings that eventually lined it. The necessity of a mall of this size in this part of Philadelphia is itself questionable, but its form was disastrous. Looking north but cut off from the northern areas of the city by the landing of the bridge and later a highway, the mall's orientation represents a profound misreading of city's original morphology; a rectangular grid with its major streets stretching between two rivers. If interested in celebrating the city's history with a mall, it would have had to be positioned east–west, parallel to (or along) Market Street. An east–west link would have tied Independence Square to the city's true beginning point, a landing at the Delaware River, and better articulated a spatial narrative of the city's history.[22]

More connected to the national network of historic parks and related tourist sites than to the history of Philadelphia, Independence Mall indicates how, at a time when metropolitan areas like Philadelphia were dissipating into the suburbs, the esthetic chosen for the symbolic areas at the center was one that put a premium on cleanliness, easy automobile access and open, verdant vistas. It was as if Penn's Greene Country Towne was finally going to be realized with a vengeance, but at a scale that could only be appreciated from a moving automobile or as part of a larger tourist's itinerary.

The Mall's misguided form follows from the order of priorities that established it, from the pragmatic to the ambiguously altruistic – that is, first traffic abatement, then the framing of hallowed shrines, and finally "urban renewal." In hindsight, it seems that the radical transformation of this urban site into a pastoral park was mired in mid-century American politics of national mythmaking and a seemingly symbiotic relationship between urban divestment, the restoration of historic structures and re-gentrification.

More generally, the Mall suggested processes by which the city's historical form and stock of historic buildings could be leveraged to stimulate both public and private reinvestment in the old heart of the city. It is in this sense – as an amalgam of transportation planning, historic "preservation" and commercial redevelopment, conceived to restore the symbolic capital of a decaying city – that the plan for Independence Mall presaged not only the larger redevelopment of Philadelphia's downtown but also the post-War focus of urban design in general.

The completion of the three-block Mall took twenty years, from 1949 to 1969, years that almost directly correspond to Edmund Bacon's highly influential tenure as Executive Director of Philadelphia's Planning Commission. Considering himself a modernist, Bacon was never comfortable with the anachronistic character of the Mall's design, which he had inherited, but he supported the larger planning goals it represented. The massive clearing and highlighting of colonial architecture set the stage for many initiatives later facilitated by Bacon, including the gentrification of the surrounding Old City and its "Society Hill."

## III. The urban design of "Better Philadelphia" under Edmund Bacon

In 1964, a heroic portrait of Edmund Bacon was featured on the cover of Time magazine, under the banner "Urban Renewal: Remaking the American City" (Figure 8.8). Now, half a century after Bacon's planning efforts were initiated, perhaps it is possible to evaluate his role in the vaunted renaissance of Philadelphia's downtown. However, a full evaluation of Bacon's theories and work in Philadelphia would not be possible here. Instead I will focus on the question

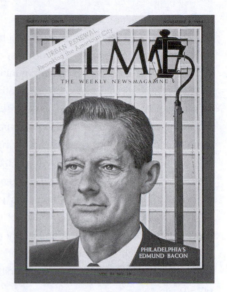

**11.8**
**Portrait of Edmund Bacon, cover:**
*Time* **Magazine, November 9, 1964**
Source: *Time* Magazine Archive

of how interventions undertaken by the city under Bacon's direction can be read, relative to both William Penn's founding principles and the multitude of historical forces acting on the form of the city subsequent to its founding. This will bring to light several interrelated questions. First, for what purpose were the boundaries of the old, central portion of the city re-inscribed and what have been the consequences of focusing so much economic, political and intellectual resources on those areas? Second, how central was the leveraging of the city's historical form and stock of colonial buildings to the downtown's redevelopment? Third, as urban design did not exist as a distinct professional activity prior to Bacon's work – Bacon was essentially an architect who became a city planner – in what ways can his work in Philadelphia be seen as constituting urban design practice as it exists today? This last question raises the issue of the degree to which urban design practice is too much invested in an historical rather than a contemporary idea of the city – that is, designing for the town rather than the metropolis.

John F. Bauman has written an account of an ideological struggle that occurred during the early 1940s among planners and others concerned with urban policies that would guide the post-War years. Bauman describes a clash between those who placed a priority on replacing slums through the rebuilding of communities spread throughout a metropolitan region, and those who stressed the remaking of the downtown and central areas of the city. The first group, emphasizing new housing as the most basic building block of a more humane city, grew out of the communitarian and reformist politics of the

1930s. Their position was that the government's resources should be focused on producing a variety of housing of a kind and quality that would, through controls over land use, zoning and utilities, spread density in a planned manner throughout the city, providing communities that could successfully compete with what was already being offered in the new suburbs. Fearful that the artificially overvalued cost of land in the most inner-city areas would undermine programs dedicated to distributing resources equitably to the greatest number of people, they warned against an overemphasis on rebuilding the centers.[23]

The second group, which Bauman called the "houser-redevelopers," viewed the provision of new housing as "the handmaiden of downtown renewal." This new breed of urbanists put great stock on the symbolic and strategic value of restoring the vitality of the downtown. They were also more aligned with the emerging federal policy and housing bureaucracy of the Cold War years, which resisted any planning policies with socialistic overtones – that is, any policies that might overly limit or compete with private commercial enterprise.

Although Bauman considered Edmund Bacon to be one of the new breed, Bacon had at the outset of his career embraced initiatives related to both the regionalist and downtown-centered positions in Philadelphia. The experiences of his early career may help to explain both his espousal of design as a tool for building consensus and the ambiguity of his ideological affiliations. Bacon grew up in Philadelphia, part of an old Quaker family. He studied architecture at Cornell in the early 1930s, and then did graduate work as a fellow under Eliel Saarinen at Cranbrook Academy. Before returning to Philadelphia, he worked in Michigan as the Supervisor of City Planning for the Flint Institute of Research and Planning. Bacon was fired from this Institute in 1939 and accused of being a communist for his advocacy of federal housing subsidies to aid the inconsistent incomes of General Motor's workers, who had staged a highly publicized sit-down strike in 1936–1937.[24]

The Philadelphia Bacon returned to in the early 1940s was in the early stages of a political transformation. Once described by the great muckraking journalist Lincoln Steffens as "Corrupt and Contented," Philadelphia and its physical decline – grimy streets, filthy drinking water, shrinking commercial venues – reflected the stronghold of an entrenched Republican political machine dominated by ward bosses and cronyism. Frustrated by the city government's resistance to the idea of active city planning, a grassroots movement of young, reform-minded individuals and civic groups formed the Action Committee on City Planning in 1939. This group later became a more permanent Citizen's Council on City Planning, with several members from its ranks appointed to important positions on the Planning Commission.[25] Bacon had been recruited back to the city by one of the civic reform groups associated

11.9
**3-D plan and key, The Better Philadelphia Exhibition, Gimbels Department Store, Edmund Bacon and Oscar Stonorov, designers, 1947**
Source: From pamphlet, *The Better Philadelphia Exhibition: What City Planning Means to You*, 1947

with the Citizen's Council to head the Philadelphia Housing Association. In 1947 the Citizen's Council on City Planning organized the "Better Philadelphia Exhibition." Bacon co-designed the exhibition with Oskar Stonorov (Figure 11.9).

Installed on the fifth floor of Gimbels Department Store in Center City, The Better Philadelphia Exhibition coordinated an ambitious, interactive display of the city and its planned projects with public programs meant to engage and inform a wide array of citizens. The exhibit was carefully choreographed using techniques drawn from both Worlds Fair pavilions and the kinds of modern retail displays found elsewhere in the department store. Heavily promoted through radio broadcasts, leaflets, newspaper and magazine articles, the Exhibition attracted over 385,000 visitors.[26]

The exhibition opened with the presentation of a 22- by 28-foot diorama, "Vista of a Better Philadelphia," a bird's-eye perspective depicting what the city and its surrounding environs would look like in 1982. Set within a converted auditorium, the diorama was supplemented by overhead images of past public works and an introductory text, "Philadelphia plans again." This narrative highlighted the ways in which changes to areas within the city's boundaries would transform them to be as compelling as the outlying suburbs, with their efficient highways and commodious industrial parks. A voice-over extolled the virtues of planning coordinated by local government, and the potential to achieve the city of civilized greenswards that William Penn had originally conceived. The city construed by the diorama, and other similar devices within the exhibition, served to orient visitors to the physical relationships between particular locales in which they lived and worked, and then, incrementally, to the larger district, city and region beyond. The exhibition featured displays explaining the specific benefits planning could offer in terms of the more everyday amenities that would improve the lives of people in the city's many neighborhoods, such as playgrounds, nursery schools, health centers and new housing.

To make the idea of a revitalized city palpable to the Exhibition's viewers, an extensive large-scale mock-up of a typical Philadelphia neighborhood composed of rowhouses was shown with new public amenities and tenant improvements to the individual houses and yards. A large section towards the end of the exhibition was devoted to the display of drawings and models made by the city's schoolchildren. Through schoolroom exercises, the students had been asked to survey their neighborhoods, make assessments of the overall quality of the environment, and develop, as individuals, an improvement plan for their part of the city. Students were then asked to work in groups to negotiate a shared plan, consulting with planning experts and city councilmen on what it would take to implement their plans. While this level of engagement in a participatory process would have been possible with a wider segment of the population, and welcomed by many reform-minded local activists in the city, it was limited to the schoolchildren's program.[27]

The Better Philadelphia diorama and the mock-up of a typical neighborhood were engaging, but the most promoted feature of the exhibition was a 30- by 14-foot model of the downtown. It contained a highly animated display of new developments projected over a 35-year period. Panels on the model would flipped over in sequence, synchronized with dialogue and spot lighting, to reveal one new initiative after another, including a series of new transportation, civic space, recreation, arts and business improvement projects. Displayed in parts, and not yet given a specific alignment, was a new expressway surrounding the entire downtown. Also included was the verdant, three-block long scheme for Independence Mall and a new boulevard between City Hall and the Main Commuter Train Terminal at 30th Street, replacing the elevated train tracks, known as the "Chinese Wall," that divided the northwestern portion of the city. A consolidated distribution facility replaced the city's waterfront food markets, and the spaces were replaced with piers and harbors for recreation and pleasure boating. The improved automobile access and open space amenities, while modeled as improvements to the city's efficiency, were also linked to new, fashionably modern housing and cultural facilities.

As Amy Menzer points out in her detailed study of the Better Philadelphia Exhibition, the spectacle of the downtown model differed in format and content from many of the other, more pedagogical displays in the exhibition, in the ease and Madison-Avenue way in which it showed the downtown transformed as if by a benevolent yet absent hand. This consumerist tone was furthered by another nearby display, consisting of a conveyor belt with a series of public projects on it, complete with price tags, under the banner "Progress Must Be Bought and Paid For."

Menzer has argued that the Exhibition contained the potential of a radical "environmental [urban] politics" in its attempt to spur citizen participation in a vision of the city that could provide a compelling alternative to suburbanization. She concedes that the exhibition, like much subsequent urban renewal, suffered from "ambivalences and missed opportunities" typical of the "post-war labor management consensus, racial and ethnic segregation and discrimination and anti-communism which undergirded a coalition of largely white male housing reformers, patrician civic leaders, socialist architects, and representatives of the chamber of commerce."[28] The Better Philadelphia Exhibition *was* radical in its attempt to take the need for visionary planning directly to the citizens, demonstrating its promise and the virtues of the initiatives it advocated. The Exhibition's subtle emphasis on the downtown and its muted take on the social inequities inherent in the city's allocation of physical resources also reflected the source of its funding; three-quarters of the $400,000 cost of the exhibition had been raised from local businesses by Edward Hopkinson Jr. Hopkinson was a financier, and, chairmen of the City Planning Commission, which covered the remaining balance.[29] The perhaps unspoken goal of the exhibit was to leverage the public interest it generated into increased support, stability and power for the recently revived Planning Commission, still fledgling under the Republican city government.

The Better Philadelphia Exhibition coincided with a period in Philadelphia when several discreet groups of civic and business leaders, fearful that the city's physical decline and reputation for corruption was beginning to stymie new business investment, joined together to form "The Greater Philadelphia Movement." Charged with the dual purpose of answering to the aroused civic interest in the city and "preserving the value of business interests," the group assembled a trust and combined assets in excess of ten billion dollars to be devoted to the transformation of the city.[30] Around the same time, the membership of Philadelphia's chapter of the Americans for Democratic Action – drawn from local labor unions and members of the community chest – was organizing independent voters in opposition to the republican regime. In 1952 they helped elect one of their members, Joseph Sill Clark Jr, as the city's first Democratic Mayor in 67 years.

A new reform-minded city government and a business community willing to cross traditional party lines empowered the Philadelphia's Planning

Commission as never before. Bacon was made Executive Director of the Commission in 1949. While his direct influence on political decisions concerning development and redevelopment is hard to assess – for example, he did not have a seat on the mayor's cabinet until the last years of his directorship in the late 1960s – his power seems to have lain in his capacity to stay ahead of the politicians. Ascribing his effectiveness to the "power of ideas," Bacon claims to have "dealt with the future beyond the view of the mayor's cabinet, and when they got there, they found me in possession: they found I had staked out the territory. By the time they became concerned with a problem, I had already developed a proposal."[31]

Almost all of proposals unveiled in the downtown model of the Better Philadelphia Exhibition were undertaken by the Planning Commission under Bacon and eventually achieved within the projected 35-year time frame. Beginning with a discreet set of projects, many of which he inherited, Bacon eventually developed a comprehensive vision of a revitalized center-city Philadelphia. The original borders of the city platted by William Penn were to be re-inscribed with a ring of expressways. New, large-scale building complexes and greenswards were to be woven into the existing streets, highlighting the monuments of the Old City (Figure 11.10).

As with Independence Mall, the accommodation of automobile circulation provided the initial impetus for planning the city. In 1952, Bacon laid out his understanding of the important relationship between traffic planning and rational redevelopment patterns in a lecture given to the College of Engineering at Rutgers University. Drawing on detailed planning commission studies which surveyed types and patterns of automobile usage and parking affecting the

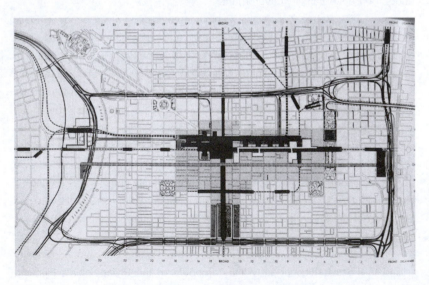

11.10
**Comprehensive plan for downtown Philadelphia, 1961**
Source: Philadelphia Planning Commission Report, 1961

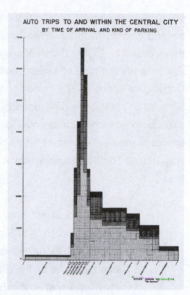

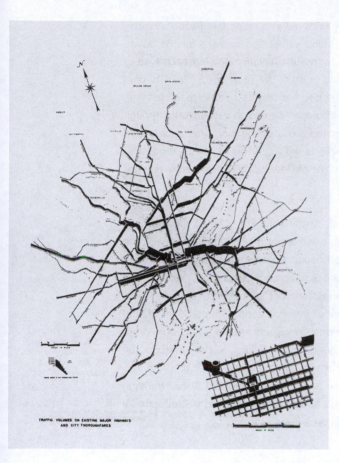

**11.11**
**Origin and destination traffic surveys, 1947. Philadelphia Planning Commission's Technical Advisory Commission, 1947**
Source: As published in Edmund Bacon, "Highway Development Related to Land Use in an Urban Area," *Spencer Miller Lecture Series: Landscape Design and its Relation to the Modern Highway* (New Brunswick, NJ; New Jersey Roadside Council/College of Engineering, Rutgers University, 1950–52)

downtown, Bacon stressed two aspects of traffic; how to analyze its effects and patterns in the city, and how to plan for it more efficiently.[32]

The study Bacon drew on sought to document "desire lines" – where people were coming from and going to, and what they were doing when they got there (Figure 11.11). His analysis showed that already at mid-century, a relatively small percentage of overall auto trips into the city was devoted to shopping, and that those trips were short in duration. He also showed evidence that although a much greater percentage of trips into the city was undertaken by those working or doing business there, they also tended to stay in the city for a much shorter duration than might be expected – less than three hours.

If the who, what and when of automobile use came first in the approach taken by Bacon, then the ways to serve more efficiently, and perhaps even increase circulation into the city followed as a response. Bacon's empirical approach to traffic analysis later found expression in plans for the downtown based on highly differentiated forms of circulation, keying each kind of use to a specific type of street, parking or mass-transit system. In his Rutgers lecture, he spoke of the need for the city not only to control road planning, but also to control the development of property adjacent to roadways through exercising eminent domain over blighted areas of the city. This coordinated approach would ensure that future projects would perform in the best possible way from a "traffic and appearance point of view, but also from a tax point of view ..."

> ... Lombard Street runs along the southern edge of the business center parallel to Vine Street on the north, and it happens that there is a band of extremely bad housing between [the] two rivers right along the route of the proposed Lombard Street highway. We have determined that if the redevelopment authority condemned all of the land involved and put it all into one control, the amount of land now occupied by *useless little alleys and streets which criss-cross this area* would be roughly equivalent to the land required for the widening of Lombard street to a six-lane highway. ... It would also be possible to prevent use of any of the Lombard Street frontage for access. All of the access could be from the North–South streets because the area would be developed as a unit.[33]

(My own italics.)

Bacon had inherited the highway plan encircling the city from the previous Planning Director. The cross-town expressway on Lombard Street was eventually shifted one block south to the original city border on South Street. Aside from the general goal of better servicing the city with highways, the specific alignments of the proposed highways to the north and south appear to follow no formal logic besides the re-inscription of the historical borders. While ward lines reinforced these historical borders, the zoning patterns tell a somewhat different story. On the South Street border there was a fairly swift transition from commercial to residential uses, but to the north there was primarily commercial and industrial use until Spring Garden Street. Had Penn's plan been completed on its northern side, with five blocks extending symmetrically in each direction from High (now Market) Street, Spring Garden Street would have been the city's northern border. Greber's plan had acknowledged this in 1917, by figuring Spring Garden Street to terminate directly into the head of the Benjamin Franklin Parkway at Fairmount (Figure 8.6). By implementing the construction of a six-lane expressway on Vine Street (completed in the early

1980s), Bacon effectively sealed off the northern border, misreading Penn's ambiguous plan and forestalling the historically established tendency of the downtown to drift north.

Having used new expressways to encase the city within the literal boundaries of Penn's plan, Bacon then went on functionally to code and optimize each element of the encased city at the scale of both the immediate project and of the downtown as a whole. Emblematic projects, separately addressing office, bureaucratic uses, shopping, and dwellings, were to be linked by overlapping but discreet networks of automobile, mass-transit and pedestrian circulation. It is almost as if each of the groups of different downtown "users" identified in the early traffic studies – shoppers, businessmen, workers, those seeking arts and leisure – might be given their own circulation network within the city.

Projects were undertaken to reinforce the hierarchical importance of the two main arteries within the downtown – Market and Broad Streets – with "super-block" projects. A roughly six-block parking lot/transit hub straddling Broad Street was projected as part of the South Street cross-town Expressway. Market Street projects included the construction of the Penn Center Office Complex to the west of Penn Square, and later the Market East Shopping Mall to the east. Each of these (now built) Market street developments incorporated complex, multi-level circulation concourses. When Penn Center was begun in the late 1950s, it was the largest mixed-use office complex undertaken in the US since the building of Rockefeller Center in the 1930s. Expressing his frustration with the difficulty of fully integrating several levels of circulation below and above the street grade at Penn Center, Bacon noted his satisfaction with the later design solution developed for the Shopping Mall at Market East (Figure 11.12):

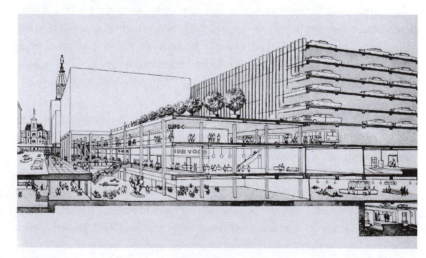

11.12
**Sectional perspective, study for Market East Urban Mall, 1960. Drawn by Willo von Moltke, Philadelphia City Planning Commission, 1960**
Source: As published in Edmund Bacon, *Design of Cities*

> The architecture of the buildings which penetrate this space rises clear from the pedestrian level [note: below grade] to the level above the street with *no expression at the street plane, so oppressively present in Penn Center* . . . The Vertebrae Structure of the bus terminal and parking garage, an architectural extension of regional movement systems, asserts itself across the composition in the background.[34]

(My own italics.)

Such an abundance and articulation of circulation could only be borne out by high levels of density, such as one might find in contemporary Asian cities. The projected 30-year population figures assumed in the traffic studies cited by Bacon in the early 1950s saw the city's population increasing until 1970 and declining slightly thereafter, with the region continuing to grow. Instead, the city's overall population stayed stagnant until 1970, and declined precipitously thereafter – dropping by almost 15 percent between 1970 and 1980 alone – and losing roughly a quarter of its mid-century population of two million people as of the Year 2000 census. It is doubtful that, even if the city had gained in population and managed to maintain a majority of those inhabitants, Bacon's duplicitous circulation schemes would have been much warranted.

Bacon's concern with functionally determining circulation was not limited to highways and mega-projects. Alongside the "super-sizing" of portions of Market Street to the east and west of Penn Square, and effectively evacuating whatever street-life previously existed in these areas, he proposed (and partially achieved) closing Chestnut Street, one block south of Market Street, to automobile traffic in order to restore its role as "the great walking street" from river to river (but proposed a new trolley there for the less hardy). If Market Street was to act as the modern, infrastructural east–west spine of the city, Chestnut Street was to serve as the main spine of an alternative, small-scale pedestrian network linked to the restored Old City, passing directly in front of Independence Hall, between the new Independence Mall and newly renovated areas of Society Hill.

Perhaps the development most responsible for changing the perception of Philadelphia within the city's general population was the gentrification of Society Hill. Drawing its name from the Free Society of Traders, an early and short-lived group given settlement privileges by William Penn, the area is comprised of roughly 15 blocks southeast of Independence Square. Adjacent to the heart of the colonial town, Society Hill had been the site of the city's finest homes during the colonial and revolutionary periods. The Park Service, which cleared all but the noteworthy colonial structures east of Independence Square, saw its strategy extended by the city, as it cleared out the old food markets on Dock Street and demolished much of the remaining "non-colonial" fabric. Having taken many properties through foreclosure and eminent domain, they were then transferred into the hands of the private Old Philadelphia Corporation, which sold roughly 600 individual houses back to private citizens at very low prices, with a stipulation that they be restored to their colonial glory. The city, along with the OPC and other private development interests, undertook the process of filling in the rest of the demolished areas with sensitively-scaled townhouse developments and residential parks, making Society Hill an attractive and affluent enclave by the 1970s.[35]

Bacon's landmark project in the area was the construction of Society Hill Towers, a luxury high-rise and townhouse project designed by I. M. Pei. Built around the site of the old Dock Street markets, atop a hill formed by a parking plinth, the composition of the Towers extended from the axis of the restored colonial market Head House. Among other claims made for this project, Bacon stated that the vertical proportions of the Tower's glass and concrete face recalled the six-over-six windows of the surrounding colonial buildings, despite the more than ten-fold difference in scale. Bacon's touting of this project as a unique and harmonious blend of the (now clichéd) "old and new" is reinforced by the picture used on the cover of Time and in many other promotions for the city: Bacon is set against a background made by the abstract grid of the towers with a colonial light-post in the foreground in-between. The viewer of this illustration was to infer that Bacon was the medium through which these two distinct historical periods were bridged (Figure 8.8).

The rapid pace of the transformation of Society Hill produced several palpable effects that other longer-term projects had yet to yield. Wealthy Philadelphians were now not only reinvesting in the city through their business efforts, but were also moving into the Old City. The 1,500 or so new and renovated residences completed by the middle 1960s formed a relatively small number compared to the general rate at which middle-class people were leaving the city's neighborhoods at that time. Nevertheless, the quaint postcard atmosphere of Society Hill had a symbolic impact, dovetailing nicely with the interest generated by the restored shrines of Independence National Park and the emerging nightlife on South Street. The area quickly began to lure significant numbers of tourists and suburban visitors eager for an adventurous outing in the "city."

By the early 1960s, Bacon's initiatives were beginning to have unanticipated effects. Expressways on the city's north, east and western eastern edge had been approved, and the long process of demolition and construction had begun. Although not yet approved, the planned cross-town expressway on South Street had by the late 1950s begun to depress investment and real estate values along the expressway's projected path. The South Street corridor had historically been an active area that welcomed immigrants to the city. Dominated by Jewish settlers and merchants from the late nineteenth century onwards, and later home to a Black community on its western extent, the area began to draw bohemians in the late 1950s, who were no doubt attracted to its cheap rents, funky atmosphere and jazz clubs. By 1963, the street's reputation was summed up in a line from a popular "Philadelphia Sound" Doo-Wop record, "South Street" by the Orlons: "Where do all the hippies meet? South Street! South Street!"

The anti-urban renewal ethos that began to emerge in the 1960s in the wake of Jane Jacob's consciousness-raising *Death and Life of the Great America City* found its local expression in Philadelphia in a fight concerning the South Street Expressway. Under the banner "Houses not Highways," a campaign to block the expressway was organized by the Citizen's Committee to Preserve and Develop the Cross-town Community. The CCPDCC was a coalition of Black residents living along and south of the proposed highway, affluent white residents from Rittenhouse Square and the recently gentrified Society Hill to the north, "hippie" homesteaders, and South Street merchants.

The Black community in particular objected in principle to the racial discrimination implied by the expressway's creation of an "effective buffer zone" between the Central Business District and the (poor) residential areas to the south. Along with the accusation of not-so-subtle racism, they faulted the city for its failure to offer a credible plan to re-house the several thousand residents that would be displaced by the highway. The coalition elicited the interest of a new generation of planners and architects – most notably Denise Scott Brown, who, having just undertaken a landmark study of "strip" urbanism in Las Vegas, was asked to develop a plan to show the viability of a revitalized South Street corridor. Sensing the political winds in 1967, then-Mayor Tate withdrew his support for the project and decided to "let the people have their victory," despite continuing pressure to build the expressway both from the city's chamber of commerce and from Bacon himself.[36] It took several more years' worth of battles before the expressway project finally died. Tired-out by the vociferous opposition of the "young liberals," Bacon retired as Executive Director of the Planning Commission in 1969.[37]

# The agency of planning and design in Philadelphia

In the critical period of economic and urban transformation that followed the Second World War, Philadelphia consistently reinvested more in its downtown than in the extended network of neighborhoods that make up the bulk of the city. It is difficult to discern the degree to which Edmund Bacon, or the Planning Commission he directed, would have been able – had they been inclined – to guide or influence these decisions in another direction. By mid-century, downtown business and real-estate interests had for years been paying taxes to the city on properties whose assessments had been maintained at artificially high levels. By bringing pressure to bear on the city's planning and redevelopment efforts, the financial establishment sought not only to reach their broader, long-term goal of stimulating new, outside investment in the city, but also to recoup their losses in property values and inflated tax payments.

The visions floated by the Better Philadelphia Exhibition may have stressed the importance of re-planning the whole city, but the substantial resources commanded by the backers of the Greater Philadelphia Movement appear to have been primarily expended on the downtown. Nevertheless, for Bacon and the group of design and policy professionals empowered by Philadelphia's reform-minded democratic city government, the emphasis on the core of the city surely must have been justified in more altruistic terms. In her assessment of the Better Philadelphia Exhibition's attempts at constructing a common ground of urban interests free of the ideological extremes of conservatism and liberalism, Amy Menzer refers to Arthur Schlesinger's roughly concurrent concept of the "Vital Center."[38] Built upon the supposed understanding of democratic notions of freedom and liberty shared by a plurality of Americans during the Cold War, Schlesinger's Vital Center was a political concept posing a "middle way" of militant liberalism against the threats of communism and totalitarianism. In 1947 Schlesinger was a founding member of Americans for Democratic Action an organization that counted among its members many of the reform-minded politicians, activists and intellectuals that took the mantle in Philadelphia at mid-century, including Edmund Bacon. It is perhaps not too far-fetched to imagine Bacon and his cohorts conceiving of the downtown's symbolic potential as a physical embodiment of the "vital center;" that is, as the common ground of an entire city's shared interests.[39] If the city's center could be revived and prosper, especially considering its historic role as the "cradle of liberty," then perhaps it could act as a catalyst for remaking the disparate communities and interests composing the rest of the city.

The "vital center" imagined by Schlesinger was more an idealistic concept than a documented, stable consensus of broadly-shared values held across a range of political constituencies. As the local struggle over the South Street cross-town expressway revealed, groups with diverging political, economic and racial interest may temporarily join forces over a shared cause, but such groups do not necessarily constitute a "vital center." Moreover, if by the late 1960s the concept of a "vital center" was giving way to more contentious models of political organization, a political figure could no longer justify his actions by claiming to represent what was never more than a fugitive political body.

The question of whether Philadelphia's downtown was revived at the cost of the rest of the city cannot be clearly ascertained here, as the factors that would have to be considered in making such a judgment go well beyond the purview of planning and design. Moreover, because very few formerly industrial American cities with profiles similar to Philadelphia's have been able to stave off population loss and physical decline, it is difficult to provide analogous examples of how better planning and design might have overcome the ravaging of much of Philadelphia outside its downtown. However, the consistent effects of urban policy in the US notwithstanding, agents of planning and design in Philadelphia, whether as visionary advocates or mere facilitators, did play a substantial role in construing the city's current form.

Bacon credits his success in transforming Philadelphia's downtown to the "power of ideas." Yet once he became Executive Director of the Planning Commission, Bacon seems to have focused little effort developing new ideas for the metropolis as a whole, and certainly no ideas with as much potential to capture the public imagination as those he advocated for the downtown. Early on in his directorship Bacon took a principled stand against the over-large, a-contextual format of federally-funded housing projects, opting instead to support programs to reinforce existing neighborhood patterns through the renovation of existing housing stock and the development of scatter-site housing. Although Bacon sought out high-caliber architects, including Louis Kahn, to do this work, and some laudable "model" projects were built, he never achieved his scatter-site scheme in any substantial way.

Today, faced with many sparsely populated neighborhoods and thousands of abandoned buildings that are literally falling down, Philadelphia's Planning Commission has undertaken an ambitious program selectively to clear many parts of the city deemed to be obsolete remnants of the city's industrial past. Harking back to the emphasis of the regionally-focused, social equity planners at mid-century, the commission is studying and implementing new, more suburban (or at least lower-density) block and settlement patterns. Unfortunately, the financial resources available at mid-century are now gone, along with the city's broader tax base. This financial circumstance has forced the planning commission to explore schemes that might have helped unify the city in the relatively more flush times at mid-century. In order to facilitate the reduction and redistribution of public amenities such as health centers, schools, libraries and public safety infrastructure, planners have begun to think beyond the boundaries of historically established neighborhoods and reconceive the city as a network of services shared across many communities.

# Taking the towne for the city: the purview of urban design

Edmund Bacon's work followed a period of unprecedented urban expansion and modernization in the late nineteenth and early twentieth centuries, when the fundamental nature of cities, Philadelphia included, had changed. The concept of urban design emerged in the late 1940s as a way for the professional apparatus of architecture better to address these changes. As the director of Philadelphia's Planning Commission, and later as the author of *Design of Cities*, Bacon played a seminal role in establishing urban design as both a discipline and an actor in the shaping of cities in the mid-twentieth century.

Bacon conceived urban design as a means to recover the civilized form of the European city within the modern metropolis, bringing the new scale and complexity of modern architecture and development under the discipline of a more humanistic order. This attitude is well-illustrated in Bacon's *Design of Cities*, where a majority of the examples are drawn from a western tradition of city building, in which Renaissance Florence is taken as the great paradigm. In *Design of Cities* and many public statements about his work in Philadelphia, Bacon devotes much rhetoric to the importance of "public process," "feedback mechanisms" and "democracy in action." Yet he states that city making is "an act of will," and draws inspiration from the harmonious design of cities executed by mostly monarchic or papal authorities. Was the "will" Bacon referred to his own, or that of the "the people," transfixed by "power of ideas?"[40] Certainly, prior to the reform movement that brought him into power, no clear public authority existed in Philadelphia, where almost since its inception private, patrician interests and commercial enterprise had shaped the city.[41] That most of great public works and monuments in Philadelphia's downtown are named after figures from the seventeenth and eighteenth centuries – William Penn and Benjamin Franklin are the most numerous – speaks not only of the way in which the city's colonial past provides the sustaining mythology of the city's importance, but of the reticence on the part of Philadelphia's citizens to put their own mark on the city in the intervening years.

Bacon's recourse to William Penn is neither innocent nor inconsequential. Rather than contend with the physical 300-year history of Philadelphia – a speculatively driven, redbrick, mercantile city – Bacon instead chose to focus on a reification of Penn's original plan for a "green county towne." An early scheme related to the Penn Center development epitomizes both Bacon's attitude toward the built history of the city that preceded him and his use of Penn as a symbolic figure. Finding fault with the inefficient traffic patterns produced by the diagonal of Greber's Benjamin Franklin Parkway (Bacon planned to replace the Parkway's function as a gateway into the city with the Vine

11.13
**Model, proposal for Penn Center and altered City Hall, Redevelopment Area Plan, Philadelphia Planning Commission, 1952**
Source: Redevelopment Area Plan, Philadelphia Planning Commission, 1952

Street expressway), Bacon terminated the Parkway two blocks before Penn Square, "restoring" the surrounding rectilinear blocks. Linked to this reorganization of traffic patterns was a proposal to tear down the imposing City Hall on Penn Square, another "inefficient" nineteenth-century structure, leaving only the tower at its center (Figure 11.13).

Conceived in an allegorical mode by Alexander Milne Calder, along with other sculptures depicting the history of the city and state, a 37-foot-high bronze statue of William Penn, Philadelphia's great patriarch, sits atop the tower of the massive City Hall.[42] The statue of Penn faces northeast, towards Penn Treaty Park, the supposed site of a treaty signing between Penn and the Lenni Lenape Indians. The Charter of Pennsylvania is held in Penn's left hand. Following the erection of the statue in 1894, a "gentleman's agreement" emerged among planners and real-estate developers, prohibiting buildings in the center-city from surpassing the brim of Penn's hat in height.[43] When Bacon proposed to remove all of City Hall, except the tower and Penn's statue, he was not only reinforcing the importance of Penn's control over the height of buildings in the city and the symbolic function of his backward glance, but also revealing two other biases. First, it showed his distaste for everything the City Hall stood for; its decadent, Second Empire style would have been anathema to a mid-century modernist such as Bacon, and redolent of the corrupt city government that had built and occupied the building in its first 50 years of existence. Perhaps more critical was the desire to manifest Penn's most enduring physical legacy in the city – the green public squares – by returning an open space to Central (now Penn) Square, thereby linking the figure of Penn to the very open space he had envisioned.

By using Penn as the animating figure for the urban design of the city, writing the "old" into the "new," Bacon was also working in an allegorical mode. Invoking the moral authority of the colonial age inaugurated by Penn, and the rather puritanical character of its architecture, he attempted to erase as much as possible the detritus of 200 years of urban speculation. In so doing, he hoped to kindle a rebirth of the city with a puritanical urbanism characterized by discreet circulation, structural clarity, visual transparency and pastoral open space. Egbert's 1928 scheme for Independence Mall had contained the entire formula: eliminate, as much as possible, all but the colonial structures, whose established historical significance and small scale made them entirely accessible to a suburban population increasingly less inclined to dense, complex forms of urbanity; optimize access, first by automobile and then by mass-transit; and finally, leverage the restored "history," new transportation infrastructure and open space to promote new commercial development – the only truly bankable form of rebirth (Figure 11.14).

While the allegory of the old colonial city giving birth to a new modern city appealed to the city's chauvinism, it was destructive in the way that it ignored those aspects of the city that had emerged during the intervening

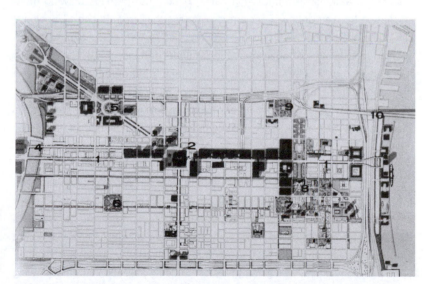

11.14
**Illustrative plan for downtown Philadelphia, 1961**
Source: Philadelphia Planning Commission Report, 1961

years, particularly the bulk of the city built in the nineteenth and early twentieth centuries. Thus the colonial allegory failed to provide a historical idea or sustaining myth that encompassed the whole city, as opposed to focusing selectively on its old center.

Louis Kahn, Bacon's contemporary and Philadelphia's most esteemed architect of the period, gave the theme of defending the old center above all else its most potent and explicit expression. During the period 1947–1962, Kahn developed a series of studies and proposals that addressed many of the same issues and assumptions as those undertaken by Bacon and the Planning Commission. Highly enigmatic and romantic in flavor, Kahn's ideas influenced many of the more seemingly sober schemes that were adopted. Most famous among Kahn's many studies for Philadelphia was one from 1953 addressing the reorganization of traffic in the center-city. Attempting to reunify the downtown through a new "order of movement," Kahn redefined streets in the existing grid by referring to the kinds of "activities" or traffic they would serve – bus, pedestrian, automobile, etc. The new order of movement was to be held in balance by encircling the original bounds of Penn and Holme's plan with large expressways. Monumentalizing the planning commission's traffic scheme, Kahn likened the expressways to the fortifying walls of the medieval city at Carcassonne, only now understood as "viaducts" channeling automobile traffic around the city. Kahn even replicated the architecture of fortifications with large, cylindrical parking towers lining the edge of the expressways. The parking towers were to act as great lithic gates to the city, keeping the hordes of automobiles from entering the city and disrupting its pedestrian life – a scheme not unlike those later adopted in pre-industrial European city centers ill-suited to automobile traffic. Anticipating Bacon, but perhaps drawing more inspiration from an Ur-city of ancient roman ruins than from Bacon's Ur-colonial city, Kahn shows the existing center-city reduced to historical monuments, circulation, and swaths of open green space (Independence Mall). Having taken the reification of the city's historic form to a greater extreme than Bacon, Kahn then reinhabited the city with space-frame-like buildings that projected a new, progressive image for the city. In one highly evocative bird's-eye perspective sketch of this scheme, the only existing building depicted is Independence Hall (Figure 11.15).

Bacon and Kahn, both highly influential figures within their respective professional communities, aimed their efforts in Philadelphia towards the retrieval of a more humanistic, pre-industrial city, as embodied in the potential of the physical layout of the old center. Kahn's rendering of the old city as a defensive fortress revealed what may have been a widely held sentiment among architects and urbanists; a fear that the old city, with its grand institutions and high culture, was going to be lost to decentralization and the growing

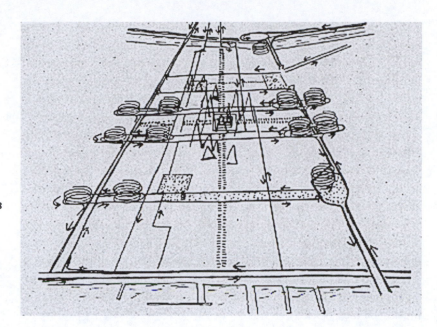

11.15
**Sketch, Louis Khan study for Philadelphia, 1953**
Source: Kahn Collection, Architectural Archives of the University of Pennsylvania, Gift of Richard Saul Wurman

popularity of suburban life. The fact that the new city walls created by the expressways corresponded to boundaries that defined well-established race and class distinctions within the city speaks two things: either these architects were naive in refusing to see that their plans materially solidified spatial, political and economic cleavages in the city, or they were acquiescing to the political and economic power of their sponsors – or both.[44] Certainly the question of who gained and who lost in the transformation of the city overseen by Bacon and imagined by Kahn is easy to answer. Downtown business interests, those wealthy enough to invest in real estate within the center-city, downtown arts and educational institutions and tourism, hospitality and restaurant industries all gained. With a few exceptions, everyone outside the downtown area lost in terms of investment in infrastructure, city services and declining land values.

The urban design of Philadelphia in the post-war period can be taken as constitutive of the historical viewpoint and methods that define urban design as a practice. The most frequent justification for concentrating on the city centers was that the centers offered a level of authenticity and dynamism that could provide an attractive counter to the lure of the suburbs. Yet the attribution of authenticity to "place" in a society characterized by mobility and change may be as fleeting as the attribution of "newness." Where the redesign of Philadelphia's center was concerned, it is certainly ironic that the monuments supposedly contributing to an authenticity of "place" were framed by an infrastructure of mobility.

The reactionary posture taken by many of the founders of urban design practice towards the new city is an aspect of their nostalgia for an historical form of city and a corresponding aversion to the "vital messy-ness" found in the "difficult whole" of the contemporary city.[45] Their nostalgia was inspired by the European cities they may have experienced as soldiers or as tourists, or perhaps by way of the European "masters" that they studied under, or conceivably was based on a longing for an apocryphal small-town America. Predisposed by their nostalgia against the seemingly endless, unbounded extents of the new metropolis, and lacking the analytical and representational tools to read the physical and programmatic patterns of these new spaces, they focused on the old centers. Urban design, as Bacon conceived it, still understood the city in static, historical terms as a center with discreet subsidiary districts. By the mid-1960s, research by figures such as Melvin Weber revealed that large cities like Philadelphia had already become something else; a complex, multinucleated network of commercial, industrial, domestic, recreational and cultural uses linked by rapidly evolving transportation and communication technologies.

William Penn had conceived of Philadelphia as a modern city, where an experiment with religious tolerance and town planning was to be financed by the selling of bonus plots to investors in Pennsylvania land. Cities were not in need of fortification by the seventeenth century, and Penn clearly foresaw an advantage in the open, ambiguous boundaries of the city. By cauterizing the city within its historical boundaries, and concentrating too much on the literal dimensions of Penn's plan, the schemes brought to fruition by Bacon overlooked the larger lessons that can be taken from Philadelphia's historical development as the outcome of Penn's broad vision. Taking Penn's scheme for Philadelphia literally, one would start by understanding the city as a center of cultural and economic exchange for a vast region. Given that the region has continued to grow exponentially since the colonial period, it follows that for the city to continue to function as not only a symbolic but also a substantive center, it too would have to expand exponentially in both scale and in the diversity of its programs and inhabitants.[46] Instead of envisioning this new metropolis, those entrusted with the urban design of Philadelphia consistently mistook the *towne* for the city.

## Notes

1 Distinctions between a town and a metropolis would typically hinge on considerations such as population size, geographic extent and other factors, including physical density and the cultural diversity of inhabitants.

2 Reps, 1965, pp. 152–153.

3 Bronner, 1962, pp. 81–82.

4 Bronner, 1962, p. 85.

5 Bronner, 1962, p. 87.

6 Bronner, 1962, p. 87.

7 Meyers (ed.), 1959, c.1912, pp. 261–273.

8 Bronner, 1962, pp. 97–101.

9 Reps, 1965, p. 161.

10 Bronner, 1962, p. 102 .

11 By 1850, just prior to the incorporation of Philadelphia county, the population of the city's adjacent liberty lands, which came to be know as the Northern Liberties district, was, combined with the more westerly Spring Garden district, approximately 100,000 people, making this area alone the sixth largest city in the U.S.

12 Reps, 1965, p. 172.

13 Penn has considered building his own house on the site.

14 At this, the country's first public, popular museum, Peale combined his portraits of luminaries from the American Revolution with paleontological finds, including the mastodon from Newburg, New York, which Peale advertised as "the great incognitum." Constructing a pre-historic lineage for America, Peale's museum reflected late-eighteenth-century efforts to legitimize the American project in the light of natural history.

15 Green, 1993, p. 197.

16 Currently the site is overseen by the National Park Service, whose renovation projects on the site continue into the present. See National Park Service, 1994, pp. 11–20.

17 National Park Service, 1994, pp. 22–28.

18 Among approximately twelve proposals developed made between 1915 and the adaptation of a plan in the mid-1940s, Paul Cret's was perhaps the most sophisticated. Clearing a half block of buildings north of Chestnut Street to Ludlow Street (one of the built-up secondary alleys), Cret proposed two similar schemes, the first with a semicircular plaza and the second with a square plaza. Cret's schemes kept the plaza small and located a flight of steps below-grade, a gesture that would have limited long views toward the diminutive colonial statehouse, thereby increasing the perception of its scale. See National Park Service, 1994, pp. 27–28.

19 National Park Service, 1994, pp. 29–32.

20 National Park Service, 1994, p. 63.

21 For an account of opposition to the wholesale clearance of the mall site on the part of the Park Service's architect, Charles E. Peterson, see Greiff, 1987, pp. 49–58; Mumford, 1957.

22 Extending the logic of the easterly portion of the National Park, Edmund Bacon later developed a meandering route to the eastern riverfront through a series of leafy, inter-block pedestrian walks.

23 Bauman, 1983, pp. 174–176.

24 Barnett and Miller, 1983, pp. 5–7.

25 Constance Dallas, as quoted in the "The Philadelphia Story," American Planning and Civic Association, 1953 pp. 13–16.

26 See "Philadelphia Plans Again," *Architectural Forum*, 1947, pp. 65–68.

27 For a detailed account of the programs associated with the exhibition, see Menzer, 1999, pp. 112–136.

28 Menzer, 1999, p. 115.

29 Menzer, 1999, p. 118.

30 Constance Dallas, as quoted in the "The Philadelphia Story," p. 15.

31 Bacon, as quoted in Barnett and Miller, 1983, p. 7 .

32 Bacon, 1950–1952.

33  Bacon, 1952, p. 56.

34  Bacon, 1974, p. 126.

35  Neil Smith has made a detailed study of the collusive political and business relationships that allowed the gentrification of Society Hill. He has shown how wealthy individuals appointed to commissions overseeing initiatives in the environs of the Center City were, at the same time, directing local banking and financial institutions making loans and guarantees in the area. Some of these same individuals were then able to buy property as private citizens at greatly reduced prices, and reap great profits after renovating them. See Smith, 1996.

36  For an account of the fight over the expressway, see Clow, 1989.

37  Bacon, as quoted in Barnett and Miller, 1983, p. 4.

38  Schlesinger, 1949.

39  Amy Menzer has argued that the Better Philadelphia Exhibition was an attempt to empower a process through which a vital political and physical "center" for the whole city could be engendered. Yet subsequent to the exhibition, the downtown, by virtue of the planning and investment processes actually undertaken, became, as a site and an idea, the de facto center.

40  Bacon, as quoted in Barnett and Miller, 1983, p. 9.

41  See Bass Warner, 1987.

42  Philadelphia's City Hall is the largest single municipal building in the U.S.

43  The agreement to not build above Penn's Hat was not broken until 1986.

44  I use the word sponsor as opposed to the larger public body design professionals are typically assumed to represent.

45  These quoted terms refer to concepts of urbanity first advocated by Robert Venturi and Denise Scott Brown in the 1960s.

46  The reform of Philadelphia might have concentrated on expanding the boundaries of the center to at least include the areas north of Vine Street – areas that were once the center of the city's residential population, but are now devastated.

Chapter 12

# San Francisco – San Francisco in an Age of Reaction

*Mitchell Schwarzer*

In San Francisco, the movement toward self-realization has reached such heights of indulgence that it is leveling the creation of inspiring urban design. Since the early 1980s, in a city that celebrates individualism, the collective discipline of architecture has taken a pounding. Here on the western shores of the North American continent, the American dream has taken a turn into activism bred on affluence and adversity. San Francisco's public planning process is lousy with naysayers. At the initial whiff of a new project, opponents spring up like oxalis, a prolific weed with yellow flowers that carpets the ground here after the first winter rains. These not-so-laidback Californians, who stymie architectural innovation in this once innovative city, defend a medley of values premised on history, esthetics, cultural politics and, most of all, an impossible-to-generalize set of self-interests. They fight to keep precious vistas and exclude new buildings – new building that add cars to the streets, new buildings that look different, any structure of monolithic stature, steely materials, odd angles. Strange that in a place distinguished by progressive politics and an artistic spirit, the reactionaries stand out when it comes to urban design.

If you're going to San Francisco, the best new architecture you see might be the International Terminal (2001) at the SFO airport, about eight miles south of city limits. Designed by Craig Hartman of Skidmore Owings and Merrill, its soaring flights of trusses and space, foregrounded by a minestrone of freeway and parking-lot structures, would likely have been grounded by the municipal planning process had the building been located in the city proper. Practically the only place within San Francisco where far-out architecture has been realized of late is the Yerba Buena Redevelopment Area, a new downtown district of convention centers, museums, hotels, and entertainment spots built atop what was once skid row. Yet Mario Botta's eyepopping San Francisco Museum of Modern Art (1995) or James Polshek's functionally expressive Center for the Arts Theater (1994) might never have risen outside redevelopment jurisdiction. Swarms of opponents would have massed like the birds in Alfred Hitchcock's film, lining up ominously at meetings and cackling that the museum's faceted brickwork and sliced cylindrical tower had no local precedents, or that the theater's collage of cubic volumes and vivid colors wasn't consistent with the historic materials and textures of the area.

Just about the only thing that flocks of people can agree on is that San Francisco is worth fighting for. The city dons a wardrobe of arresting visages. San Francisco, gridded, whitish, wooden and stucco, rolls up and down over 40 hills, the building-enhanced last dance of the California Coast Ranges as they shoot down to the sea. Many valuable struggles have been undertaken in the name of these beauties and intricacies – against billboards that mar the skyline, chain stores that put local stores out of business, and unfair tenant evictions that force poorer people out. Yet some San Franciscans are loving a traditionalist esthetic vision of the town to death.

Love is often blind. Because many of San Francisco's vocal citizenry came to this city from elsewhere, and because they came here not by accident but by intention, they hold particularly strong attachment to early impressions, memories of youthful romps from bay to breakers, and carefree days spent in small cream-colored flats that rented for pittance. Proposed changes threaten people's core identities. If San Francisco doesn't look the way it did, they too will have changed. The love of older architecture and hatred of the new expresses a fear of aging and the loss of one's lodestar. Someday the city might be looked at as a museum to the region's cult of perpetual youth, just as Venice, Italy, has become a museum of Renaissance *coloratura*. And as in Venice, in San Francisco tourism sways the urban design process. San Francisco holds greater claim (through frequent use) to the nickname "America's Favorite City" than any other place. In the media, million-dollar images treat the city as a cable-car ride to the stars or a spin under the Golden Gate Bridge. Not only do famous sites like the bridge, Transamerica Pyramid or Coit Tower hold court; ridges of Victorians and Edwardians also file out peaked, turreted, and reliably recognizable rhythms. Alas, postcard San Francisco makes it hard for the real city to grow. Through mass exposure in magazines, films, and television, San Francisco is immediately and spectacularly identifiable, branded,

12.1
**A steely prototype for the narrow lot, 1022 Natoma Street, Stanley Saitowitz architect**
Photo by Pad McLaughlin

12.2
**The bane
of the bay
window, recent
condominiums,
16th and Missouri
Streets**
Photo by Pad
McLaughlin

marqueed, a reel of appetizing scenes. The success of tourism encases "Baghdad by the Bay" in imagistic scaffolding that blocks deeper visual grains.

While tourism has been a part of San Francisco's mix since the nineteenth century, the city's architectural vision turned from the future to the past during the 1970s – the decade during which tourism once and for all eclipsed shipping and manufacturing as the number one industry. Nowadays, factories, warehouses, dry docks, and bridges embody a little noticed industrial San Francisco. Despite their showcasing in movies, like Clint Eastwood's *Dirty Harry* series, such structures hardly figure in public debate about the city's architectural identity. The Eastern Waterfront is left to rot, a vast memory-tomb of the city's former working classes and mechanical innovations. Out of benign municipal neglect, some innovative architecture has been built in these coarser warehouse and factory barrens. In particular, Stanley Saitowitz's loft projects propose an inventive typology of continuous living space expressed through large clear-span windows and assertive industrial materials. However, implausible as it sounds, even amid the decaying hulks of manufacturing and shipping some other designers sweeten their facades with Victorian finery and lace. In a Potrero Hill complex completed in 1999 bay windows protrude out of a loft, despite the fact that the nearest residential building with bay windows is several blocks away and the immediate surroundings stare back corrugated metal, cracked cement, and clumps of anise weeds. If architecture that expresses contemporary lifestyle and historical industry can't be built here, then where?

Certainly not in the other new city district – besides Yerba Buena – of the past twenty years, South Beach, located along what had been a working waterfront of piers and warehouses south of downtown. Past the palm-lined Embarcadero, South Beach revels in patent-yuppie historicism. When the San Francisco Giants baseball team decided to build a new ballpark (completed in 2000) there, the architectural team, Hellmuth Obata and Kassebaum, looked for inspiration to nearby brick warehouses and not nearby concrete warehouses. In spite of the fact that brick bearing wall construction makes no sense in earthquake country and was abandoned after the 1906 earthquake, brick veneer covers most of the ballpark's forceful concrete and steel skeleton as well as other new buildings in the vicinity. Along with fake stone copings and a clock tower, Pacific Bell Park (while a wonderful place to watch a baseball game) looks from the outside like any other retro ballpark or a Rouse festival marketplace, a neo-Baltimore by the San Francisco bay.

Two major urban design controversies of recent years stand out. In 1999, needing to replace their seismically-damaged building, the M. H. de Young Museum proposed a new building for its site in Golden Gate Park. With great foresight, the museum's trustees chose the firm of Herzog & de Meuron. Known

12.3
**Bring me back to the old ball game, Pacific Bell Park, Third and King Streets, Hellmuth Obata Kassebaum architects**
Photo by Pad McLaughlin

for their approach to building skin as an urban-scale screening room, the architects unveiled a façade of glass and dimpled/perforated copper that would generate intricate textures playing off light and nearby flora. Nonetheless, the feat of getting their proposal for a new de Young approved by the city has approached the magnitude of Hercules's fifth labor cleaning the Augean Stables. Through several seasons of public meetings, opponents argued that the design didn't harmonize with the natural context of the park, even though no building presumably could meet that demand, and despite the fact that the park's tall cypress, pine, and eucalyptus trees are themselves an artificial terrain, planted during the nineteenth century atop an unglamorous landscape of shrubs, grasses, and sand dunes. Some citizens loudly advocated resurrecting the Museum's former Spanish Revival design on the grounds that its historicism better matched the traditions of the city, and ignoring the fact that such period revivals bring back to life architectural symbols of colonialism offensive to some Latinos and Native Americans. Finally, their arguments faltering, diehards settled on battling the education tower proposed by Herzog & de Meuron. Incredibly, after several millennia of cultures around the world erecting towers so that they could be viewed from long distances and provide a focal point for a place, the diehards felt the only appropriate tower should be one that can't be seen from afar. Eventually, the museum was forced to cut the height of the tower from 160 feet to 144 feet.

In 2002, a second controversy came to a close. After a long planning process, the Lesbian Gay Bisexual Transgender Community Center opened on Market and Octavia Streets. Designed by Jane Cee and Peter Pfau, the building's polychrome glass curtain walls brilliantly express the different shades of the LGBT community as well as their travails and triumphs. Unfortunately, only part of the center as originally proposed was built. Because a Victorian occupies the corner lot, the city's preservation community rose up in arms at the first mention of its possible demolition. Though the three-story wooden building has no striking architectural or historical features, and hundreds like it grace the streets, preservationists argued that it forms a unique trapezoidal response to Market Street's diagonal clash with the grid. A photo that shows the building standing at the edge of devastation caused by the 1906 fire also stirred emotions. These appeals worked, and the building was given landmark status. The architects had to forsake the far grander possibilities of using the corner, and instead settle for the mid-block lot. Together the two buildings look separated by more than just a century. They embody the city's quibbling march to the future.

Given all that has been said so far – the power of tourism, tradition, and all the trimmings – it's no wonder that the preservation of modernist architecture has been a low priority. In 1996, the Red Cross Building by Gardner Dailey, one of the city's leading mid-century architects, was demolished with little opposition. In 2001, the same fate befell the Daphne Funeral Home,

12.4
**Building a diverse community, Lesbian Gay Bisexual Transgender Center, Market and Octavia Streets, Jane Cee and Peter Pfau architects**
Photo by Pad McLaughlin

designed by the noted Los Angeles firm of Jones and Emmons. Even though the Daphne – the only small-scale public example of an open plan in the city – was a far more important work of architecture than the LGBT's corner Victorian, the battle to save it went down to defeat. The reason has to do with the fact that for preservationists, modernism has long been the enemy. Despite the current rise of worldwide interest in a revamped architectural modernism, postmodernism still reigns in San Francisco.

How did this reactive state of affairs acquire such tidal force? To understand the anti-modernism of the past twenty years, one has to go back several decades. In the late 1950s, San Francisco was the first American city to begin dismantling plans to throw a spaghetti-jumble of freeways atop the small 46-square-mile city. During the early 1970s, the term "Manhattanization" came into vogue as part of an attack on highrise towers. Referendums were held, and allowable building height and bulk came down. No downtown skyscraper would ever again approach the heights of the Bank of America (779 feet) or Transamerica Pyramid (853 feet), completed respectively in 1969 and 1972. Nor would historic buildings, like the lost Montgomery Block (a longtime artistic haven) or City of Paris Department Store, be demolished any longer. Plans for slab, super-block urban renewal similarly shrank in scale, even though areas like the Western Addition had already been severely torn apart. As elsewhere,

12.5
**The great ornamental leap backward, apartment building, 21st Street and South Van Ness Avenue**
Photo by Pad McLaughlin

the autocratic ways of modernist urbanism brought about citizen reactions and urban design re-evaluations. More than elsewhere, the San Francisco counter-attack hardened into dogma.

The *Urban Design Element* of the city's Master Plan has been the bible of San Francisco's architectural philosophy since its completion by the City Planning Department in 1971. Boldly, it shifts the focus of architectural design from issues of art, structure, and function to those of historic and geographic context. Much of the plan makes sense. For instance, architects are encouraged to preserve the city's precipitous landforms by grouping towers on the tops of hills instead of on their sides, where they would flatten the topography. However, the costs outweigh the benefits. Architects are pushed to replicate the contextual features of adjacent buildings in any new design. Even though most new buildings are far larger than their Victorian or Edwardian predecessors, the plan encourages that their massing be broken up to match the small lot sizes in vogue a century ago. But should transitions between old and new buildings reduce the latter's design to dull reiteration? Are visually strong buildings that contrast severely with their surroundings such a bad thing? If these policies had been followed earlier in the city's history, they would have prevented any serious architecture. San Francisco would never have seen the likes of Willis Polk's Hallidie Building (1918) – one of the world's first glass curtain walls – or Timothy Pflueger's 450 Sutter Street building (1930) – a streamlined appliqué of glass and terracotta Mayan ornament onto a steel frame.

After more referendums, a subsequent planning document, the *Downtown Plan* (1985), extended the use of design guidelines. A highpoint of the plan is its strict preservation of over 500 significant historical buildings, setting a national standard. The *Downtown Plan* also mandates several conservation (or preservation) districts, intended to prevent new buildings whose scale and composition would overwhelm older structures. The plan goes too far, however, by telling architects *how* to compose, forcing them to clad steel frames with tops and veneers that cause new tall buildings to look all too much like wedding cakes. In their zeal to bring back the good old days of skyscrapers, the planners overlooked the fact that their model era, 1906–1933, wasn't any longer than the age of modernism, 1945–1975. In reality, the city's urban design policies regulate not as much on the basis of context – for the modern context is routinely excluded – but on preferred temporal style.

This post-modern ideology leaves out the critical post-war period of San Franciscan cultural ascendancy. In almost every artistic arena, from poetry to architecture, San Francisco came into its own after the Second World War – not before it. No reasonable San Franciscan would disavow such local post-war painters as Clyfford Still, Elmer Bischoff, Jay DeFeo, and Joan Brown; photographers like Minor White and Ansel Adams; poets such as Kenneth Rexroth, William Everson, and Michael McClure; independent filmmakers including James Broughton, Bruce Baillie, Bruce Connor, and Sidney Patterson; and landscape architects like Thomas Church and Lawrence Halprin. Why, then, should the debate on the city's architectural identity omit the important contributions of William Wurster, Joseph Esherick, Moore Lyndon Turnbull and Whittaker, Anshen and Allen, and Skidmore Owings and Merrill, all of whom built important buildings in the city and vicinity between the war and the 1970s? Why, moreover, should forceful engineering structures not be considered part of our urban design heritage? Eliminating modernism from the municipal debate on urban design cuts San Francisco off from its own artistic legacy, the great international works of the past century, and the most vital contemporary architectural discourse.

Since the 1980s, forward-thinking architectural discourse has been noticeably absent in San Francisco planning. After a history of proposing Utopian schemes and then retrenching into downzoning and design guide-lining, the city has practically given up on long-range planning. Instead of moving forward and adjusting the reactive strictures of the 1970s and 1980s, instead of realizing that the reaction to modernism was as extreme as modernism itself, city planning in San Francisco has shriveled to permit processing and a regulatory scholasticism. One local architect compares going to the Building or City Planning Departments for permit approval to Franz Kafka's description of K.'s dealings with the authorities of *The Castle*.

In large part, as mentioned above, the planners are merely responding to vocal activists. Before the 1970s, San Franciscans were so preoccupied with their dream city, they didn't have time to wallow in details. Yet nobody in his or her right mind would say that the city of late hasn't cultivated a weighty self-image. San Francisco's gentrified neighborhoods are hotbeds of opposition to architectural innovation or densification, masters of the arcane detail – whether architectural, historical, or legal. Merely mentioning the Telegraph Hill Dwellers or Noe Valley Neighbors is enough to strike fear into the heart of any progressive architect. Paradoxically, in such neighborhoods (and there are lots of them in the city) the disconnect between exuberant interior lifestyle and stolid exterior expression couldn't be greater. Gobs of money are spent on kitchen and bathroom remodeling, but, thanks to planning policies and neighborhood activists, gut-rehabbing homeowners go to great lengths to keep facades familiar. Maybe living lavishly indoors induces people to pretend, at least from the outside, that all's as modest as it was 100 years ago. Or possibly those San Franciscans who have cut ties to tradition and family find it more comforting to live behind traditional facades, the same look of building that their faraway families inhabit.

Sometimes planning shortsightedness has no neighborhood activist to blame. In 1999, the Prada Company hired Rem Koolhaas to design a flagship building on the corner of Grant Avenue and Post Street, in one of the *Downtown Plan* conservation districts. At a meeting of the San Francisco Planning Commission to approve the project in 2001, the City Planning Department, citing its interpretation of the guidelines for the conservation district, recommended disapproval. The basis for their negative recommendation? The proposed building didn't copy the compositional strategies of its older neighbors, cornice line for cornice line. Even worse, they stated that the proposed building stood out in excess of its public importance – whatever that means. Effectively, the planners were saying that new architecture in a conservation district established because of its prior architectural inventiveness must not be inventive or conspicuous. They couldn't see that Koolhaas's design actually advances the creative energies of its context. For starters, the Prada building's height and shape, and its articulation into a frame, fit squarely in the mainstream of the district. But Koolhaas wouldn't settle for meek replication. His proposed stainless-steel façade is composed of transparent holes and opaque discs that would create fantastic light effects on the interior and variable clouds of luminosity on the exterior. What makes these urban design gestures successful is that they ramp up the tradition of innovative illumination on Grant Avenue. During the district's reconstruction after the 1906 earthquake and fire, tone-setting buildings had simple facades and large square windows that responded to needs for illumination and exhibition. In sync, Koolhaas's unusual fenestration plays off today's different needs for retail pomp through architectural spectacle.

**12.6**
**Towards a
new shopping,
proposed Prada
Store, Grant
Avenue at Post
Street, Rem
Koolhaas architect**

Amazingly, in a city drowning in process and regulation, decades of planning can be tossed aside when powerful interests intrude. Atop Potrero Hill, the view north toward downtown San Francisco is the stuff car commercials are made of. Steep streets cut straight sightlines toward gleaming skyscrapers. While tall buildings make the panorama exciting, if a local government official has his way no further monuments of architecture will spoil the prospect. In March of 2002, with little more than a few telephone calls, State Senator John Burton stopped construction of a planned 17-story dormitory for the new University of California at San Francisco's campus at Mission Bay. No matter that the 700-bed dormitory would have helped to ease a drastic affordable housing crunch. No matter that the proposed building's 160-foot height met the guidelines of the Mission Bay Plan, approved in 1998 after 15 acrimonious years in the making.

How could the desires of one politician and a few hill residents for an unchanged view trump the greater need for affordable housing? Why should the planning process make it so difficult to build challenging architecture? Have earlier struggles against historic demolitions, freeways, urban renewal, and skyscrapers carried over to a permanent war against anything new and different? While few San Franciscans dispute the sentiment that the city possesses an incomparable landscape and that architecture and engineering have improved this physical setting in the past, its citizens seem incapable of agreeing on how to enhance it in the future.

Such indecisiveness proves costly. From 1996 until 2001, dot-coms, dot-commers, and their martini-and-loft lifestyle overtook large parts of the city. San Francisco, along with nearby Silicon Valley, was ground zero for the Internet revolution, and as the economy boomed, the city underwent one of its most traumatic periods of upheaval. Ironically, in a city that thought it had regulated large-scale change out of existence, an economic gale blew into town and brought about as much dislocation as the great urban renewal efforts of the 1960s.

As the dot-com boom has busted, San Francisco's pivotal urban design challenge is to overcome the climate of opposition. Over the past twenty years, in any given situation, the naysayers have never held great numbers. Thanks to the city's exhaustive neighbor notification program and permit appeals process, even a single opponent can generate considerable hurdles. The problem has always been that the few people with an axe to grind are far more dogged than those in support of a project. Yet in some of the recent urban design controversies, an encouraging development has begun to manifest itself. Increasing numbers of citizens are fed up with design mediocrity, and are becoming more vocal. The long wave of architectural conservatism may have crested. The Herzog and de Meuron museum is proceeding, in part because of the intervention of local artists and architects. Despite the planners, the more visionary ordinary citizens who sit on the planning commission approved Koolhaas's Prada Building. International architects like Thom Mayne, Renzo Piano, and Daniel Liebeskind are in the final stages of designing significant museums and public buildings. Downtown, several elegant glass-curtain-wall skyscrapers have risen in the past few years, including Gary Handel's sleek Four Seasons Hotel (2001). Hopefully, in a few years time, the new wealth of world-class architecture might cause more San Franciscans to see their city in a new light, as a place of the future as well as of the past.

After all, the city doesn't have a long history. Founded only a century and a half ago, San Francisco's reactive preoccupation with its visual image might be understood as a momentary (although two-decade long) crisis in self-confidence. The climate for urbanistic experimentation is better in newer cities, like Houston or Phoenix, that don't dwell too much on their past identity. It's also better in older cities like London or Paris, where any new building joins an architectural assemblage impossible to generalize, centuries of building activity that defeat any idea of a singular urban image. In both cases, youthful and

12.7
**Curtain walls for our time, Four Seasons Hotel, Market Street at Grant Avenue, Gary Handel architect**
Photo by Pad McLaughlin

mature, the urban climate accommodates new ideas and appearances. By contrast, San Francisco has seemed lately like an overly responsible 30-something, all too eager to cut off its wild years for a static ideal of ancestral foundations.

In retrospect, the age of reaction has been as severe as the preceding age of progress. From the late 1940s till the early 1970s, proponents of

Utopian modernism cast their vision of the city in bi-polar terms like blight *vs* renewal, or outdated *vs* new. Then, from the mid-1970s onward, reactive post-modernists similarly used oppositional frameworks like small *vs* large, or harmonious *vs* contrasting. The past was seen by modernists as an impediment to the future, while post-modernists turned the tables to recast the future as an impediment to the past. Ultimately, aren't these visions opposite sides of a coin? The modernist highway to the future and the post-modernist detour to the past each offer limited and exclusionary understandings of the city.

Struggles against new architecture discussed in this article point out the dark side of urban design in conditions of affluence. For all that San Francisco's recent confrontational design politics (with its potent use of adjectives) suggests, what it yields really is the ethos of individualism. The neighborhood activist's view of the city is of a neo-city, nurtured not by a love of density, monumentality, and change, but by a power to control swathes of space, the signal quality of American suburbia – not social interest but defense of private interest, not people caught up in their desires to participate in a city but in their fears of the city intruding upon them. The activists see San Francisco as a patchwork of neighborly villages, yet in reality the city they envision is infected by a romantic sense of timelessness, a city without change, the same tomorrow as today, lovely, tidy, a closed canon. Do San Francisco's fringes, its non-traditional families, lifestyle experimenters, and counter-cultures add up to a reduction when it comes to urban design, the hot life chilled in reports, meetings, referendums, the protocols of mediocrity and resignation? Does the sum of individuals equal nothing more, nothing new?

In the first decade of the twenty-first century, one can do no better than expose this predicament of reactionary urban design. A city's context can never be a closed canon – indeed, the idea of canonical thinking is inimical to urban growth and vitality. If San Francisco's individuals truly want to build out from the city's context, they must acknowledge its complexity, volatility, and frequently severe contrasts. San Francisco's visual appeal has never rested on smooth transitions or steady repetition. Compare the stylistic and textural jumble of buildings on Russian Hill with the smooth monotonies on Sunset District streets. The glorious moments of the city abruptly contrast water with land, grid with topography, valleys with heights, nature with building, and buildings with each other.

The crux of architectural reaction in San Francisco can be traced to a narrow and superficial definition of urban design context. While the city's *Urban Design Element* takes into account pre-war architecture and topography, it ignores post-war design, infrastructure, technology, economics, and society. The energies that can inform the design on any given parcel of land extend far beyond issues of façade and massing conformity. Urban contexts are like individuals before they congeal into the norms of identity, when they are still open to multiple affiliations, experiences, and energies. Urban contexts must be sought out in the moment like scents, the pungencies of San Francisco's natural environment, food culture, ethnic diversity, hi-tech economy, and complex history – Victorians and Moderns, tourist landmarks and neighborhood nooks, walking streets and driving streets. For example, the idea of the regional context has long been over-simplified. In the past, Bay Region architectural movements looked closely at local materials such as redwood and cedar trees. Yet the city of San Francisco never had such trees. Its native flora, nonetheless, offers other inspirations for design: looking at the chaparral alone – and its associations with fire, sand, wind, cool sea air, serpentine soil, and drought – inspires a wide range of colors, shapes, and patterns. San Francisco, as its internationally recognized food culture demonstrates, can realize original style out of the cornucopia of local substance. What's more, the city's population, to an unprecedented extent, represents all corners of the globe. What's local is most likely an import from somewhere else. But why aren't the visual symbols and design strategies of Asia, where over one-third of the city's residents trace their origin, or Latin America, where the largest group of Californians trace their ancestry, a larger part of the debate on the city's architectural identity? How long must we recycle the same Victorian or Colonial details? San Francisco,

12.8
**When structure mattered, Battleship Gun Crane, Hunters Point Naval Shipyard**
Photo by Pad McLaughlin

12.9
**The unseen
landmark, Sutro
Tower**
Photo by Pad
McLaughlin

as the Internet revolution in communication shows, needs to search for other images, forms, and dispositions of itself.

How refreshing it would be to re-imagine the city through its lesser-known industrial monuments. The most notable of these is certainly the unloved Sutro Tower (1968), a 977-foot television and radio tower. Perched atop a hill (and thus reaching 1,390 feet in the sky), the steel colossus dominates the city. Since it looks like the mast of a galleon, the Sutro Tower could symbolically guide San Francisco over the stormy seas of self-interest to new collective design destinations. Another striking and unrecognized landmark is the re-gunning mole crane (1947) at the Hunter's Point Naval Shipyard, at one time the world's mightiest hoisting machine. Visible from much of the southern part of the city and especially the bay front, the cantilever arms of the 200-foot steel-truss crane once lifted the turrets of guns onto the largest Second World War battleships. It's tempting to think of how the crane's power could be used metaphorically to raze bureaucratic gridlock and raise the city from its urban design doldrums.

## Chapter 13

# San Diego/Tijuana – An Urbanism Beyond the Property Line

*Teddy Cruz*

A central urban crisis facing us today is inequality. Any discussion on architecture and urbanism that does not begin by engaging the asymmetry of urbanization today between enclaves of wealth and sectors of marginality would simply perpetuate the powerlessness of design. The context of pressing socio-political realities worldwide and the conditions of conflict have redefined the territory of intervention. It is unsettling, in fact, to witness some of the most "cutting edge" practices of architecture rush unconditionally to China and the United Arab Emirates to build their dream castles, and in the process reduce themselves to mere caricatures of agents of change, camouflaging, as they do, gentrification with a massive hyper aesthetic and formalist project. I certainly hope that in the context of urbanism's and architecture's euphoria for the "Dubais" of the world in recent years, and the seemingly limitless horizon of design possibilities they inspired, we now can be mobilized by a sense of dissatisfaction, a feeling of "pessimistic optimism" that can provoke us to also address, head on, the sites of conflict that define and will continue to define the cities of the twenty-first century.

One of the primary conflicts in our time is the one generated by the current gap dividing institutions of Urbanization and the Public. "Where is the PUBLIC today?" is a fundamental question that must frame the point of departure to revitalize our conversation about the future of the city. The shrinking relevance of the public has become evident mainly since 2008 when the public bailed out the architects of the economic crisis only to receive as repayment millions of foreclosures in addition to unprecedented spending cuts in education, housing, and infrastructure.

While this anti-public agenda is nothing new to the politics and economics of urban development in the construction of the city, so are the periods in history when the search for a collective imagination has been central to the formation of institutions of urbanization. While there are similarities between the economic downturns of 2008 and 1928, the decades following the Great Depression years witnessed the emergence of the New Deal and with it new institutional synergies across government, philanthropy, and civil society, which represented a collective commitment to investment in public housing, infrastructure, education, and services with the goal of generating a more equitable distribution of economic and civic resources. Our current period of crisis has been defined by exactly the opposite. The consolidation of power today is not only economic but also political, changing the terms very dramatically by polarizing institutions and publics in unprecedented ways.

So, because I do not think FDR will come back any time soon, and the restoration of a top-down Public Project is unattainable in today's political climate driven by de-taxing of the wealthy and institutional atrophy, we must begin this conversation by imagining other publics and their operational dimension in the context of today's inequality. As the concentration of resources has been diverted, once more, so dramatically from the many to the very few, the essential question is, what do we do in the meantime? As architects, we cannot continue perpetuating the notion of a "free imagination" as our creative prophylactic, keeping us at a "critical distance" from the crisis of the public and the institutions in today's conflicts. What we need is an "urgent civic imagination" provoked by a "critical proximity" to the very conditions that produced the crisis in the first place. How to intervene in the gap between the top-down and the bottom-up while reconnecting art to the drama of the socio-economic and political realities shaping the city today is an essential task, as an anti-immigration, anti-taxes, anti-public, anti-infrastructure society today continues to blindly defend a strange version of democracy as the almighty right to be left alone.

What follows is a discussion in two parts: first, a general outline of the border conditions that define the San Diego/Tijuana nexus and, second, a discussion of what might be done to address the inequities so central to this nexus to impart an understanding of the city through a discussion of practice.

# The camouflaging of crisis: 60 linear miles of local transborder urban conflict

"There is no such thing as a natural disaster," the landscape architect and theorist Anudartha Mathur has declared often, in the context of her work on the Mississippi River. Disasters, she declares, happen when the logic of natural systems is encroached on by stupid urban development. Every disaster yielding human loss, socio-economic and environmental degradation, and political strife can be traced to collisions provoked by either institutional idiocy or discrimination, as top-down forces of urbanization and/or militarization clash with bottom-up natural and social networks.

Much of my research on the transborder urbanisms that inform my practice began as a desire to critically observe and trace the specificity of such conflicts inscribed in the territory of the border between San Diego, in the US, and Tijuana, Mexico, one of the most contested borders in the world. This observation has not only enabled a practice of research, a sort of projective forensics of the territory, but has also revealed the need to seek expanded notions of architectural design. The revelation was simple: without retroactively tracing and projectively altering the backward exclusionary policies that have guided the construction of this territory over recent years, our work as architects will continue to be a mere camouflaging (decorative at best) of selfish, oil-hungry urbanization from China to Dubai to New York to San Diego.

Moving from these broad conceptual meditations to the specificity of the San Diego–Tijuana border, one oscillates back and forth between two radically different ways of constructing a city. At one pole we find in San Diego some of the wealthiest communities in the world. At the other pole and barely 20 minutes away we find some of the poorest settlements, which have emerged in the many informal settlements that dot the new periphery of Tijuana. These two different types of suburbia are emblematic of the incremental division of the contemporary city into enclaves of megawealth surrounded by rings of poverty. I am interested in processes of mediation that can produce critical interfaces between and across these opposites, exposing conflict as an operational device to transform architectural practice. Critical observation of this border region transforms it into a laboratory in which we can trace the current politics of migration and citizenship, labor and surveillance; the tensions

13.1
Radicalizing the local: 60 linear miles of transborder conflict (installation on the façade of the US pavilion, 2008 Architecture Venice Biennial). A 60-linear-mile cross-section, tangential to the border wall, between these two border cities compresses the most dramatic issues currently challenging our normative notions of architecture and urbanism. This transborder "cut" begins 30 miles north of the border, in the periphery of San Diego, and ends 30 miles south of the border. We can find along this section's trajectory a series of collisions, critical junctures, or conflicts between natural and artificial ecologies, top-down development and bottom-up organization

between sprawl and density; the contrasts between formal and informal urbanisms, and wealth and poverty. All these elements incrementally characterize the contemporary city everywhere. Border areas such as the Tijuana–San Diego region are the sites where the forces of division and control produced by these global zones of conflict are amplified and physically manifested in the territory, producing, in turn, local zones of conflict.

A 60-linear-mile cross-section, tangential to the border wall, between these two border cities exposes the most dramatic issues challenging our normative notions of architecture and urbanism. We can find along this section's trajectory a series of collisions, critical junctures between natural and artificial ecologies, top-down forces of urban development and bottom-up organizational systems, all anticipatory of territorial crises. These conflicts are made spatial as a large freeway and a military infrastructure collides with watershed systems, gated communities with marginal neighborhoods, formal urbanization with informal economies, and dense slums with sprawling enclaves. This transborder cut begins 30 miles north of the border, on the periphery of San Diego, and ends 30 miles south of the border, at the point where the fence sinks into the Pacific Ocean.

## +30 miles: San Diego

The only interruptions along an otherwise continuous sprawl, 30 miles inland from the border, occur where the military bases that dot San Diego's suburbs overlap with environmentally protected lands. This produces a strange montage of housing subdivisions, natural ecology, and militarization. The conflict between military bases and environmental zones has been recently dramatized in mock Afghan villages, equipped with hologram technologies to project Afghan subjects, now being erected here as vernacular military-training sites.

## +25 miles: San Diego

A large freeway and mall infrastructure runs the length of coastal San Diego, colliding with a natural network of canyons, rivers, and creeks that descend toward the Pacific Ocean. A necklace of territorial voids is produced out of the conflict between large infrastructure and the watershed. As the politics of water will define the future of this region, the recuperation of these truncated natural resources is essential to anticipate density.

## +20 miles: San Diego

Top-down private development has instantiated a selfish and oil-hungry sprawl of detached McMansions everywhere. The conflict between masterplanned gated communities and the natural topography flattens the differential landscape of San Diego's edges and encroaches on the natural cycles of fire-prone areas. This archipelago of beige tract homes also exacerbates a land use of exclusion into a sort of apartheid of everyday life.

### +15 miles: San Diego

San Diego's downtown has reconfigured itself with exclusive tax-revenue, redevelopment powers, becoming an island of wealth delimited by specific zoning and budgetary borders. Luxury condos and hotels, stadiums and convention centers, surrounded by generic commercial franchises, compose this stew of privatization from New York to San Diego. The proximity of wealth and poverty found at the border checkpoint is reproduced here in the conflict between powerful downtowns and the neighborhoods of marginalization that surround them. It is in these neighborhoods that cheap immigrant labor concentrates, conveniently becoming the service sector that supports downtown's massive project of gentrification.

### +10 miles: San Diego

The conflict between the formal and the informal emerges as immigrants fill the first ring of suburbanization surrounding downtown, retrofitting an obsolete urbanism of older, postwar detached bungalows. Informal densities and economies produce a sort of three-dimensional land use that collides with the one-dimensional zoning that has characterized these older neighborhoods.

### 0 miles: San Diego–Tijuana

At the border itself, the metal fence becomes emblematic of the conflict between these two border cities, re-enacting the perennial alliance between militarization and urbanization. This territorial conflict is currently dramatized by the hardening, after the attacks of September 11, 2001, of the border wall that divides this region, incrementally transforming San Diego into the world's largest gated community. As we cross the border into Mexico, we immediately see how the large infrastructure of the Tijuana River clashes with the border wall. This is the only place where an otherwise continuous metal fence is pierced and opened as the river enters San Diego. A faint yellow line is inscribed on the dry river's concrete channel to indicate the trajectory of the border. But as the channel moves beyond the fence and into San Diego's territory the concrete disappears, and the channel becomes the Tijuana River estuary, a US ecological reserve, which frames the natural ecology of the river as it flows freely to the Pacific Ocean. What dramatizes this conflict between the natural and the political is the fact that the border checkpoint is at the exact intersection of both, punctuating the environmentally protected zone with a matrix of border patrol vehicles, helicopters, and electrified fences.

### −10 miles: Tijuana

Many of the sites of conflict found in San Diego are reproduced and amplified in Tijuana. As Tijuana grows eastward, for example, it is seduced by the style and glamour of the masterplanned, gated communities of the US, and builds its own version – miniaturized replicas of typical suburban southern California tract homes, paradoxically imported into Tijuana to provide "social housing." Thousands of tiny tract homes are now scattered around the periphery of Tijuana, creating a vast landscape of homogeneity and division that is at odds with this city's prevailing heterogeneous and organic metropolitan condition. These diminutive 250-square-foot (23-square-meter) dwellings come equipped with all the clichés and conventions: manicured landscaping, gatehouses, model units, banners and flags, mini setbacks, front and backyards.

### −15 miles: Tijuana

The conflict between the formal and the informal is re-enacted here, as these mini tract homes quickly submit to transformation by occupants who are little hindered by Tijuana's permissive zoning regulations. While the gated communities of southern California remain closed systems due to stringent zoning that prohibits any kind of formal alteration or programmatic juxtaposition, residents in Tijuana fill in setbacks and occupy front and backyards and garages with more construction to support mixed use and provide more usable space.

### −20 miles: Tijuana

These mini American-style masterplanned communities are intertwined with a series of informal communities or slums, and both surround enclaves of maquiladoras. The conflict between cheap labor and informal housing is produced here as these factories extract cheap labor from nearby slums without contributing any support for dwellings. As these favela-like sectors grow ever larger, they encroach on the natural ecology of Tijuana's delicate topography, also re-enacting the conflict between the informal and the natural.

### −30 miles: Tijuana

As we reach the sea on the Mexican side of the border territory, the metal border fence sinks into the Pacific Ocean. As the poles of this militarized artifact descend into the depths of the water, the site is simultaneously strangely poetic and hugely tragic, physically manifesting the contradictions that characterize the border landscape and amplifying the most dramatic of all territorial collisions across this 60-mile section: the conflict between the natural and the jurisdictional.

It is in the midst of these metropolitan and territorial sites of conflict that contemporary architectural practice should reposition itself. Each of these physical junctions needs to be unfolded to reveal hidden institutional histories, the missing information that can allow us to piece together our anticipatory research, enabling the reorganization of the fragmented and discriminatory policies that have created this archipelago of division. In other words, no meaningful intervention can occur in the contemporary city unless we first expose the conditions, the political and economic forces (of jurisdiction and ownership), that have produced these collisions in the first place.

## Practices of encroachment: post-bubble urban strategies where urban waste moves Southbound, illegal zoning seeps into North

By zooming further into the particularities of this volatile territory, traveling back and forth between these two border cities, we can expose many other landscapes of contradiction where conditions of difference and sameness collide and overlap. A series of "off the radar" two-way border crossings – North–South and South–North across the border wall – suggest that no matter how high and long the post-9/11 border wall becomes, it will always be transcended by migrating populations and the relentless flows of goods and services back and forth across the formidable barrier that seeks to stop them. These illegal flows are physically manifested, in one direction, by the informal land use patterns and economies produced by migrant workers flowing from Tijuana and into San Diego, responding to a demand for cheap labor in Southern California. But, while "human flow" moves Northbound in search for dollars, "infrastructural waste" moves in the opposite direction to construct an insurgent, cross-border urbanism of emergency.

## South to North suburbs made of non-conformity: Tijuana's encroachment into San Diego's sprawl

The shifting of cultural demographics in American suburbs has transformed many immigrant neighborhoods into the site of investigation for our practice, challenging the politics of discriminatory zoning in San Diego. Our research and work in the US has focused, in fact, on the impact of immigration in the transformation of the American neighborhood, arguing that the future of Southern California's urbanism will be determined by tactics of retrofit and adaptation.

Tactics of encroachment: as the Latin American Diaspora travels Northbound, it inevitably alters and transforms the fabric of San Diego's older subdivisions, generating non-conforming mixed uses and high densities that retrofit Levittown with difference.

Non-Conforming Buddha: a tiny post-war bungalow in a San Diego mid-city nieghborhood has been transformed from a single-family residence into a Buddhist temple.

An urbanism 70' deep: thirty some tunnels have been dug beneath Homeland Security in the last eight years. One of the largest ones was discovered last year. It had retaining walls, water and air extraction systems and electricity. It connected a house in Tijuana and a factory in San Diego.

South to North: Neighborhoods made of non-conformity. Tijuana's informal land use patterns encroach into San Diego's sprawl.

North to South: Neighborhoods made of waste. San Diego's Housing waste is recycled into Tijuana's slums.

Migrant housing: Mexican builders recuperate post-war bungalows that are slated for demolition in San Diego, and bring them across the border. Once imported into Tijuana they are assembled above one story steel frames. These floating houses define a space of opportunity beneath them, that will be filled with other uses.

Housing urbanism made of waste: one city recycles the leftover of the other into a second hand urbanism. Used garage doors and wooden crates make wall systems.

Recycled rubber tires are cut and dismantled into folded loops, creating a system that threads a stable retaining wall.

13.2

**Border research.**
**Trans-border informal urban dynamics: as illegal zoning seeps into the North to retrofit the large with the small, urban debris flows Southbound to construct a housing urbanism made of waste**

# North to South suburbs made of waste: San Diego's Levittown are recycled into Tijuana's slums

As people move North, the waste of San Diego flows southbound to construct an urbanism of emergency, as one city recycles the "left over" of the other into a sort of "second-hand" urbanism. Our research in San Diego/Tijuana has perforce studied the relationship of shanty towns, emergency housing, and the politics of cheap labor, as maquiladoras (NAFTA factories) settle in the midst of these slums.

Our research suggests a double project of retrofit by which the recycling of fragments, resources, and situations from these two cities reveals new ways of conceptualizing housing and density. The research of these transborder urbanisms that have informed our practice at the San Diego–Tijuana border has inspired the rethinking of the role of architecture within geographies of conflict. Different conceptual procedures are needed to straddle two radically different ways of constructing the city. Most emblematic of this contrast has always been the thought that, as far as I know, at no other international junction in the world can one find some of the wealthiest real estate, such as that found in the edges of San Diego's sprawl, so close to some of the poorest settlements in Latin America, manifested by the many slums that dot the new periphery of Tijuana. These two different types of suburbia are emblematic of the incremental division of the contemporary city and the territory between enclaves of megawealth and the rings of poverty that surround them. We are interested in processes of mediation that can produce critical interfaces between and across these opposites, expose conflict as an operational device to transform architectural/urban practice.

This has led us to focus on the micro-scale of the border neighborhood, proposing it as the urban laboratory of our time. The forces of control at play across the most trafficked checkpoint in the world has provoked the small border neighborhoods that surround it to construct alternative urbanisms of alteration and adaptation, searching for a different meaning of housing and public infrastructure. Fostering experimental collaborations with community-based NGOs such as Casa Familiar in San Ysidro and Alter Terra in Tijuana, our practice has fostered a small-scale activism that alters the rigidity of discriminatory urban planning of the American metropolis, and searches for new modes of sustainability and affordability. Through this practice we have come to understand that the future of the city should not be framed in terms of objects like buildings but by the fundamental reorganization of socio-economic relations, and that architects have a role in designing alternative institutional protocols. In other words, our current crisis can inspire ways of imagining counter-spatial procedures and political and economic structures that can produce a new civic imagination. Without altering the exclusionary policies that have facilitated a selfish, oil-hungry urban development in the last years, architects will continue being subordinate and remain mere decorators of exclusionary urbanization. This suggests the pressing need for expanded notions of architectural practice that can engage the shifting socio-political and economic domains that have been ungraspable by design.

## San Ysidro: the neighborhood as a socio-economic and political unit

The micro-urbanisms that are emerging within small communities across the city, in the form of non-conforming spatial and entrepreneurial practices, are defining a different idea of density and land use. It is from the particularities of these issues that a different idea of participation and representation emerges. Our work has engaged with the question, how can the human capacity and creative intelligence embedded in communities be amplified as the main armature for rethinking sustainability? We contend that the tactics of adaptation and retrofit across many immigrant neighborhoods in the US are the DNA for the transformation of discriminatory zoning and exclusionary economic development in the contemporary city.

13.3
**An urbanism of co-existence: designing political and economic process**

The exhausted recipes of global urban development based on exclusionary top-down economic models, discriminating homogeneity and privatization need to be redefined in order to transform the very political and economic

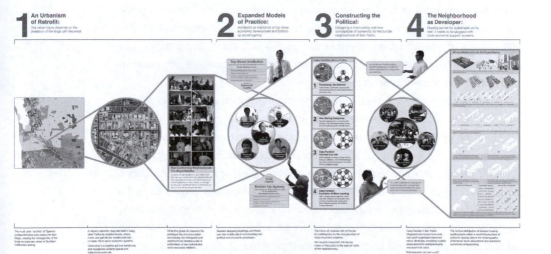

13.4
Designers of political process, part 1.
The multi-color "confetti" of Tijuana's compacted land uses seeps into San Diego, altering the homogeneity of the large exclusionary colors of Southern California's zoning.
  A migrant urbanism deposits itself in many older California neighborhoods, where mono-use parcels are transformed into complex micro socio-economic systems. Citizenship is a creative act that transforms and reorganizes existing spatial and institutional protocols.
  While the global city became the privileged site of consumption and display, the immigrant local neighborhood remains a site of production, of new cultural and socio-economic relations

institutions responsible for the current crisis. In the process of rethinking the top-down financial frameworks that have caused today's economic crisis and the spread of uneven urban development in the last years, our practice has been researching new interfaces between top-down recipes of urbanization and bottom-up socio-economic relations.

         This is why we need to focus on the translation of the socio-cultural and economic intelligence embedded in many marginal immigrant neighborhoods in order to propose more inclusive land use and economic categories that can support new forms of socio-economic sustainability. The hidden value (cultural, social, and economic) of these communities' informal transactions across bottom-up cultural activism, economies, and densities continues to be off the radar of conventional top-down planning institutions. It is in the context of these conditions where a different role for art, architecture, and environmental and community activist practices can emerge, which goes beyond the metaphorical representation of people, where only the community's symbolic image

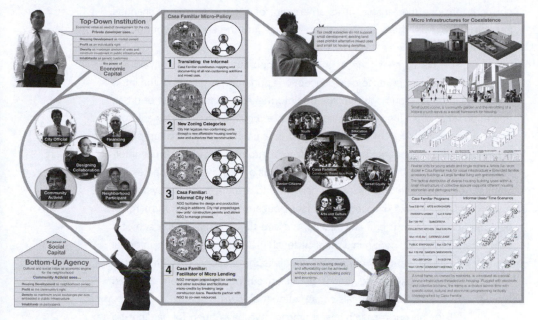

**13.5**
**Designers of political process, part 2.**
**Besides designing buildings, architects can also collaborate in constructing new political and economic processes.**
The future of urbanism will not be led by buildings but by the reorganization of socio-economic relations. We need to move from the neutral notion of the public to the specific rights of the neighborhood.
Casa Familiar in San Ysidro: neighborhood-based community non-profit organization becomes micro-developer, translating invisible socio-economic entrepreneurship into economic value.
The tactical distribution of diverse housing building types within a small infrastructure of collective spaces allows the choreography of temporal socio-educational and economic community programming

is amplified instead of mobilizing its socio-economic entrepreneurship to produce new models of urban development. These marginal communities' invisible urban praxis needs artistic interpretation and political representation and this is the space of intervention for our architectural practice.

In other words, behind the façade of poverty that characterizes the marginal communities, such as San Ysidro, on both sides of the border, there is a more complex idea of housing, a complexity we need to translate and make accessible to produce new urban policy. Across these neighborhoods, housing is conceived not as generic units of dwelling thrown in the territory, but as a relational system grounded on social organization. A new paradigm can emerge here about sustainability, threading environmental, economic, and social issues, where housing can become the main armature to construct public culture and infrastructure. In fact, a main pursuit of our practice has been to act as facilitators of a different conception of density that is less abstract and more specific, moving from a paradigm that measures density as an amount of "units–people" per acre into one that enables it as an amount of socio-economic exchanges per acre. Also, from the neutrality of the "public" into the specificity of rights – to the neighborhood.

In this context, one of the most important issues underlying our research has been to produce new conceptions and interpretations of the informal. Instead of a fixed image, we see the informal as a functional set of urban operations that allow the transgression of imposed political boundaries and top-down economic models. We are interested in a practice of translation of the actual operative procedures behind the informal into new tactics of urban intervention. We see the informal not as a noun but as a verb, which detonates traditional notions of site specificity and context into a more complex system of hidden socio-economic exchanges. Primarily, because of our work in marginal neighborhoods in San Diego and Tijuana, we see the informal as the site of a new interpretation of community and citizenship, understanding the informal not as an aesthetic category but as praxis. This is the reason we are interested in the emergent urban configurations produced out of social emergency, and the performative role of individuals constructing their own spaces.

Through our research-based practice we have been forwarding the notion of citizenship as a creative act that reorganizes not only stagnant institutional protocols but the spaces themselves in the city. All of this desire amounts to a redefinition of the architect-citizen and the citizen-architect, defined less by a professional identity, and more by the willingness to construct a course of action, a political will to produce new critical interfaces across divided institutions, jurisdictions, and communities. We are interested in a practice of mediation intervening in the debate of the public and public debate: how to construct a new civic imagination? A public culture that builds the city from the ground up, across tactical small gestures, emphatic and persuasive enough to have large, strategic urban implications: from the scale of the parcel in the neighborhood we can reimagine a region. For us this has meant enabling expanded models of urban pedagogy and practice that mediate the large and the small, the top-down and the bottom-up.

Our work has been inspired by the realization that no advances in housing design can be accomplished without advances in housing policy and economy. Also, by the need to expand existing categories of zoning, producing alternative densities and transitional uses that can directly respond to the emergent political and economic informalities at play in the contemporary city. It is, in fact, the political and cultural dimension of housing and density as tools for social integration in the city that has been the conceptual armature of our work. How to enable an urbanism of transgression beyond the property line, a migrant, micro-urbanism that can alter the rigidity of the discriminatory public policies of the American city? The effort has been to create a participatory practice that can enter into the politics of information and public debate in the border cities: what do we mean by density? What is the meaning of affordable housing? How do we re-energize the American public to embrace the notion of the Public itself, so that public housing is not a forbidden construct in the US?

Also, one pressing challenge in our time, primarily when the paradigm of private property has become unsustainable in conditions of poverty, is the need to rethink existing conditions of ownership: the transformation of the mythology of the American dream in the context of home-ownership. This means redefining affordability by amplifying the value of community participation: more than "owning" units, residents, in collaboration with community-based, non-profit agencies, can also co-own and co-manage the economic and social infrastructure around them. In other words, how to amplify the value of social capital (people's participation) in urban development, enhancing the role of communities in producing housing. Housing configurations that enable the development and emergence of local economies and new forms of sociability, allowing neighborhoods to generate new markets "from the bottom up," within the community (i.e. entrepreneurial efforts that are usually off the radar of conventional top-down economic recipes), as well as to promote new models of financing to allow unconventional mixed uses.

We have articulated this research not only as a form of discourse that has enabled new critical conversation and debate across different constituencies, from academics to activists and politicians, but into tangible processes of collaboration with community-based non-profit organizations and physical interventions in neighborhoods on both sides of the border. In recent years, the work has been shaped by promoting creative collaborations with community-based non-profit organizations on both sides of the border. The most important collaboration that serves as a case study for our practice unfolded through our work with Casa Familiar, a community-based non-profit organization in the border neighborhood of San Ysidro, on the US side. This collaboration has been grounded on researching and enacting alternative political and economic frameworks that can generate tactical housing projects inclusive of these neighborhoods' informal patterns of mixed use and density. This has resulted in the design of micro-political and economic protocols with Casa Familiar as the foundation for housing.

This collaboration has brought to our attention the need to produce new corridors of knowledge exchange between the specialized knowledge of architectural practice and the ethical knowledge of communities. To act as facilitators of this bottom-up intelligence means mobilizing the ethical knowledge specific to a community into new communicational systems, urban pedagogy, and micro-political and economic armatures: an urbanism at the scale of the neighborhood and community as political and economic unit. Our process with

Casa Familiar transformed the neighborhood of San Ysidro into a site of experimentation, to investigate actual economic and spatial tactics in order to mobilize dormant sources of funding and blur certain obsolete boundaries separating public and private resources. A tactical new zoning policy was proposed to the city of San Diego that would pertain to this neighborhood as a site of exception, expanding limited, existing categories of land use. This is one of the reasons this collaboration has been recognized internationally: it forwarded the possibility that in times of crisis, experimentation must be enabled at small scales and that zoning must be conceived as a generative tool to organize activity rather than a punitive tool that prevents socialization.

This process has led to the tactical design and organization of a series of community dialogues and workshops, which in turn generated the idea of a micro-zoning policy, providing the fertile political ground from which alternative hybrid projects and their sources of funding could emerge. This presented the possibility to the City of San Diego for the necessary partnerships and interfaces with local non-profit organizations to enable them to co-own the resources of development and become the long-term choreographers of social and cultural programming for housing. In other words, this opened a process that intensified the role of the community-based as local experts and sources of innovation. The foundation of the Casa Familiar Micro-Policy was the proposition to seek a new role for many NGOs in neighborhoods to develop housing. These are the mediating agencies that translate otherwise invisible neighborhood dynamics: they can connect tangible housing needs to specific community participants, and support and generate new economies that emerge from the community itself and enhance social service capabilities to be plugged into housing. Agencies like Casa Familiar can mobilize the internal entrepreneurial energies and social organization that characterize these neighborhoods toward a more localized political economy latent in these migrant communities. These socio-economic agendas can be framed by particular spatial organization.

The micro-policy for San Ysidro included the proposition to San Diego's municipality that Casa Familiar become an informal City Hall, capable of facilitating and distributing information, permits, financing, and services to the community. A few of its main parameters include the documentation of all stealth illegal additions and small informal economies sprinkled through the neighborhood in order to legitimize their existence, enabling the approval of a new affordable housing overlay zone for the neighborhood. The second part of the policy included the partnership of Casa Familiar with property owners who cannot afford to sustain their own properties – the production of social contracts within the community to produce a new form of shared ownership and insurance is essential here. Then, Casa Familiar will be enabled by the City to pre-package construction permits to replace the precarious existing illegal dwelling units as well as tax credit subsidy-based proformas to support their designation as affordable housing.

Since tax credit subsidies do not currently support small development, Casa Familiar also proposes the pre-bundling of all proposed small housing units sprinkled throughout the neighborhood into one affordable housing proforma, enabling the breaking apart of large tax credit subsidies, pertaining to equally large housing buildings, into smaller loans with social guarantees to support the retrofitting and new building of incremental density for San Ysidro. This facilitation of entitlement and lending amplifies the notion that marginal communities need political and economic representation by agencies like Casa Familiar. This opened up a small-lot ordinance process in San Diego, seeking to infill transitional and suburban areas of the city, while enforcing an incremental densification and supporting community-led small development.

The affordable housing prototype Living Rooms at the Border emerged from this micro-policy and has served as an architectural prototype to enable Casa Familiar to further transform zoning regulation for the border city of San Ysidro. Both the micro-policy and this small architectural project convey to the San Diego municipality the need to foster the relationship between socio-political and economic strategies and specific spatial tactics in order to shape a new notion of affordability. The main aspiration of this project was to convey housing beyond shelter and conceive it as an economic engine for the community: the neighborhood as a site of production, a small urbanism of co-existence. After nine years, we have finally secured the funding and the zoning variances that will enable the construction of these projects in San Ysidro in 2013.

## Living Rooms at the Border frames the following principles:

1   Density is no longer sustainable as an amount of objects per acre; density must be redefined as an amount of social exchanges per acre and housing as a system of economic and cultural interactions.

2   Housing is more than units only: it needs to be plugged with economic and cultural support systems.

3   Housing is embedded within an infrastructure of flexible social and pedagogical spaces: open frames are equipped with electricity, collective kitchens, and movable urban furniture; Casa Familiar injects them with specific cultural and economic programming.

4   Small parcels are conceived as small infrastructures that mobilize social entrepreneurship into new spaces for housing, cultural production, and political participation.

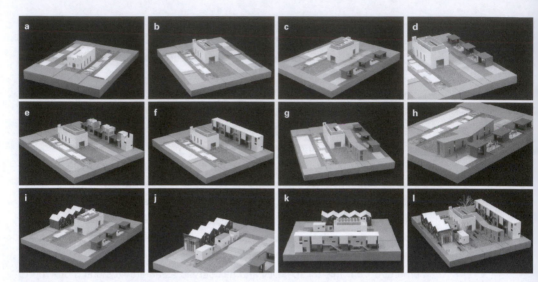

13.6
The neighborhood as a site of production.
Located in the border neighborhood of San Ysidro, community-based NGO Casa Familiar has evolved from social service provider into alternative developer of affordable housing. Estudio Teddy Cruz's collaboration with Casa Familiar has conceived the neighborhood as producer of new housing policy and economy, focusing on designing parcels as small infrastructures that mobilize social entrepreneurship into new spaces for housing, cultural production, and political participation.
a
Casa Familiar acquired a large parcel with an old church and then subdivided it into smaller slivers, anticipating a finer pixelation of property and circulation
b
The church is retrofitted into an incubator of cultural production where Casa Familiar will generate new categories of socio-economic programming. For Casa Familiar, housing is not sustainable as units only. It needs to be plugged with economic and cultural support systems
c
Open frames, conceived as social rooms, are equipped with electricity, collective kitchens and movable urban furniture. Casa Familiar injects them with specific cultural and economic programming. The church, social rooms, collective kitchens, and community gardens are the small infrastructure for housing
d
Here, the void is more than open space for private housing growth, it is the site made available for injecting specific collective programming to support informal economies and social organization. This tactical programming enables new interfaces with the public, across time: Thursdays, new community workshops; Saturdays, framing informal markets; every day: collective kitchens – supporting entrepreneurship
e–f
Housing type 1: young couples; single mothers with children. More than just renting or owning units, dwellers are participants in co-managing socio-economic programs
g
Housing type 2: Live–work duplex for artists. The exchange of rent for social service: artists and Casa Familiar choreograph pedagogical interfaces with children and families, plugging education and other resources
h
Integrating artists toward new models of financing, social contracts, and unconventional mixed uses: artists engage urban pedagogy as well as partner with dwellers as co-producers
i
Housing type 3: large families with grandmothers. Housing equipped with shared kitchens to support two small extended families. Casa Familiar partners with families, promoting economic entrepreneurship

5   Other modes of property are enabled by activating small lots into economic and social systems.

6   Small building envelopes and open spaces produce a gradation of housing economies and social interaction, from individuals to collectives, public to private uses.

7   Residents are not customers, they are participants and co-managers of socio-economic programs.

## Epilogue: designers of political process?

The evolution of our work in recent years has occurred in tandem with the need to question our role as architects within geographies of conflict, searching for a more meaningful socio-political role for architecture, in terms of advocacy and activism in the US. Through these projects we seek the design of political and economic processes and systems toward the democratization of development: can a neighborhood be the developer of its own housing?

It is clear that no advances in building design can occur without reorganizing the existing political structures, economic resources, and social relations that can promote alternative systems of cohabitation. Architecture can mutate from the designing of buildings or environments as ends in themselves (the normative task of architectural practice) into a more meaningful creative process that transforms them into relational social systems.

The urgency to transform our own creative procedures during these times of crisis inspires this last reflection: ultimately, it does not matter whether contemporary architecture wraps itself with the latest morphogenetic skin, pseudo neoclassical prop or LEED-certified photovoltaic panels, if all of these approaches continue to camouflage the most pressing problems of urbanization today.

---

j
Housing type 4: accessory buildings as alternative housing. Small sheds become flexible spaces for extended families: for example, a nephew studies at local community college, rents studio and living space; a niece, recently married, rents a studio temporarily and uses a small shed for office space; or Casa Familiar subsidizes a room for the gardener who collaborates with dwellers to maintain vegetable beds
k–l
Casa Familiar: the performance of a small parcel – a social infrastructure of small buildings and spaces produce a gradation of housing economies and social interactions, activating small lots into economic and social systems

Chapter 14

# Shenzhen – Topology of a Neoliberal City

*Adrian Blackwell*

Estimates in 2010 place the population of Shenzhen at 15,250,000 people. Not only is it one of the most populous cities in the world, it is also the largest municipality in the world's biggest urban agglomeration – the Pearl River Delta (PRD) – whose population of just over 50,000,000 lives in one contiguous band of urbanization, a horseshoe-shaped megalopolis.[1] Even more astonishing than its world-historical scale is the speed with which it was constructed. In China, "Shenzhen tempo" once referred to its unprecedented speed of construction – one floor of an office building every 2.5 days – but it can equally be applied to the pace of urbanization itself.[2] Shenzhen grew from an urban and rural population of 300,000 living in fishing villages and small towns to its current population in just over 30 years; this amounts to an influx of approximately half-a-million new people every year and requires a development and construction industry designing and building structures to accommodate them. Shenzhen is an unprecedented event in the history of urbanization, but it has also played an important role in the transformation of architectural theory.

In 2005, the architectural historian Jianfei Zhu wrote an essay that instigated an intense debate among both Chinese and non-Chinese architectural theorists, historians, and practitioners. "Criticality in between China and the West, 1996–2004" argued that the flow of architectural ideas between China and Europe and North America functioned as a two-way exchange, through which the incredible pace of development in China was exported as a model for operational and projective practices in the West, while critical theory

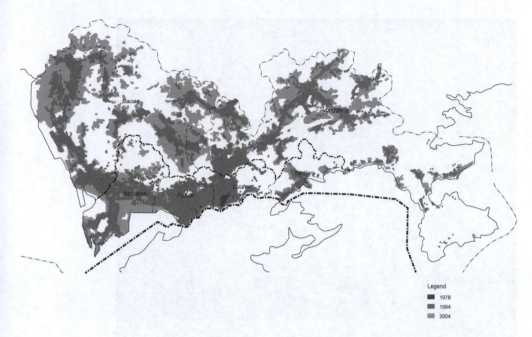

Legend
■ 1978
■ 1994
■ 2004

**14.1**

**Shenzhen urban growth 1975–2004**

Source: Google historical aerial imagery; drawing Song Deng/Adrian Blackwell

was imported to China as way to develop and position its emerging architectural practices. Zhu's essay was a brave intervention into existing discussions about Chinese architecture, challenging stereotypes about its derivative character. The key players in Zhu's revalorization were Chinese architects Yung Ho Chang and Ma Qingyun. Zhu argued that they imported architectural theory to China, while Rem Koolhaas exported new ways of studying and theorizing the city to the West.[3]

The first iteration of the Harvard "Project on the City," Koolhaas's teaching and research program, was called *Great Leap Forward* and focused on the urbanization of the PRD. Zhu points to this work as the tipping point of a significant change in the study and practice of architecture and urbanism.[4] Koolhaas's research on China almost entirely abandons the still historical mode he used in his 1995 text, "Singapore songlines," attempting instead to theorize the city through a synchronic analysis of the radical transformation of territory.[5] Koolhaas's stated aim was to develop a new starting point for the theorization of the unrecognizable subject of contemporary urbanization. The unprecedented development of the PRD was the stimulus he used for this move.

In his response to Zhu's essay, George Baird has argued that the late 1990s marked a change in the tone of Koolhaas's writing, a moment when the heroic timbre of a contemporary Le Corbusier, audible in his earlier texts, gives way to a more ambivalent, first-person narrative style.[6] But this period also marks a real turn outward for Koolhaas's work, as if the concept of "Bigness" that anchored *S,M,L,XL*, and represented the apotheosis of Koolhaas's longstanding

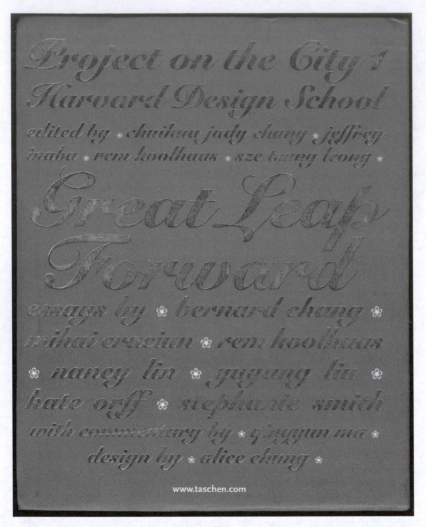

14.2
Cover of Koolhaas
et al. (eds.), *Great
Leap Forward*
(Harvard
University
Graduate School
of Design/
Taschen, 2001)

interest in architecture as a surrogate for the city, had given way to a curiosity about a potential beyond architecture: the actual processes of urbanization themselves.[7] This move in Koolhaas's thinking paved the way for projective practice, landscape urbanism, and the larger geographical turn within architectural education.[8] It is to Zhu's credit that he localizes this shift not in Koolhaas's oeuvre as a whole, but at the specific moment when he began his research on Shenzhen, where the ironic internalization of the city within the architectural artifact is abandoned in favor of a more pragmatic engagement with the problem of urbanization.[9]

# Shenzhen, capital of neoliberalism

Koolhaas's 1997 contribution to the exhibition and catalog of *Documenta X* was a text printed over a set of images of the Pearl River Delta. It was a first draft for the longer glossary of concepts published four years later in *Great Leap Forward* and was used to describe a new historical process of urbanization.[10] The most important of this rich series of concepts is "City of Exacerbated Difference," which opens the Documenta text, forms the conclusion of a longer essay published in 2000's *Mutations*, and is the title of his succinct introduction to Great Leap Forward.[11] Certainly it is a powerful term to describe the new cities developing in the PRD in the 1990s, but in Koolhaas's texts the concept's incisive charge is diffused as a simple description of the different functions of the cities that circle the PRD. However, the "City of Exacerbated Difference" points to a much more significant problem, one that is paradigmatic of contemporary urbanization – the exacerbation of differences in the value of labor between constrained markets. What is so important about Shenzhen as an urban experiment is that it represents the most extreme design of this difference in labor value, at the foundation of capitalist production in general, and the intensification of class differences specific to contemporary neoliberalism. Despite its apparent semi-peripheral status in the network of global cities, Shenzhen is the neoliberal city par excellence, the city that has innovated most intensively in its urban strategies of economic differentiation.

In *The New Imperialism*, David Harvey argues that neoliberal ideology has sanctioned a renewal of primitive accumulation, or what he calls "accumulation through dispossession," a process of labor and resource expropriation designed to recentralize wealth in the hands of the capitalist class.[12] While neoliberalism appears to favor the reduction of government and the privatization of public resources, it also involves the apparently contradictory process of state rebuilding and expenditure. In their 2002 essay "Neoliberalizing Space," geographers Jamie Peck and Adam Tickell argue that mature neoliberalism is a Janus-faced regime of market regulation, under which the state is "rolled back" to privatize resources, while at the same time new state institutions are "rolled out" to manage the inequality produced by privatization.[13] Hui Wang recontextualizes this phenomenon within China in his book, *China's New Order*, explaining that there is no contradiction between neoliberalism and neo-authoritarianism and in the process offering an explanation for the incredible success of the reforms of the socialist market economy over the last 20 years. Wang argues that neoliberalism became hegemonic on a global scale in the wake of the massacre of June 4, 1989 in Tiananmen Square and that its proliferation was the result of this severe repression more than the spirit of market liberalization promoted by some of the protesters.[14] Economist

Minqi Li, a participant in those demonstrations who was imprisoned for two years as a result of his activism, argues that for much of the twentieth century China acted as one of "the last strategic reserves" of the world economy and that its reintegration into the capitalist market has acted as the foundation for the neoliberal resurgence of capitalism as an enormous new economic frontier.[15] A close relationship to Western neoliberalism can be seen in four specific dimensions of China's reform period: first, the temporal coincidence of their birth in the late 1970s and mutual acceleration in the early 1990s after the fall of the Iron Curtain;[16] second, the emergence of an immense new labor force in China that has helped to drive down global wages for industrial work; third, China's over-production of commodities that has driven down consumer costs, allowing an increasingly impoverished working class in the rest of the world access to cheap commodities; and finally China's trade surplus that has been invested in US bonds, allowing the US economy to coast forward on easy credit.[17]

The urbanization of Shenzhen holds a special place in this history. In 1979 the Party Central Committee announced its intention to initiate the creation of four "Special Export Zones" in the south of China, and by August 1980, it had established three "Special Economic Zones" (SEZs) in Guangdong; of these three Shenzhen was by far the largest, with an area of 327.5 square kilometers.[18] The function of these SEZs was to attract foreign direct investment,

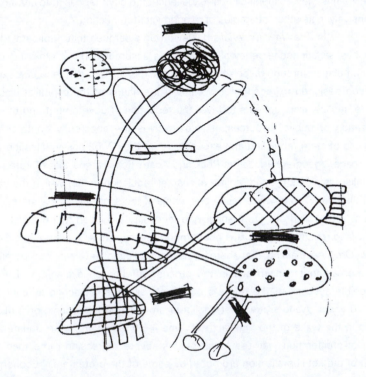

14.3
**Rem Koolhaas's drawing of the "City of Exacerbated Difference" from** *Great Leap Forward,* **image courtesy of OMA**

especially from wealthy Chinese investors living outside the People's Republic of China (PRC), so each was carefully located adjacent to capitalist economies in Hong Kong, Macau, and Taiwan. This proximity was crucial and explains why Shenzhen was the most successful of the SEZs, located as it was directly adjacent to the world financial, manufacturing, and logistics center of Hong Kong.

Shenzhen takes its place as the preeminent neoliberal city for two principal reasons: first, it really is the "City of Exacerbated Difference," the location of the greatest coincidence of separation and proximity between a capitalist class in Hong Kong and a ready supply of cheap labor and land in the PRC; and second, with its minimal indigenous population, all its workers live in the greatest possible state of precariousness, in temporary accommodation hundreds of kilometers from their home villages. It is at once a city where inequality is heavily structured by urban form and at the same time it relies on the most radical contingency. In this sense it is entirely organized along the axis that connects two tendencies of contemporary capitalism: neo-authoritarianism and neoliberalism. What follows is a topological description of Shenzhen, through four coupled neoliberal urban forms: borders and migration, axes and infrastructures, work camps and urban villages, and fakes and creative industries. These seemingly contradictory vectors of the neoliberal city are in fact its complementary technologies, tools to produce the "City of Exacerbated Difference." They are apparatuses to design a city oriented away from itself, for production, not reproduction, a city without citizens.

**14.4**
**Key map of Shenzhen showing sites discussed in this chapter, drawing Song Deng/Adrian Blackwell**

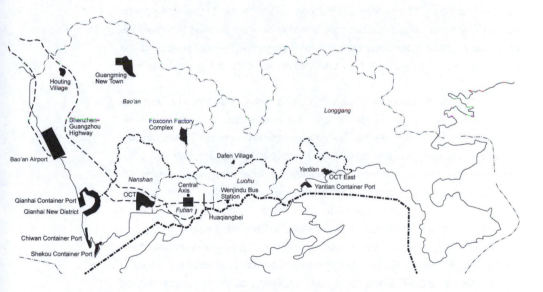

# Regulating the population: borders and migration

The Shenzhen Special Economic Zone bears a striking similarity to Koolhaas's thesis at the Architectural Association: Exodus, or the Voluntary Prisoners of Architecture.[19] The walled district he proposed in the center of London served as a prototype for his investigation of the islands that populate *Delirious New York*, from the actual islands, Manhattan, Roosevelt and Coney, to the autonomous blocks in the Manhattan grid, to the contrasting floors of the Downtown Athletic Club.[20] Exodus served as a first architectural manifesto for a "City of Exacerbated Difference." Like it, Shenzhen was designed as a space with specific privileges and restrictions. Workers flowed into Shenzhen to work for higher wages than elsewhere in China, but in exchange for this privilege they were met with a new system of labor management. The 1980 document "Regulations on Special Economic Zones in Guangdong Province" states: "staff and workers employed by enterprises in the special zones are to be managed by the enterprises according to their business requirements and, when necessary, may be dismissed."[21] While this sounds like business as usual today, it is important to recall that China was still a communist state in 1980, so this legislation was complete reversal of China's "iron rice bowl," in which industrial workers were its privileged citizens, guaranteed jobs for life and comfortable homes. The jobs in Shenzhen could not compete with the secure living conditions of China's working class, but they provided new possibilities for ambitious young peasants and university graduates willing to risk the vicissitudes of the market system, and over time they undermined the communist covenant with labor.

Shenzhen's unique history is a direct result of its three borders and their distinct histories. It was designated as a Special Economic Zone in 1980 because of its location on the border between the PRC and the British territory of Hong Kong, and although Hong Kong is now part of China, this remains the first and most important of the three, because it structures the proximate differential between capital surplus and labor supply. In 1984, the Chinese government completed the construction of an 86-kilometer "second border" between the SEZ and the rest of China.[22] This 2.8-meter-tall security fence with multiple checkpoints was ostensibly built to control the flow of black-market goods from the SEZ to the rest of China,[23] but it also functioned to control the two-way flow of labor in and out of the zone, restricting entry to those selected by the government's labor management bureau, or to those who passed examinations set by foreign-owned companies. By controlling access to Shenzhen's jobs through special work permits, the government collaborated with the foreign-owned enterprises to discipline a migrant labor force.[24] Although the second border was progressively decommissioned between 2003 and 2008, and today remains as a physical remnant of earlier policies,[25] the control over the flow of labor that it pioneered has been universalized through the *hukou* system. This household registration system ties all citizens to their home towns, while dividing all citizens into one of two categories – peasants and urban residents – and requiring all migrant farmers to acquire temporary work permits in order to work in urban areas. China and Hong Kong were unified in 1997 after the expiry of the British lease on the New Territories, so the Hong Kong border became a third Chinese border, creating three distinct economic regions within one country directly adjacent to one another: the Special Administrative Region of Hong Kong, the Special Economic Zone of Shenzhen, and the rest of China, including Shenzhen's own counties of Bao'an and Longgang. These three zones each have different roles to play in the regional economy, with Hong Kong as a global city of financial, management, and logistics expertise, the periphery of Shenzhen and adjacent Dongguan as the epicenter of global export-oriented production, and the SEZ as an interface between the other two, housing high-tech manufacturing, as well as being the mainland base for the creative, financial, and logistics sectors. The "City of Exacerbated Difference" was initially produced through the construction of three physical borders that functioned to control the flow of labor, turning it on and off as required.

Since 2005, artist and curator Ou Ning has made a sequence of works that examine Shenzhen's border zones for the Shenzhen and Hong Kong Biennale of Urbanism/Architecture. In "City: Open Door," the inaugural 2005

**14.5**
**Shenzhen's first and second borders, drawing Song Deng/Adrian Blackwell**

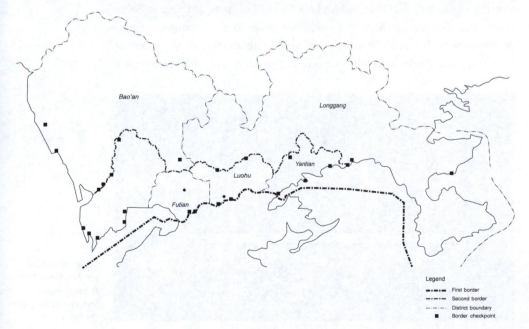

Legend

—■—■—■—  First border
—·—·—·—  Second border
— · · —  District boundary
■  Border checkpoint

event, Ou presented Border, Illegal Zones & Urban Villages, a three-screen projection just inside the entrance to the main exhibition hall. The piece, one of the most powerful works in the exhibition, focused on Shenzhen's internal and external edges – its double border, informal and black-market economies, and high-rise urban villages in the central city. While the exhibition was designed to celebrate the urban experiment of Shenzhen, Ou's work made it clear that Shenzhen's doors were not simply open, rather the city was topologically complex, bounded at its edges, but with holes throughout its surface. For the second biennale, Ou collaborated with an animator, Lei Lei, to produce The Border Project, which focused exclusively on the near obsolete border between the SEZ and the rest of Shenzhen. The artists produced hand-animated videos describing seven checkpoints along the border. Each starts by showing the checkpoint as it currently functions and then transforms it to accommodate new urban uses that reflect the illegal zones and urban villages that Ou examined in his earlier work. Informal housing, markets, and new public spaces are built on and around the obsolete checkpoints. Finally, in 2009 Ou was chosen as the chief curator for the third biennale, which he titled "City Mobilization." In his introductory essay he described the way the border zone incites movement through the story of his little sister, who was drawn to Shenzhen to work in the service and manufacturing industries. Her story highlights the complementary face of border urbanism – migration.[26]

The differences produced by the three borders described above set in motion not only large sums of investment from Hong Kong into China, but also the movement of millions of workers from other parts of China to Shenzhen. This migration has been unprecedented, creating a city made up mostly of non-citizens. The 2000 Shenzhen Statistical Yearbook counts 74 percent of Shenzhen residents as temporary workers, but because temporary workers are

14.6
**Ou Ning and Lei Lei, still from *The Border Project*, image courtesy of Ou Ning**

likely to be missed in the census, their actual percentage may be much higher.[27] Most of Shenzhen's permanent residents are also strangers to the city, so up to 95 percent of the city's population is made up of migrants.[28] Shenzhen is indeed a city of exodus. Michael Hardt and Antonio Negri, the authors of *Empire* (2000), use the word exodus to describe contemporary migration as a form of revolt or escape from specific burdens of capitalism. "A specter haunts the world and it is the specter of migration. All powers of the old world are allied in a merciless operation against it, but the movement is irresistible."[29] In her 2005 book *Made in China*, sociologist Ngai Pun echoes this observation, applying it to the Shenzhen context by arguing that the migration of female peasants to the factories of Shenzhen is an active choice, not a simple case of deception. "Attempts at transgression, such as escape to the city for work, or refusal to go back home for marriage, worked to challenge the patriarchal power of the family and submissive images of Chinese women."[30]

The result of this influx has been the incredible cosmopolitanism of Shenzhen, with foreigners arriving from outside China to manage factories, creative industries and financial services, but more importantly an incredibly diverse workforce arriving from across China, speaking many dialects, eating diverse food, and coming from very different living situations. Jia Zhangke's 2003 film, *The World*, portrays the lives of migrants working in a theme park in Beijing. The film was inspired by its star Zhao Tao's experience working in the Window on the World theme park in Shenzhen for a year before becoming an actor.[31] While on the one hand the film illustrates the confined lives of temporary workers, without access to the world outside the park, its title also confirms the way in which China itself is a world, with vast differences between its regions, comparable to those between countries in Europe. Shenzhen is typical of the cosmopolitanism of many global cities in which productive complexity is in fact deeply divided by class, creating an image of hybridity atop a deeply segmented social and economic structure.[32]

# City of lines: axis and infrastructure

In his analysis of OMA's proposal for the French new town of Melun-Sénart, Alejandro Zaera-Polo points out that every contemporary approach to the city must acknowledge its essential linearity; it is dispersive and infrastructural, not centralized.[33] Despite this, contemporary urbanization does not embrace dispersion tout court, it also practices a complementary recentralization within newly gentrified commercial, financial, and residential centers.[34] The Chinese city is no exception in this regard, developing numerous pedestrian shopping streets, new Central Business Districts (CBDs), and cultural clusters. However, one of the most distinctive strategies of recentralization in China has been the production of ceremonial central axes. This practice is especially clear in the three largest cities in the Pearl River Delta: Guangzhou, Dongguan, and Shenzhen.[35] In each city a new axis has been deliberately planned away from the city's historical center in order to provide a new vector for real estate speculation, while at the same time allowing for the production of an urban form powerful enough to assert state control in the midst of market chaos. The axis is one example of what architect and professor Zhou Rong calls "a nostalgia for utopia" in contemporary China, through which three different utopias are often confused: the ritual utopia of classical Chinese capitals, the monumental utopia of Soviet realism, and the utopia of modernization.[36] As a sign, the axis refers seductively to both Chinese and Western forms of power. While it appears in plan to mimic Chinese imperial architecture, such the forbidden city in Beijing, Zhu Jianfei makes it very clear in his analysis of Tiananmen Square that the open visual form of these contemporary axes are much more closely allied with a modern European tradition of perspective and visibility than to the Chinese Imperial spaces in which the opacity of the emperor was paramount.[37] The axis is more closely indebted to urban plans of the Italian Baroque, seventeenth- to nineteenth-century France, American City Beautiful, and even to postmodern plans for sites like La Défense in Paris.

Shenzhen's central axis, located in Futian district, six kilometers west of the city's historic core in Luohu, is the young city's primary symbolic space and a crucial expression of government power within the spectacle of the capitalist city. Futian was designated as the future municipal center in the early 1980s by the Shenzhen Urban Planning Bureau. In 1989 the municipal government initiated a more detailed planning process, specifying the form of an axis in a collaborative process involving local, Hong Kong, and Singaporean consultants. It was finally given its signature form in 1996, when John M. Y. Lee/Michael Timchula Architects of New York City won an international competition to design it.[38] The axis begins on a large hill at its north terminus.[39] At its top is a statue of Deng Xiaoping, striding toward Hong Kong, leading the charge for its repatriation. Deng looks out toward the swooping roof of the Shenzhen Civic Center designed by John Lee.[40] Between the hill and this structure is a square lined with cultural institutions, on the west side is the Shenzhen Cultural Center, a library and concert hall designed by Japanese architect Arata Isozaki, and to the east a childen's palace and the still unfinished Museum of Contemporary Art and Planning Exhibition Hall, won by Coop Himmelb(l)au in a 2007 competition. South of the Civic Center is a vast open square and park bounded by the city's new CBD to the west, residential buildings to the east, and an immense conference hall at its southern end.

The axis produces centrality as a vector, directing motion, which is why it is a fundamentally modern solution to the problem of urbanization. In

14.7
**Model of Shenzhen at the Shenzhen Civic Center, photo Adrian Blackwell**

Shenzhen the axis is over-coded with symbolic functions. Clearly, its north–south orientation refers directly to the tradition of imperial capitals, and to Beijing specifically. However, the popularity of the governmental axis in southern cities, especially those built up from almost nothing, like Dongguan and Shenzhen, may also be explained by the national axis of power that runs from the north to the south. If all the SEZs were designed to be as far from the country's political center as possible, the axis can be seen as a project of symbolic reintegration, monumentalizing the famous southern tour (Nanxun) Deng made in 1992. Finally, in the local context the axis also refers to the repatriation of Hong Kong into the PRC. Formally Shenzhen's axis is a pre-emptive cut in the urban fabric. The axis represents the force of urban and economic planning to intervene in a contingent world. Through these layered meanings the axis functions as a line through time from the ideological justification of the past toward a knowable future.

If the north–south axis is the symbolic and geographic center of the new metropolis, its metropolitan infrastructure began with a perpendicular vector of linearity. Since its inception Shenzhen has had four masterplans, in 1982, 1986, 1996, and 2007. The first concentrated development in 30 square kilometers between the first industrial development in Shangbu and the border crossing at Luohu. The second 1986 plan proposed the city's innovative linear development along Shennan Avenue connecting six urban clusters parallel to the Hong Kong border: Qianhai, Nantou, Overseas Chinese Town, Futian, Luohu-Shangbu, and Shatoujiao.[41] This plan was revolutionary in China, departing radically from the concentric developments of historic planned cities. Celebrated by professors and professionals and referred to as "clustered linear

14.8
**Statue of Deng
Xiaoping Striding
to Hong Kong on
top of Lotus
Mountain, photo
Adrian Blackwell**

planning,"[42] the city formed a dense urban corridor following the east–west axis of Shennan Road and bounded by the Beihuan expressway to the north and the Binhai/Binhe expressway to the south. The third masterplan in 1996 extended the concept of linearity to the districts of Bao'an and Longgang, which were amalgamated into the municipality in 1994. This "Network Model" was based on three new north-to-south axes of development – western, central, and eastern – planned to rationalize and contain the industrial sprawl being built outside the boundaries of the SEZ.[43] A key aspect of the western axis was a toll expressway financed by Hong Kong developer Gordon Wu. Built as a raised structure floating above the territory, it connected the Hong Kong border in Futian with Guangzhou, stimulating an explosion of industrial development in Northern Bao'an and Dongguan in the 1990s, turning this zone outside the SEZ into the world's largest factory territory.[44] The highway now includes a ring that encircles Guangzhou and extends down the western side of the Delta. The last segment of Wu's plan, a cross-delta causeway that would turn the PRD from a "U" into a ring, is still in the planning stages. Inside the SEZ Metro lines one and two were planned in 1998 and opened in 2004.[45] The latest masterplan, Shenzhen 2030, is "polycentric" and aims to emphasize regional connectivity, around an equally large green infrastructure of recreational and ecological spaces that form the core of the plan. It proposed far-reaching improvements to the Shenzhen Metro system, including lines three, four, and five, which had all opened by 2011,[46] and new commuter lines designed to connect two centers, Qianhai and Futian, with five subcenters located in Bao'an, Longgang, and Yantian.[47]

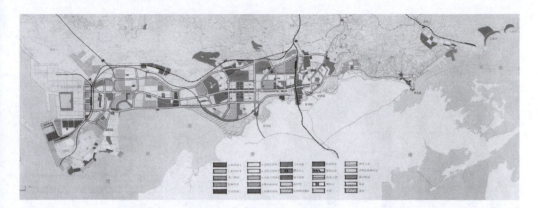

14.9
**1986 plan for Shenzhen within the Special Economic Zone, image courtesy of the Shenzhen Center for Design**

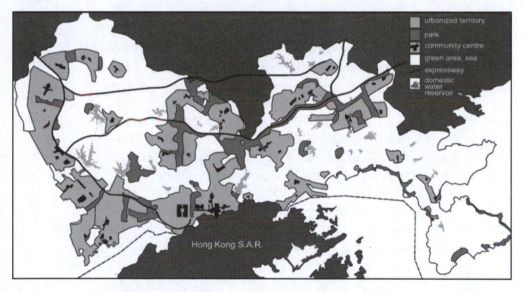

14.10
**1996 Shenzhen municipal plan, image courtesy of the Shenzhen Center for Design**

But the city's infrastructural systems are not simply city-building tools; they are also the crucial prerequisite for the circulation of commodities. Shenzhen's status as the factory of the world has been contingent on the production of a dense logistics network from Shenzhen to the rest of the world. As Wu's highway already suggests, this network is fundamentally outward-looking, it is ungrounded and involves not only the rail and road networks mentioned above, but also air and sea networks. Shenzhen's Bao'an International Airport is currently the fifth busiest in China, and the city is planning to double its size

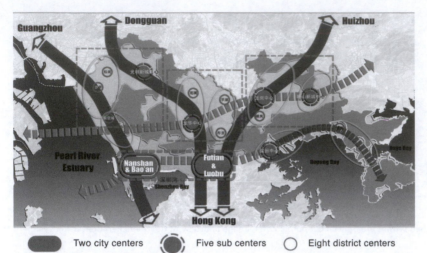

Two city centers ⬤ Five sub centers ◯ Eight district centers

with a new terminal designed by Fuksas architects. Planned to open in 2012, the airport is an example of parametric design at an unprecedented scale. Reminiscent of Norman Foster's immense Beijing airport, Fuksas's structure has a much more complex skin whose scales vary parametrically at different sections of the building, modulating the smooth space of this transit non-place. Shenzhen's three ports, Yantian, Shekou, and Chiwan, make the city the third largest container port in the world, behind only Singapore and Shanghai. In 2010 the PRD was already the world's largest shipping hub with 58.76 million TEUs, far larger than the Yangzi Delta (42.47 million) or Singapore (28.43 million).[48]

In 1996 Manuel Castells argued that the PRD was a megacity that was "not yet on the map" and that "is likely to become the most representative face of the twenty-first century."[49] It seems clear 15 years later that his predictions are substantively true – not only is the inner ring of the PRD the

14.12
The new Shenzhen airport by Massimiliano and Doriana Fuksas Architects, image courtesy of Massimiliano and Doriana Fuksas Architects

world's largest urban conurbation, but it is also the most important strategic location in the contemporary global economy. He makes two crucial points about the PRD: first, it exists as a megacity insofar as it looks away from itself, a city for production before consumption; and second, it is an "interdependent unit" in which its different parts require one another, a fact that makes it distinct from Jean Gottman's characterization of the northeastern US seaboard as a megalopolis.[50] The resonance with Koolhaas's "City of Exacerbated Difference" is clear here. However, the violent reality of neoliberal infrastructures are perhaps best described by Stephen Graham, whose work on splintering urbanism calls out the cold logistics spaces of contemporary margins as the physical monuments of our contemporary political and economic paradigm.[51]

## Peripheral urban forms: worker camps and peasant villages

What this distant examination of the city's infrastructure has missed is the resolutely industrial nature of Shenzhen in its piecemeal patterns of development outside the SEZ. Just over a decade ago this zone was primarily a rural area filled with fish farms, and even after its intense urbanization and integration into the fabric of Shenzhen, it remains a zone of indistinction between urban and rural space. This vast territory is dominated by two urban forms: factory compounds and farmer's villages, with only occasional shopping malls, hotels, nightclubs, or government buildings interrupting their monotonous repetition. This peripheral urbanization houses most of Shenzhen's population. It is a city of migrant youths who have come to make money and escape the farm villages where they grew up. Its built form is a strange mixture of top-down and bottom-up development, in which foreign firms build highly structured factory compounds to accommodate single workers in dormitory housing, while the village

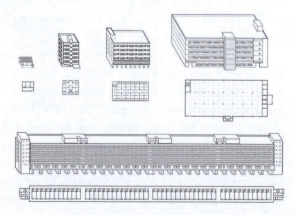

14.13
**Building types found in the Factory Territory, drawing David Christensen/Adrian Blackwell**

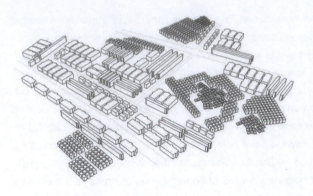

14.14
**Typical composition
of building types in
the Factory Territory,
drawing David
Christensen/Adrian
Blackwell**

collectives develop their land into high-rise apartments to rent to married migrant families. The factory/dormitory camps are rigidly planned and tightly controlled, with walls, gates, guards, and curfews, while the villages seem open and self-organizing by comparison.

Ngai Pun and Christopher Smith have called the industrial urbanism that dominates this territory a "dormitory labour regime,"[52] as its compounds combine spaces of both production and reproduction. These compounds bear a superficial resemblance to the communist work units that acted as the base units of urbanization in China from 1949 until the end of the 1970s, but are radically different in architectural intention and actual functioning. The *danwei*[53] of the communist period were designed to actualize the revolution's goal of improving people's lives and though they provided only modest accommodation, it was modern in comparison to the housing that had been ravaged by a half-century of war and instability. In contrast, the dormitory labor regime has been introduced to fulfill a very different function. It houses migrant workers who are interpellated as peasants according to the *hukou* system, and are considered temporary guest workers in cities like Shenzhen. As a result, dormitories provide the absolute minimum requirements for the worker's reproduction: a bed to sleep in and cafeteria to eat in. A single dormitory can house hundreds or even thousands of workers, often living in bunk beds, with 12 or more workers to a room.

This regime has been one of the key features of Shenzhen's urbanism since the region was tapped as an SEZ. A widely published photograph of the first industrial development on Huaqiangbei Street in 1981 shows factories and dormitories that are typologically identical to contemporary examples, with 5–7-story factory buildings sitting next to dormitories of a similar height.[54] This form is one of Shenzhen's unique contributions to the history of urbanism, yet it seems to have arrived fully formed. While dormitories have been used to house seasonal workers in rural industries since capitalism began, their application in urban spaces has been less common. Smith sees the origins of their use in urban areas within emergent Japanese capitalism. In the 1920s the Japanese introduced a system of "board apprenticeships" to China in order to house rural female workers. This system allowed for the substitution of more expensive or rebellious workers with cheaper and more precarious ones; women replaced men, and farmers replaced urban residents.[55] As Smith points out, the secret of the dormitory is its specific combination of mobility and immobility. It allows workers to move easily into a new work environment in the city, but then ties their accommodation to work, making it very hard to leave the job and giving employers close surveillance over their workforce.[56]

This vernacular urban form is so completely driven by pragmatic concerns that it has been almost entirely beyond the influence of innovative urban designers. However, in 2000 Yung Ho Chang, of Atelier Feichang Jianzhu, designed a municipal building in Dongguan that takes the ubiquitous paired slabs of the dormitory and factory to create an asymmetric building with a covered porch between its two wings. Like many projects by his firm, the building modifies everyday precedents to create architecture for new programs. In a brilliant critique of the "nostalgia for utopia" criticized by Zhou Rong, the project models the most honorific structure in the territory on the repetitive forms that surround it.

14.15
**Street between Factory/Dormitory compounds in Houting Village, Bao'an District, photo Adrian Blackwell**

In contrast to the disciplinary structure of the dormitory factory complexes, the endogenous development of rural villages has played a complementary role in the urbanization of the delta. The communist legacy of the strict division between urban and rural space has created conditions in which rural villages have little government support but strong land use rights. In most places the villager's control over rural land provides only the minimal security of subsistence, but at the fringes of large cities, where land values are quickly increasing, land use rights have allowed some farmers and village collectives to make money developing land. Rural land is allocated to farmers in two forms: farm land can be expropriated by paying six to ten times the average income produced on it over the last three years, but house land is more difficult to expropriate, because of its higher value and the necessity to provide replacement housing.[57] During the process of land development inside the SEZ, farm land was quickly expropriated for urban use while houses were left untouched, so that village fabric was quickly swallowed into the city. Resourceful peasants, unable to transfer their rights or change the use of their properties, leveraged the capital gained from selling their farmland to add floors to their homes. When the government attempted to control this process through a series of laws, villagers often responded by breaking them. Each new law precipitated an acceleration of transgressions that were tolerated because the villages provided the only accommodation available to migrant families, absolving the state

14.16
**Atelier Feichang Jianzhu, municipal building in Dongguan, image courtesy of Atelier Feichang Jianzhu; photo Shu He Architectural Photography Studio**

14.17
**Gangxia Urban
Village, Shenzhen,
image courtesy of
Urbanus
Architecture &
Design**

of its responsibility to construct affordable housing. Through this process some buildings reached heights of 20 stories, and most villages were built far too densely for sufficient light, ventilation, or fire safety.[58] The resultant phenomenon has been called *Chengzhongcun* (village in the city).

Outside the central cities, villages have also controlled the development of much of the industrial land in Shenzhen. This practice has its roots in the Maoist division of labor. Mao attempted to solve the deep economic divide between the countryside and the city by bringing industry to the countryside, rather than allowing farmers to migrate to the city. One of the key policies of the Maoist period encouraged rural communities to start small factories, called "commune and brigade enterprises," which allowed villages to diversify their economies and make use of seasonal farm labor. After the opening of the special economic zones in the early 1980s it was these small industries (renamed "town and village enterprises" (TVEs)) that formed a beachhead for foreign capital. Peasants in Shenzhen and Dongguan entered into a relationship of *sanlai yibu*, literally, "three supplies and one compensation," with family members living in Hong Kong.[59] The Hong Kong investor would supply material, equipment, and plans to the local enterprise, which would provide labor, land, and infrastructure. When the product was manufactured the investor would compensate the TVE for its work. As products became more sophisticated and the economy more developed, the TVEs became less competitive and new joint ventures and foreign-owned enterprises pushed them out, so the village collectives turned their attention from industry to land development. Planner John Friedmann has called this dispersed and decentralized pattern of urbanization "endogenous development," emphasizing the self-organizing character of the Chinese state's economic miracle.[60] George C. S. Lin has described the pattern of urbanization as "urbanism from below."[61] But this particular city from below is also a profit-making machine for local farmers who develop property for migrant housing and transnational industries, and in a refrain that seems all too common in the neoliberal city, the informal sector is called upon to replace basic functions provided by the state during the Fordist period.

In 2005 Urbanus Architects made three theoretical proposals to renovate villages within the boundaries of the SEZ. All three called for the preservation of the bulk of the built form in the village, and the superimposition of a new infrastructure on top, or alongside them. This strategy flew in the face of mainstream planning, which argued that the villages were crime-ridden and blighted neighborhoods that needed to be torn down and rebuilt. Urbanus's embrace of the complexity of urban form in these spaces provided a strong critique of the over-scaled streets, buildings, and open spaces of official urbanism in Shenzhen. In a catalog essay for the 2009 Shenzhen Biennale, Ou Ning related his experience of living in the village in the city:

> I found that these communities, built by the original residents on their own land, formed a world that was independent and open, where they accepted outsiders, but also maintained autonomy, using their own wisdom to create a kind of inexpensive and convenient, but also rich and rowdy street life.[62]

14.18
**Proposal for a new apartment building in Xinzhou Village, in Futian District, image courtesy of Urbanus Architecture & Design**

So, despite its non-utopian realpolitik, the village in the city still acts as a model for a different kind of city, one that privileges the everyday practices and lives of people over a purely economic logic.

## The persistence of modes of production: from *shanzhai* to creative industries and financial services

In 2007, construction was completed on a museum designed by Urbanus Architects in Dafen in Longgang district, a village with a unique export economy based on hand-painted copies of famous and obscure paintings from around the world. The village employs roughly 8,000 migrant workers in 500 companies, producing five million paintings each year and generating total revenue of 300 million RMB.[63] The museum functions as gallery and community center for the village's cottage industry. Its ground floor houses a painting market and auditorium for public events; its second floor contains a sequence of galleries dedicated to the exhibition of "original" paintings; and the top floor, modeled on the gridded form and dimensions of the village in the city, consists of a set of studios, workshops surrounding outdoor public spaces.[64] If art is still understood as a practice of subjective creativity, then an art gallery in an industrial village specializing in forgeries appears at first as a contradiction, and it is

14.19
**Art Museum in Dafen Village, Longgang District by Urbanus Architecture & Design, image courtesy of Urbanus Architecture & Design**

precisely this coincidence of copies and originals that seems to most confound the European imagination in contemporary China. But Chinese culture has a very long history of mass production and as a result places a very different value on productive repetition. In *Ten Thousand Things*, Lothar Ledderose argues that the modularity of characters in the Chinese written language facilitated a way of thinking that allowed for the mass production of cultural objects that have been the basis of Chinese export production for centuries.[65]

When Shenzhen was founded as an industrial city earmarked for export processing, it was clear that the expertise would be foreign, and that the local villagers would only supply labor and real estate. Industries began by repetitively assembling cheap products, such as toys and clothing, using tools and machines and designs imported for this purpose. Deng Xiaoping was clear from the beginning that the SEZs were designed to function as "a window of technology, management, knowledge and foreign policy," stating: "we can then import technology and learn various kinds of knowledge including management techniques."[66] Over a 30-year process of technology transfer, Chinese manufacturers have learned to run the plants, build machines, and design products themselves. 2005 was a benchmark year in the successful process of technology transfer, when the Lenovo Group bought out IBM's personal computing department.[67]

Today when entering Shenzhen from the Hong Kong subway, visitors pass through the Luohu Commercial Center, which sells counterfeit products made in the PRD. The fabrication of fakes (*shanzhai*) has certainly served an important role in this process, allowing factories contracted to make brand products to continue production when their orders dry up and new factories without contracts to open shop.[68] But under Postfordism it has also become more difficult to point to an "original." The world's largest computer and phone manufacturers are not brand name companies, but subcontractors such as Foxconn, Hon Hai Precision, Quanta Computer, and Compal, each of which has, or has had, large manufacturing centers in Shenzhen, and each of which is currently moving at least part of its operations either inland to Chongqing or Chengdu, or outside China to Vietnam.[69] These Taiwanese giants make products for multiple brand name companies, and each brand contracts multiple subcontractors to manufacture its products. Finally, the subcontractors are not only responsible for manufacturing, but also for research and development. So in this context copying is not the opposite of invention but its necessary complement.

Despite the fact that modern architecture emphasized the multiple, the copy and the fake seem to be tied to postmodern fashions in architecture and urbanism and they have proliferated in Shenzhen, just as they have in North America and Europe. Theme parks have almost become a theme of the city itself. Their greatest density can be found in Oversea Chinese Town (OCT), a district developed by the OCT Group to accommodate foreign investors and managers working in Shenzhen. OCT is serviced by a one-way monorail circuit. Starting from the Crowne Plaza Shenzhen, "the first international Venetian style hotel in China,"[70] the tiny train passes Window on the World, Splendid China Miniature Park, China Folk Culture Village, and the amusement park Happy Valley. In 2007 OCT East opened in Yantian district with three new theme parks: Knight Valley, Tea Stream Valley, and Wind Valley. Each of these parks is constructed of copies of existing buildings from around the world.

Throughout the downtown of Shenzhen one can also find fakes, or *shanzhai* architecture, where ideas borrowed from other buildings around the world come to life.[71] This is Photoshop urbanism, designed by the renderer as much as by careful design. In his glossary of the PRD, Koolhaas lists Photoshop as a key concept of contemporary urban design: "The facility that allows PHOTOSHOP to combine everything into anything – uncritical accumulations of desire – is applied literally in the PRD as urbanism."[72] Like in the world of industrial production, the copying of foreign and Chinese buildings and the production of contract documents for designs by foreign firms are two practices that have been used by outsiders to illustrate the backwardness of the Chinese architecture and urban design industries.[73] However, in this context, Koolhaas's argument is refreshing for its lack of moralism. As his 2001 essay "Junkspace" illustrates, uncritical repetition is by no means a Chinese phenomenon, but a universal condition, practiced with a special verve and intensity in the Chinese context.[74] In this situation, as in many others, Shenzhen is not just one step ahead in China, but one step ahead of the rest of the world.[75] While Koolhaas famously valorized the incredible productivity of Chinese designers, his analysis did not explain the intention and results of this process, which has been to learn through practice, resulting in an exponential increase in the quality of Chinese architectural culture in the past decade.[76]

Since the turn of the new millennium, Shenzhen has undergone a cultural and financial turn. Like China as a whole, the municipality is now focusing on cultural and creative industries in the hope that it can diversify its successful industrial economy. In November 2008, UNESCO appointed Shenzhen China's first "City of Design." The report cites a list of Shenzhen's characteristics as justification for its new status: its diversity,[77] its proximity to Hong Kong, its early industrialization, its leadership in high-tech industries, fashion and software, its renowned designers and architects, and its progressive environmental policies.[78] The shift can be seen in the fabric of the city itself. The city boasts 20 creative industry clusters. One of the best known is OCT-LOFT, the site of the first two Shenzhen/Hong Kong Biennales of Urbanism/Architecture. The former factory complex was converted into galleries, event spaces, and office space for creative businesses between 2003 and 2005 by Urbanus Architects, who now have their Shenzhen offices there. This renovation was a pioneering project of adaptive re-use in China, in which factory buildings were overclad and reroofed, and the entrance to a multi-story factory was transformed with surgical interventions.[79] In 2009 Urbanus collaborated with OMA to win a competition to renovate the vast square south of its Shenzhen Civic Building. Named "Crystal Island," their project proposed a circular pedestrian path floating above the square. The ring would connect a sequence of creative clusters: design administration, tourism center, design retail, design campus, and a leisure park. Within the ring the city's ceremonial square would be preserved, and at its geometric center, on an island in Shennan Avenue, would be the site and infrastructure for a future design expo.[80]

As Fredric Jameson argues in his writing on postmodernism, a cultural turn always follows a financial turn, which provides the surplus capital for the luxury of culture.[81] Nowhere is this relationship more evident today than in Shenzhen. Since 1978 the city has been transformed from an industrial hinterland for Hong Kong into a financial center in its own right. There are only two stock exchanges in China, in Shanghai and Shenzhen. Both opened in the fall of 1990, and by the first half of 2011 both cities were ranked in the top 15 financial centers in the world by the Global Financial Centres Index.[82] Shenzhen's neighbor, Hong Kong, is currently considered the third pillar of the global financial system along with London and New York City.[83] Combined, Shenzhen and Hong Kong constitute one of the most formidable sites of financial services in the world.[84]

Jameson goes on to argue that real estate speculation is simply the effect of the financial turn on urban space.[85] This has been illustrated through the short history of Shenzhen's development. It was the first city in China to sanction a land market in 1987, and its rapid development has made real estate

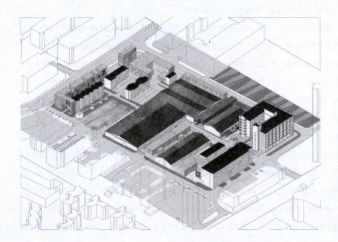

14.20
**OCT East Factory Area Rehabilitation by Urbanus Architecture & Design, image courtesy of Urbanus Architecture & Design**

**14.21**
**Shenzhen Eye/**
**Crystal Island,**
**cultural center by**
**OMA and Urbanus**
**Architecture &**
**Design, image**
**courtesy of**
**Urbanus**
**Architecture &**
**Design**

one of its primary industries.[86] Today, development is more challenging because of scarcity of land, and as a result it is also more lucrative. Important new residential developments are currently being planned in Guangming New Town, Qianhai, Dameisha in Yantian, and the new CBD. The 2007 competition for Guangming New Town was won by a young Austrian firm, Rainer Pirker ArchiteXture. Rather than fill the city with high-rise buildings, their proposal calls for a series of clustered towers up to 300 meters tall, floating in a sea of medium-density fabric.[87] The Dutch firm MVRDV was the competition's runner-up with "Superwindow," a "Park Avenue" of tall buildings, surrounding the central park, with medium-rise fabric filling in the rest of the town. Both firms will contribute to the final design.[88] The competition for Qianhai proposed an immense development area of 4,500 acres and 1.5 million people, ringing a bay facing east across the delta. It was won in 2010 by Field Operations, whose project, "Creating the Water City," organized development between a series of radiating tributaries into the bay. These park spaces will function to accommodate and clean storm-water runoff, while also greatly extending the water frontage and real estate value.[89] Dameisha, in Yantian, is the home of OCT East, but it is already famous in the architectural press for Steven Holl and Li Hu's horizontal skyscraper, a multi-pronged mixed-use structure floating 9–14 meters above the ground. Finally the most developed of these new zones is Shenzhen's new CBD, located on the west side of the central axis in Futian.[90] Planned by Skidmore, Owings, and Merrill in the late 1990s, the CBD is now nearing completion. Its most important building, located on the corner closest to the civic centre and on the intersection of the city's two main axes, is Shenzhen's new stock exchange, which will be finished at the end of 2011. Designed by OMA, the project is based on a very simple idea: to illustrate both the speculative nature of finance in general and the virtual form of Shenzhen's exchange, OMA decided to float the trading services in a podium 36 meters above the ground, creating a public plaza at grade and clearly signifying the deterritorialized and ungrounded nature of finance capital.[91]

14.22
**Masterplan for Qianhai Bay by James Corner Field Operations, image courtesy of James Corner Field Operations**

In 30 short years, Shenzhen has completed an arc that took New York City almost two centuries: from nascent industrialization to a Postfordist economy of speculation. However, this progression is not a simple case of succession; rather, as Paolo Virno observes in *The Grammar of the Multitude*,

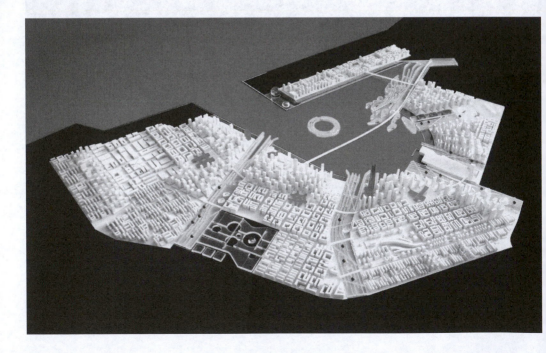

14.23
**Shenzhen Stock Exchange by Office for Metropolitan Architecture, image courtesy of OMA**

under contemporary capitalism "the production models which have followed one another during this long period (of capitalist development) re-present themselves synchronically."[92] It is not that Shenzhen was Fordist in 1980 and finally neoliberal today, but that its industrial rise was as much a part of neoliberalism as its emergence as a world city is today, and its exemplary status as a neoliberal city lies precisely in this complex uneven development. The exacerbation of differences that Shenzhen's first and second lines produced in its early days has been internalized within the municipality itself, so that Shenzhen has managed to maintain its preeminence as a locus of proximate differential within labor markets.

## Shenzhen time

If neoliberal urbanism runs in two directions, from liberalization to a new authoritarianism, neoliberal time is organized along a line that runs between poles of permanence to absolute contingency: from the incontrovertible arrest of Margaret Thatcher's "There is no alternative" and Francis Fukuyama's "The End of History," to the absolute flexibility of its mode of production and the precarious instability of its labor force. But what alternatives exist to this double bind of the present? What time might organize Shenzhen after neoliberalism? American economist Giovanni Arrighi has charted the historical periodization of capitalism in relation to the rise of China. The trajectory of his investigations offers us a framework in which to consider three possible urban futures for Shenzhen: first, a regressive time that travels backwards, shrinking the city; second, a new stasis of Chinese domination; or third, the political time of urban revolution.

In *The Long Twentieth Century* (1994), Arrighi writes the history of capitalism as a sequence of cycles of systemic accumulation, each governed by different states: Genoa, the Dutch United Provinces, England, and the US. These four long centuries have each consisted of two phases: the first in which hegemonic power is built through the territorialization of wealth in fixed assets required for production, a period of growth and expansion that always eventually ends in over-production and falling profits; and a second in which wealth is deterritorialized as finance capital, creating a new surge of wealth that has always eventually led to the waning of the state's political and economic power.[93] Neoliberalism is simply the name we use for this second stage in our current cycle of American dominance. According to this scenario, Shenzhen's financialization will also usher in its decline; the once formidable "window on the world" will be rendered obsolete as a manufacturing center and all its largest and most profitable manufacturers are now deterritorializing, leaving abandoned industrial areas in their wake. Philipp Oswalt's *Shrinking Cities* exhibition and publications powerfully reflected on this situation in four regions, Detroit, Manchester/Liverpool, Halle/Leipzig, and Ivanovo.[94]

Arrighi opens up a slightly different possibility in his final book, *Adam Smith in Beijing* (2007), arguing that the US turn toward financialization in the late 1970s led to the current decline of its economy, the impossibility of a "New American Century," and the emergence of China as the center of the global market economy. But for Arrighi the prospect of a long Chinese century suggests a very different world market. He makes a clear historical distinction between China's dominance during the 500-year peace of the East Asian market system between 1428 and 1894 and the militarism of Europe's competitive nation states during the same period,[95] and he hopes that the contemporary rise of a Chinese market economy will learn from this past in order to distinguish itself from capitalism in four ways: "self-centered market-based development, accumulation without dispossession, mobilization of human rather than non-human resources, and government through mass participation in shaping policies." Arrighi concludes that our most optimistic hope for the future lies in the possibility of Chinese global leadership faithful to these principles, arguing the rise of the Asian market economy may evolve to function more equitably than capitalism as we now know it.[96] As the locus of China's emergence within Western capitalism, Shenzhen could become a key command and control center in the transition to the new dominant center of the world market system. Koolhaas's ambivalent work on the PRD and OMA's recent projects in China both seem to begin from this position.

However hard Koolhaas and many of the practices that have followed in his wake have worked to describe the world, when the situation of contemporary urbanism appears as dire as it does in Shenzhen, the point is not simply to maintain the status quo, but to change it.[97] Not only has Koolhaas distanced himself from this responsibility but, despite their seduction, his analyses of contemporary urbanization have been less illuminating than they might at first seem. On this count, his most incisive critic has been the geographer Matthew Gandy, whose analysis of The Harvard Project on the City's research on Lagos points to the methodological limits of Koolhaas's ahistorical perspective.[98] Gandy cautions that it is naive to valorize the desperation of an informal urbanism as ingenious, when it was generated through the violence of the World Bank and IMF restructuring in the 1980s and 1990s.[99] The *Great Leap Forward* suffers from similar problems. In its description of incredible urban vitality, it fails to acknowledge the production of the dormitory labor regime as the engine of the city's unprecedented growth. In his spirited critique of Jianfei Zhu's "Criticality in between China and the West," Tao Zhu dismisses many of Koolhaas's assumptions about the PRD.

> Unchecked "market forces" have constituted an agonizing lesson for China during this period of development; today in order for Chinese society to survive at all, there has to be a set of intervening, if not to say "critical," forces mediating between the unrestrained impulses of exploitation, the authoritarian power structure, all-too-limited natural resources and the vulnerable public sphere.[100]

In a third scenario that builds on Arrighi's research, Minqi Li analyzes global capitalism from a position less sympathetic to the Chinese state, arguing that China will not become the new global hegemon, but that the current rise of China will instead lead to the end of the capitalist world economy. Not only will expansion into the Chinese labor and consumer market be capitalism's last great spatial fix, but the emergence of an enormous consumer market will test the Earth's environmental capacity.[101] In a posthumously published essay, co-written with Beverly Silver, Arrighi concurs, arguing that the next systemic cycle will necessarily be truly global and integrate the real costs of reproduction "of labour and of nature," within its operation.[102] In this scenario, Shenzhen's future will hinge on the ability of its inhabitants to contest the exacerbated differences that until now have been the foundation of its urban development. So it is the social forces of the city that threaten to have the greatest impact on both its

temporality and spatiality. Between January and May 2010, 13 workers at iPhone manufacturer Foxconn's Bao'an plant attempted or committed suicide. This unprecedented and tragic refusal of work had concrete effects on the situation of labor in Shenzhen's industrial districts. Foxconn increased the base wage to 1,200 RMB a month in June 2010, still only 9 percent above Shenzhen's minimum wage. At the same time Foxconn strategically accelerated its plans to relocate one-third of its Shenzhen workforce of 450,000 to Chongqing.[103] Beverley Silver and Lu Zhang have documented recent workers' protests in China, calling the country an "emerging epicenter of labour unrest."[104] Second-generation workers are becoming less tolerant of the exploitation of the dormitory labor regime. Their resistance will radically change patterns of development in the delta, opening up possibilities for new architecture and urbanism, organized along a different temporal frontier than neoliberalism's horizon of eternal precarity.

14.24
**Foxconn factory complex in Bao'an District, Shenzhen**
© 2012 Google/ Digital Globe

## Notes

1   Demographia, 2011, p. 13.
2   Campanella, 2008, p. 37.
3   Zhu, 2009, pp. 129–146.
4   See Koolhaas *et al.*, 2001.

5  Koolhaas *et al.*, 1998, pp. 1009–1091.

6  Baird, 2009, pp. 147–149.

7  Aureli, 2011, pp. 218–219.

8  See Jameson, 1984; Corner, 1999; Gissen, 2008; as well as the Harvard-based journal *New Geographies*.

9  Koolhaas *et al.*, 1998, pp. 2–21; see also Koolhaas, 1978.

10  Koolhaas and Mau, 1997, pp. 556–592.

11  Koolhaas and Mau, 1997, pp. 557–558; Koolhaas *et al.*, 2000, p. 334; Koolhaas *et al.*, 2001, pp. 27–28.

12  Harvey, 2003, pp. 145–152. See also Duménil and Lévy, 2004.

13  Peck and Tickell, 2002, p. 389.

> No longer concerned narrowly with the mobilization and extension of markets (and market logics), neoliberalism is increasingly associated with the political foregrounding of new modes of "social" and penal policymaking, concerned specifically with the aggressive reregulation, disciplining, and containment of those marginalized or dispossessed by the neoliberalization of the 1980s.

14  Wang and Huters, 2003, pp. 43–45.

15  Li, 2008, pp. 12–13.

16  There is a close coincidence between Deng Xiaoping's initiation of market reforms in China at the third Plenum of the Eleventh Party Congress in December 1978 and the first moves of neoliberalism in the West – the election of Conservative Margaret Thatcher as prime minister of Great Britain in May 1979, Jimmy Carter's appointment of Paul Volcker as chairman of the Federal Reserve in August 1979, and Reagan's election as president of the US in January 1981. See Harvey, 2005, p. 1.

17  Li, 2008, pp. 67–92.

18  Vogel, 1989, pp. 126–127; Li 1995, p. 200.

19  See Koolhaas and Mau, 1997, pp. 2–21.

20  Koolhaas, 1978.

21  http://novexcn.com, 2011.

22  The border was later expanded to 130 kilometers. Zeng, 2006, p. 3.

23  Lai, 1985, p. 74; Vogel, 1989, p. 148; Zeng, 2006, p. 3.

24  Lai, 1985, pp. 76–78; Zhong, 2009, pp. 165–166.

25  Business Alert China, Shenzhen, 2003.

26  Ou, 2009, pp. 70–72.

27  Kaiming Liu, 2007, p. 27.

28  Kaiming Liu, 2007, p. 32.

29  Hardt and Negri, 2000, p. 213.

30  Pun, 2005, pp. 63–65.

31  Young, 2005.

32  For a description of this phenomenon in Toronto, see Goonewardena and Kipfer, 2004.

33  Zaera-Polo, 1998, pp. 404–407.

34  Sassen, 1992.

35  This concept of axial development was developed in many conversations with Tsui Kin, a professor of art history at the Sichuan Art Profession College.

36  Zhou, 2006, pp. 44–47.

37  Zhu, 2009, pp. 75–104. See also Zhu, 2004, pp. 28–44 for a description of the Beijing city plan as ideology.

38  Cartier, 2002, pp. 1523–1525.

39  The axis of the Forbidden City in Beijing is bounded to the north by Jingshan Hill, and this
    is a typical feature of Imperial Capitals, as well as the contemporary axes in Guangdong.
40  Cartier, 2002, p. 1523.
41  Bruton *et al.*, 2005, p. 231.
42  Zacharias and Tang, 2010, p. 217.
43  Ng, 2003, pp. 438; Zacharias and Tang, 2010, p. 218.
44  Koolhaas *et al.*, 2001, pp. 479–487.
45  Koolhaas *et al.*, 2001, p. 236.
46  *Shenzhen Post*, 2009.
47  Lu, 2009, p. 2, see diagram "Urban Spatial Structure Plan 2009–2020."
48  World Shipping Council, 2011.
49  Castells, 1996, pp. 436–439.
50  Castells, 1996, p. 439.
51  Graham, 2004, pp. 162–183.
52  Smith and Pun, 2006; Pun and Smith, 2007.
53  *Danwei* means "work unit" in Mandarin. For an excellent description of this system of
    planning, see Bray, 2005.
54  *Urban China*, 2007, p. 58.
55  Smith, 2003, p. 338.
56  Smith, 2003, p. 339.
57  Tian, 2008, p. 285.
58  Wang *et al.*, 2010, pp. 960–964.
59  Lin, 2006, p. 37.
60  Friedmann, 2005, pp. 38–51.
61  Lin, 2006, pp. 50–51.
62  Ou, 2009, pp. 73–74.
63  Wong, 2010, p. 30.
64  Elsea, 2008; Wong, 2010, p. 31.
65  Ledderose, 1998.
66  Ng and Tang, 2004, p. 192.
67  Chuanzhi Liu, 2007, pp. 573–577.
68  Feng *et al.*, 2011, pp. 74–80.
69  Culpan *et al.*, 2011.
70  OCT Hotel, 2003. From the description of the Crowne Plaza Shenzhen on the OCT Hotels
    website.
71  Campanella, 2008, p. 36. Shenzhen's first skyscraper, the International Foreign Trade
    Center, was the tallest building in China at 53 floors when it was finished in 1985. Topped
    with a revolving restaurant, it was modeled on Gordon Wu's Hopewell Center in Hong
    Kong and it in turn became the prototype for copycat towers in many other Chinese cities
    including Guangzhou and Beijing.
72  Koolhaas and Mau, 1997, pp. 560–561.
73  Muynck, 2006.
74  Koolhaas, 2001, pp. 408–421.
75  *One Step Ahead in China* is the title of Ezra Vogel's history of Shenzhen in the 1980s.
76  UNESCO, 2009, p. 3. The report argues that through this process, modern Chinese design
    was born in Shenzhen.
77  See UNESCO, 2009, p. 2, "*Admire creativity, Encourage diversity* and *Be tolerant of
    failure*."
78  UNESCO, 2009, pp. 2–5.
79  Urbanus Architecture & Design, 2005.

80   Archdaily, 2009.

81   Jameson, 1998, pp. 136–161.

82   The Z/Yen Group, 2011.

83   Overholt, 2011, p. 9; The Z/Yen Group, 2010.

84   William H. Overholt points out that Hong Kong, Shanghai, and Shenzhen consistently
     outpace all global exchanges except NASDAQ in their primary function, the ability to raise
     capital. Overholt, 2011, p. 3.

85   Jameson, 1998, pp. 162–190.

86   Ng, 2003, p. 434.

87   Rainer Pirker ArchiteXture, 2007.

88   Liauw, 2008.

89   Archdaily, 2010.

90   Steven Holl Architects, 2006.

91   OMA, 2006.

92   Virno, 2004, p. 105.

93   Arrighi, 1994.

94   See Oswalt, 2005.

95   Arrighi, 2007, pp. 309–350.

96   Arrighi, 2007, 389.

97   Scott, 2007, pp. 265–266.

98   Gandy, 2005, p. 42.

99   Gandy, 2005, p. 46.

100  Zhu and Zhu, 2007, pp. 199–203.

101  Li, 2008.

102  Silver and Arrighi, 2011, p. 67.

103  Chan and Pun, 2010.

104  Silver and Zhang, 2009, p. 174.

Chapter 15

# New Urbanism

*Edward Robbins*

Some critical ideas that have shaped our cities are the product of our experience of actual physical forms and designs rather than self-conscious design principles: Las Vegas and Los Angeles come to mind. Others often are the result of a judicious mix of actual design and the writings that accompany them: Hausmann's Paris and Cerda's Barcelona are examples. Still others are movements better known for their writings and organizational activities and the effects these have had on the larger discourse about urbanism rather than the projects that they have brought to fruition. The New Urbanism is just such a phenomenon. Since its founding in 1993 as the Congress of the New Urbanism, the New Urbanism has addressed a whole range of challenges posed by contemporary urbanism: the automobile, connectivity, growth, sustainability, sprawl, regionalism, and equity, among others. From the beginning it has been a movement dedicated to: "The poetics of small town life, the virtues of sustainable communities, and the appeal of environments that emphasize the pedestrian over the automobile."[1] Few, though, of the many and different projects New Urbanists claim as theirs have been fully realized and none have met the goals set out in their various charters and written texts.

Nonetheless, any discussion about urban design and the city in the early twenty-first century would be incomplete if it did not include the "New Urbanism." It has taken center stage as the most discussed architectural response to the plight of our cities in the last few decades and has grown from a relatively small movement to one that today has over 3,100 members in 20 countries and 49 states. Among its proponents can be found mayors, federal cabinet secretaries, and state governors. The architecture critic of the New York Times called the New Urbanism "the most important phenomenon to emerge in American architecture in the post-Cold War."[2] At the same time it has been argued that "this emperor may have no clothes."[3] While the New Urbanism has expanded its horizons, moving from more small-scale to more regional design and planning, its reputation and its influence still primarily rest on its initial formulations laid out in the Charter of the New Urbanism (2000).[4] What follows is just such a discussion of this foundational perspective, its relation to earlier thinking about urban design, and a critical analysis of why the New Urbanism has received so much attention and whether it has or can deliver on its promises. Along the way, I will also briefly address some of the newer interests and ideas set forth in the many discussions of the CNU.

## Conceptual roots

While there is much that is unique and new about the New Urbanism, it owes much to older approaches to urban design. The New Urbanists, most crucially, are directly bound to their forebears by their faith in their own all-encompassing vision for the design of a better world. It is, in their view, the only answer to the critical problems that our contemporary cities face. If Le Corbusier argued that it was either "architecture or revolution" (that is to say, his architecture), Leon Krier, one of the heroes of the New Urbanism, has argued similarly that "If the United States is to solve its social and environmental problems in the future, it must revise the whole national philosophy of settlement, the very notion of civil society."[5] That whole new philosophy is embedded within the Charter of the New Urbanism, which New Urbanists argue "provides a powerful and enduring set of principles for creating more sustainable neighborhoods, buildings and regions."

The design of housing and the residential landscape has been associated throughout the twentieth and twenty-first centuries, especially in the US and UK, with the development of better citizens and a better society as much as it has been concerned with the design of commodious and aesthetically pleasing residential developments. Like so many urban designers before them, the New Urbanists "speak of community and neighborhood as physical rather than social activities, as if community resulted from the built form rather than from people who inhabit it".[6] As Gwendolyn Wright writes: "For centuries Americans have seen domestic architecture as a way of encouraging certain kinds of ... social life."[7] In England, too, from at least the middle of the nineteenth century, commentators like Friedrich Engels and Samuel Kingsley linked housing with the moral state of its inhabitants.[8] As Kingsley argued as early as 1857, the social state of the city depends on its moral state and that, in turn, depends on the "lodging of its [the city's] inhabitants."[9] In the twentieth century, too, architects as different as Ebenezer Howard and Le Corbusier, Tony Garnier and the designers of failed developments like Thamesmead in England and Pruitt–Igoe in St. Louis, have offered their design visions as the singular answer to the social and cultural problems of urban life. The legacy of Patrick Geddes, Ebenezar Howard, Raymond Unwin,[10] and German town planners of the 1920s looms large in the work of New Urbanists. What binds these designers is a "belief in the scale and spatial organization of the traditional town as the basic building block for human settlement."[11] The New Urbanist emphasis on density and compactness also echoes the 1940s fondness of British planners for dense old villages and small towns. It was felt that these kinds of dense and enclosed spaces fostered community and more energetic urbanity; the desire for active streets with mixed use, greater density, and neighborhood coherence was the order of the day long before the New Urbanists came on the scene.[12]

In their search, the New Urbanists have been strongly influenced by Werner Hegeman and Elbert Peets and their taxonomy of different types of urban places, plazas, intersections, and gateways, and road arrangements that provide a sense of the civic scale and civic art.[13] So too did the New Urbanists borrow the notion of the relatively self-contained neighborhood as a critical scale of design from planners such as Clarence Stein, at Radburn among other places, and Clarence Perry. They, like the New Urbanists, placed great importance on and gave new life to the idea of the neighborhood and the priority of the pedestrian over the car in order to make a social and hospitable community. As Perry argued as early as 1929: "By some sociologists the automobile has been regarded as a destroyer of neighborhood life ... Thus the automobile menace has set up an imperative demand for a definition and standardization of the neighborhood district."[14] The New Urbanists' strong emphasis on the streetscape and street use is part and parcel, as well, of a long and continuous concern with street life[15] that re-emerged again in the 1960s. In the work of Jane Jacobs, the Smithsons, Gordon Cullen, and, more recently, Robert Venturi and Denise Scott Brown there is a strongly stated desire to return to an emphasis on life in the street in contrast to the thinking of modernists like Le Corbusier.[16] For these commentators, the street is critical to urbanity and community, even if the streets to which each architect saw us returning varied from the building corridors of the Smithsons to the strip of Venturi and Scott Brown and the nostalgic main street of Cullen.

In many ways, though, the most influential urban design movement is, ironically, the one that the New Urbanists most vilify, that is, modernism.

## Modernism and the New Urbanism

The New Urbanists acknowledge their legacy from, even their connection to, the modernists, at least in part. They readily admit that "In important ways the

Congress for New Urbanism is modeled on CIAM [The Congress of Modern Architecture] ... Our methodology is the same." But they also emphasize that they offer a critical antidote to the errors of modernist thinking about city making. As one of the founding fathers of the New Urbanism has succinctly put it, "Our ideology is different."[17]

New Urbanism has borrowed the structure of CIAM and adapted it to contemporary circumstances. Mirroring CIAM practices, there are annual congresses where members discuss and debate old and new approaches to the task of urban design and renew their allegiance to the general principles of the New Urbanism. There are working groups to discuss and report on particular issues. Most notably, proponents of the New Urbanism have produced a founding Charter of the New Urbanism (2000), which has much in common with the Charter of Athens (1933) so central to the work of CIAM. The charters of both groups address similar issues such as reforming the chaos of existing cities, linking physical with economic and social issues, and providing clear guidelines on how to proceed in practice. Both set out to create community and social good through their designs. In practice, members of the CNU, similar to CIAM, work assiduously to influence government agencies and other important groups central to the development of urban projects. Also like CIAM, they have produced more publicity, more publications, and more interviews and programmatic statements than projects that have been realized.[18]

Unlike CIAM, which limited its membership to architects and designers and remained relatively small, the CNU is open to anyone who wants to join and receive their publications and participate in their work. At CNU gatherings one will find students, developers, community organizers, politicians, and city administrators along with architects, urban designers, and planners participating actively in both the official and informal discussions and activities. There is an active effort to capture the press and broadcast media by inviting them to CNU events and programs. The CNU accepts much of the organizing principles of CIAM but rejects its elitism.

Even though New Urbanists insist that their thinking and approaches critically contrast with those of modernism, they share many substantive ideas with it as well. Indeed, as John Dutton points out so succinctly: "The irony is that the New Urbanism is in many ways a resurrection of modernism but cloaked in the dress of the pre-modern era."[19]

The CNU, like CIAM, focuses not only on design but also on reforming the building industry to get it to understand the advantages and superiority of their design approach in comparison to more conventional design. Similar to CIAM there is also a strong belief in the efficacy of standards, codes, and written conventions. Like the modernists, the New Urbanists also are willing to work with big developers in realizing their goals but at a scale of design that is less monumental than that of the modernists. New Urbanists also share with CIAM an interest in the making of community through the design of town centers, and like many members of the MARS group, an offshoot of CIAM, they believe that urban design has to address the design of the street. And, it bears repeating, like CIAM, the CNU has a fundamental and almost evangelical belief in the role of design not only in forming a better city but also in shaping a better society.

Still, it is clear that in many ways the New Urbanism is a rejection of modernist approaches to urban design. Unlike CIAM and other modernists, the CNU seeks to work with people who are not professional architects but who are willing to join in the effort to realize the New Urbanist project. New Urbanists also repudiate the notion central to modernist ideology that one single architectural genius is and should be responsible for the design of the totality of any project, be it at the scale of a house or of a whole city like Le Corbusier's Plan for Algiers.

Most crucial to the popularity of New Urbanists among many of its followers and the media, New Urbanists eschew the modernist aversion to popular taste and traditional building types. They reject the reliance on a single masterplan that works from universal ideas about the city, often ignores, even at times obliterates, the traditional urban fabric, and makes no reference to the surrounding street grid and adjacent buildings. In contrast, the New Urbanists have looked to the particular and local because:

> Each community shared a local vision and language of how to build
> their world ... They shared common customs and culture that led them
> to create places that were a part of a larger, coherent, ordered and
> intrinsically beautiful whole.[20]

## How do they do it?

Contemporary urbanism for New Urbanists is characterized by urban sprawl, placelessness, the domination of the automobile, and mediocre urban design[21] that create suburbs that are noteworthy not only as aesthetic failures but also "as civic environments [that] ... do not work."[22] New Urbanists promise to remedy this condition through their own good design principles and practices and to reintegrate dwelling, working, schooling, worshipping, and recreating, and to put an end to the domination of the automobile. In the place of the classic suburb – less a community in their eyes than an alienating agglomeration of houses – the New Urbanists assure us that their design principles will create a sense of place, which will re-engage the spirit of the traditional American small town and reinvigorate urban community.[23]

Vision will be made reality if one follows a set of design approaches central to New Urbanist thinking and practice. At its core is a series of scales that New Urbanists believe essential to the generation of good urban environments – the region, the neighborhood, and the street – and a set of town-making principles and an architectural lexicon that provide a methodology for practice.

**The region, neighborhood, and street**

New Urbanists contend that it is essential that designers and planners engage the regional scale if they are to address the problems of air quality, water, issues of economic equity, urban decay, sprawl, social segregation, and the growing importance of the metropolitan culture in general. Without a regional plan, for example, neighborhood- and village-scaled developments can create the very sprawl and social segregation that should be prevented. Nonetheless, designers have as yet "no framework for this new reality, no handle to guide it."[24]

Although it is continually alluded to, the region is not rigorously defined by New Urbanists. It may be bounded by topography, watersheds, coastlines, river basins and other natural features of the landscape, or may be described as consisting of cities, towns, and villages; regions may also defined by reference to economic, political, and cultural attributes. There are, however, a number of principles that derive from addressing the region.

For the New Urbanists, designers should respect the edges of the metropolis so that sprawl and development do not replace agricultural and natural landscapes. With this in mind, they place great emphasis on infill development within existing areas rather than development of marginal or peripheral areas to the core city.

Where possible all development should be contiguous with existing urban boundaries. Noncontiguous development should be designed as towns and villages with their own employment, civic, and cultural base rather than as bedroom communities to avoid sprawl. Development should respect the local historical patterns of urbanism and the physical organization of the region should be supported by a transportation structure that provides for mass transit, pedestrian movement, bicycles, and any other means of transportation that lessens the use of the automobile.

The neighborhood for New Urbanists is the essential element of development and redevelopment in the metropolis. It is critical that neighborhoods be compact, pedestrian friendly, and provide for mixed use. Neighborhoods are to be designed and to be seen as coherent wholes. Districts, though, within a neighborhood should emphasize a single use as a civic or commercial center, for example. As many activities as possible, shopping, schooling, using parks and local governmental facilities, should be accessible by walking, especially by the young and the old. Other desirable features of a neighborhood are easy access to mass transit, codes that provide guidelines for building, and the dispersion of parks, ballfields, gardens, and such throughout the neighborhood rather than being concentrated in one single-use area.

It is also important that within neighborhoods a broad range of housing types, from single family to multi-family, from more to less expensive, be made available so that people of diverse backgrounds and incomes can find a place to live within the development. But to make a neighborhood work, it is crucial that the streets that make up a neighborhood be designed to allow for the elements that need to be accommodated and in an aesthetically pleasing way.

For the New Urbanists, whether correctly or not, the "fault line between Modernism and traditional urbanism" is in the respect that traditional design and the New Urbanism show for the street.[25] Any designer that thinks that "urban squares are obsolete, or that traditional, figural spaces clearly shaped and defined by buildings are somehow irrelevant" has another think coming.[26] A primary task of architecture and urban and landscape design, according to New Urbanists, is to ensure that streets are designed as places of shared and mixed use. These streets should be designed seamlessly with their surrounding streets, and not as isolated pods so common to contemporary design. Local context and precedent should always be taken into account and the design of any street should be undertaken in relation to the overall plan.

Streets should be designed to be safe and secure without the use of overt signs of policing. Rather, such things as human presence through elements such as front porches and windows facing the street and street dimensions and scales that encourage congeniality are better ways to create a sense of security. Visibility, good lighting, well-maintained public spaces, and the legibility with which one street or neighborhood site connects with another are other ways to make people comfortable with using what they will sense to be secure and inviting streets.

Clearly, New Urbanists are aware that cities have to accommodate the automobile. But in neighborhoods, the use of the automobile must be made to respect the pedestrian. This implies the use of such elements as on-street parking to protect the pedestrian from auto noise, traffic calming devices that slow the auto in densely used pedestrian areas, narrow street widths, and fewer traffic lanes, among other things.

## Town-making principles, codes, and lexicon

There is at the heart of New Urbanism a professed set of town-making principles as a guide to town design. These, they claim, are based on observations of patterns revealed by looking at traditional American communities. The principles describe the fundamental physical elements that embody community, although the principles are flexible in relation to local landscapes and programs.[27]

At the core of any urban design is a masterplan; a composite drawing that includes all the critical information needed to develop a town plan. It attempts to exemplify the patterns of what the New Urbanists claim to be the typical American town: a geometrically located town center surrounded by an interconnected street network. The town is made up of, in the parlance of the New Urbanists, a series of "neighborhoods and villages"; in effect smaller quarters that connect to create a whole. In larger towns, the plan will also account for the ascending scales of urban development: the neighborhood, the village, the town, and the region.

Commercial activity and workplaces are concentrated in the town center. Civic spaces and buildings like schools, parks, and community centers are distributed throughout the neighborhoods. Each neighborhood, mirroring the earlier work of designers like Clarence Perry, is planned so that from edge to center is a quarter-mile or a five-minute walk.

Street size, depth, and length are developed so that building lots front the street and traveling distances are reasonable. All the streets, at least all that are possible, should connect and the street layout should allow for connections to new streets so as to create a regional network of streets. Along with streets there should be pedestrian paths that connect civic spaces as well as, where possible, alleyways that also provide alternative pedestrian routes through the neighborhood. The street section provides carefully detailed building heights, parking lanes, and street landscapes to ensure that the scale of the elements that surround the street make it attractive to pedestrian use.

It is also crucial that dwellings, shops, civic uses, and workplaces be in close proximity to each other and that squares and parks be distributed throughout the neighborhoods. Civic buildings should be prominently sited to serve as nodes or landmarks and as terminating places. The goal of all these design principles is to encourage active social use of the streets and other spaces of the neighborhood.

What the New Urbanists hope by the instantiation of their town-making principles is that issues of growth, traffic, and affordability are addressed through physical design: traffic by the design of streets, affordability by preventing large-scale, single-income tract housing, and encouraging homes over stores, garage apartments, and other forms of mixed use usually prohibited by the design of most new suburban tracts.

The town-making principles are embedded within a series of codes that regulate and ensure that the principles embodied in New Urbanist town making are implemented. Much of suburbia is already the product of codes and conventions. The New Urbanism rewrites these codes and conventions to restructure the nature of urban and suburban development. New Urbanist codes are a series of ordinances that regulate everything from the masterplan to the streetscape, the building types and distribution to the architectural design of all building types.

There are five basic documents that lay out the codes. The Regulating Plan sets out the terms of the masterplan in detail, and outlines where residences, civic spaces, and commercial activities are to be located. What are called Urban Regulations delineate such things as how much of a building must be on a common frontage line and where parking is allowed, encourage such elements as porches and stoops, and provide for rentable outbuildings. It tends to be prescriptive rather than proscriptive. Architectural Regulations set out such things as materials, methods of construction, and acceptable architectural elements to insure that there is harmony among the building types. They vary from strictly deterministic to more open-ended, depending on the development. Street Types and Landscape Regulations set out the rules that govern everything from street widths and alignments to encouraged street plantings.

The codes do not set out the design in exact detail; they are guidelines and limits to design within which architects can work. They are used to control the shape and the social reality of neighborhoods by providing not only boundaries for what is allowable but also strong suggestions about what is considered admirable and complementary to the neighborhood as a whole.

In 1999, to provide a more exhaustive guide for the analysis of urban space and to create standards for a common urban language, Andrés Duany and Elizabeth Plater-Zyberk, central figures in the New Urbanist movement, developed what they called a Lexicon of the New Urbanism.[28] It sets out a taxonomy of urbanism and provides a terminology with which to describe the form of the city and its structure from the regional scale to the building type. The Lexicon also provides a strategy for implementation and ideas about how best to represent urban plans.

More recently, there has been a discussion about the scale at which New Urbanists should work. For some New Urbanists there has been a turn to more regional planning and what they call the "Transect," which is a categorization system that organizes all elements of the urban environment on a scale from rural to urban. While according to the New Urban News it was developed by Andrés Duany and DPZ,[29] the Transect is rooted in earlier planning thinking for in many ways it is a play on the Valley Section of Patrick Geddes. For these New Urbanists there needs to be a critical shift away from the more local and small-scale Lexicon of the New Urbanism to the Transect. As Andrés Duany is quoted as stating:

I am convinced that the Transect will do the job, not The Lexicon as we thought.... The Lexicon has advocates, but I have come to realize that it is wrong. The Lexicon is too specific and complete to be a standard. The real matrix, I believe, is the Transect.[30]

More recently, it should be noted, there have been efforts among New Urbanists to link with other urban planning movements that address issues of sprawl, sustainability (e.g. LEED), equity, and other contemporary urban challenges. It should also be noted that as New Urbanists shift their interest, the tone and direction of their discourse does not become more modest. Rather, even as doubts arise about this or that approach, the confidence in their new approaches as the answer remains as strong as ever. And even as the movement shifts in one or another direction and creates new and different links, its core philosophy as expressed in their charter remains. It is what makes the New Urbanism at its core a movement and what makes it unique.

## Whence the popularity/why the criticism?

Whether the combination of scales, town-making principles, code, lexicon, and Transect works in practice and what kind of world it is creating are the issues that are most often debated about the New Urbanism. It is noteworthy that these are usually debated in the abstract, with pieces of various projects, often unbuilt, used as examples of this or that point in favor or against the New Urbanism. In a way, it is arguable that the New Urbanism both benefits and suffers from the fact that it has not been systematically adopted anywhere and consists of a number of different and independent projects. They vary from pattern books to block-long projects, from whole towns or villages to single mixed-use developments, from slum-renewal projects like HOPE VI to high-end shopping malls, and from projects that have been realized to projects that are still only broad suggestions. Even with this range of projects, New Urbanist schemes make up only a small percentage of worldwide building development. What the New Urbanists do produce are many texts, guides, discussions, and publicity for their theories. What we need always to keep in mind when speaking about the New Urbanism is that it claims so many different approaches to the city in its name – everything from brownfield development to clearfield development – that what constitutes a New Urbanist project is at best elusive.

It is thus difficult in a sense to come to any general understanding about the success or failure of the New Urbanism on the basis of any one or another particular project. The most written about projects associated with the New Urbanism are at best problematic as archetypes for critical review.

Seaside, celebrated or denigrated, depending on your point of view, in the movie The Truman Show, is a vacation development and not an everyday community. Celebration, built by Disney, is not strictly speaking a New Urbanist community in the way it was created and designed even though it has become one of the icons of the movement in the popular press. Other "iconic" projects, as we shall see, also raise serious issues about just what New Urbanism is and why one or another development is New Urbanist. Nonetheless, the New Urbanism is not without its strong support and equally strong criticism. What this debate revolves around for the most part are the core beliefs and suggestions of the New Urbanism as defined in its Charter and Lexicon: it is that which is sui generis about the New Urbanism. Other arenas that New Urbanism addresses, such as sprawl as a general phenomenon and urban renewal, are not specific to the New Urbanism and debates about these issues do not focus on New Urbanist ideas alone. Thus it is to the core beliefs that I will turn, with some brief comments on other areas where appropriate.

## The support

There are many reasons for the apparent celebration of the New Urbanism among designers, developers, and the wider public. For some proponents, the New Urbanism, as the former mayor of Milwaukee John O. Norquist points out, is a significant part of the resistance to continued urban sprawl and fragmentation.[31] New Urbanism provides a voice for those fed up with inner-city decline, the social alienation produced by conventional suburbs, and a world that seems to be increasingly dominated by the automobile. The call for towns and neighborhoods that build community suggest a regional order less dependent on the car and more amenable to pedestrian traffic; it serves as an anodyne to the prevailing planning and development practices responsible for our current plight.

For many people, the apparent concern New Urbanists have with community voices and attitudes is a salutary alternative to the often dictatorial and unresponsive design strategies of many urban designers and planners of the modernist and also bureaucratic mode. In an attempt to include local visions and languages, New Urbanists often try to work with the local community in design charrettes to develop a contextual solution grounded in local circumstances and attitudes. Whether this is a marketing strategy or a genuine attempt to include locals in developing the design or a bit of both is open to question. That it is an attractive element of New Urbanist practice and ideology is not.

For those developers that support the New Urbanism, it is not only an answer to sprawl and reliance on the automobile, it allows for, indeed encourages, development of sites that, previous to the New Urbanism, would have had fewer units in the same size tract. Real estate developers embrace the New Urbanism in the name of community development but, as Norman Blankman, writing in Real Estate Finance Journal, makes clear,

> The single most important thing that should be done to bring affordable housing within reach for millions of people is to change zoning laws to permit more compact development. The first steps have been taken by a nationwide movement [i.e. the New Urbanism] to reform US urbanism.[32]

Also, as one CEO of an important development firm once told me, the New Urbanism, by providing more restrictive building codes, alleviates many of the problems of customer choice associated with new suburban development and the complications and increased costs that such choice generates. It simplifies the developer's design process. Issues of access, house type, lot and street configurations, front door location, and other such decisions are limited and as a result so are the ensuing problems that this often causes between potential neighbors, as well as between customers and the developers of new suburban and urban tracts.

There may be a more profound explanation for the New Urbanism's popularity and the support that it appears to engender. Throughout the nineteenth and twentieth centuries, architects and urban designers, whether modern or postmodern, radical or conservative, have tried to realize an Enlightenment dream to forge a satisfactory city through the cauldron of design and thereby produce good citizens.[33] One continually reappearing vision in that quest is that of a tidy, small, and genteel urban place, which in the words of Prince Charles would "nurture human life and imbue people with a sense of … community."[34] As David Harvey so aptly puts it:

> Faced with the innumerable problems and threats that urban life poses, some analysts … have reached for one simple solution – to try and turn large and teeming cities so seemingly out of control, into urban villages where, it is believed, everyone can relate in a civil fashion to everyone else in an urban and gentle environment.[35]

The New Urbanism in a sense makes a kind of Freudian trade-off.[36] Freud in his *Civilization and Its Discontents* (1930) argues that civilization provides freedom from fear and guarantees what he calls in German *Sicherheit* in exchange for accepting certain constraints on the self and individual liberty. *Sicherheit*, as Zygmunt Bauman suggests, is more than just "security." It also refers to "certainty and safety."[37] Security guarantees us that what we have gained or possess will retain its value and that the world, and how we have learned to act in it, will remain dependable. Certainty provides us the knowledge that the distinctions between, let us say, useful and useless, proper and improper will allow us to act in ways we will not regret, will tell us what is a good life and what is not. Safety is the awareness that if we behave correctly we will experience no danger or threats to our bodies, our property, our home, or our neighborhood.

In a critical way this is precisely what the New Urbanist vision offers many people. It proffers security by establishing a set of limits that helps to establish and guarantee the value of the home that has been purchased. The restrictions that are set by the codes also appear to guarantee that the community will not change its physical form and appearance. New Urbanism sells a vision of community, rooted in our nostalgic memory of small-town life, that sets out a notion of the good life and provides assurances that this life will be maintained. It also sets out to make us feel safe through the notion of the eyes on the street, the familiarity with our neighbors, and the bounded, if not gated, form of the neighborhood letting us know who belongs and who doesn't. The emphasis on traditional house types and urban aesthetics that signifies memories of a certain and controllable past suggests that this world can be resurrected. The assurances that tradition seems to convey also appear to provide a place for safe investment in a neatly bounded universe in a world that is increasingly diverse and threatening.

In exchange for Sicherheit, the New Urbanists ask that as a member of their development one accepts strict codes and conventions. These strictly limit individual freedom to use and design a house and property in any way an owner might see fit and insist on a number of standards that prescribe what your neighborhood can look like and on the necessity of a strong sense of neighborhood control – albeit often informal – over public practices. In some New Urbanist developments, when and how one could place political signs and how often one could have garage sales are among the regulations set for the community. In other New Urbanist projects, the color of houses, the type and height of fences, the range of ornament for homes, even the types of curtains one could have are regulated by codes. As the architect Robert Stern put it:

> In a free-wheeling Capitalist society you need controls – you can't have community without them. It's right there in de Tocqueville; in the absence of community of an aristocratic hierarchy you need firm rules to maintain decorum. I'm convinced these controls are actually liberating to people. It makes them feel their investment is safe. Regimentation can release you.[38]

This is a statement with which so many of the residents of New Urbanist developments could agree or, if not agree in principle, in which they could at least find some comfort in practice. For critics though, such sentiments raise serious questions about whether the New Urbanism is worthy of the praise it has received.

## The critiques

The questions about the New Urbanism revolve around a number of issues both technical and ideological and in many ways go to the heart of so much discussion about contemporary urbanism as a physical and social reality. If for no other reason, it is why the New Urbanism has been so central to architectural debates.

Most often voiced within the architectural community is a critique of the traditionalist architectural bias of the New Urbanism. For many architecture critics the nub of the matter is what they see as a tacky populist reliance on traditional house types and a spurning of more modern and adventurous housing and architectural forms. New Urbanism's greatest sin in this view is that it is boring, commonplace, and without any formal or aesthetic merit. The criticism is easily shrugged off by the New Urbanists as the ramblings of an elitist minority without concern for the larger issues that face people in their everyday lives in the city. But there are criticisms that are not as lightly rejected.

There are a number of critics who do not challenge the architectural and aesthetic qualities of the New Urbanism but argue that what the New Urbanists propose cannot alleviate the very problems they claim to solve. So far, these critics contend, the New Urbanism offers more in rhetoric than reality. And their rhetoric holds a number of assumptions that stands in want of serious questioning.[39]

Few, if any, projects built by the New Urbanists provide all that they promise. In one of the most publicized, Kentlands (which has gone belly-up a number of times), the village relies on a conventional mall, which is based on regional automotive traffic for its economic survival and to which the residents of the Kentlands go to shop for necessities like food. Laguna West has neither its promised commercial center nor its rapid transit link to Sacramento; residents still drive to work and shop. Visits to New Urbanist developments suggest that driving is still an important aspect of living in those communities. Seaside finally has its commercial center in place but it is dependent on tourism based on the automobile. On the way to Seaside, the highway is littered with poor copies of Seaside that increase not decrease sprawl. Certainly, the New Urbanists cannot be held responsible for weak imitations. Seaside, Kentlands, and Laguna West, among others, remind us, however, that the New Urbanists have as yet been unable to deliver the kind of regional plans they promise. They have yet to integrate the proliferation of small pedestrian-based places in a way that does not also produce sprawl, fragmentation, and the domination of the automobile.

The failure of Kentlands and Laguna West to "concentrate commercial activities, including shopping and working, in town centers"[40] and the
regional traffic problems that Seaside poses are not accidents. Nor is the failure
of the New Urbanists to take a critical look at these problems. Such commercial
centers are not viable. Communities of 5,000–10,000 people cannot support
economically feasible town centers that will adequately serve the shopping
needs of its populace. At best, they might provide centers for the sale of convenience goods and personal services. The densities of population needed for a
serious shopping street or center are simply not possible if one designs a community based on single-family dwellings in today's commercial market, as
studies by the Urban Land Institute make clear.[41] Also, a typical catchment area
for a general convenience shopping area is usually about 3–6 miles, which is far
outside conventional walking distances. Such pedestrian-based commerce is
more likely in a city with higher densities, large multi-family buildings, and larger
populations.

Developing places where people would walk to work is just as problematic. Even in neighborhoods and cities with the densities to support a jobs/
housing balance, it is unlikely that people would work where they live. Robert
Cervero has illustrated that even where counties develop a job/housing balance,
two-thirds of those who work in such counties live elsewhere and two-thirds of
those people who live in those counties work elsewhere.[42] In my own city of
Boston, one of three cities with more jobs than people, 31 percent of its citizens work outside its municipal boundaries. Clearly, many people cannot or
would not choose to live and work in the same place. Even if people could be
persuaded to work walking distance from where they live, unless one divided a
metropolitan region into company-based towns, the possibility of designing
such relationships is questionable at best.

For argument's sake, let us say that such pedestrian-based communities could be built. There are still questions begging answers: How do the New
Urbanists plan to guarantee work for a community's residents near where they
live? Do people have to move if they change jobs to employers that are not within
walking distance of their homes? What are families with two working adults to do
if the firms for which they work are far apart? How do the New Urbanists plan to
guarantee homes to new employees if a company grows and people who have
changed employers or retired do not move? Design principles are clearly not
enough. What would be needed is a frightening scenario of an almost "1984-ish"
control of residential choices and management of economic practices.

Just as the New Urbanists cannot make thriving commercial centers
or guarantee that there will be enough jobs within walking distance for residents even if they wanted to walk to work, they cannot provide sufficient civic,
religious, and recreational facilities within easy walking distance for residents.

But, let us assume for the moment that the New Urbanists had succeeded in building the suburban metropolitan region following their principles. A
region of a million people would have 200 neighborhoods of 5,000 or so people.
A region of five million would have 1,000 such communities. If each community
housed only five denominational churches that would be 1,000 churches in the
first metropolitan region and 5,000 churches in the second. (The Boston/Cam-
bridge area of over 600,000 residents and a nearby region of another 2.4 million
residents has 532 churches representing over 50 denominations.) These hypo-
thetical cities would have 200 to 1,000 swimming pools, health clubs, movie
theaters, libraries, and sports fields, among other things. Even this would not
prevent auto traffic, unless one assumed that use patterns and social interactions
were limited to the community in which one resided. Picture such a regional plan,
and then think of the sprawl as 200 to 1,000 separate communities each with its
own town center spans the metropolitan landscape. In effect, as Robert Bruegmann points out, the New Urbanists have created not so much an anodyne to
urban deconcentration but "really just a kind of more attractive sprawl."[43]

Even if the New Urbanists do not meet all their goals, they might
still succeed, as Vincent Scully argues, "in creating an image of community"
that will overcome the social dissolution that, he and other New Urbanists
claim, is plaguing our society.[44] The New Urbanist belief that it is through
neotraditional design that their developments can resurrect a lost sense of
community has come under significant criticism. At the core of New Urbanist
thinking and design practice is

> The presumption ... that neighborhoods are in some sense "intrinsic,"
> and that the proper form of cities is some "structure of
> neighborhoods," that neighborhood is equivalent to "community," and
> "community" is what most Americans want and need.[45]

It is a presumption that is open to serious question. Many Americans love living
in the anonymous suburbs as well as in urban towers. Effective community can
be and has been created by people who live in different neighborhoods, and
even different cities through mutually shared interests. It is especially noteworthy that the members of the CNU, a community of like-minded designers from
all parts of the country, have through their shared efforts created a major force
in the American, indeed, international discussion about urbanism. As Thomas
Bender points out, trying to recapture community by imputing it to locality-
based social activity regardless of the quality of human relationships is mislead-
ing. And, "if community is defined as a colonial New England town" or as some
other nostalgic vision of small-town America, as it is by the New Urbanists,
"then the prospect for community today is indeed dim."[46] It trivializes the

complex and sensitive mix of social cultural practices and attitudes that go into making a community and it assumes that community should be or must be place-based. What few studies of New Urbanist developments there are suggest that community is no more likely to develop there than in other types of developments and urban and suburban places.[47]

Even where community is created, it may not always be the cure for urban problems. It might be useful in a time of increasing fragmentation, conflict, and a fast-growing dual economy to ask whether creating small well-designed places built around their own commercial and social center, whether in the urban core or periphery, is the best way to deal with our urban condition. This is especially important as ever more community groups are beginning to reach out for more citywide strategic planning rather than mere community-based development. The need for ties between communities is growing in a world in which bigness at the corporate and political level is growing.

New Urbanist design militates against the notion of broad-based community alliances. Even in the way they visualize their developments suggests a fully bounded and singular community that is not represented as part of the wider world. This is unlike, for example, the representations of neighborhood design by such as Clarence Perry, where the neighborhood is represented as part of an almost infinite urban region. Moreover, so many New Urbanist designs, if they are not gated, have monumental entrances, clearly demarcating their setoff from the urban context that surrounds them. If boundaries set out who and what we include in our world and who we are appearing to reach out to and encourage being with us, then New Urbanist designs and representations appear to suggest exclusivity.

Creating "urban villages," even if it were possible to do so, may create more problems in our cities than it would solve. There are questions about how best to insure cultural and social diversity. Commentators and citizens alike argue about whether it is better to mix peoples of different ethnic and racial backgrounds or to work within social enclaves to maintain tradition. While most of us would criticize creating islands of class privilege and underclass misery, it is not obvious that intermixing people of upper-middle-class backgrounds in the same place as the poor will either create community or overcome privilege. More crucially, creating such a mix does not simply come about as a result of good design principles. The minimum price for a house in Kentlands, outside Baltimore, is over $150,000, more than ten times the median income of people in Baltimore.[48] In Seaside the prices are significantly higher. This does not augur well for the notion of economic diversity.

In Kentlands as well the number of minority residents is significantly lower than for the region at large.[49] Although Andrés Duany suggests that it is the aim of the New Urbanism to create diverse communities, there is little evidence that they have done so. He also has said that he is not interested in designing communities that will not be built. Thus, diversity not only would appear to threaten their market, as Gerald Frug has argued, it ironically runs counter to the American small town they yearn for with its clear social divisions and class and racial segregation.[50] It is of note that even as the New Urbanists call for class and economically mixed communities, they also brag that house prices in their developments invariably are higher than in surrounding developments not based on New Urbanist design.

The more recent suggestion of the Transect is one way the New Urbanists might argue they are facing the problem of fragmentation. While the Transect might set in place a plan for a regional system that organizes all elements of the urban environment on a scale from rural to urban, it does not really address the issue of the smaller communities and how they would deal with the conditionalities suggested above. It sets out a regional plan but at a relatively abstract level and as a result simply sidesteps the critical issues that the core New Urbanist philosophy raises. The love of the small town or village has recently been re-emphasized. In a recent talk, Andrés Duany was reported to be trying "to push the body of planners and architects toward a small-town America that more closely resembles pre-1850 America than pre-1950" with his call for an "agrarian urbanism."[51] At its core the original concerns that critics have with the New Urbanism remain.

Also, it should be noted that the concern of critics and commentators like John Kaliski that the New Urbanism is, after one moves away from the Charter for the New Urbanism, an amorphous set of concerns with a strong institutional frame is still apt. If one examines the more recent CNU Congress one sees the vast range of issues that the New Urbanists claim to command, issues that are neither unique to the New Urbanists – for example, Smart Growth and sustainability – nor ones to which, other than their suggestions for village-based design and such abstract notions as the Transect, they have little more to offer than anyone else concerned with these issues.

Finally, the most telling criticism has been that the New Urbanists, like so many architectural practitioners and theorists before them and especially the modernists whom they scorn, are guilty of a kind of designer hubris. The New Urbanism, like modernism, can be accused of a kind of essentialism, in which all aspects of the complex and diverse urban world is reduced to a set of singular and authoritative principles summarized in a set of simple statements and strategic visual and verbal discourses. Even more arrogant, in the view of critics, is the belief that these principles and discourses are crucial to, indeed determinative of, better social and cultural practices; a questionable assumption at best. Finally, at its core is an authoritarian sensibility similar to that of the modernists. The New Urbanist belief that their design solutions are the one and only answer to the problems that beset us is not only a conceit but a dangerous conceit. In their unquestioned belief in their own good works, New Urbanists try to close off discussion of alternative visions of urbanism and urban design. They try to limit the range and diversity of the discourse about a subject that can only be strengthened by more rather than fewer potential approaches to what has become an increasingly intractable problem: what to do about our cities and suburbs.

# Conclusion

The New Urbanists have raised many critical issues facing our cities both publicly and successfully. They have, unlike so many of their postmodern brethren in design, not walked away and refused to face substantive problems to which design may be able to offer a solution. They have not hidden behind an apolitical relativism and elitist poetics but rather have been willing to join some of the most political and quotidian realities facing people today. Like the modernists, they are relevant and important, they are engaged and energetic. In many ways they have made discussions of urban design a crucial part of the larger discussion of whither the city, and urbanism. Their contribution to the debates about the city should not be underestimated or go unappreciated.

But the opportunity opened by the New Urbanists should not force all those concerned with the future of urbanism to get on their bandwagon. It should generate a critical debate about new solutions for what have been and still are seemingly intractable and complex problems. Designers should learn from their past that there are no singular solutions to our urban problems and that no single one-dimensional approach to urban design can or should shoulder such a monumental and intractable task. Rather the hubris of the New Urbanists, like the hubris of the modernists, should teach designers to approach the problems of our cities open to a range of ideas and approaches to urban problems, which will provide the basis for flexible, creative, and appropriate responses to the urban condition.

## Notes

1 Kaliski, 1999, p. 69.
2 Quoted in Anderson, 2001, p. 102.
3 Robbins, 1997, p. 61.
4 *Charter of the New Urbanism*, 2000.
5 Krier, 1991, p. 119.
6 Southworth, 1997, p. 43.
7 Wright, 1981, p. xv.

8  Engels, 1958.
9  Kingsley, 1880, p. 187.
10 Geddes, 1915; Howard, 1898; Unwin, 1909. For an insightful overview of their work, see Hall, 1988.
11 Krieger, 1991, p. 12.
12 See, for example, Glendinning and Muthesius, 1994.
13 Hegeman and Peets, 1992.
14 Perry, 1929, pp. 31–32.
15 For an elucidating discussion of the street in design thinking and practice, see Vidler, 1978.
16 Jacobs, 1961; Cullen, 1968; Venturi and Scott Brown, 1977. See Glendinning and Muthesius, 1994, for a discussion of the Smithsons' notion of streets.
17 Duany, 1997, p. 48.
18 Duany, 1997, p. 48.
19 Dutton, 2000, p. 31.
20 Bothwell, 2000, p. 51.
21 See Kunstler, 1993, for an energetic, at times even vitriolic polemic against the American city and suburb and its design.
22 Duany and Plater-Zyberk, 1992, p. 28.
23 Duany and Plater-Zyberk, 1992.
24 Calthorpe, 2000, p. 15.
25 Solomon, 2000, p. 122.
26 Solomon, 2000, p. 123.
27 Lennertz, 1991, p. 21.
28 It is discussed and reproduced in Dutton, 2000.
29 Steutville, 2000.
30 *Better Cities and Towns*, 2000. "Transect applied to regional plans," September, 1.
31 Norquist, 1998.
32 Quoted in MacCannell, 1999, p. 109.
33 For a discussion of this effort see Vidler, 1978.
34 Quoted in Donald, 1997, p. 182.
35 Harvey, 1996, p. 424.
36 The discussion that follows borrows heavily from a brilliant discussion of public space by Bauman, 1999.
37 Bauman, 1999, p. 17.
38 Quoted in MacCannell, 1999, p. 112.
39 For example, see Robbins, 1998, from which much of what follows is taken.
40 Duany and Plater-Zyberk, 1994.
41 Urban Land Institute, 1985.
42 Cervero, 1996.
43 Bruegmann, 2005, p. 153.
44 Scully, 1994.
45 Harvey, 2000, p. 171.
46 Bender, 1982, p. 4.
47 For discussions of the extent to which New Urbanism leads to community, see Andersen, 2001; Frantz and Collins, 1999; A. Ross among others. For a more detailed analysis of community and design, see Robbins, 2000.
48 Harvey, 2000.
49 Andersen, 2001.
50 Frug, 1997.
51 Lindsay, 2010.

# Bibliography

## Introduction

M. de Certeau, 1984. *The Practice of Everyday Life*. University of California Press.

T. Gieryn, 2000. A place for space in sociology. *Annual Review of Sociology*, 26, 463–496.

H. Lefebvre, 1991. *The Production of Space*. Basil Blackwell.

## Chapter 1  Abu Dhabi and Dubai – world city doubles

Mohammed Al-Fahim, 1995. *From Rags to Riches: A Story of Abu Dhabi*. The London Center of Arab Studies.

Essam Al Tamimi, 2003. *Setting up in Dubai*. Cross Border Legal Publishing.

Frederick F. Anscombe, 2003. An anational society: eastern Arabia in the Ottoman period. In: *Transnational Connections and the Arab Gulf* (Madawi Al-Rasheed, ed.), pp. 21–35. Routledge.

Iain Boal, T. J. Clark, Joseph Matthews, Michael Watts, and Retort, 2005. *Afflicted Powers: Capital and Spectacle in a New Age of War*. Verso.

Fernand Braudel, 1992. *The Structures of Everyday Life: Civilization and Capitalism 15th–18th Century*. University of California Press [reprinted from Librairie Armand Colin, 1979].

Mike Davis, 2005. Dubai: sinister paradise. *Mother Jones*, July 14. Online: www.motherjones.com/commentary/columns/2005/07/sinister_paradise.html.

*The Economist*, December 7, 2006. Glittering towers in a war zone.

Peter Hall, 1971. *The World Cities*, McGraw-Hill.

Frauke Heard-Bey, 2004. *From Trucial States to United Arab Emirates: A Society in Transition*. Motivate Publishing [first published by Longman, 1982].

Sulayman Khalaf and Saad Alkobaisi, 1999. Migrants' strategies of coping and patterns of accommodation in the oil-rich Gulf societies: evidence from the UAE. *British Journal of Middle Eastern Studies*, 26(2), 271–298.

Roland Marchal (ed.), 2001. *Dubai, cité globale*. CNRS.

Roland Marchal, 2003. Dubai: global city and transnational hub. In: *Transnational Connections and the Arab Gulf* (Madawi Al-Rasheed, ed.), pp. 93–110. Routledge.

Robin Moore, 1976. *Dubai*. Doubleday.

Kenichi Ohmae, 2000. The rise of the region state. In: *Globalization and the Challenges of a New Century* (Patrick O'Meara, Howard Mehlinger, and Matthew Krain, eds.). Indiana University Press.

Saskia Sassen, 1991. *The Global City: New York, London, Tokyo*, Princeton University Press.

## Chapter 3  Barcelona – re-thinking urbanistic projects

Ajuntament de Barcelona, 1983. *Barcelona: espais i escultures*. Publicacions Ajuntament.

Ajuntament de Barcelona, 1983. *Barcelona: La segona renovació*. Publicacions Ajuntament.

Ajuntament de Barcelona, 1983. *Plans i Projectes 1981–82*. Publicacions Ajuntament.

Ajuntament de Barcelona, 1987. *Barcelona: Plans cap al 92*. Publicacions Ajuntament.

François Ascher, 1999. *Metrópolis: ou l'avenir des villes*. Odile Jacob.

Eve Blau and Monika Platzer, 2000. *L'idée de la grand Ville*. Prestel.

J. Borja, 1989. *El espacio público: ciudad y ciudadanía*. Diputación.

Fernand Braudel, 1972. *The Mediterranean and the Mediterranean World in the Age of Philipp II*. University of California Press.

Joan Busquets, 1992. *Barcelona: Evolución urbanística de una ciudad compacta*. Mapfre.

Joan Busquets and J. L. Gómez Ordóñez, 1983. *Estudi de l'Eixample*. Publicacions Ajuntament.

Joan Busquets and J. Parcerisa, 1983. Instruments de projectació de la Barcelona suburbana. *Annales ETSAB*.

Joan Busquets *et al.*, 2003. *The Old Town of Barcelona: A Past with a Future*. Publicacions Ajuntament.

Gianfranco Canniga, 1979. *Composizione architettonica e tipologia edilizia*. Cluva.

Ildefonso Cerdà, 1992. *Cerdà y Madrid, Cerdà y Barcelona*. Facsímil. Ajuntament de Barcelona + MOPT.

Ildefonso Cerdà, 1995. *Trabajos sobre Cerdà*. MOPT.

Fabián Estapé, 1971. *Teoría General de la Urbanización*. Instituto Estudios Fiscales.

Fabián Estapé, 1977. *Cerdà 1876–1976: Construcción de la Ciudad*.

Jole Garreau, 1991. *Edge City: Life on the New Frontier*. Doubleday.

David Harvey, 2000. *Spaces of Hope*. University of California Press.

Patsy Healey *et al.*, 1995. *Negotiating Development*. Spon.

Laboratori d'urbanisme, 1978. *Ensanches I y II*. Publicacions UPC.

Laboratori d'urbanisme, 1992. *Trabajos sobre Cerdà y Barcelona*. Ajuntament de Barcelona + MOPT.

Aldo Rossi, 1982. *Architecture of the City*. MIT Press.

## Chapter 4  Brasilia – city as park forever

Robert W. Berger and Thomas F. Hedin, 2008. *Diplomatic Tours in the Gardens of Versailles under Louis XIV*. University of Pennsylvania Press.

Ítalo Campofiorito, 1989. Brasília Revisitada. *Revista do Patrimônio Histórico e Artístico Nacional*, 7, 36–41.

Le Corbusier, 2006. Le Logis, prolongement des service publics. In: *Conférences de Rio: Le Corbusier au Brésil – 1936*, pp. 118–138. Flammarion.

Lucio Costa, 1995. *Registro de uma vivência*. Empresa das Artes.

Osvaldo Peralva, 1988. *Brasília: Patrimônio da Humanidade*. Ministerio da Cultura.

José Pessôa Cavalcanti de Albuquerque, 1958. *Nova Metrópole do Brasil*. Imprensa do Exército.

Martino Tattara, 2011. Revendo a Memória Descritiva do Plano Piloto. In: *Seminário: Lucio Costa, Arquiteto*, pp. 69–84. Casa de Lucio Costa.

## Letters and decree laws

Lucio Costa to Oscar Niemeyer, undated. Casa de Lucio Costa Archives, Rio de Janeiro, III.B.04–03362.

Lucio Costa to Oscar Niemeyer, undated. Casa de Lucio Costa Archives, Rio de Janeiro, VI.A.01.

Lucio Costa, 1987. Brasília Revisitada, Anexo I of Decree Law No. 10.829/1987. Brasilia: Federal District Government.

Federal District Government Decree-Law #10.892, October 14, 1987 and IPHAN Portaria # 314, October 8, 1992.

Hugo Gontier to Le Corbusier, telegram, June 2, 1955. Fondation Le Corbusier Archives, Paris, I1.1.XX.7.

Juscelino Kubitschek to Rodrigo Mello Franco de Andrade, June 15, 1960. Casa de Lucio Costa Archives, Rio de Janeiro, III.B.11–00692.

Oscar Niemeyer to José Aparecido, October 4, 1989. Oscar Niemeyer Foundation Archives, Rio de Janeiro.

## Chapter 5  Chicago – superblockism: Chicago's elastic grid

James Silk Buckingham, 1842. *The Eastern and Western States of America*. Cited in John Reps, 1965. *The Making of Urban America*. Princeton University Press.

Bureau of Land Management (Washington, DC), 1947. *The Manual of Surveying Instructions of 1947*.

Chicago Plan Commission, 1945. *Chicago Looks Ahead: Design for Public Improvements*. Chicago Plan Commission.

Alan Colquhoun, 1971. The Superblock. Reprinted in: Colquhoun, 1985. *Essays in Architectural Criticism: Modern Architecture and Historical Change*. MIT Press.

Carl Condit, 1973. *Chicago: 1910–29*. University of Chicago Press.

Sigfried Giedion, 1944. Need for a new monumentality. In: *New Architecture and City Planning* (Paul Zucker, ed.). Philosophical Library.

Bertrand Goldberg, 1985. Marina City. In: *Goldberg on the City* (Michel Ragon, ed.). Paris Art Center.

Bertrand Goldberg, 1985. The critical mass of urbanism. In: *Goldberg on the City* (Michel Ragon, ed.). Paris Art Center.

Homer Hoyt, 1933. *One Hundred Years of Land Values in Chicago: The Relationship of the Growth of Chicago to the Rise of Its Land Values, 1830–1933*. University of Chicago Press.

Jane Jacobs, 1961. *The Death and Life of Great American Cities*. Vintage.

Hildegard Binder Johnson, 1976. *Order upon the Land: The U.S. Rectangular Land Survey and the Upper Mississippi Country*. Oxford University Press.

Rem Koolhaas, 1984. *Delirious New York*. Monacelli Press.

Katherine Kuh, 1971. *The Open Eye: In Pursuit of Art*. Harper & Row.

Phyllis Lambert (ed.), 2001. Bas-relief urbanism: Chicago's figured field. In: *Mies in America*. CCA and The Whitney Museum of American Art.

Kevin Pierce, 1998. IIT at a crossroads. *Competitions*, 8(2).

Albert Pope, 1996. *Ladders*. Princeton Architectural Press and Rice School of Architecture.

John W. Reps, 1965. *The Making of Urban America: A History of City Planning in the United States*. Princeton University Press.

Ron Shiffman, 2002. Quoted in: Lynne Duke, 2002. A wellspring of grief and hope. *Washington Post*, September 9.

Frank Lloyd Wright, 1901. Home in a prairie town. *Ladies' Home Journal*, February 18.

Alfred B. Yeomans, 1916. *City Residential Land Development: Studies in Planning*. University of Chicago Press.

## Chapter 6 Detroit – Motor City

Michel de Certeau, 1984. *The Practice of Everyday Life.* University of California Press.

Ze'ev Chafets, 1990. *Devil's Night: And Other True Tales of Detroit.* Random House.

*Chicago Tribune*, 2000. Census should show if Detroit is successful in its comeback. June 5, pp. A1, 10.

City of Detroit City Planning Commission, August 24, 1990. *Detroit Vacant Land Survey.*

*The Economist*, 1993. Day of the bulldozer. May 8.

Michael Hays, 1995. *Modernism and the Posthumanist Subject.* MIT Press.

Jerry Herron, 1993. *AfterCulture: Detroit and the Humiliation of History.* Wayne State University Press.

Ludwig Hilberseimer, 1945. Cities and defense, 1945. Reprinted in: *In the Shadow of Mies: Ludwig Hilberseimer, Architect, Educator, and Urban Planner* (Richard Plommer, David Spaeth, and Kevin Harrington, eds.). Rizzoli/Art Institute of Chicago.

Ludwig Hilberseimer, 1949. *The New Regional Pattern.* Paul Theobald & Co.

Dan Hoffman, 2001a. Erasing Detroit. In: *Stalking Detroit* (Georgia Daskalakis, Charles Waldheim, and Jason Young, eds.), pp. 100–103. ACTAR.

Dan Hoffman, 2001b. The best the world has to offer. In: *Stalking Detroit* (Georgia Daskalakis, Charles Waldheim, and Jason Young, eds.), pp. 48–56. ACTAR.

Sanford Kwinter, 1994. Mies and movement: military logistics and molecular regimes. In: *The Presence of Mies* (Detlef Mertins, ed.). Princeton Architectural Press.

Sanford Kwinter and Daniela Fabricius, 2000. Contract with America. In: *Mutations: Rem Koolhaas, Harvard Project on the City, Stefano Boeri, Multiplicity, Sanford Kwinter, Nadia Tazi, Hans Ulrich Obrist* (Rem Koolhaas, Stefano Boeri, Sanford Kwinter, Nadia Tazi, and Hans Ulrich Obrist, eds.), p. 600. ACTAR.

*Metropolis*, 1998. Dismantling the Motor City. June.

Richard Pommer, David Spaeth, and Kevin Harrington (eds.), 1988. *In the Shadow of Mies: Ludwig Hilberseimer, Architect, Educator, and Urban Planner.* Rizzoli/Art Institute of Chicago.

Witold Rybczynski, 1995. The zero density neighborhood. *Detroit Free Press Sunday Magazine*, October 29.

Joseph Rykwert, 1988. *The Idea of a Town: An Anthropology of Urban Form in Rome, Italy and the Ancient World.* MIT Press.

Patrick Schumacher and Christian Rogner, 2001. After Ford. In: *Stalking Detroit* (Georgia Daskalakis, Charles Waldheim, and Jason Young, eds.), pp. 48–56. ACTAR.

Thomas Sugrue, 1996. *The Origins of the Urban Crisis.* Princeton University Press.

Andrey Tarkovsky, 1986. *Sculpting in Time: Reflections on the Cinema.* The Bodley Head.

Paul Virilio, 1986. Overexposed city. *Zone*, 1–2.

Charles Waldheim, Jason Young, and Georgia Daskalakis (eds.), 2001. *Stalking Detroit.* ACTAR.

## Chapter 7 Hong Kong – aformal urbanism

Peter Reyner Banham, 1976. *Megastructure: Urban Futures of the Recent Past.* Thames & Hudson.

Mike Davis, 2004. Planet of slums: urban involution and the informal proletariat. *New Left Review*, 26, 5–34.

Christopher DeWolf, 2011. A sleepy area caught between slow gentrification or mass development. *South China Morning Post*, March 27.

Adam Frampton, Jonathan Solomon, and Clara Wong, 2012. *Cities without Ground*, Oro Editions.

Government Property Agency, Audit Commission, Hong Kong, 2008. Commercialization and
     utilization of government properties, March 25, chapter 2. Online: www.aud.gov.hk/pdf_e/
     e50ch02.pdf.
Fredric Jameson, 1984. Postmodernism, or the cultural logic of late capitalism. *New Left
     Review*, 146 (July/August), 53–92.
Hidetoshi Ohno, 1992. Hong Kong: alternative metropolis. *Space Design*, 330 (March), 55–77.
John Portman, 2010. Peachtree Center. In: *Workbook: The Official Catalog for Workshopping –
     An American Model of Architectural Practice, the US Pavilion for La Biennale Venezia, 12th
     International Architecture Exhibition*. Princeton Architectural Press, the High Museum of
     Art, and 306090.
James C. Scott, 1998. *Seeing Like a State: How Certain Schemes to Improve the Human
     Condition Have Failed*. Yale University Press.
Barrie Shelton, Justyna Karakiewicz, and Thomas Kvan, 2010. *The Making of Hong Kong: From
     Vertical to Volumetric*, Routledge.
Jonathan Solomon, 2010. Learning from Louis Vuitton. *Journal of Architectural Education*, 63(2)
     (March), 67–70.
Jonathan Solomon, 2011. Looking for megastructure: a partial archeology of the present. In
     *Banham in Buffalo* (Mehrdad Hadhigi, ed.). ORO Editions.
Jonathan Solomon, 2012. It makes a village. In: *Aspects of Urbanisation in Asia* (Gregory
     Bracken, ed.). Amsterdam Press.
Zaiyuan Zhang, Stephen Lau Siu Yu, and Lee Hoyin, 1997. The central district of Hong Kong:
     architecture and urbanism of a laissez-faire city. *Architecture and Urbanism*, 322 (July),
     13–16.

## Chapter 8  Los Angeles – between cognitive mapping and dirty realism

Theodor W. Adorno and Max Horkheimer, 1994. *Dialectic of Enlightenment*. Continuum.
Stephanie Barron and Sabine Eckmann, 1998. *Exiles + Emigrés: The Flight of European Artists
     from Hitler*. Los Angeles County Museum of Art.
Jean Baudrillard, 1984. Precession of the simulacra. In: *Art After Modernism: Rethinking
     Representation* (Brian Wallis, ed.). New Museum of Contemporary Art.
Jean Baudrillard, 1987. Forget Baudrillard: an interview with Sylvère Lotringer. In: *Forget
     Foucault*. Semiotext(e).
Marco Cenzatti, 1993. *Los Angeles and the L.A. School: Postmodernism and Urban Studies*. Los
     Angeles Forum for Architecture and Urban Studies.
Dana Cuff, 2000. *The Provisional City: Los Angeles Stories of Architecture and Urbanism*. MIT
     Press.
Mike Davis, 1990. *City of Quartz: Excavating the Future in Los Angeles*. Vintage Books.
Mike Davis, 1998. *Ecology of Fear: Los Angeles and the Imagination of Disaster*. Metropolitan
     Books.
Michael J. Dear, H. Eric Schockman, and Greg Hise, 1996. Preface. In: *Rethinking Los Angeles*
     (Michael Dear, H. Eric Schockman, and Greg Hise (eds.). Sage Publications.
Stephen Dobney, 1997. *The Master of Architect Series III: Johnson Fain Partners – Selected and
     Current Works*. The Images Publishing Group.
Umberto Eco, 1987. *Travels in Hyperreality*. Picador.
Nan Ellin, 1999. *Postmodern Urbanism*. Princeton Architectural Press.
Robert M. Fogelson, 1967. *The Fragmented Metropolis: Los Angeles, 1850–1930*. University of
     California Press.

Hal Foster, 1996. *The Return of the Red: The Avant-garde at the End of the Century*. MIT Press.

Michel Foucault, 1993. Of other spaces: utopias and heterotopias. In: *Architecture Culture 1943–1968: A Documentary Anthology* (Joan Ockman and Edward Eigen, eds.). Rizzoli Press.

William Fulton, 2001. *The Reluctant Metropolis: The Politics of Urban Growth in Los Angeles*. Johns Hopkins University Press.

Mario Gandelsonas, 1996. *X-Urbanism: Architecture and the American City*. Princeton Architectural Press.

Sir Peter Hall, 1998. *Cities in Civilization*. Pantheon.

Dolores Hayden, 1995. *The Power of Place: Urban Landscapes as Public History*. MIT Press.

Anthony Heilbut, 1998. *Exiled in Paradise: German Refuge Artists and Intellectuals in America from the 1930s to the Present*. Viking.

Greg Hise and William Deverell, 2000. Preface to the Master Plan. In: *Eden by Design: The 1930 Olmsted–Bartholomew Plan for the Los Angeles Region*. University of California Press.

Catherine Ingraham, 1998. *Architecture and the Burdens of Linearity*. Yale University Press.

Fredric Jameson, 1988. Cognitive mapping. In: *Marxism and the Interpretation of Culture* (Cary Nelson and Lawrence Grossberg, eds.). University of Illinois Press.

Fredric Jameson, 1991. Postmodernism or, the cultural logic of late capitalism. In: *Postmodernism or, the Cultural Logic of Late Capitalism*. Duke University Press.

Fredric Jameson, 1994. *The Seeds of Time*. Columbia University Press.

Charles Jencks, 1993. *Heteropolis: Los Angeles, the Riots, and the Strange Beauty of Hetero-Architecture*. Academy Editions.

Norman Klein, 1997. *The History of Forgetting: Los Angeles and the Erasure of Memory*. Verso.

Richard Lehan, 1998. *The City in Literature: An Intellectual and Cultural History*. University of California Press.

Jean-François Lyotard, 1984. Foreword. In: *The Postmodern Condition: A Report on Knowledge* (trans. Geoff Bennington and Brian Masumi). University of Minnesota Press.

John McPhee, 1989. Los Angeles against the mountains. In: *The Control of Nature*. Farrar, Straus, and Giroux.

Carry McWilliams, 1946. *Southern California: An Island on the Land*. Gibbs Smith.

Elizabeth Moule and Stefanos Polyzoides, 1994. Five Los Angeleses. In: *World Cities: Los Angeles* (Maggie Toy, ed.). Academy Editions.

Office for Metropolitan Architecture, Rem Koolhaas, and Bruce Mau, 1995. *Small, Medium, Large, Extra Large: Office for Metropolitan Architecture, Rem Koolhaas, and Bruce Mau* (Jennifer Sigler, ed.). Monacelli Press.

Leonard and Dale Pitt, 1997. *Los Angeles: A to Z – An Encyclopedia of the City and County*. University of California Press.

Thomas Pynchon, 1965. *The Crying of Lot 49*. Lippincott.

Dagmar Richter, 1991. Reading Los Angeles: a primitive rebel's account. *Assemblage* 14, MIT Press.

Colin Rowe and Fred Koetter, 1975. *Collage City*. MIT Press.

Charles G. Salas and Michael S. Roth, 2001. *Looking for Los Angeles: Architecture, Film, Photography, and the Urban Landscape*. The Getty Research Institute.

Allen J. Scott and Edward W. Soja, 1996. Introduction to Los Angeles. In: *The City: Los Angeles and Urban Theory at the End of the Twentieth Century*. University of California Press.

Edward Soja, 1989. *Postmodern Geographies: The Reassertion of Space in Critical Social Theory*. Verso.

Edward Soja, 1996. *Thirdspace: Journeys to Los Angeles and Other Real-and-Imagined Places*. Blackwell.

Michael Sorkin, 1992. *Variations on a Theme Park: The New American City and the End of Public Space*. Hill and Wang.

Douglas R. Suisman, 1989. *Los Angeles Boulevard: Eight X-rays of the Body Public*. Los Angeles
    Forum for Architecture and Urban Design.
Douglas R. Suisman, 1992. *Wilshire Boulevard, L.A.* Casabella.
Roemer van Toom, 1999. Architecture against architecture: radical criticism within the society of
    the spectacle. In: *Ctheory* (Arthur and Marilouise Kroker, eds.). Online: www.ctheory.net/
    text.file?pick=94.
Kazys Varnelis, 2003. Los Angeles, cluster city. In: *Future: City* (Jürgen Rosemann, Stephen
    Read, and Job van Eldijk, eds.). Routledge.

## Chapter 9  New Orleans – ecological urbanism

Leon Battista Alberti, 1988. *On the Art of Building in Ten Books* (trans. Joseph Rykwert, Neil
    Leach, and Robert Tavernor). MIT Press.
Alan Berger, 2006. *Drosscape: Wasting Land in Urban America*. Princeton Architectural Press.
Ila Berman and Mona el Khafif, 2008. *URBANbuild: Local Global*. William Stout.
Richard Campanella, 2010. *Delta Urbanism and New Orleans*. American Planning Association,
    Planners Press.
Jeffrey Hou, 2006. Hybrid landscapes: toward an inclusive ecological urbanism on Seattle's
    central waterfront. In: *Getting Real: Design Ethos Now* (Renée Cheng and Patrick J. Tripeny,
    eds.), pp. 245–250. Association of Collegiate Schools of Architecture.
Peirce F. Lewis, 1976. *New Orleans: The Making of an Urban Landscape*. Ballinger.
Ian L. McHarg, 1969. *Design with Nature*. Natural History Press.
Elizabeth Mossop, 2011. Landscape Agency in Urban Revitalization: recent projects in New Orleans.
    Public lecture at the School of Architecture, Illinois Institute of Technology, March 30.
Mohsen Mostafavi, 2007. Ecological urbanism. In: *Intervention Architecture: Building for Change*
    (Aga Khan Foundation, ed.). I. B. Tauris.
Mohsen Mostafavi and Gareth Doherty (eds.), 2010. *Ecological Urbanism*. Graduate School of
    Design, Harvard University/Lars Müller.
Ned Sublette, 2008. *The World That Made New Orleans: From Spanish Silver to Congo Square*.
    Lawrence Hill Books, Chicago Review Press.
Charles Waldheim (ed.), 2006. *The Landscape Urbanism Reader*. Princeton Architectural Press.
Raymond Williams, 1976. *Keywords: A Vocabulary of Culture and Society*. Oxford University Press.

## Chapter 10  Oslo – the triumph of zombie urbanism

Agency for Planning and Building Services, 2007. *Bjørvika. The New City within the City*. Online:
    www.prosjekt-fjordbyen.oslo.kommune.no/getfile.php/plan-%20og%20bygningsetaten%20
    (PBE)/Internett%20(PBE)/Dokumenter/arsberetning/Bjorvikabrosjyre_engelsk.pdf (accessed
    October 8, 2011).
Agency for Planning and Building Services, 2008. Information leaflet, August. Online: www.
    prosjekt-fjordbyen.oslo.kommune.no/getfile.php/fjordbykontoret%20%28FJORDBYEN%29/
    Internett%20%28FJORDBYEN%29/Dokumenter/dokument/folder_tfc_061108_web_small.
    pdf (accessed October 8, 2011).
Agency for Planning and Building Services, 2009. *Oslos bærekraft og vekst. Overordnet
    arkitekturpolitikk for byen og hovedstaden* [*Oslo's Sustainability and Growth: Overall
    Architectural Policy for the City and the Capital*]. Online: www.byradsavdeling-for-
    byutvikling.oslo.kommune.no/getfile.php/plan-%20og%20bygningsetaten%20
    %28PBE%29/Internett%20%28PBE%29/Dokumenter/Filer%20utlagte%20saker/2009/
    arkitekturpolitikk-lett.pdf (accessed October 8, 2011).

Ulrich Beck and Johannes Willms, 2004. *Conversations with Ulrich Beck*. Polity Press.

Bjørvika Development Ltd./Bjørvika Infrastructure Ltd, 2011. *Get to Know Bjørvika – the New City within the City*. Online: www.bjorvikautvikling.no/english (accessed October 8, 2011).

Bjørvika Development Ltd., 2011a. *Operaallmenningen* [*The Opera Common*]. Online: www. bjorvikautvikling.no/Byrom-i-Bjørvika/Operallmenningen/07F5AFCA-2136-42AA-A4D4-F6C4E26E3C3A/1 (accessed October 8, 2011).

Bjørvika Development Ltd., 2011b. *Stasjonsallmenningen* [*The Station Common*]. Online: www. bjorvikautvikling.no/Byrom-i-Bjørvika/Stasjonsallmenningen/A82821E5-BF38-4A6E-83AB-729087E12FD8/1 (accessed October 8, 2011).

Bjørvika Infrastructure Ltd./Gehl Architects ApS, 2006. *Byrumsprogram Havnepromenaden* [*Public Space Program Harbor Promenade*]. Online: www.bjorvikautvikling.no/ Byromsprogram/53EBBE5D-6CCE-47FF-B63C-90F9D8DC902E/1 (accessed October 8, 2011).

Graeme Evans, 2006. Branding the City of Culture: the death of city planning? In: *Culture, Urbanism and Planning* (Javier Monclús and Manuel Guàrdia, eds.), Ashgate.

Richard Florida, 2002. *The Rise of the Creative Class: And How It Is Transforming Work, Leisure, Community and Everyday Life*. Basic Books.

Nicholas Gane, 2004. Ulrich Beck: the cosmopolitan turn. In: *The Future of Social Theory* (Nicholas Gane, ed.). Continuum.

Gehl Architects, 2005. *Bjørvika*. Online: www.gehlarchitects.dk/files/projects/100414_Bjorvika_ Competition_LS_ENG.pdf (accessed October 8, 2011).

David Harvey, 1989. From managerialism to entrepreneurialism: the transformation in urban governance in late capitalism. *Geografiske Annaler* 71 B 1.

Charles Landry, 2000. *The Creative City: A Toolkit for Urban Innovators*. Earthscan Publications Ltd.

Malcolm Miles, 2010. After the creative city? Paper presented at Metropolis Laboratory 2010, Copenhagen.

Steven Miles and Ronan Paddison, 2005. Introduction: the rise and rise of culture-led urban regeneration. *Urban Studies*, 42(5/6).

Oslo Waterfront Planning Office, 2005. *Byrom i Bjørvika: Åpen konkurranse. Juryens rapport* [*Urban Space in Bjørvika: Open Competition. Jury Report*]. Online: www.prosjekt-fjordbyen. oslo.kommune.no/getfile.php/Fjordbykontoret/Internett/Dokumenter/rapport/juryens%20 rapport%20151204.pdf (accessed October 8, 2011).

Leonie Sandercock, 1998. *Towards Cosmopolis: Planning for Multicultural Cities*. John Wiley & Sons.

## Chapter 11 Philadelphia – the urban design of Philadelphia: taking the towne for the city

American Planning and Civic Association, 1953. *American Planning and Civic Annual*. American Planning and Civic Association.

Edmund Bacon, 1950. Highway development related to land use in an urban area. In: *Spencer Miller Lecture Series: Landscape Design and its Relation to the Modern Highway* (James Carter Hanes and Charles H. Connors, eds.). New Jersey Roadside Council/Rutgers University.

Edmund Bacon, 1974. *Design of Cities*. Penguin Books.

Jonathan Barnett and Nory Miller, 1983. Edmund Bacon: a retrospective. *Planning*, December.

John F. Bauman, 1983. Visions of a post-war city: a perspective on urban planning in Philadelphia and the nation, 1942–1945. In: *Introduction to Planning History in the United States* (Donald A. Krueckeberg, ed.). Rutgers University Press.

## Bibliography

Edwin Bronner, 1962. *William Penn's "Holy Experiments."* Temple University Press.

David Clow, 1989. *House Divided: Philadelphia's Controversial Crosstown Expressway.* Society for American City and Regional Planning History.

Jack P. Green, 1993. *The Intellectual Construction of America: Exceptionalism and Identity from 1492–1800.* University of North Carolina Press.

Constance M. Greiff, 1987. *Independence: The Creation of a National Park.* University of Pennsylvania Press.

Samuel Hazard (ed.), 1850. William Penn's Instructions to Commissioners. In: *Annals of Pennsylvania from the Discovery of the Delaware 1609–1682.* Hazard and Mitchell.

Franz Kafka, 1926. *The Castle.*

T. McGee and I. Robinson (eds.), 1995. *The Mega-Urban Regions of Southeast Asia.* University of British Columbia Press.

R. Marshall, 2002. *Emerging Urbanity: Global Urban Projects in the Asia Pacific Rim.* Spon Press.

Amy E. Menzer, 1999. Exhibiting Philadelphia's "Vital Center": negotiating environmental and civic reform in a popular post-war planning vision. *Radical History Review*, 74.

Albert C. Myers (ed.), 1912. Letter from William Penn to the Committee of The Free Society of Traders, 1683: A Short Advertisement of the City of Philadelphia and the Ensuing Plat-form thereof, by the Surveyor General. In: *Narratives of Early Pennsylvania, West New Jersey and Delaware 1630–1707.* Charles Scribner & Sons.

Lewis Mumford, 1957. The skyline: Philadelphia – II. *New Yorker*, February 9.

National Park Service, 1994. *Cultural Landscape Report: Independence Mall, Independence National Historic Park.* US Dept of the Interior.

M. Perry, 1998. The Singapore growth triangle in the global and local economy. In: *The Naga Awakens: Growth and Change in Southeast Asia* (V. R. Savage, L. Kong, and W. Neville, eds.), pp. 87–112. Times Academic Press.

Philadelphia plans again. *Architectural Forum*, 1947.

John W. Reps, 1965. *The Making of Urban America: A History of City Planning in the United States.* Princeton University Press.

P. Rowe, 2001. A difference of degree or a difference in kind: hyperdensity in Hong Kong. In: *Hong Kong: Defining the Edge* (J. Brown, E. Mossop, and R. Marshall, eds.), pp. 14–39. Harvard University Graduate School of Design.

Arthur Schlesinger, 1949. *The Vital Center: The Politics of Freedom.* Houghton Mifflin Co.

Neil Smith, 1996. *The New Urban Frontier: Gentrification and the Revanchist City.* Routledge.

D. Sudjic, 1993. Bangkok's instant city. *Blueprint*, 99, 19.

United Nations Department of Economics and Social Affairs, 1998. *World Urbanization Prospects: The 1996 Revision.* United Nations.

Paul Virilio, 1986. *The Overexposed City*, from *L'espace critique* in *ZONE 1–2*, 1986. In: K. Michael Hays (ed.) 1998. *Architecture Theory Since 1968.* MIT Press.

Sam Bass Warner, 1987. *The Private City: Philadelphia in Three Periods of Its Growth*, 2nd edn. University of Pennsylvania Press.

World Bank, 1993. *The East Asian Miracle: Economic Growth and Public Policy.* Oxford University Press.

## Chapter 14  Shenzhen – topology of a neoliberal city

Archdaily, 2009. OMA's new landmark for Shenzhen: Crystal Island Competition. Online: www.archdaily.com/25450/oma%C2%B4s-new-landmark-for-shenzhen-crystal-island-competition (accessed July 15, 2011).

Archdaily, 2010. James Corner Field Operations to design Qianhai. Online: www.archdaily.com/66650/james-corner-field-operations-to-design-qianhai (accessed July 15, 2011).

Giovanni Arrighi, 1994. *The Long Twentieth Century: Money, Power, and the Origins of Our Times*. Verso.

Giovanni Arrighi, 2007. *Adam Smith in Beijing: Lineages of the Twenty-First Century*. Verso.

Pier Vittorio Aureli, 2011. *The Possibility of an Absolute Architecture*. MIT Press.

George Baird, 2009. A response to "Criticality in between China and the West." In *Architecture of Modern China: A Historical Critique* (Jianfei Zhu, ed.), pp. 147–149. Routledge.

David Bray, 2005. *Social Space and Governance in Urban China: The Danwei System from Origins to Reform*. Stanford University Press.

Michael J. Bruton, Sheila G. Bruton, and Yu Li, 2005. Shenzhen: coping with uncertainties in planning. *Habitat International*, 29(2), 227–243.

Business Alert China, 2003. Shenzhen, Zhuhai ease frontier control. *Business Alert China*, 7 (July 1). Online: http://info.hktdc.com/alert/cba-e0307b-3.htm (accessed July 7, 2011).

Thomas J. Campanella, 2008. *The Concrete Dragon: China's Urban Revolution and What It Means for the World*. Princeton Architectural Press.

Carolyn Cartier, 2002. Transnational urbanism in the Reform-era Chinese city: landscapes from Shenzhen. *Urban Studies*, 39(9), 1513–1532.

Manuel Castells, 1996. *The Rise of the Network Society*. Blackwell Publishers.

Jenny Chan and Ngai Pun, 2010. Suicide as protest for the new generation of Chinese migrant workers: Foxconn, Global Capital, and the state. *Asia-Pacific Journal*, 37(2). Online: http://japanfocus.org/-Jenny-Chan/3408.

James Corner, 1999. The agency of mapping. In: *Mappings* (Denis Cosgrove, ed.). Reaktion Books.

Tim Culpan, Zheng Lifei, and Bruce Einhorn, 2011. Foxconn leads the race for the interior. *Chinadaily*, May 7, 2011. Online: www.chinadaily.com.cn/business/2011-05/07/content_12463331.htm (accessed July 15, 2011).

Demographia, 2011. *Demographia: World Urban Areas (World Agglomerations)*, 7th annual edn. Online: www.demographia.com/db-worldua.pdf (accessed July 15, 2011).

Gérard Duménil and Dominique Lévy, 2004. Neoliberal income trends: wealth, class and ownership, in the USA. *New Left Review*, 30, 103–133.

Daniel Elsea, 2008. Dafen art museum. *Architectural Record China* 01.

Feng Wei, Lin Yu, and Yi Tianzhu, 2011. Research on the phenomena of "SHAN ZHAI" and the corresponding intellectual property rights strategies of China. *International Management Review*, 7(1), 74–80.

Hal Foster, 2002. *Design and Crime: And Other Diatribes*. Verso.

John Friedmann, 2005. *China's Urban Transition*. University of Minnesota Press.

Matthew Gandy, 2005. Learning from Lagos. *New Left Review*, 33, 37.

David Gissen, 2008. Architecture's geographic turn. *LOG 12*, pp. 59–67.

Kanishka Goonewardena and Stefan Kipfer, 2004. Creole city: culture, class and capital in Toronto. In: *Contested Metropolis* (R. Paloscia, ed.). Birkhäuser Publishing Ltd.

Stephen Graham, 2004. Flowcity. In *Urban Mutations: Periodization, Scale, Mobility* (Tom Nielsen, Niels Albertsen, and Peter Hemmersam, eds.). Arkitektens Forlag.

Michael Hardt and Antonio Negri, 2000. *Empire*. Harvard University Press.

David Harvey, 2003. *The New Imperialism*. Oxford University Press

David Harvey, 2005. *A Brief History of Neoliberalism*. Oxford University Press.

Steven Holl Architects, 2006. *Horizontal Skyscraper: Vanke Center*. Online: www.stevenholl.com/project-detail.php?id=60&worldmap=true (accessed July 15, 2011).

Fredric Jameson, 1984. Postmodernism, or the cultural logic of late capitalism. *New Left Review*, 146.

Fredric Jameson, 1998. *The Cultural Turn: Selected Writings on the Postmodern, 1983–1998*. Verso.

Rem Koolhaas, 1978. *Delirious New York: A Retroactive Manifesto for Manhattan*. Oxford University Press.

# Bibliography

Rem Koolhaas, 2001. Junkspace. In *The Harvard Design School Guide to Shopping* (Chuihua Judy Chung, Jeffrey Inaba, Rem Koolhaas, and Sze Tsung Leong, eds.), Taschen.

Rem Koolhaas and Bruce Mau, 1997. Pearl River Delta. In *Politics, Poetics: Documenta X, the Book* (Catherine David and Jean-François Chevrier, eds.), pp. 556–592. Cantz.

Rem Koolhaas, Stefano Boeri, Sanford Kwinter, Nadia Tazi, and Hans Ulrich Obrist, 2000. *Mutations: Rem Koolhaas, Harvard Project on the City, Stefano Boeri, Multiplicity, Sanford Kwinter, Nadia Tazi, Hans Ulrich Obrist*. ACTAR.

Rem Koolhaas, Chuihua Judy Chung, Jeffrey Inaba, and Sze Tsung Leong (eds.), 2001. *Great Leap Forward/Harvard Design School Project on the City*. Taschen.

Rem Koolhaas, Bruce Mau, Jennifer Sigler, and Hans Werlemann, 1998. *Small, Medium, Large, Extra-Large: Office for Metropolitan Architecture, Rem Koolhaas, and Bruce Mau*. Monacelli Press.

C.-F. Lai, 1985. Special Economic Zones: the Chinese road to socialism? *Environment and Planning D: Society and Space*, 3, 63–84.

Lothar Ledderose, 1998. *Ten Thousand Things: Module and Mass Production in Chinese Art*. Princeton University Press.

Gucheng Li, 1995. *A Glossary of Political Terms of the People's Republic of China*. Chinese University Press.

Minqi Li, 2008. *The Rise of China and the Demise of the Capitalist World Economy*. Pluto Press.

Laurence Liauw, 2008. Leaping forward, getting rich gloriously and letting a hundred cities bloom. *Architectural Design*, 78(5), 6–15.

George Lin, 2006. Peri-urbanism in globalizing china: a study of new urbanism in Dongguan. *Eurasian Geography and Economics*, 47(1), 28.

Chuanzhi Liu, 2007. Lenovo: an example of globalization of Chinese enterprises. *Journal of International Business Studies*, 38(4), 573–577.

Kaiming Liu, 2007. Chapter 1: the hierarchical mode of Shenzhen's population and labor structure. *Chinese Economy*, 40(3) (May–June), 24–46.

Jia Lu, 2009. Spatial planning in Shenzhen to build a low carbon city. Paper in The 45th ISOCARP Congress.

Bert de Muynck, 2006. Creative China: cutting and pasting? Online: http://movingcities.org/bertdemuynck/cccp.

Mee Kam Ng, 2003. City profile: Shenzhen. *Cities*, 20(6), 429–441.

Mee Kam Ng and Wing-Shing Tang, 2004. The role of planning in the development of Shenzhen, China: rhetoric and realities. *Eurasian Geography and Economics*, 45(3), 190–211.

OCT Hotel, 2003. *Crowne Plaza Shenzhen*. Online: www.octhotels.com/eng/octHotels/interlaten30/hotel_30.html (accessed July 14, 2011).

OMA, 2006. Shenzhen Stock Exchange. Online: www.oma.eu/index.php?option=com_projects&view=portal&id=631&Itemid=10 (accessed by July 15, 2011).

Philipp Oswalt (ed.), 2005. *Shrinking Cities, vol. 1: International research; vol. 2. Interventions*. Hatje Cantz.

Ning Ou, 2009. A city called Shenzhen. *City Mobilization 2009 Shenzhen and Hong Kong Biennale of Urbanism/Architecture Guide Book*.

William H. Overholt, 2011. Hong Kong's financial vitality continues. *Hong Kong Journal*. Online: www.hkjournal.org/archive/2011_summer/2.htm (accessed July 15, 2011).

Jamie Peck and Adam Tickell, 2002. Neoliberalizing space. *Antipode*, 34(3), 380–404.

Ngai Pun, 2005. *Made in China: Women Factory Workers in a Global Workplace*. Duke University Press.

Ngai Pun and Chris Smith, 2007. Putting the transnational labour process in its place: the dormitory labour regime in post-socialist China. *Work Employment and Society*, 21(1), 27–46.

Rainer Pirker ArchiteXture, 2007. *Guangming New Town Centre*. Online: www.rainerpirker.com (accessed July 15, 2011).

Saskia Sassen, 1992. *The Global City: New York, London, Tokyo*. Princeton University Press.

Felicity Scott, 2007. *Architecture or Techno-utopia: Politics after Modernism*. MIT Press.

*Shenzhen Post*, 2009. Shenzhen Metro. Online: www.szcpost.com/2009/01/shenzhen-metro.html (accessed July 15, 2011).

Beverly Silver and Giovanni Arrighi, 2011. The end of the long twentieth century. In: *Business as Usual: The Roots of the Global Financial Meltdown* (Craig Calhoun and Georgi Derluguian, eds.). New York University Press.

Beverly Silver and Lu Zhang, 2009. China as an emerging epicenter of world labor unrest. In: *China and the Transformation of Global Capitalism* (Ho-Fung Hung, ed.). Johns Hopkins University Press.

Chris Smith, 2003. Living at work: management control and the dormitory labour system in China. *Asia Pacific Journal of Management*, 20(3), 333–358.

Chris Smith and Ngai Pun, 2006. The dormitory labour regime in China as a site for control and resistance. *International Journal of Human Resource Management*, 17(8), 1456–1470.

Li Tian, 2008. The Chengzhongcun land market in China: boon or bane? – A perspective on property rights. *International Journal of Urban and Regional Research*, 32(2) (June), 282–304.

UNESCO: Creative Cities Network, 2009. *Shenzhen: City of Design, Fast Facts*. United Nations Educational, Scientific and Cultural Organization.

*Urban China*, 2007. Regenerating Shenzhen. *Urban China*, 24.

Urbanus Architecture & Design, 2005. OCT East Factory Area rehabilitation. Online: www.urbanus.com.cn/public_class.php?action=project&num=4&aid=45&saction=sclass (accessed July 15, 2011).

Paolo Virno, 2004. *A Grammar of the Multitude: For an Analysis of Contemporary Forms of Life*. Semiotext (e).

Ezra F. Vogel, 1989. *One Step Ahead in China: Guangdong under Reform*. Harvard University Press.

Hui Wang and Theodore Huters, 2003. *China's New Order: Society, Politics, and Economy in Transition*. Harvard University Press.

Yaping Wang, Yanglin Wang, and Jiansheng Wu, 2010. Housing migrant workers in rapidly urbanizing regions: a study of the Chinese model in Shenzhen. *Housing Studies*, 25(1), 83–100.

Winnie Won Yin Wong, 2010. After the copy: creativity, originality and the labor of appropriation: Dafen Village, Shenzhen, China 1989–2010. PhD dissertation, Department of Architecture, MIT.

World Shipping Council, 2011. *Top 50 World Container Ports*. Online: www.worldshipping.org/about-the-industry/global-trade/top-50-world-container-ports (accessed July 15, 2011).

Yvonne Young, 2005. Entering Jia Zhangke's world. *HK Magazine Online*, June 2.

The Z/Yen Group, 2009. *The Global Financial Centres Index 6*. City of London Corporation, September.

The Z/Yen Group, 2010. *The Global Financial Centres Index 7*. City of London Corporation, March.

The Z/Yen Group, 2011. *The Global Financial Centres Index 9*. City of London Corporation, March.

John Zacharias and Yuanzhou Tang, 2010. Restructuring and repositioning Shenzhen, China's new mega city. *Progress in Planning*, 73(4) (May), 209–249.

Alejandro Zaera-Polo, 1998. Notes for a topographic survey. In: *1987–1998 OMA/Rem Koolhaas*, pp. 404–407. El Croquis Editorial.

Guoying Zeng, 2006. The urban segmentation problem of Shenzhen. Paper in *The 42nd ISOCARP Congress*.

Lena Zhong, 2009. *Communities, Crime and Social Capital in Contemporary China*. Willan.

Rong Zhou, 2006. Upon the ruins of utopia. *Special Issue Ubiquitous China*, 2, 44–47.

Jianfei Zhu, 2009. *Architecture of Modern China: A Historical Critique*. Routledge.

Jianfei Zhu, 2004. *Chinese Spatial Strategies: Imperial Beijing, 1420–1911*. Routledge Curzon.

Tao Zhu and Jianfei Zhu, 2007. Critical dialogue: China and the west. *Journal of Architecture*, 12(2), 199–207.

## Chapter 15  New urbanism

Bengt Anderson, 2001. Making territory in urban America: new urbanism and Kentlands. In *Hovedfagsstudentenes Årbok*. Årbokredaksjonen.

Zygmunt Bauman, 1999. *In Search of Politics*. Stanford University Press.

Thomas Bender, 1982. *Community and Social Change in America*. Johns Hopkins University Press.

Stephanie Bothwell, 2000. Six. In: *Charter of the New Urbanism*, pp. 49–52. McGraw-Hill.

Robert Bruegmann, 2005. *Sprawl: A Compact History*. University of Chicago Press.

Peter Calthorpe, 2000. One. In *Charter of the New Urbanism*, pp. 15–22. McGraw-Hill.

Robert Cervero, 1996. *Subcentering and Commuting: Evidence from the San Francisco Bay Area, 1980–1990*. University of California Transportation Center.

*Charter of the New Urbanism*, 2000. McGraw-Hill.

Gordon Cullen, 1968. *Townscape*. Reinhold.

James Donald, 1997. Imagining the modern city. In *Imagining Cities: Scripts, Signs, Memory* (Sallie Westwood and John Williams, eds.). Routledge.

Andrés Duany, 1997. Quoted in: Urban or suburban: a discussion at the GSD. *Harvard Design Magazine*.

Andrés Duany and Elizabeth Plater-Zyberk, 1992. The second coming of the American small town. *Wilson Quarterly*, 16(1), 19–51.

Andrés Duany and Elizabeth Plater-Zyberk, 1994. The neighborhood, the district and the corridor. In: *The New Urbanism* (Peter Katz, ed.), pp. xvii–xx. McGraw-Hill.

John A. Dutton, 2000. *New American Urbanism: Re-forming the Suburban Metropolis*. Abbeville Pub. Group/Thames & Hudson.

Friedrich Engels, 1958. *The Condition of the Working Class in England*. Allen Unwin.

Douglas Frantz and Catherine Collins, 1999. *Celebration USA: Living in Disney's Brave New Town*. Henry Holt and Company.

Gerald Frug, 1997. Urban or suburban? A discussion. *Harvard Design Magazine*, Winter/Spring, 46–63.

Patrick Geddes, 1968 (1915). *Cities in Evolution*. Ernest Benn.

Miles Glendinning and Stefan Muthesius, 1994. *Tower Block: Modern Public Housing in England, Scotland, Wales and Northern Ireland*. Yale University Press.

Peter Hall, 1988. *Cities of Tomorrow*. Basil Blackwell.

David Harvey, 1996. *Justice, Nature and the Geography of Difference*. Oxford University Press.

David Harvey, 2000. *Spaces of Hope*. University of California Press.

Werner Hegemann and Elbert Peets, 1992. *The American Vitruvius: An Architects' Handbook of Civic Art*. The Architectural Book Publishing Co.

Ebenezar Howard, 1898. *Garden Cities of Tomorrow*. Faber.

Jane Jacobs, 1961. *The Death and Life of Great American Cities*. Random House.

John Kaliski ... *Design Book Review* Berkeley.

Samuel Kingsley, 1880. *Sanitary and Social Lectures and Essays*. London.

Alex Krieger, 1991. Since (and before) Seaside. In: *Towns and Town-Making Principles* (A. Duany and E. Plater-Zyberk, eds.). Rizzoli.

Leon Krier, 1991. Afterword. In: *Towns and Town-Making Principles* (A. Duany and E. Plater-Zyberk, eds.), pp. 117–119. Rizzoli.

James Kunstler, 1993. *The Geography of Nowhere*. Simon & Schuster.

William Lennertz, 1991. Town-making principles. In: *Towns and Town-Making Principles* (A. Duany and E. Plater-Zyberk, eds.). Rizzoli.

Greg Lindsay, 2010. New urbanism for the Apocalypse. Fast Company.Com, May 24.

Dean MacCannell, 1999. "New urbanism" and its discontents. In: *Giving Ground: The Politics of Propinquity* (J. Copjec and M. Sorkin, eds.). Verso.

John O. Norquist, 1998. *The Wealth of Cities: Revitalizing the Centers of American Life*. Addison Wesley.

Clarence Arthur Perry, 1929. The neighborhood unit: a scheme of arrangement for the family-life community. In: *Neighborhood and Community Planning, Monograph One*. New York Regional Plan Association.

Edward Robbins, 1997. The new urbanism: unkept promise. *Harvard Design Magazine*, Winter/Spring, 61.

Edward Robbins, 1998. The new urbanism and the fallacy of singularity. *Urban Design International*, 3(1), 33–42.

Edward Robbins, 2000. Can/should designers foster community? *Designer/builder*, March.

Vincent Scully, 1994. Architecture of community. In *The New Urbanism* (P. Katz, ed.), pp. 221–230. McGraw-Hill.

José Luís Sert, 1933. The town planning charter. Fourth CIMA Congress, Athens, 1933. *Can Our Cities Survive?* Harvard University Press.

Daniel Solomon, 2000. Nineteen. In *Charter of the New Urbanism*, pp. 13–126. McGraw-Hill.

Michael Southworth, 1997. *Streets and the Shaping of Towns and Cities*. McGraw-Hill.

Robert Steutville, 2000. The New Urbanism: an alternative to modern automobile-oriented planning and development. In *New Urban News*, 2000.

Raymond Unwin, 1909. *Town Planning in Practice*. Princeton Architectural Press (reprinted 1994).

Urban Land Institute, 1985. *Shopping Center Development Handbook*. Washington, DC.

Robert Venturi and Denise Scott Brown, 1977. *Learning from Las Vegas: The Forgotten Symbolism of Architectural Form*. MIT Press.

Anthony Vidler, 1978. The scenes from the street: transformations of ideal and reality, 1750–1871. In *On Streets* (S. Anderson, ed.), pp. 29–112. MIT Press.

Gwendolyn Wright, 1981. *Building the Dream: A Social History of Housing in America*. Pantheon.

# Index

Note: Page numbers in *italics* denote figures